AMERICA

ESCAPE FROM AMERICA

Moe and Joe had a candy store,
Selling fortunes behind the door,
Policeman come and they all run out,
Brother Moe he begin to shout,
Run Joe ...run as fast as you can,
Run Joe ...policeman holding my hand.

A Caribbean song from the 1950's "Run Joe"

MANHATTAN
LOFT
PUBLISHING

This book is available from Manhattan Loft Publishing Company
738 East Burnside Portland, Oregon 97214 USA
Order Line: Toll Free USA 888-314-1592
Information Line: 503-460-9313

WebSite Address: http://www.escapeartist.com
Data URL: http://www.escapeartist.com/going/home.htm

Includes index.
ISBN: 0-9656709-3-7

Printed in the United States of America

10 9 8 7 6 5 4 3 2

First Edition

For Hurricane Suzy

Table of Contents

WARNING

The earth has an area of 197 million square miles. It has a human population of roughly six billion. Two hundred years ago there were only 900 million people on the earth. It is doubtful that anyone who was alive two hundred years ago is still alive. What's happening? Almost a billion people gone? Five billion people show up to take their place? What a strange place and what strange people we are. We have never planned ahead very well. Besides that, we keep dying.

It is almost certain that someone who is reading this book will break their arm in a foreign country. Others will go broke. We'd like to believe that everyone reading this book will accomplish their wildest dreams and find the liberty and happiness they seek. But not everyone will. So, we'd like to make an agreement with the reader. If you promise to wait two hundred years before you sue me for any stupid mistakes you make as a result of reading this book we'd like to advise you that we did our best to make this book as factual as possible. If on the other hand you are the type of person who sues people every time your throw a tantrum we'd like to inform you that we just told you the first lie. We've included many in this book. So every time you think the advice given is factual, check it out for yourself.

Additionally, we want to advise those who live by suing others that the best country in the world for lawsuits is the United States. So, stay home. You don't want to be an expatriate. It will save you a lot of grief if you never leave the house.

We'll give you a another peice of advice. If you want to sue others who read this book you had better do it now before they leave. It will probably be almost impossible to sue those who follow the lessons in this book once they've left you behind. Their assets may soon be beyond the reach of monetary predators.

Only those who have the ability to make their own judgements and accept self-responsibility for their actions have what it takes to be an expatriate. If you don't fall into that category you should not become an expatriate. If you do have the substance and the courage to make your own judgements, then let's get started. There is a real world out there and it's an exciting one.

AN INTRODUCTION
ESCAPE FROM AMERICA

Do people really want to escape from America? What kind of people?

The answer to the first question is an unequivocal yes, people really want to escape from America and for many of them, the sooner they can escape the better. The answer to the second question is that the kind of people who want to escape are America's best and brightest.

How many? ...and why?

The surprising answer is that millions of Americans want to leave and would... if they only knew how. (statistics show that of people queried; almost three million *would* leave America *if they only knew how to do it and where to go.* Of that number the largest percentage [82.3%] had a college education.)

How could this seemingly amazing situation ever have come to be?

The answer is both complex and simple, it involves a number of profound changes that have taken place in the world over the last several years including such seemingly disparate things as the end of the cold war and the advent of the Internet's world wide web of computer communication.

Where do they want to go?

They want to go where there is a 'better quality of life' and where there is 'much less government intervention' into their lives. America, for many people has become intolerable. The taxes burdensome, the crime overwhelming, the violence rife, the ambience impoverished and the future bleak. It is becoming a has-been nation with one of the most powerful standing armies in the world. Requests for information recieved by foreign consulates cite "social unrest," "fear of violence," "racial tensions," and the decline of moral standards in America as reasons for interest in settling elsewhere. But there is also another factor: opportunity. For the first time in America's history it is easier to make more money outside of America than it is to make money inside of America. The new expatriates are going to smaller economies, that are moving faster. They are also going to peaceful pristine nations where real estate is still a bargain. In America most people now feel there is no longer any hope of even staying financially even, let alone getting financially ahead. However, more than any other reason for those who are going, is the simplest yet most enigmatic reason of all; people now want to have a life.

Does what they seek exist?

Yes.

CHAPTER ONE

ESCAPE FROM AMERICA

"All language is a set of symbols
whose use among its speakers assumes a shared past."
-Jorge Luis Borges

WHERE WE ARE GOING

USING THIS BOOK TO FREE OURSELVES

Jorge Luis Borges, the Argentine, tells a story, (or perhaps it's a parable,) about a location in the universe where everything is simultaneously visible. We are reminded of that story as we write the opening section to this book. For if this book is about anything, it is a book about the entire world. While none of us actually believe that the world can fit inside of a book or even a library of books, there are many like myself who spend an inordinate amount of time looking inside of books for a world we've somehow lost.

In a way this is a book about a world we've lost, or to be more precise, about a world some of us have lost and others of us never knew existed. It is about the world outside of the United States of America. It isn't a complex book. This book is intended to be a sensible sort of dream book that includes enough facts to give credibility and ammunition to the act of building our dream of becoming expatriates. For some of us the act of leaving America and going to greener pastures is fraught with dread. We want reassurance. Is it safe? Can we get stuck there? Lose our money? Get thrown in jail? Beyond the harms, what about the opportunities? We've heard about the increased opportunities opening up abroad, but can we make a living if we don't know the rules? If we can manage to make a living can we get rich? Buy real estate? ...and what about the logistics? If we find it difficult to move from Detroit to Seattle, what's it like moving from Seattle to Rio de Janeiro?

The facts are as accurate as we can make them in a constantly changing world. As for the dream, the dream of moving abroad is more realistic today than it has ever been in America's history and we are going to prove that to the reader.

Of course no one can predict the future. Those who say they can predict the future are charlatans and those who believe what they say are fools.

ESCAPE FROM AMERICA

Do I really believe that one can do well in a foreign country? I believe that one can do more than just well in a foreign country, I believe that one can do *better* in a foreign country than one can do in America and I'll tell you why. Americans are some of the most innovative people on the face of the earth. Other First-World countries might look down their nose at us but the truth is we have more daring, more guts, and more ideas than the rest of the world combined. I was talking with a Frenchman on a train in Europe some years back and he was criticizing Americans because he considered them facile. I nodded my head in solemn agreement. Who was I to argue with a Frenchman, these are the people who admittedly have been willing to recognize artists and artistic talent decades before the rest of the world. If anyone should be able to recognize the brutal face of the facile, it has to be the French.

I asked him what he considered of value, if anything about Americans. His reply startled me, for he too looked solemn for a moment. "Your ability to innovate." he replied. "Innovate, innovate what?" I asked him. "Everything." he said. " The hoola hoop even. No one in France could ever have thought of such a thing. It may not seem amazing to you, but it is to us. When I go to California, I see young people who are not stumped by anything. What they cannot buy they create, whether it is a hobbie-craft or a skate board. We have no capacity for such things. We can be honest to our tradition and slowly improve on it, but for you tradition is a thing that you find a dozen ways to bend and turn into some game, gimmick or commodity. The whole world sees this odd creative capacity in Americans. But Americans do not seem aware of it in themselves, as if it were a natural attribute. It is not."

I've always remembered this conversation and have considered its meaning many times over the years since it occurred. I am relating the story to the reader of course because it answers part our rhetorical question regarding our chances in a foreign country, but there is more to the answer than this simple cracker-barrel wisdom. We need four things to really blow 'em away in a foreign country; we need money, we need know-how, we need a plan and we need to stay with whatever we start for a couple of years.

Money. It is easy to hear the muttering in the distance: if we had money we'd just go and hang out on the beach. Well, most of us can give a qualified agreement to that. However what is meant by our needing money as one of our four requirements is a quantitative statement. As readers might suspect every human being on the planet is going to have a different opinion of how much money qualifies as enough money. But let's take a stab at answering the question anyway. Enough money, is a statement that depends on intention. One of the major hamburger chains in Brazil is called *BOB'S*, we know because we've been there and eaten their hamburgers. (which we recommend, along with their Brazilian fresh fried potato chips). An acquaintance of ours in Brazil told us that *BOB'S* was started by an American hippy back in the 60's. A guy named Bob was living on the beach in Brazil, couldn't get a hamburger, which he really, really, really, really, wanted. (...or so the story goes). What happened is obvious; he opened a little hamburger stand on the beach and now he's a millionaire. We have to confess that we have never been able to verify this story. Its the sort of story one hears in the waterfront bars of Belize City, but we like it.

Is it any more incomprehensible than a dixie-cup salesman from Chicago named Ray Kroc buying an obscure hamburger stand in Beaumont, California with the improbable name of *McDonalds*?

The time isn't over for hamburger stands in America... its still possible. Rags to riches can happen anywhere. Success is based on a slippery combination which we call 'luck.' Luck can be defined as being in the right place at the right time, working twice as hard as everyone else, and still being successful despite those things. Add to that innovation, and bingo.

Being successful for Roy Kroc consisted of those factors. Precisely so. Look at the timing that Roy Kroc had going for him. A factor which does not detract from the fact that he worked very hard and was a very astute individual. There is nonetheless a great deal of difference between what was timely in the early 1950's in the USA and what was timely in the late 1960's. If our hippy friend Bob of Bob's in Brazil would have opened a hamburger stand in say Pismo Beach, California in the late 1960's rather than in Rio de Janeiro he might be on welfare today. Fortunately for Bob he was in Brazil and he had timing and place going for him. So, what to do? How to analyze what we want to do? What should be made clear to the expat, is that the cost of starting up a business is considerably less in Tegucigalpa than it is in Tacoma. So much less that the two ventures are barely comparable. Knowing how much money we have is probably more relevant than deciding how much we need. There are places in the world where we can make success possible for us on a shoestring if we know how to work for ourselves mentally. We can think of a half dozen countries waiting for hamburgers. Some of them right under our noses. We were astounded while doing the research for this book, to learn that the American Virgin Islands didn't have a place to rent motorbikes. The island of Saint John's still doesn't from what we've been told. Saint John's is an island with miles of back-country roads, a shortage of cars, a surplus of tourists and no place to rent a mountain bike or motor-bike.

Determining how much money it would take to start up a motorbike rental shop in Saint John's is easier to calculate than the cost of setting up a hamburger stand in Tegucigalpa. Also it is more expensive. But our obvious intention is to convey a point to the reader, no?

We've also heard from reliable sources that no one, we repeat, no one is supplying fresh produce or vegetables on any of the American Virgin Islands. Produce has to shipped into the Virgins from afar at great shipping cost. (causing the available pro-duce in V.I. markets to be high in price and dated in flavor.) The reason for the lack of locally grown produce, or so we've been told, is a scarcity of water. There are several ways to grow fresh vegetables hydroponically that utilize low water-consump-tion methods. As a matter of fact, upon hearing about that lack of fresh produce in the Virgins we spent several days reading about hydroponic methods and thinking about what it would take to set up such a venture. It was a rather intriguing few days. It would be lots of hard work, but in our opinion it would be fun, in addition to it's having the potential of being extremely lucrative. There are numerous nearby is-lands that would also be interested in purchasing fresh produce. The venture would take some serious research. Hydroponics is a science; but it isn't rocket science and we believe that anyone with a brain could learn what is required to be successful.

We realize that we have not given the reader a satisfactory answer to the question regarding venture capital. It's an impossible question. The variables are as numerous as the number of readers who read this book. But it is quite possible that we can design a simple technique for reaching our own individual answers by viewing a variety of expatriate venture possibilities and calculating their cost requirements. Can we determine how much capital it would take to begin growing produce in the Virgin Islands using low-water hydroponics? Yes, we most probably can. Let's see what it would take to answer that sort of question.

It is no secret that the methods of gaining *'current'* information have recently changed because: [1] the volume of information has radically increased, [2] the perspective of what constitutes relative information is now global rather than local, and [3] the timeliness of information has become a dynamic factor that radically affects the value of the information recieved. Specific world wide information that is current is difficult to get from traditional sources such as a local library. Today whether we like it or not, most current information comes by way of a PC, or personal home computer. We want to stress the use of the word 'current,' which in this context can mean anything from 24 hours to six months depending on the type of information we are searching for. It is impossible to make any kind of meaningful venture-decision in todays world with information that is over a year old. (an issue we will discuss at length in just a moment.) By keying-in the word *hydroponics* on our PC just now we were able to bring up 100 separate pieces of relevant information on the subject of hydroponics in the time it took us to write one sentence.* (we actually just did this a moment ago as we were writing in order to time the search.) The information we recieved including the on-line addresses of several data-libraries that we can query regarding specific issues about hydroponics. One of these databases included the **Library of Congress.** We were also offered access to a series of instructional videos on the science & techniques of hydroponics we could purchase right over the internet.

Next, if we are to continue our scenario for venture cost analysis, we could do the same type of search on other issues, including the Virgin Islands themselves: subjects as varied as; climatic conditions, soil types, business permits, land prices, water availability, water pumps, building material, local phone numbers, airline ticket information, moving costs and any other relevant questions.

With an Internet search we can get pretty close to knowing what it would take to become hydroponic farmers living on a Caribbean Island. It costs less than a opening a Caribbean resort hotel, more than a hamburger stand in Tegucigalpa. Are the bags packed?

---

*Note: since writing the above we have added software that allows us to bring up over a thousand pieces of information on *hydroponics* (or any other query) in 3 or 4 minutes by accessing 23 search engines simultaneously.

Because they are especially important tools for expats, this book has a section on computers and the new science of *telephony*. It is not a large section. It contains no obscure computer lingo and we try to avoid incomprehensible terms and acronyms. It's our guess that many readers are pretty sick of hearing about computers. We empathize. Our observations about computers involve communications technology and how that technology is of special value to the expat. It should be pointed out that many people will go their entire lives without ever owning a computer, just as many people can go their entire life without ever owning a car. A computer is no more pertinent than a telephone or a fax machine. They are tools. Their goodness or badness, value or lack of value is an aspect of our personal selves. It is entirely possible to become an expat without using a computer.

As we've just pointed out, using a computer as a research tool we are able to answer questions regarding the viability and possible costs of a venture. But does the information we are able to gather answer the question of what it would cost to become an expat for someone who wants to move to the Virgin Islands, get a job as a wine steward in a fine restaurant and live in treehouse? (Which is exactly what my daughter did. Treehouse and all.)

Obviously, both the question of capital outlay and the use of a computer is something that has to be answered individually. Just as it is possible to become an expat without a PC it is possible to go abroad without money. My daughter dropped out of college, used what money she had to buy a one-way ticket to the Virgin Islands, lived with two girlfriends in a treehouse *'a-la-Swiss Family Robinson,'* (complete with electricity, running water, etc..) and spent most of her time sailing, diving, dining and dancing. Two years later she did the same thing in Australia, then after another two years: Europe. (Fortunately, for my fatherly peace-of-mind, she married someone sane and stable.)

Becoming an expat does not need to be a complex undertaking, especially for someone who is single and is intent simply on enjoying themselves. However, today my daughter has a husband and twin daughters of her own. It is highly unlikely that my son-in-law and my daughter would go anywhere on a one-way ticket without resources and a plan. For the larger number of us, knowing where we are going, knowing what's there and knowing what we're going to do to make a living when we get there is an absolute requirement. And that, of course, is the *raison d'être* for this book.

WHERE WE ARE COMING FROM

"...the migration to rural/resort real estate [now taking place in the United States] will extend everywhere on the face of the globe. Primitive countries will benefit the most, and property prices there will reflect the influx of buyers."

-Doug Casey

This book has a couple of predecessors that were pretty fine books in our opinion. One, written by Robert Hopkins was published in 1972, and titled *I've Had It; A Practical Guide to Moving Abroad.* It was a closely researched book, thoughtful in its approach to the subject, a harbinger to events that are much more apparent today then they were twenty-five years ago. The second book, *The International Man* by Douglas Casey was published in 1978 in hard back, reappearing the following year as a paperback in a new edition and with a new name; *The Expatriate Investor.* Much has changed in the world since these books were written and much of the information in them is now dated. Even so, if the reader is lucky enough to find a copy of either book in a used bookstore they are well worth the read. We will occasionally be referring to these two books throughout this book; and we will certainly be recommending Casey's current book, *Crisis Investing For The Rest of the 90's,* an investment book with much information that today's expatriate will find of value. Casey still focuses on international investing with an emphasis on mining and mining stocks. He has visited 110 countries and lived in seven of them. Hence, the man knows whereof he speaks. He has given some time recently towards trying to establish a new country, or to the establishment of a system of liberty within an existing country. He has consulted with heads of state around the world on this issue.*

When Robert Hopkins and Douglas Casey wrote their books half of the world was under the oppressive blanket of communism. Today, a place like **Prague** and much of **Czech & Slovak** might well be considered one of the better destinations for the expatriate. Prague has recently been compared to the Paris of the 1920's, with artists and others now moving there for the historical ambience and the cheap rents.

Also in the years since these books were published we have seen the globalization of the world economy and the advent of immensely improved telecommunications which heralded the home-office/ telecommuting revolution. These factors alone have radically changed the nature of choosing where we *'want'* to live by changing where we *'have'* to live. But these factors, although primary factors, may be just the more obvious part of the iceberg that is showing; we are today witnessing innovations occurring at a phenomenal rate of speed on a worldwide scale. Innovations so unprecedented in nature that it is safe for us to assume that nothing will ever be again

*There seem to be a large number of people seeking a free nation and the idea is looking more and more feasible as time goes by. The issue of a new nation is unresolved at this time. We are monitoring this situation and we will update readers in our fax-on-demand system as the situation changes.

as it was before. Any further advances in ultralight aircraft will soon make them as usable as an automobile at half the cost and twice the proficiency. Roads may soon become inconsequential in determining where we must live, allowing us to finally choose where in the world we want to live.

Writing in his recent book about the explosive expansion to technology and its effect on creating the coming global village, Douglas Casey states, "...the migration to rural/resort real estate [now taking place in the United States] *will extend everywhere on the face of the globe. Primitive countries will benefit the most, and property prices there will reflect the influx of buyers.*" He adds that the very last people who will become aware of the global migration will be the people who have been living sheltered lives in those very regions that will be the target destinations of the new expatriates. "...the big profits accrue to the person who capitalizes on the trend, not to the original owner of the land." However, far from being a loser, workers from the Third World may finally begin to realize dreams of their own as the new American expatriates leave job vacancies behind them as they seek further and further afield for global homesites.

There may well be an exchange of places, a sort of global game of musical chairs; as we seek a more tranquil life in Third World countries working where we choose to live, so Third World workers may continue their traditional immigration into America, willing to work longer and harder than us for a wage we no longer find interesting. Although we surely are seeking more than the higher wages by going further afield.

"It seems that we have finally begun to seek what might be called 'a life'."

For the Third World worker tired of trying to live without a refrigerator and other simple amenities, 'a life' might mean: a clean and well lit studio apartment in Los Angeles, an assembly line job, and the ability to make car payments on a new car. For the new expatriate, 'a life', might mean being able to live on a Caribbean Island or a mountain-side ranch in Chile while doing market research or designing for that very same assembly line company in Los Angeles, but from a spot halfway around the world and at a different pace.

Hopkins and Casey each discussed the reasons why Americans were becoming disenfranchised with America. Hopkins pointed out that in 1967 America became an emigrant as well as an immigrant nation for the very first time since the civil war. (Although the number of Americans moving abroad each year had not yet exceeded the number of other nationalities immigrating into the United States). However, Hopkins then proceeded to drop a bombshell with some statistical changes of a slightly more disturbing nature; "Following the 1968 Democratic Convention, with its attendant televised violence," Hopkins tells us, " inquiries to the Australian consulates in the United States jumped from a trickle to 8,000 in one month, and continued to climb. Two years later, the 1970 figures show that Australia recieved 120,000 requests for immigrant information. Requests for information recieved by foreign consulates cite "social unrest," "fear of violence," racial tensions," and the decline of moral standards in America as reasons for interest in settling elseswhere."

Casey's book, published a half dozen years later, showed a continuing numerical increase in the number of Americans leaving American. Casey's analysis of the eroding enchantment with America was cautious and closely reasoned. He examined freedom around the world from a number of differing perspectives and concluded that while America was becoming a decreasingly attractive place to live, it still had a high degree of freedom. He then added the rather apocalyptic comment; "...but you may want to get a second passport now; just in case, ...or to beat the last minute rush."

A comparative look at the procurable statistics from the U.S. State Department show that in 1971 when Hopkins published his book, there were approximately 1.5 million American civilians living abroad. Today the U.S. State Department claims that there are 2.5 million; but they are basing those figures on expatriate Americans who are paying taxes.* The number of American's who may have chosen to quietly escape from the burden of paying into a system that will *not meet* their needs because it *cannot* meet their needs could easily triple the number of expatriate Americans. The U.S. Government has created a 5 trillion dollar debt, which works out to $20,000.00 for every man, woman and child in America. Any person who assumes that there is going to be any sort of Social Security, Medicare, or other U.S. Government programs twenty years hence may well be in for a big surprise.

When the politicians began asking Americans to play what amounts to a chain-letter game with a time-bomb attached to it, many prudent Americans decided it was time to simply pack up and leave quietly. And who can blame them? What sane person wants to subject their precious family or themselves to a system that takes away over half of their earnings (with promises to provide services in exchange), and then somehow cannot account for almost 70 percent of the money taken.**

* I spoke with the U.S. State Department's public affairs office in Washington DC regarding this issue; they confirmed that the figures did indeed come from Americans who had *registered* in some way with a U.S. Government agency. They also based their estimates on numbers that the Foreign Service Office gathered from foreign-based American Chamber's of Commerce and from private organizations of American's abroad, such as **FLAGG**, Resident's Assistance Associations, and senior citizens groups. When I said that I believed that the number of Americans abroad was double of triple their estimate, they concurred that they believed this also. When I said that I believed there were millions of Americans who had simply slipped away because they had quit paying taxes, they laughed heartily and replied cryptically, "That may well be.

[2] Bureaucracy 'operates' on 70 percent of each dollar it collects; returning 30 percent as services. And then to add insult to injury, the remaining 30 percent of the confiscated funds that hasn't been lost in the shuffle, is returned as a sort of 'booby prize for fools' in purely appalling services, from the shamefully low academic standards of our schools, to the astronomic money 'giveaways', such as a Foreign Aid Program that somehow resembles an incomprehensible series of ransom payments more than it does any kind of aid.

VIA CON DIOS

Are Americans walking away from America without saying goodbye?

It is instructive to look at the 'official estimates' of American expatriates living abroad; certain curious discrepancies are made noticeable by their absence. It was claimed that there were 172,134 Americans living in Canada in 1969. In 1971 that figure jumped to 240,500; an increase of 68,366 persons overall, or 34,183 per year; a 20 percent annual increase. The 'official' figure today [for 1995-96] is 381,535 Americans living in Canada. Something seems wrong with these figures. If the increase of departing Americans between 1969 and 1971 was 20 percent per year and those years were prior to the acceleration of departing Americans, then even with no acceleration it would mean that the figure today would be closer to 13 million. Do I believe that the figure is 13 million? No, emphatically not. But if we had to hazard a guess as to how many Americans have joined what Hopkins labeled, 'The quiet exodus', we would probably be foolish to believe that the number is not at least triple the 'official' estimates.

Other countries showed similar increases of departing Americans coming to roost between 1969 and 1971, and in some cases with numbers even exceeding Canada's 20 percent. Italy, for instance, increased by 21 percent each year during that two year period, Belgium 25 percent, Australia 22 percent, and Israel by an astounding 77 percent! Italy today shows an 'official' expatriate American population of a mere 121,500; up only 70 thousand Americans since 1969. Yet the increase from 1969 to 1971 was 22,076; 11 thousand for each year. An increase of 11 thousand persons for each of the 26 years since 1969 would produce a current total population figure of 337,850. We suspect the number is much higher than even this adjusted figure.

What's happening? Is the U.S. State Department lying? Are they exceedingly poor at mathematics? Or does the answer have to do with something else, something unprecedented in American history? Are Americans walking away from America without saying goodbye?

It was far from easy for the families of my father and my mother to leave Italy, a land that they loved and which they never quit loving. But they were motivated to emigrate by a crushing poverty and by conditions so backward that progress was not merely improbable as it was totally inconceivable. My father was ever vocal as I grew up in singing the praises of America. I cannot remember how many times I heard him say, '...this is the greatest country on earth,' I am sure he used the phrase at least twice a week for forty years. Today, when I ask him if this is still the greatest country on earth, he pauses reflectively before his reply; "...Yes, still the greatest," he will say with pride, but there is a sadness in his eyes as he continues, "...but we have troubles, ... big troubles."

Italy today, more or less leads the common market, or is second after Germany; depending on which set of statistics we choose to believe. * A nation no longer divided by regional language differences, but united by a common television dialect, it has sprug forth from centuries of slumber to take its place as one of the worlds leaders. Glancing through a contemporary medical book, we find that about 15 percent of the entries resulting from medical research are Italian; a number that is profound when we consider per capita contribution. Italy has managed to pull towards the front of the pack in many sectors from industrial and fashion design to manufacturing with the verve and style of a Farari driver winning the Grand Prix. It is not the Italy my father left, not even close. And the Americans who emigrate to Italy to live these days are not impoverished immigrants trying to pull themselves up from a morass of abject poverty. It's a whole new ballgame. As Hopkins wrote in 1972, "Americans are perhaps the first people in history who have been able to afford the luxury of voluntary emigration unforced by famine, disease, imminent danger, religious intolerance, or the gnawing desire for economic betterment." It seems that what was once inconceivable is now reality. The countries that our parents left behind are quickly becoming more desirable places to return to and to live in for many of us, than living in American. The culture, the ambiance, the pace, the attitude of the people; whatever it is we are seeking, no longer seems available in America. The 'greatest country on earth' has lost its charm. We would rather sit at a sidewalk café or piazza than a McDonalds.

"We shall not cease from exploring,
and the end of all our exploring,
will be to arrive where we started,
and know the place for the first time"

So goes a T.S. Eliot poem. Perhaps his poetic forecast was more than just clever metaphor; we may indeed be seeing the equivalence of some cultural sunbreaks. We have come full circle and we like ourselves; and what is more important, we are perhaps finally willing to admit the unthinkable; that at long last after thousands of years of preparation, we are now prepared to shed the confines and concept of government, like a living thing shedding a dying skin.

---

*The Paris-based Organization for Economic Cooperation and Development, sets the average share of the 'submerged market' economy in its member states at 4 percent of their gross domestic products. Italy, according to most international experts, has a 'submerged' economy responsible for a whopping 30 percent of its production.

WORLD WITHOUT BORDERS
THE END OF THE NATION STATE

Two important books were recently published with the very same title; each book was called *"The End Of The Nation State."* One was written by Kenichi Ohmae a well known Japanese businessman and published in 1995, the other by Jean-Marie Guéhenno a French Diplomat was published in 1993.* Both books deal with the same subject, which as the title[s] imply has to do with the coming borderless world. These books discuss among other things the effect that the global economy is having on the way individuals (and corporations) view the world. In his book Guéhenno discusses what he calls *'deterritorialization,'* a phenomena which reflects the result of an almost global change in the traditional view of three interrelated factors: the *strategic, economic* and *moral* interests of nations. According to Guéhenno these three parts; strategic interests, economic interests and moral position no longer evenly overlap as they once did. Borders have suddenly become not much more than meaningless lines drawn on maps by governments. Governments out of touch with their own people. The borderlines depicting nations, keep the governments in business but act as an impediment to the real business of human beings. In strategic terms the borders have become a very expensive ring of defenses against an enemy who is no longer as dangerous as the idea of government itself. They are a ring of defenses around nothing.

In America, **Microsoft** President Bill Gates also recently mentioned the phenomena of changing attitudes towards borders, though in a slightly different context. Talking about what he calls the 'information superhighways' in his recent book, *'The Road Ahead"* Gates' writes that, "...the highway will ease the current stress on urban infrastructures by providing more people the opportunity to telecommute, working from home via the network instead of commuting to the office each day."

---

*The explanation for the identical titles is that while Guéhenno's book was published first as *La fin de la démocratie*, it wasn't translated from French until 1995, and then republished in English on almost the same date as Ohmae's. Jean-Marie Guéhnno is France's Ambassador to European Union. He gave a talk on **Public Radio's Talk of the Nation** on October 2, 1996. The entire talk can be downloaded live audio at: **URL**: http://www.realaudio.com/contentp/npr/ne1002.html

These seemingly disparate factors taken in combination seem on their way to changing much of what we now take for granted. If Gates is correct and we believe he is, then what each of us need to address is the question of where in the world our home or our home office could, should and will be located. Does it make as much or more sense to locate our home office in Bakersfield, the Bahamas, Boston, or Baton Rouge as it does in Bahia, Belize City, or Buenos Aires? With no historic precedence to guide us, what are the factors that will help us make these types of decision? What we seek may be as widely varied as a need for pleasure, a concern with our natural environment, schools for our children, beaches to play on, population trends, crime factors, business possibilities, political stability, freedom from government control, telecommunication (and internet) access, good looking women, good looking men, good music, a brighter future, a life with more promise and joy, access to the sporting areas we prefer, farm land, access to Paris, access to Rio, or perhaps all of the above, some of the above, or none of the above.

The fact is that there are an almost overwhelming number of issues which need to taken into consideration when (and if) we do decide the time has come for us to relocate. If it is true that we can finally live where we want to live and do what we want to do; where in the world do we want to live and what is it we really want to do? In addition to the intriguing complexity of these questions, much like a kid in a candy store we are faced with the fact is that every location in this vast world changes the logistics involved in the decisions that we are asking ourselves to make. (Even while the logistics involved in the possibilities are growing exponentially at the same time.)

I myself feel excited by the possibilities and challenges that these decisions may bring to my future and I find their numerical complexity intellectually invigorating. But I am aware that not everyone feels the way I do. We can choose to be overwhelmed by the possibilities opening up before us, or we can celebrate in the numerous new pleasures that seem to be inherent in our new liberty. There is no question that too much liberty can be frightening to many of us; for liberty does entail the obligation of self responsibility and that of course means that we are going to have to be responsible for our own failures as well as our own successes. With no government safety net beneath us, it is not surprising that some of us may experience moments of hesitation. However it is safe to assume that the good old government safety net many of us are so accustomed to in America is not going remain what it is in any case. It is easier to prepare for the inevitable with a sense of joy and anticipation by our being prepared than it is to bury our head in the sand hoping that tigers prefer to eat grass.

The so-called government safety nets of our youth were tenuous and built on a monetary fault. No government in the world has any magic other than slight of hand. No one can borrow from Peter to pay Paul forever. When the time comes to make the Pipers payment who do you think that the United States government employees will be turning to in order to place the blame? They will be looking for humans like us. It is safe to assume that the safety nets we pretend are there are either going to go away entirely or they are going to become so tight that they will strangle all the incentive out of those who remain. (Or perhaps create a trap that they won't be able to escape from.)*

Robert A. Heinlien once said that when humanity goes to the stars the 'culls' will remain behind. I have a European-born acquaintance who insists that America was populated by culls; those who couldn't make it in Europe went to America. I have given some thought to the double-bind that these two disparate statements create. It is certainly true that those who came to America were for the most part those who were impoverished or who were escaping the heavy hand of political oppression. But look at the nation they created. Was it just the increased economic liberty that made America the powerful nation it became? Or was it the quality of it's people? If it was the former, then what will happen now? It is no secret that it is exactly that very important freedom which is quickly eroding in America at the precise moment that a wider degree of freedom is increasing almost everywhere else in the world.

*There is every reason to believe that United States government will move to stop flight capital. Imagine if it was you personally who were guilty of running up a 5 trillion dollar debt with borrowed money and you needed more money to keep yourself in business and you could take anyone's money with impunity, wouldn't you try to stop your victims from escaping with their money if you considered their money to be yours? If you answered No to this question, then perhaps you don't belong in today's political arena. Further, what is perhaps more frightening, but certainly possible, is that the United States government may move at a certain point to stop a 'brain drain' such as the one experienced by Great Britain (which was caused by very much the same monetary-political causes.) What I am saying, is that the United States government might try at a certain point to stop people from leaving by way of legislation, ...especially if it's losing it's best and it's brightest people to better opportunities abroad. Although they'll have a different name and different explanation for the 'emergency' 'security' legislation that they will be 'forced' to impose. (i.e.They might just be holding you prisoner in America to save your children from harm.)

In purely relative terms, Americans do not have a long history to draw on (in the broadest sense of the concept of history.) This fact is especially true in the area of emigration. Americans have nothing in their past which enables them to see that the other side of the border may have better possibilities than the side they live on. Additionally, all of these changes we are discussing have happened rather suddenly. Last year Prague was where the Soviets had their tanks parked, this year we're parking our Mercedez there.

It may well be that what has begun as a silent emigration out of America on the part of intelligent Americans may become a stampede. As we mention elsewhere; if it is now possible to run a global business from a 50 acre ranch in Argentina or from an island off the coast of Belize and the real estate in those places is cheaper and better; then how long does the reader assume it will be before other Americans realize the same thing?

What is required of the reader is to quit *imagining* that the world is now global. It no longer has anything to do with imagination. It's a fact. We are just 'in' on the early stages of it and our perspective isn't complete. Looking back on the event twenty-five years from now it will be obvious that we only live on one planet and that the borders were meaningless. What kind of real estate we own then and where we are living is going to have a lot to do with how perceptive we are now.

CHAPTER TWO

TREASURE ISLAND
Tax Havens & Offshore Banks

"Privacy is perhaps the greatest human value. With it we can aim at greatness. Without it we have nothing ...or less than nothing."

WARNING

It is now appropriate to admonish the reader to check and verify all facts with an attorney prior to putting coins in a parking meter. Here is our warning to readers: If you are too stupid to make your own decisions then stay home. Whatever you do, not go abroad where you will come face to face with the responsibility of making independent judgements. Anyone who cannot make independent judgements should stay in America. That will save you the trouble of trying to sue me for your mistakes. The fact is that everyone who was alive two hundred years ago is now dead. The world seems to have some sort of strange habit. There seem to be pitfalls. People keep smashing their toes, going broke, hitting walls, falling off cliffs and dying. Being alive is learning to miss the big drop offs and trying to hit the big jackpots. Jackpots can consist of love, money, freedom, or of their opposites depending on what it is we are attracted to. As Borges said, there are those who will even find hell inadequate. When we wrote this section we fully believed that the information it contained was accurate. After thinking about the possible lawsuits we changed our mind. Read it as fiction. Perhaps like *Treasure Island*. But do so only if your attorney says that it's alright to read it that way.

ROGER'S INVESTMENT RULES

1. The laws of probability gain their final shape and their definition by whatever it is that is least probable.
2. No matter what we look at, or how we look at it, it is impossible to see it all.
3. If an act is involuntary; somewhere, somehow, a pistol is involved.

OF FIELD MICE, HAWKS & THE ISLAND LIFE

We are considered field mice. It's certainly not a very flattering thing to be called, is it? But that is what they call us in the greater world, there amidst the tree tops, where the hawks live. There are few hawks and many field mice and the hawks live by eating the field mice. I didn't invent this parlance, any more than I invented the world.

STUPID STORY TIME

Let me tell you a story. It's sort of a boring story but we need the story to develop a point of reference, so please indulge us by wading through it.

Once upon a time in the midst of looking at the world, we [meaning: I and possibly you] discovered the fact that most of the world's chromium comes from the country of **Rhodesia**. (now called **Zimbabwe**) At the time of our discovery, a civil war was heating up in Rhodesia. The reasons for this civil war, at least ostensibly, was that the white minority in Rhodesia and the government under their control, had much too much and the black majority had much too little. That's what we were told. Each day the situation appeared to be growing worst for the white Rhodesians who had been abandoned by the rest of the world for their sins and were being maligned by the media. They were fighting a lonely losing battle. While watching these events unfold (and feeling an appropriate amount of sympathy for both sides,) the thought occurred to us that the price of chromium was about to go sky high. Believing this, we purchased a 'futures contract' for chromium. When we purchased this contract, we did so with a process that involved inserting a 'stop-loss' into the purchase order. A stop-loss as you may or may not know, is a method of insuring that in the unlikely event of a decline in price of one of our market investments, our loss would be kept to a specific minimum (as spelled out in the terms of the stop-loss instructions.) As an example of this procedure, let us imagine an imaginary futures contract in silver. For our scenario, let us suppose that the price of silver is $5.00 per ounce, and we assume that in the near future, it is going to rapidly ascend to $10.00 per ounce and make us rich. Knowing this, we purchase a forward contract, or futures contract, (an agreement to buy silver at $5.50 at a specified date in the near future, say three months in the future.) In order to purchase a forward contract, we put up a percentage (or down payment) on the contract, this downpayment is called a *margin*. This margin is a percentage of the contract, usually 20% of the total contract. Once done, unless there is a drastic fluctuation, we simply sit back and wait for our commodity to rise in price so that we can become rich.

We can cash in our contract any time we feel we are prepared to do so. If, by some good fortune the price of silver has gone to $10.00 per ounce, as it was supposed to, we can, as a result of our foresight, cunning, (and by right of contract,) buy it at $5.50 per ounce; even though the going price is $10.00 per ounce. This gives us an obvious profit of $4.50.

Of course forward contracts are purchased in large lots, such as 10,000 ounces. So, our forward contract with a $4.50 increase would then be worth $45,000 more than the price we agreed to pay for it. A nice profit. (It is simpler to view forward contracts as a 'promise to buy' at a given price, with a small downpayment made by the purchaser to insure that the purchaser is obligated to perform.) By buying a forward (or futures) contract to purchase, we can purchase a commodity in advance. We buy whatever it is we want to buy ahead of time; in three months, six months, or whatever time-frame we choose because we believe that what we are purchasing in advance is going to rise in price. Essentially, what we are really purchasing is a *guaranteed price*. A guaranteed price that is insured by our contract to purchase, which we have purchased from a seller who has contracted with us to sell, at that guaranteed price.

If we are foolish, greedy and sure of ourselves, we can get an even larger contract, somewhere on the order of 100,000 ounces, or 500,000 ounces, or perhaps more. The problem with such a contract, is that if the price happens to fall, then we are still obligated to purchase the commodity at the price agreed for in the contract. A silver contract of 500,000 ounces having fallen by $1.00 an ounce creates a half million dollar debt. Of course silver can't fall by a dollar, right?

It is interesting to note, that on a 500,000 ounce contract, a fall in price of only five cents (.05¢) produces a $25,000 loss. Knowing this, what we do to protect ourselves from unstoppable loss, is that we inform our broker or Swiss Banker, that we want to place a 'stop-loss' on our forward contract, our intention being that in the event the price of silver falls by a specific amount, (five cents or whatever we deem prudent,) we want our forward contract sold automatically to protect us against further loss.

Armed with this much wisdom I entered the futures market for chromium. After all, Rhodesia produced the majority of the world's chromium and chromium was a necessity. Rhodesia was engaged in a deepening civil war and we could clearly see that the mining operations within Rhodesia were facing a imminent shutdown. These facts were not some pipe-dream, they were the facts regarding chromium, Rhodesia, and the world, It was easy to see that the price of chromium had to rise! Additionally, in the remote possibility that I'd somehow made a miscalculation and that I was wrong, well, I was so smart that I'd placed a five cent stop-loss on my forward contract. Smug I was when I purchased my forward contract.

Here is what happened: the price of chromium fell by eight cents, I lost my margin deposit of $25,000, and then the price of chromium turned around, headed upwards and went through the roof.

After I picked myself up and dusted myself off, I asked my banker what the hell had happened.

"Well," he said, "...well nothing happened. They just shook out the field mice by whip-sawing and then they picked up the loose change."

Whip-sawing? Field Mice?

What had happened was simple. The world can be rather simple once you understand the rules. Its just that no one bothers to tell us the rules until we get caught off base. The world consists of the hawks and the field mice. The hawks have the ability to make a market go downwards, (or upwards) and will do so even when a market is poised to go in the opposite direction. Why? Because they know that field mice do not have the resources to withstand large fluctuations of a given price in a commodity and are forced out of the market. i.e. their bread crumbs fall to the ground while they scurry for cover. The hawks then simply swoop up the bread crumbs on the way to the picnic.

EXPLANATION: If the price of a commodity has stayed in one price range for a long period of time and it appears to be about to rise, then hundreds of thousand of little field mice enter the market and buy futures contracts on that commodity. These little fellows are awfully shy, so they place a stop loss, **usually in the amount equal to 50% of their margin payment** and then they sit shyly on the sidelines with their beady little eyes and wait for the hawks to move. The hawks do move. They cause the price of the commodity to fall, by selling their huge holdings of the commodity, then when it dips below the margin level of the cute little field mice, the hawks hold out their talons and all the money that the field mice put there drops obediently into the hawks waiting claws.)

Here is what we learned for only $25,000: We learned that in the world of investment (or anywhere else we may care to look,) nothing is totally perceivable, that there is *always* more to be seen. No, there is no conspiracy. It's just that our frame of reference to things can never be large enough to encompass everything. Does that mean we should throw in the towel and quit? Or, does that mean we should broaden our perspective as much as possible and be the better player? After all, just because we cannot see it all doesn't mean we cannot learn to see better than most.

Does all this have anything to do with Tax Havens? Yes, it does. What is a tax haven? A tax haven by definition has several different categories, which we'll soon describe, but before we do so let's take a look at one particular type of tax haven. Imagine a country where you could place your money that didn't tell anyone back home what you were doing. Imagine that all of the money earned there was tax free: (on interest earnings, profit from stocks, bonds, whatever.) Wouldn't that be a great place? For any foreign investor in the world, such are exactly the conditions within the United States. The United States is the world's biggest tax haven. People from all over the world bring their money to the United States and invest it with impunity, knowing that their own governments will not find out, and knowing that the US government will not charge them any taxes on anything they earn in the United

States while they are hiding out from the bad old folks back home. With this nice scheme just about everyone is making out like a bandit in the deal.

Well... just about everyone. It doesn't work for field mice. The United States is the only government in the world which taxes its own citizens on income worldwide to begin with and to top it off the poor field mice inside the US who are American have to pay 40% to 60% taxes on everything they earn, if they are able to earn anything, because the tax haven isn't for them, it's for foreigners only. Also, just to rub in a little more salt, the other governments of the world don't tax their citizens on any foreign income, although its true that some of them do have exchange controls, however their citizens are able to turn to their good friend the US government who keeps their hidden deposits and profits secret. The American citizen field mice are the only ones who pay, and they better pay, ...if they don't pay, their property is confiscated.

Perhaps our eyes are opened wider. It is better to know the rules, because it broadens our perspective and helps us see better, even when the playing field isn't too even.

Let me tell you about the playing field. The playing field is large, it consist of the entire world; but Americans find themselves trapped in a narrow valley where the hawks are thick and vicious; additionally, Americans have not had a tradition of escaping from the valley, so no one passed on the information of what the valley looked like from afar, or what conditions were like beyond the valley.

Imagine that there is a river at the far end of the valley and that all we have to do to gain our freedom is to swim across that river and be free. Next to the river lives the bald eagle. If we are spotted crossing the river, the eagle will swoop down and gobble us up. Such is the challenge faced by the new expatriates. How to escape America with our assets intact and reach the far shore of freedom. It is as difficult or as simple as we care to make it. Do we have a right to do so? If we don't, then we have lost our right to live. Within our own country, we are not even entitled to the same rights and privileges as a foreigner. The US government wants their money here, so it creates a huge tax haven for the world which we ourselves can't utilize, nor are we even allowed to flee to a haven of our choosing with our assets intact. The reason of course, is that we're field mice and being field mice we don't count; our purpose is keep our eyes closed and to serve the wishes of our masters.

SOAP BOX TIME

It also important to note that in becoming an expatriate not all of us will need tax havens. Not everyone wants to spend all of their time making or worrying about money. Many of us would just like to have a real life. In this context, how many of us are even remotely content with life in America? We cannot imagine a prison more horrible than to live without imagination. Yet, with each passing day America seems to become more and more devoid of imagination. Or, perhaps it is only becoming devoid of the spirit of imagination. The effect is the same. And it isn't just one person's imagination, somehow we all seem to sense what is happening, even if we can't put our finger on it. How wonderful it would be to live a life like we've always dreamed. A real life. A life where there are new things to discover and the freedom to do the simplest of things. We know it sounds trite to mention this, but Americans can't even own chickens anymore. Christ, but its difficult to imagine a country where you can't even own chickens. Don't tell me about the reasoning and the rules. I'm as sick to death with the reasoning and the rules as everyone else. We've been legislated to death; and what has died is our imagination and our freedom to live. So, for some of us, the mere freedom to be able to live a simple, healthy life free of government supervision would constitute freedom. However, some of us do have more stressful financial worries; (real or imagined) and hence greater tax problems and shelter needs. None of us want to lose our hard-earned assets. What if our total assets are so great as to place us in the position of being afraid to move? How can we insure some form of asset protection from the irrationality of government? How do we maintain the right to advance our assets without the undue consequence and jeopardy of having to deal with any government that we might consider morally or financially bankrupt? How do we get free of government? Perhaps we are seeking a place where we can continue to operate our business without the added expense of giving away 60% of each dollar we earn as ransom to the hawks. Perhaps what we need is a tax haven. Let's take a look at what they are and what they do and try to figure out if a tax haven is really what we need.

TAX HAVENS AND OTHER DESTINATIONS

Here are the rough overall criteria which more or less describe the basic advantages of a tax haven:

✓ Some existing level of Freedom from Taxation
✓ Banking, Corporation, & Transaction Secrecy Laws that protect both Privacy and Assets.
✓ An absence of Exchange Controls and other governmental handicaps to doing business.

Before we continue, it should be pointed out that most professional tax specialists are in agreement that not everyone needs a tax haven and it is not always to our benefit to use one. Because there is no standard index to follow in evaluating ones need of a tax haven, the decision to use one must be weighted on an individual case by case basis.

Tax Havens have different categories. The simplest being the **No-tax tax-haven**. A no-tax tax-haven is a country (or jurisdiction) that has no income, capital gain, or wealth taxes of any sort and in which there are facilities and legislation under which we can incorporate and/or form trusts. This type of tax haven is a pure tax haven. The countries that fulfill this definition include; Anguilla, the Bahamas, Bahrain, Bermuda, the Cayman Islands, Cook Islands, Djibouti, Turks and Caicos, Vanuatu and perhaps a few more which we will discuss throughout the book. The government of these countries most usually earns its revenue by charging fees on: documents of incorporation, the value of corporation shares, registration fees and so forth. We can operate a business from one of these countries without any income taxes

There are some special considerations which must be observed, but for all intents and purposes, **No tax Tax Haven** countries are tax-free.

Next, in degree of taxation levied, we have the **No-tax-on-foreign-income tax-havens**. These countries (jurisdictions) do impose income taxes, both on individuals and corporations, but only on locally derived income. The countries that fulfill that definition include; Hong Kong, Liberia, Panama, Philippines, Venezuela, Shannon International Airport, Jersey, Belize, Guernsey, Isle of Man, Gibraltar, and a few others whose rules and regulations regarding income will be discussed throughout this book.

Some countries establish fixed rates of taxation. These countries are called **Low taxation tax-havens**. They generally tax a small amount on corporate income and have double-taxation agreements with many high-tax countries that when taken in combination and structured correctly work to reduce the overall degree of taxation. This is best for individuals who are not going to become permanent expats, but may some day want to return to the US once its government officials have been imprisoned. The countries which more or less fulfill the Low Tax definition are Cyprus, the British Virgin Islands, Liechtenstein, Oman, Switzerland, Jersey, Guernsey, and other countries which we will be discussing throughout the book.

Then there are the special incentive privileges to off-shore companies and qualified holding companies that are given by tax havens such as Luxembourg, the Netherlands, the Netherland Antilles, and Singapore. Plus the international business company tax reductions given by Antigua, Barbados, Grenada, Belize and Jamaica.

Additionally, there are the **Free Trade Zones (FTZ's)** that are now located in countries around the world. These FTZ's offer a number of benefits that are similar to a traditional tax haven but are geared more towards (but not strictly to) manufacturing. An FTZ can work as a sort of stand alone type of tax haven or it can be used in conjunction with a traditional tax haven for added benefit and protection. Let's look at an imaginary scenario in order to better understand Free Trade Zones and see how they might be used in conjunction with traditional tax haven corporate structuring.

STUPID STORY TIME

--The Terrorism of Privacy

An imaginary couple, Harold and Olivia run a Telephone Answering and Corporation Services Center for other offshore corporations. Let us imagine that they operate their center out of the Free Trade Zone in Jamaica. Let us further imagine that they use the latest in computer & telephone technology to make their service 'state of the art' and totally 'data encryptinated.' What this means is that Harold and Olivia have as their true product the commodity of privacy. It would be suspected that they have all the business they can handle from the growing number of global expats looking for business privacy. (I'd be happy to find such a service!) Because Harold and Olivia operate out of the **Montego Bay Free Trade Zone**, they are entitled to the following:

WHAT WE CAN EXPECT FROM A FREE TRADE ZONE

✓ A 100 percent tax exemption forever
✓ Complete exemption from import licensing
✓ Exemption from import duties
✓ Full freedom to repatriate profits up to original capital without approval of the Central Bank

Additionally, Harold and Olivia have done something else. They have formed a **Cayman Island** Corporation. Their corporation, does all its billing by debiting their clients offshore debit accounts directly. Therefor all of the money they take in from their clients goes directly into an offshore bank located in a "no-tax jurisdiction" outside of Jamaica (and away from any eyes other than that of their offshore bank.) Their own checks that are written inside of Jamaica are written by Harold and Olivia themselves to pay their employees and for other local expenses. Because Montego Bay has the huge **Jamaica Digiport International (JDI)** earth-satellite station, the answering service Harold and Olivia is more than just top rate. Their Corporation Services Center can do: credit authorization, reservation services, toll-free numbers, image processing, electronic publishing, mailing lists, and a host of other telephony services most corporation services have not a clue to. Additionally, they can provide these services with a degree of privacy that does not and can not exist in the United States. (There are a great many government agencies inside the United States that are set up to protect us against privacy, because it is assumed that anyone who wants privacy in the United States is a terrorist.) Because Harold and Olivia provide jobs for sixteen Jamaicans, the island of Jamaica has little to complain about and much to be happy for. Harold and Oliva have happy clients, whose privacy and intelligence is respected in a way that is uncommon in today's world; their clients are respected as if a human beings privacy and intelligence really mattered.

We can see that by operating inside of a Free Trade Zone Harold and Olvia have much of the benefits we might assume would only be available from operating out of a traditional tax-haven. But the Free Trade Zone allows them to operate 'on site,' while a tax-haven is usually just a 'jurisdictional site' which exists more in paper reality than in corporal fact. (What today we might lovingly call 'virtual reality.') Using an FTZ combined *with* a tax-haven gives us the best of both worlds. Let's take a look at that.

In order to take our scenario further and make a nice bakers dozen out of one scenario, let us imagine that Harold is of Irish descent. One of his grandparents was born in Ireland. This entitles Harold to Irish citizenship without having to fulfill any residency requirements, nor does it require him to pay any money out of pocket for a second passport. So, Harold and Olivia (the former by right of descent, and the latter by right of marriage), become Irish Citizens and carriers of Irish Passports. However, just to play it safe, only Harold renounces his American citizenship. Olivia keeps her American citizenship; their intention in keeping at least one American Passport is their way of hedging their bets. No one can predict the future even when it applies to a stable country like Ireland.   (...remember our friend who knew that the price of chromium 'had' to go up?) As long as Olivia does not earn more than $70,000 per year she is exempt from US taxes. So, the corporation only pays her $70,000 a year. (we will return to this exemption in a moment) Harold is not a US citizen, he doesn't pay US taxes but he is now entitled to invest inside the United States without being taxed on his returns. (Although his wife might theoretically be taxed on half of such profit). Additionally, Harold and Olivia own a very nice property in Ireland where they spend a part of the year. They also own a home in Jamaica and they spend some time in Colorado each year at a home that is registered in the name of a Swiss bank. They do not have to pay Irish taxes, because [1] their money is earned outside of Ireland and [2] because they reside in Ireland less than six months out of the year. [3] They don't pay Jamaican taxes for much the same reason. The Cayman Islands is where their corporation tax jurisdiction exists (in virtual reality) and [4] the Cayman Islands charges no taxes. [5] If the US government or the IRS did decide for any reason to try to confiscate the properties of Harold and Olivia they would have to find something that Harold and Olivia owned inside of a geographical area over which the U.S. Government or the IRS had jurisdiction. Because the house in Colorado is in the name of a third-party entity, to wit: a Swiss bank; it will not show up on the County Assessors Tax Role as a property belonging to an individual named Harold or Olvia. Meaning that the US government is going to play hell trying to discover or prove ownership.

Let's return to the issue of the $70,000 earned by Olivia. To our understanding, there is a foreign earned income exclusion provision in the US tax code. (please verify this with a professional before acting upon it, for while we have read the code regarding the exemption #2555 of the Internal Revenue Code regarding this issue, we are not tax consultants, nor are we legal consultants) To our understanding, this section of the code specifically allows for any US citizen who works and lives outside the United States, to exclude from their gross income, up to $70,000 of foreign-earned income. (Additionally, employer-provided housing allowance can be excluded from this amount.) This provision states that each member of a married couple can exclude $70,000 of foreign earned gross income. Note, that this does imply a deduction, credit or deferral, but an outright exclusion of the total foreign income from gross income. For a couple, that equals $140,000 tax free income. (We are hopeful that no one would foolishly be paying taxes to a foreign government on their income.)

According to the IRS, your tax home is specified by *where you work and not by where you live*. If we lived in Mexico and drove across the border each day to a job in the United States than we would not qualify for the $70,000 exclusion. Further, if we work and live outside the United States, but we maintain a residence inside the United States; the IRS construes this to mean that we are disqualified from the exclusion. In order to qualify, *we must establish both a principal place of business and an absolute residence outside of the United States.* We have seen others claim that it might help us to rent out an existing house we owned inside of the United States to prevent misunderstanding and possible exclusion from earning the deduction. We cannot agree less. To our way of thinking, any property left inside the United States is open to confiscation *when* the IRS changes its policy, or when the IRS decides to disagree with someone's interpretation of the exclusion law, or for any other reason under the sun. In the scenario involving Harold and Olivia, even though we assume that they are acting within the law; the IRS may decide to take a different view. We know from studying IRS history, that someone doesn't actually have to be guilty of anything to find themselves spending years battling the IRS in court. It seems safe to assume that the IRS has little incentive to battle anyone whose assets are absolutely and totally out of reach and whose citizenship has been changed. The IRS may be willing to spend $100,00 to collect $4,000, but it seems highly unlikely that they will spend a great deal of time pursuing a situation where there is absolutely nothing of value to be attained. They can't even extradite Harold with impunity, he is after all an Irish citizen, as is Olivia. To be sure, Olivia's maintenance of US citizenship by way of dual-citizenship makes her slightly vulnerable. But Ireland would take a dim view of any US action to extradite someone such as Olivia unless there was just cause. Perhaps she might be extradited for murder, or espionage; but for a technicality in a tax code? Congress wants your money not your blood; and the popularity of the IRS has fallen to such a low that there is a great deal of talk in political circles about scraping it for a better system. The IRS prefers tangible assets.

In any event, for someone who maintains their US citizenship to qualify for the $70,000 exclusion **they must have their primary place of residence outside of the United States**. To pass the IRS test on this issue, we must be outside of the United States for 330 days out of every 12 consecutive months. We have heard that the IRS actually has a number of rules for counting days. If we are to use the $70,000 exclusion we must learn the IRS rules and comply with them. If the taxpayer prefers, the IRS is also willing to use a subjective test, rather than counting the days to determine foreign residency, but it involves so many personal questions that we'd have to be a total fool to consider it. It involves questions I wouldn't tell my priest, let alone some young kid with an IRS badge trying to act like Dick Tracy.

If we are self-employed there are additional IRS rules. Would you believe that? As we understand it, for self-employed individuals it is net income that is applied towards the exclusion limit and not gross income. We must once again carefully stress that a qualified professional should be consulted for those of us who wish to fully explore using the foreign-income exclusion. Tell your tax attorney what your intentions are; the tax form that must be used for the exemption is Form 2555. Your tax attorney will be able to tell you about additional perks, such as tax credit options, housing deductions, using more than one offshore residency and claiming both as exemptions, self-employment benefits, and so forth. Because the IRS uses no clearly defined definition as to what constitutes housing expenses your tax attorney may advise you that the same standard used inside the United States may apply offshore, because, after all, such an assumption seems reasonable. This would seemingly include: rent, utilities, insurance, lease fees, rent for furniture and accessories, repairs, parking fees and whatever your tax attorney deems appropriate to include.

Having a second offshore home included within the exemption is also a possibility. To accomplish this is a bit tricky. We must demonstrate that our primary foreign tax home is subject to adverse conditions. The conditions must be "dangerous, unhealthful, or otherwise adverse." What immediate comes to mind is a state of war or civil insurrection, however it can also and perhaps more accurately be meant to imply locational dangers, such as unsafe conditions existing on a construction site for instance, (which can be construed to be too dangerous for one's entire family to use as a place of residence.) We will need a tax attorney to help us define the precise definition of "adverse conditions" as it applies to our individual situation. It would seem to us that the amount of petty crime in Rio de Janerio might mean we need an additional residence in the resort city of Cabo Frio for our family residence. Talk to a professional.

There are provisions which exempt offshore workers from Social Security Tax. There are also provisions which exempt offshore workers from the social security taxes of the foreign host nation. These provisions are called totalization agreements. They dictate that US citizens who are temporarily working offshore are subject only to the US social security tax and are exempt from the host countries tax. The US has signed agreements regarding this exemption with twelve countries; they are: Canada, Belgium, France, Germany, Italy, the Netherlands, Norway, Portugal, Spain, Sweden, Switzerland, and the United Kingdom. We can get around paying local social security in many other countries by presenting proof that our employment is temporary and that we are covered by US social security. To qualify for any of these social security exemptions, US or foreign, we must obtain a certificate prior to the foreign assignment from the US Social Security Administration, Office of International Policy, P.O. Box 17741, Baltimore, Maryland 21235

If we are *not* US Citizens and if we have our tax jurisdiction in a tax haven and we are living in a country *other than our tax jurisdiction*, there might be some way to avoid foreign social security taxes, but we have not figured out how to set up such an arrangement because it seems unnecessary to us. There are too many better ways to earn a living than working for a wage. But if we do work for a wage, we can probably assume that it is possible to legally avoid foreign social security taxes if it is worth the trouble to figure out how. However, in our opinion it's probably unwise to squeeze the lemon that hard.

The $70,000 exemption for foreign income is of interest to the expat who does not want to sever ties with the US. We personally see little sense in using such an exemption from US government taxes if we are of a mind to simply turn around and place ourselves in a position to be unfairly taxed by a foreign government. Regarding unfair taxation we should give our definition of fair: fair taxation is a sum paid in taxes to a government that does not exceed in value the benefits returned in goods and services by that government to the taxpayer. If as an expat we contribute to a foreign host country by bringing jobs and expertise, we add to that countries wealth and evolution. Most countries will be exceedingly happy with a productive expats presence and why shouldn't they be? Greedy countries will simply have to come up with a better way of attracting talented people to their shores. With so many nations now willing to provide citizenship and passports, and so many countries joining the tax-haven corporation-vending 'league of nations' willing to provide privacy, banking and corporate services as their method of gaining revenue, it would be foolish to place all our eggs in anyone's basket but our own personal one. **While more and more nations are providing privacy, the nation in which we are domiciled has a bearing on our method of avoiding undue taxation.**

Most countries of the world tax on the basis of residency (or domicle.) While the rules vary from nation to nation, most of today's nations consider anyone who has established a place of abode inside their country for more than six months to be a resident. Here are our options: If we are working for someone other than ourselves and if those for whom we work have a policy of paying their employees *inside* the host country *and* of reporting the amount of that payment to the host government we can try the following options. We can ask our employer if we can hire-on as independent contractors, having them make payment to our 'company,' located in a third nation, rather than to pay us personally. Our 'company' of course will be our own, with its corporate headquarters domicled in a tax haven. Once payment is made to our corporation, our corporation can then in turn pay us an amount sufficient to live on in our foreign host nation, with the remainder of the funds remaining in our corporate account, **just as it is with every other corporation in the world.** We believe it rational to assume, that the amount of money we are personally paid, is the amount of money our host nation has to use to determine the amount of the taxation levied against us and not the money paid to our corporation.

If our employer declines to hire us on a contractual basis, if for instance we are working for the Australian government as statisticians; then we probably will have to pay Australian taxes. To be exempt from a host country's tax, we must qualify as a 'detached worker." A detached worker is one whose assignment in the host country is expected to last less than five years.

Being self-employed usually presents more creative options for us. Not all nations will be as enthusiastic about our methods of avoiding unfair taxation. A government is like a Yellowstone Bear, once it starts eating garbage it is difficult to get it to eat a more wholesome diet. Additionally, much depends on the source of our income and how payment is made. Our obligation to ourself and our family is to avoid as much unnecessary and unfair taxation as possible by every means globally possible. With so many new tax haven opportunities coming available globally, it is no longer necessary to go without some method of reducing at least a portion of our global tax obligations.

Thus far we have restricted our discussion of tax havens to their primary use, of being a place to base paper entitles, (such as a corporation, trust, or bank account,) and we have discussed how in such a capacity, tax havens serve to act as an interface between our financial selves and the bureaucratic world. However, there may very well come a day when we ourselves will find that having our home and personal residence located *inside* of a tax haven will enhance the quality and freedom of our personal life. While the issue of choosing a haven for our personal residence is not thorny, the issue of choosing such a haven is slightly cloudy; which is a consequence of the changed attitudes among nations. **With each passing year more and more countries qualify for what we would want and what we would need to attain financial freedom in a residential haven.** So the issue of what constitutes a residential haven is today one of degree and deciding on which haven accomplishes our ends, now depends on the ends sought.

Considering that most nations do not tax foreign source income most nations would act as a residence haven for those of us who choose to work globally. In the Americas, only the United States, Venezuela, Brazil, and the Dominican Republic tax on foreign source income; and in the case of the Dominican Republic, there are so many FTZ's (27 and counting,) that we should have little trouble finding a way of avoiding the foreign source income regulation there. Brazil is developing FTZ's; and from my experience in Brazil, I would classify it along with Italy as a country in which just about anything is possible. Both Italy and Brazil are blessed with a great disparity between theory and practice. Italy once hired IBM to computerize its tax rolls in an effort to make the system function. Thanks to massive noncooperation by the people of Italy, IBM had to abandon the project in total failure after two desperate years of struggling against a people who consider tax evasion a national sport. This does not mean we are recommending you go to Italy or Brazil and attempt to hoodwink the local governments. Such a practice could earn you a jail term, a loss of property, or both. What we are saying, perhaps poorly; is that there is a disparity between theory and practice and as we live in a foreign country we gradually learn the ways of the locals. Once learned, those ways might give us a panoramic view of the valley between the letter of the law and the spirit of the law. Use caution in that valley!

A further note regarding this subject: foreigners are often treated differently than locals in either a positive or a negative way. As an example of such differences; consider the Haitian who is mistreated by the same bureauracrat who manages to gain for a foreigner a special permit to do business. In this case, the local citizen is mistreated, and the expat is treated with special preference. Or, consider the gringo thrown in a jail for having a few ounces of cocaine in his pocket in an area of the world where cocaine is the major cash crop. In this case, the expat is singled out and treated discordantly. Legality, is a local custom, subject to its own weather patterns. The old saying, 'when in Rome...' may apply in Italy, but we should use caution when trying to apply it in Zaire. Additionally, if we make undue trouble for the US government, officials in the US government would have little problem bribing officials of another country to have an expat thrown in jail or shot. We must remember that the United States invaded Panama with impunity in order to perform a 'drug bust' on a noisy field mouse, (and killed hundreds of Panamanian civilians, including women and children, in the process.) So it is merely wishful thinking on our part to assume that the brutality of the US government knows any limits. We must also remember, that at the exact moment of the invasion of Panama, the president of the United States was in Washington announcing new high-technology sales to China [and] the plans to lift a ban on loans to Iraq. This should clarify Washingtons moral position for all of us who are not wilfully blind. Any assumptions regarding some (or any) degree of morality within the US government is purely wishful thinking. In a world where the butchers of Beijing and Baghdad are friends, while someone who has too much evidence regarding the complicity of high level officials in Washington DC is the enemy, noisy field mice should be careful where they tread.

Where to tread? In the Americas; Belize, Argentina, Uruguay, Chile, Guatemala, Panama, Honduras, Costa Rica, Mexico, and a host of other countries do not tax foreign source income. In Europe, the situation is much the same. Ireland and the United Kingdom are considered high tax countries, however both have a system of "resident but not domiciled" in their tax laws. We will address these factors in the special sections many of these countries have elsewhere in this book. Numerous countries in Europe do not tax on foreign source income. In fact, the practice of taxing foreign source income is an anomaly; with the United States being the worst offender. Even the United Kingdom, with some of the highest taxes in the world, doesn't practice taxing foreign source income against its own citizens. Few countries have citizens who would stand for it. This said, we will return to the seed issue. Are there places in the world so unique that they entail inherent safety by their very nature? Are there havens with great and vigorous freedom in today's world?

Yes.

CAMPIONE D'ITALIA

The first pure haven we remember reading about was a city on the shores of **Lake Lugano** in **Switzerland**, called **Campione D'Italia**. We can't recall where we first heard about Campione, because it was a number of years ago, but we do remember being fascinated with the anomalous nature of the city; yes even somewhat amazed that such a place could actually exist.

When we take the time to look at a map of Southern Switzerland, or of Northern Italy, we will see that the Swiss city of **Lugano** is located on the shores of Lake Lugano some distance away from the Italian border. Yet, directly across the lake from the city of Lugano is an Italian city. That city is Campione D'Italia and it is entirely inside the borders of Switzerland, surrounded on all sides by Switzerland and even at its closest point almost twenty miles away from Italy itself. Yet, Campione is part of **Italy**.

Some 13 centuries ago in the year 787 AD, that area of Lugano was ruled over by a local ruler who so appreciated the craftsmanship of the Milanese designers, that he ceded the site of Campione to the church of San Ambrogio in Milan. Since that date, Switzerland has complied with this unique grant. Which means that today, happily situated within the country of Switzerland is an Italian city that is subject entirely to Italian law.

This unique situation creates some very unique opportunities. Switzerland does not as a rule grant residency to anyone who is not Swiss. Additionally, Swiss taxes are relatively high. In Campione, foreigners have no problem gaining residency. Campione, although part of Italy, has no personal income or municipal taxes. Nor is Campione subject to any of Switzerland's agreements with the United States and Canada regarding income tax. Campione has the best of both worlds. While it is Italian, it uses Swiss banks, Swiss post offices and mailing systems, Swiss telephone companies, telephone numbers and telephone systems, as well as Swiss telegraph. Everything that is good about Switzerland and everything that is good about Italy live inside the city of Campione without any of the concomitant negatives. There are no borders, no border guards, yet when we enter the city of Campione, we enter Italy.

When we form a company in Campione, we have all the advantages of Switzerland. Switzerland appears on our letterhead, our telephone is Swiss, we can walk to a Swiss bank and perform any normal business function; yet our company is formed with a minimum of capitalization in Milan. There is nothing complex about our corporation, it is not exotic, however by nature of the fact that our residence is in Campione, we can operate tax free, unless we are doing business inside of Italy rather than globally. If we did choose to include Italy within the scope of our business dealings, we would then simply use a Swiss or Liechtenstein corporation as an intermediary for those parts of our global interactions that were Italian and thereby avoid Italian taxation.

Foreigners can purchase real estate without restriction in Campione. Residency is a simple matter, especially when compared to Switzerland. Unfortunately, for most of us, Campione is the most expensive tax haven in the world. Real estate in Campione is almost on a par with Tokyo. It is a prosperous place filled with prosperous people, (as befits a land without the heavy hand of government intervention in human affairs.) Unless we are extremely wealthy we probably shouldn't bother to consider Campione as a potential residence. If we feel we are wealthy enough, then we might consider visiting Campione and spending some time there.

The language in Campione is predominantly Italian. Most Swiss speak several languages, so it is usually relativity easy to find someone who can answer our questions; however to live there as a full time resident would probably necessitate our learning Italian. Children of Campione residents go to Swiss schools. There are numerous sporting activities in proximity to Campione; golf, fishing, skiing and so forth; additionally we are only an hour away by freeway from Milan. My Campione telephone directory lists numerous fine restaurants, stores and other services just minutes away in the City of Lugano, so even though Campione is only a small town with a small population it's not isolated. Within Campione is a casino which is run by the municipality of Campione itself. This lake front casino has a spectacular view of Lugano across the water. The revenue raised by this casino are what provides the citizens of Campione with their municipal services; that is why they have no taxes.

Doesn't it feel good to hear of such a place?

Perhaps someday we will all deserve to be without governments Perhaps someday all the world will know the joyfulness of a city like Campione D'Italia. We are hopeful.

Entry Requirements: For information on entry requirements to Switzerland, travelers may contact the Embassy of Switzerland at 2900 Cathedral Avenue N.W., Washington D.C. 20008, tel. (202) 745-7900, or the nearest Swiss Consulate General in Atlanta, Chicago, Houston, Los Angeles, New York, or San Francisco.

Medical Facilities: Good medical care is widely available. Doctors and hospitals often expect immediate cash payment for health services. U.S. Medical insurance is not always valid outside the United States. Travelers have found that in some cases, supplemental medical insurance with specific overseas coverage has proved to be useful. Information on specific health matters is available through the Centers for Disease Control and Prevention's hotline for international travelers at (404) 332-4559 or via the CDC home page on the Internet:http://www.cdc.gov.

Crime Information: Switzerland has a low rate of violent crime. However, pickpocketing and purse-snatching do occur during peak tourist periods (such as summer and Christmas) and when major conferences, shows, or exhibits are scheduled in major cities. Most crime is restricted to specific localities in major cities that are avoided by the prudent traveler and residents, such as areas frequented by drug dealers and users, the vicinity of train and bus stations, and some public parks. Travelers may wish to exercise caution on trains, especially on overnight trains to neighboring countries. Even locked sleeping compartments can be entered by thieves who steal from passengers while they sleep.

Road Safety: Although many roads are mountainous and winding, road safety standards are high.

Registration/Embassy and Consulate Locations: U.S. citizens may register and obtain updated information on travel and security in Switzerland at the locations below:
The U.S. Embassy in Bern is located at Jubilaeumstrasse 93, telephone (41)(31) 357-7011.
The U.S. Consulate General in Zurich is located at Zollikerstrasse 141, telephone (41)(1) 422-2733. At this time only emergency services are available. The U.S. Consulate General will be closing on September 15, 1996 to be replaced by a part-time consular agency offering limited consular services to U.S. citizens. Limited consular services for U.S. citizens are offered by a part-time consular agency in Geneva located at the America Center of Geneva, World Trade Center II, Geneva Airport, Route de Pre-Bois 29, telephone (41)(22) 798-1605 or 798-1615.

ANDORRA

Another haven somewhat like Campione exists high in the Pyrenees, between France and Spain. The Pyrenees are a high mountain range that stretches from the Bay of Biscay on the Atlantic, to Côte Vermille on the Mediterranean. This spectacular range of mountains, over 250 miles long, contains scenery that is paralyzingly beautiful and worth a trip totally in their own behalf. Geographically, the Pyrenees lie within three countries; Spain, France and the country of **Andorra**. Consisting of no more than 178 square miles, the little-known country of Andorra, lying between Catalonia and Ariége, is another anomaly. Andorra is a *condominium*, which is evidentially a *terme de politique* used to describe an area over which sovereignty is exercised jointly by two or more states. In the case of Andorra, the purported honor is shared by the Spanish Bishop of Seo d'Urgel and the President of the French Republic; whereas in actual fact Andorra has been independent for centuries and is ruled internally by a body of 28 elected counsellors. We remember first reading about Andorra in Douglas Casey's book, *The Expatriate Investor*, published in 1978. As Casey put it, Andorra is a country devoid of professional politicians, labor unions, political parties, armies and most other similar banes. Much has changed in the world since Casey wrote about Andorra, but what he wrote is worth repeating. Andorra at that time was very isolated because of the hours or winding roads between it and **Barcelona**, (the closest city with an international airport.) Casey reported that Andorra had one of the lowest costs of living in Europe, largely due, he said, to the general lack of a having to support a huge government coupled with the total absence of any burdensome taxes. His description of laid-back Andorra made Andorra sound like the middle of nowhere; and he debated the question of Andorras possible growth. Hang on to your seatbelts!

Today Andorra is called the 'Mega-Store in the Mountains.' Forget laid-back, **Andorra la Vella**, the capital of Andorra now has not just one, but several, brand new American style shopping malls. The shopping activity, and the crowds, are described as frenzied. The highways leading from Spain and to France are bumper-to-bumper traffic-jams with everyone trying to reach Andorra to buy the bargains. And bargains there are. Tourists from all over the world come to shop the busy streets of Andorra la Vella, and prices are significantly lower than either France or Spain, so the locals are in on the bidding. We have heard that prices are not set lower than distant free ports like Hong Kong; but are merely lower than countries in proximity. We have also heard repeated warnings of 'buyer beware,' because of counterfeit merchandise, brand name pirated goods and post-dated consumer items.

What happened to Andorra? Well, the good news is that it's still there. Off the main roads the countryside is still idyllic, the living is still 'low-government pleasant' and there still aren't any heavy taxes. If we can put up with the annoying influx of shoppers on the main roads and in the capital, then Andorra still holds it's capacity to act as a tax-free residential haven. Undoubtedly the prices of property are ten times what they were eighteen years ago; but that's par for the course in much of Europe. We would certainly recommend seeing the Pyrenees if we were traveling in Europe in any event and Andorra is right in the center.

31

FACTS AT A GLANCE ON ANDORRA

Local Name: Vallée d'Andorre (French) Valls d'Andorra (Spanish)
Timezone: GMT+1
Area: 181 sq mi
Population: 63,930 (July 1994 est)
Capital: Andorrala Vella
Language: Catalan (official) Spanish [Castilian,] French Ethnic groups: Catalan (50%) Andorran (29%) French 8%) Portuguese (7%)
Religions: Roman Catholic (94%)
Economy: Tourism remains the mainstay of Andorra's economy and accounts for roughly 80% of GDP. An estimated 13 million tourists visit Andorra annually, attracted by Andorra's duty-free status and by its summer and winter resorts. The banking sector, with its tax-haven status, also contributes substantially to the economy. Agricultural production is limited by the scarcity of arable land, and most food has to be imported. Manufacturing consist mainly of cigarettes, cigars and furniture.
GDP: $760 million (1992 est) GDP Per Capita: $14,000
Freedom House Rating: Political Rights: 1 Civil Liberties: 1
TELECOMMUNICATIONS & WWW:
Andorra has a website homepage at:
URL: http: //www.xmission.com/dderhak/andorra.htm
Notes: Andorra became a sovereign nation in 1993 and now has UN membership.
U.S. State Department Information for Andorra is included in the section on Spain.

CUETA AND MELILLA: PARADISE LOST

Much of what once made **Ceuta** and **Melilla** appealing resident-havens no longer applies; nonetheless we will discuss them for what they still may have to offer. Ceuta and Melilla are two Spanish enclaves on the North African side of the Mediterranean within **Morocco**. For hundreds of years Spain has had control over five islets, the three Jaafariya Islands off the Cap de L'Eau, the Peñon de Ahucenas, and two freeport Moroccan cities; Ceuta and Melilla; all of which are collectively and commonly referred to as Spanish Morocco. The past appeal of Ceuta and Melilla was in their low rate of taxation on residents, which is but half of that levied on the Spanish mainland. Ceuta and Melilla are considered duty-free ports and many Spaniards make the crossing to take advantage of the duty-free shopping. We have been led to believe that Ceuta and Melilla make excellent places to keep a yacht because of their freeport status.

The writer **Adam Starchild**, describes a method of using the Ports of Ceuta and Melilla which may have some appeal to the European based expat. Because rents are low in these enclaves and becoming a resident there fairly simple, by using either of these enclaves as our de facto legal residence and hence paying Spanish taxes at a fifty percent discount, we exempt ourselves in some cases from further taxation. Because no one monitors the activities into and out of these busy ports, no one monitors where or how we spend our time. The enclave address on our tax return and our residence card, according to Starchild, is what gets us the tax break, not our physical presence. The implication of this being that we might be spending considerably more time elsewhere.

32

Ceuta, the larger of the two freeports, is only twelve nautical miles from the Strait of Gibraltar, a one hour ride on a transport ferry, with swifter-moving hydrofoils available when the weather is calm. Boats leave about a dozen times a day from Algeciras and Tarifa in **Spain**, from the port of **Gilbratar**, and from Sète in **France**. Ceuta is about 19 sq km, (11.5 sq mi) in size, half of which is used by the Spanish military. The population is about 75,000 about a third of which is made up of Muslims (to all intents and purposes Berbers, and not Moroccans, but officially, 'Spanish Muslims'.) The city has a Andalusian feel to it, and its Spanish speaking Muslim population give it an other-worldly air. The port activity and traffic is extremely heavy, as more and more people have come to prefer entering Morocco via Ceurta in order to avoid the punks and hoodlums who hang around Tangier. There are numerous stores and shops in Cueta selling 'duty-free' goods. The town depends mainly on the traffic for commerce; it's other industries being fishing, tourism and smuggling. Spain has recently began the process of granting such regions as Ceuta and Melilla a larger degree of political autonomy and there is much talk of a free trade agreement between the European Community and Morocco, which agreement would pretty much knock Ceuta out economically. (as well as Melilla.) This has caused uncertainly amidst Spanish residents and has led some to migrate to the mainland.

How this would affect Adam Starchilds residential scheme is uncertain. If we can use either of the enclaves for a de facto address and be taxed at a 50% discount, then the local economy would not seem to be a crucial matter. Nonetheless we would approach this situation with caution until such issues are resolved.

Melilla is slightly smaller than Ceuta. It has also been pushed into a cloud of uncertainty, with a recent drastic increase in the Muslim population and new fears of the city being handed over to Morocco. The economy is said to be shattered and the city becoming run down, along with the ever increasingly presence of Muslims entering the city each day from the surrounding countryside who are either underemployed or jobless.

Melilla is more isolated then Ceuta, takes longer to reach and has less vehicle traffic. It takes an eight hour ferry ride to reach Malaga, Spain and even longer to reach Almería. There is however an airport, and **Iberia**, the Spanish National Airline has numerous daily flights (except in bad weather) on a 46 seat Fokkers. There's a daily flight to Almería and six daily flights to Madrid. As a de facto tax-residence Ceuta has some advantages over Melilla. It is easier to disappear in the crowd, it's access to Europe is scant minutes away, the boat basin allows yacht owners a pleasant degree of anonymity and the prices of some commodities are actually a bargain. Starchild reports that we can buy a Mercedes Benz automobile in Ceuta or Melilla for a price that is even below what the car would cost us in Germany. However, there is a stipulation that we drive the car locally for one year before we can take it to Spain without tariff duties.

FACTS AT AT A GLANCE ON MOROCCO

Entry Requirements: For information concerning entry requirements for Morocco, travelers may contact the Embassy of Morocco at 1601 21st St., N.W., Washington, D.C. 20009, telephone (202) 462-7979 to 82, or the Moroccan Consulate General in New York, telephone (212) 758-2625.

Areas of Instability: The sparsely-settled Western Sahara (formerly Spanish Sahara) was long the site of armed conflict between the Polisario Front and Morocco on the issue of independence versus Moroccan sovereignty. Although a ceasefire is presently in place, several violations have occurred and the area cannot be considered safe. There are reports of thousands of unexploded mines in the Western Sahara and in areas of Mauritania adjacent to the Western Sahara border. Exploding mines are occasionally reported, and have caused death and injury. Transit to the Western Sahara remains restricted; persons planning to travel in the region may obtain information on clearance requirements from the Moroccan Embassy.

Medical Facilites: Medical care in Morocco is available, although not all facilities meet high quality standards and specialized care or treatment may not be available. Travelers planning to drive in the mountains and other remote areas may wish to carry a medical kit and a Moroccan phone card for emergencies. Doctors and hospitals often expect immediate cash payment for health care services.

Crime Information: Morocco has a moderately high crime rate in urban areas. Criminals have targeted tourists for assaults, muggings, thefts, pickpocketing, and scams of all types. Commonly-reported crimes include falsifying credit-card vouchers, and shipping inferior rugs as a substitute for the rugs purchased by the traveler. The Embassy and Consulate have also received reports of thefts occurring in the vicinity of ATM machines. Some travelers have been befriended by persons of various nationalities who have offered them food, drink, or cigarettes which are drugged. Harassment of tourists by unemployed Moroccans trying to be "guides" is a common problem. Prudenttravelers hire only official tour guides through hotels and travel agencies. Traveling alone in the Rif Mountain area is risky. Driving on the highway at night can be dangerous. In Casablanca, persons have thrown large rocks at cars from overpasses. These incidents have led to several accidents and at least one death.

Currency Information: Travelers checks and credit cards are accepted at some establishments in Morocco, mainly in urban areas. Drug Penalties: U.S. citizens are subject to the laws of the country in which they are traveling. Penalties for possession, use, or trafficking in illegal drugs are severe, and convicted offenders can expect jail sentences and fines.

Registration/Embassy Location: citizens are encouraged to register at the Consular Section of the U.S. Embassy or Consulate General. Updated information on travel and security within Morocco may be obtained at the Embassy. The U.S. Embassy in Rabat is located at 2 Avenue de Marrakech in the capital city of Rabat, telephone (212) (7) 76-22-65. The American Consulate General in Casablanca is located at 8 Boulevard Moulay Youssef, telephone (212) (2) 26-45-50.

THE STEALTH EXPAT APPEARS

There is one rather innovative way of completely avoiding taxes that was thought up some years ago by **Harry Schultz**, the investment writer who we have mentioned elsewhere in the book. Harry came up with the rather simple, but highly original concept of being a perpetual traveler, or **P.T.** We have heard a dozen definitions of the acronym P.T. Perpetual tourist, previous taxpayer, practically transparent, privacy trained, permanent traveler, possibility thinker, parked temporarily, prepared thoroughly and so on. Essentially, a P.T. is someone who is 'passing through' different countries without any sort of a permanent residence. This illusion, is accomplished through creative paperwork and we are happy to report that we know for a fact that the P.T. concept is *fait accompli,* with many of today's more experienced expatriates actually using the principal with good success. It is very difficult to hit a moving target, especially when it is a stealth expat.

We leave it to your creative imagination to figure out how to equip your expat jet with 'stealth equipment', or a Klingon 'Cloaking Device,' whichever you prefer. Without creative imagination you will find yourself inadvertently 'Decloaking' in front of Romulan War Birds and you know what that means.

HOLDING REAL ESTATE TITLE OFFSHORE

As expats and private investors we can gain immense benefits by establishing an offshore company to hold our real estate investments. Most tax havens allow this, (with the possible exception of Luxembourg.) Holding our real estate investments in company fashion makes the best kind of business sense; it preserves a degree of respectable anonymity for us and it allows us to take advantage of a number of creative business techniques not available to those who hold their investments as individuals. It can limit eventual capital gains tax liability by the expedient of selling the shares in the company that owns the real estate rather than selling the real estate itself. In some cases, it is possible for us to invest in local tax-haven real estate through our company, hence enjoying many of the benefits unavailable to individual residents. (how's your Matter/Anti-Matter Containment Field?)

A massive amount of foreign real estate is held by offshore corporations; even real estate within the United States. Additionally, it is possible to set up an intermediary company or trust to handle the 'management affairs' of the company properties, particularly where these properties are located in high-tax jurisdictions. If the intermediary company's/trust's management can be shown to operate and manage the properties — a significant amount of pre-tax profits can be transferred through management fees to the tax haven, thereby reducing any excess foreign tax debts. Additionally, when company properties are sold, capital gains tax in the high-tax jurisdiction may be deferred if the ownership is registered in the tax-haven and the company can demonstrate that ultimate capital gains will be paid to the country of the companies tax-residence after the benefits of deferral. Additionally, if new ownership is taken by way of stock purchase as mentioned above, there will not actually be a transfer of real estate title. The stock purchasers will own the stocks which own the real estate. Essentially the same company will own the real estate as before the stock purchase. More importantly, the company stock will be the stock of a foreign offshore company not located either territorially or politically within the high-tax jurisdiction where the real estate is located. We would be surprised, if not shocked, if anyone outside of the tax-haven in which the company is registered would have access to the names of the company stockholders. Such information is privy and often **not even of public record within the tax-haven itself**. Which is why people use tax havens.

We would also like to point out that the tax-benefits derived by foreigners or 'international investors' owning and 'managing' real estate inside of the United States through the expedient of holding title in an offshore tax-haven can be referred back to the problems faced by the American field mouse. Foreigners are in a position to reduce U.S. tax liabilities that the American field mouse cannot. Additionally, it is possible to use a network of tax havens with differing tax treaties and structures to obtain the best features of each, gaining thereby more than the sum of the disparate parts through the symbiotic relationship derived from the use of the global whole.

OFFSHORE BANKING

A very important issue we will need to consider in taking our banking offshore, is how to analyze an offshore bank as to its credibility and its financial strength. Some of the best tax-havens are distantly connected to the United Kingdom and operate under the so called UK Code of Banking Practice. The UK Code of Banking Practice is to some degree is based on the Tournier decision, an early 20th century British court case regarding the inappropriate release of information by a British bank without the consent of the depositor. Theoretically, in a British bank, if it is determined that the holder of the account is not a British resident, no inspector is allowed to examine the account further. Additionally, the British government require an auditing of all banks; this auditing reveals the creditworthiness of the bank, so that we can make a decision regarding its safety as a depository for our funds. In Switzerland it is often possible to get a liquidity rating of a bank. Such a rating is a rough determination of the assets the bank could quickly turn into cash versus its liabilities outstanding. In the event that all of the customers of the bank would demand immediate payment at the same instant, they would at the very least receive an amount equal to the amount of the banks rated liquidity. If, as in the United States the bank had a liquidity rating of only 1.2%, as does the FDIC then as depositors we would receive $12.00 for every $1000.00 we had there in deposit.

Fortunately for expats, Swiss Banks have a liquidity rating that on 'average' is usually in the 30% to 40% range and is quite often much higher. We will have the names of several banks whose liquidity rating is one hundred to two hundred times greater than that of most American banks, so that hopefully readers will not be among the many who stand to lose their lives savings *if and when* the house of cards tumbles. All Swiss banks are obligated by Swiss law to report their liquidity twice a year to the Swiss government unless they are a private bank. The way in which liquidity ratings are kept high is determined by the method of investment carried out
36

by the bank, and by the amount of assets owned by the bank. Not all Swiss banks are conservative (or wealthy) in this way; but the number of Swiss banks operating within this range is adequate enough for us to choose among several. (We have heard of many Swiss banks with liquidity far exceeding 150%)

It is important to note that not all tax havens have Swiss Bank and many of us may want to use tax havens. (Switzerland is *not* a tax haven.) We need to consider some of the possibilities we might run into in these circumstances.

Before we go further it is important for us to state that we consider the issue of bank liquidity and stability a primary issue. It does not exist within the United States. It's lack is part of the reason that the United States may fall apart. We are not prophets so we'll stay out of the prophecy business. We prefer to give friendly advice. We suggest that you may find it prudent to get your money out of American banks that have no assets and put it into a bank that has assets.

If we choose to use a British tax haven such as the Bahamas, Anguilla, Cayman Islands, Bermuda, Belize and so on, it must be stressed that not all of these havens are under the UK Code of Banking Principles. Those that are, like Anguilla, have a different problem which we must discuss. If a bank is audited by the British government, then we can determine its assets. However, we may not be the only ones who can determine its assets. If the British government has information regarding our account, then it is the possible that such information is no longer a totally private matter. That is not to say that the British government would give information out as a matter of practice, but we are not really as concerned with matters of practice as we are with matters of contingency. Information *has* been given out by British banks, however reluctantly, because those banks happened to have assets inside another country that wanted information and threatened to confiscate the banks assets inside that country if the information was not forthcoming. Such things can happen. Therefore we will only list and recommend banks which tend to have assets in countries that respect property rights; or preventing that, we will point out any caveats we should be aware of.

We have a concept that we feel might well be applied to those whose intention it is to open an offshore bank for the growing market in expat customers. Rather than have a government entity perform an audit, an offshore bank might consider contracting with a proficient insurance agency, perhaps one of the Swiss insurance companies, perhaps Lloyds of London, or any insurance company that performed determinable sound insurance practices by rational definition. The insurance company would have total access to audit the investments of the bank and all of the banks assets and debts *on demand* and the insurance company would then issue a liquidity rating based on its judgement. The bank would have to pay the insurance company for the privilege, but the insurance company itself would be liable to the depositor, up to the amount of its liquidity report. Or, alternatively, the depositor might pay a portion of the insurance on a prorated basis, sharing the cost with the bank, but increasing the depositors safety proportionate to the depositors premium. The **FDIC** operates by the principal of insuring a pool of risks for a fraction of the total amount of risk outstanding. This principal might work with automobile insurance where it is mathematically improbable than everyone in the United States will get in a wreck on the same day. Insuring banks with this technique is the worst violation of insurance principals. When and if the bank of cards collapses, it is probable that the event will be a chain reaction. Because the FDIC has only 1.2% of the insurance payment funds available for the total of the money that is deposited inside all U.S. banks, the possibility of us getting our money is nil. Less than one and one-half of a percent of the total money owed to the American people would probably be just enough money to pay for the funeral costs of the Directors of the FDIC and all of the of the nations major Bank Presidents that didn't escape to Brazil.

We are admittedly ambivalent about many Caribbean tax havens banks. We like them because to their proximity to the Americas, however we are having a difficult time finding stand-alone banks to recommend that fall within our guidelines.* For example, we found a bank called **European Union Bank** operating from **Antigua**, that had a Web Page on the Internet. It offered the convenience of online service (and a range of banking services via the telephone, fax, telex and post in addition to its online access.) We wrote them and asked for literature describing the banks services. We also asked some simple qualitative questions: we asked for instance, if they were a Swiss Bank or a European Bank and if not, what guidelines they used to report their liquidity rating? One month went by without a reply, so we faxed them again; asking the same questions and included a cordial note asking why we had not heard from them. As you might guess, we have still not heard from them. This does not mean 1] that they are not a legitimate bank practicing sound banking services; it doesn't mean 2] that they are not in an actual European bank, it doesn't mean 3] that they are not liquid, it does not mean 4] that they could not repay us our money in the event they lost their money playing the horses; all that it does mean is: that we have absolutely no way to know anything about them whatsoever. It would be better for us to flush our money down a toilet than to place it in an unknown (and unknowable) entity. If European Union Bank feels maligned by our herein stated position, they can remedy our view by clarifying their position. We would be happy to recommend their bank in subsequent editions of this book, or through our fax-on-demand service. But only if we have any possible way to know what it is that we would be recommending.

Operating a bank as an offshore corporation, having an offshore banking license, or operating under a so-called secrecy banking charter, regardless of the country of domicile, does little to reassure us. European Union Bank makes the statement in their web-site literature they were "established in Antigua by **Swiss Investment Association** and incorporated in Antigua under the International Business Corporations Act (IBC) of 1982." What is Swiss Investment Association? Is that the name of an offshore corporation incorporated in Belize? Does it have anything whatsoever to do with Switzerland? Are the principals Swiss? We cannot know the answers to any of these questions because no one from EUB will reply to our inquires. This is unfortunate, because EUB's idea of using telecommunications is a sound one and they are moving (at least conceptually) in precisely the direction we might most admire. We will update our readers as to liquid banks with our fax-on-demand system.

* See the footnote on page 41 regarding this same issue.

ANGUILLA

"Anguilla may be on it's way to becoming a very viable tax-haven. It offers a zero-tax jurisdiction. No corporate, income, or resident taxes are levied for residents, nor for non-residents who use an Anquillan Corporation to engage in International business."

Despite some recent bank closures on Anguilla, we believe that the offshore business community of Anguilla has moved in a positive directions. Perhaps we should state that *because* of the bank closures, we feel that Anguilla has moved in a positive direction. The closures were the result of licences being revoked. The revocations themselves resulted from two separate causes; the first being poor or nonexistent auditing statements, the second being that some of the banks were being operated by individuals undesirable to the Island of Anguilla and to the British government which holds jurisdiction over Anguilla.

Anguilla (the word means 'eel' in Spanish,) is located in the Lesser Antilles and is the most northern of the Leeward Islands. It is near the U.S. Virgin Islands next to St. Martin and approximately 170 nautical miles due east of Puerto Rico.

Timezone: GMT-4
Area: 60 sq mi
Population: We have seen population figures that range from 7,052 (1994) to 9,660 (1992) depending on the source of the statistic. The population density is low and the population growth rate under one (1%) percent. (24.25 births /1,000 population)
Capital: The Valley (Yes, the actual name of the Capital City is The Valley)
Language: English
Geography & Climate: Flat low lying island of coral and limestone with a tropical climate moderated by northeast trade winds.
Coastline: 40 miles
Literacy: 95%
GDP: $56.5 million
GDP PER CAPITA: $6,800 [1991 est]

Anguilla has few natural land-based resources (other than its very resourceful people) and the economy of Anquilla depends to a good part on the sea. The Anguillans are master boat builders, experts at lobster fishing and are said to be the best sailers in the entire Caribbean. In recent years the economy has also benefited from a boom in tourism and construction; however the Anguillans have decided to restrict tourism to small inexpensive resort-hotels, hence preserving the very thing that is lovely about the island. We applaud this. Anguilla's beauty is other-worldly, it is a serene remote place with crystal-clear blue-green water, empty white-sand beaches and skies as open as a broken clock.

Interestingly, in 1967 they declared war on Great Britain, all 7000 unarmed Anguillans.

Britain responded by invading Anguilla on March 19, 1969. The heavily armed British forces were met at Sandy Ground, by children bearing flowers and candy bars and by smiling parents singing, "God Save the Queen." Needless to say, Britain lost.

Anguillas rebellion was based on the following facts: Anguilla had been 'lumped into" statehood with St.Kitts and Nevis, whom they detested. They had been 'dumped out of" the British Commonwealth, where they preferred to be. The UK not understanding any of this, knew only that it didn't need any advice on how to run its affairs from an upstart island. They miscalculated the Anguillans, and suffered a major defeat of shame in what Time Magazine called: "Britain's Bay of Piglets." Anguilla was post-haste reinstated into the Commonwealth and now has the fortunate arrangement of governing itself with funding from the UK. i.e. The UK handles the judiciary and foreign affairs, as well as the regulation and supervision of banking. The local government handles all other local affairs and couldn't care less about foreign policy. For the expat, this happy situation is a mixed blessing; on the one hand it works to insure accountability in banking practices, on the other it means that the UK could theoretically access an expats affairs. This is improbable, but within the realm of possibilities. Of course, this same possibility exists in many Caribbean havens to one degree or another. As stated previously, we would prefer to see offshore fiduciaries make their auditing and business activities available to an entity other than a government agency. However, all this aside, Anguilla may be on it's way to becoming a very viable tax-haven. It offers a zero-tax jurisdiction. No corporate, income, or resident taxes are levied for residents, nor for non-residents who use an Anquillan Corporation to engage in International business.

As a possible home Anguilla may be a worthwhile destination. It has a very low population, full employment, and an extremely peaceful society. It is crime free and drug free for the most part. These factors and its pristine natural environment make it a very attractive destination for small scale, low key, individuals to use either as an corporate tax jurisdiction or as a place to live. Obviously, Anguilla cannot support a burgeoning population, but we don't think this will happen in any event. Its small airport does not carry international air traffic, (access is by way of San Juan, Puerto Rico) it has no town to speak of and no nightlife. (...although we hear there's a jump-up on Saturday night.) The few resorts are very low key, very exclusive, or both. Anquilla is off the beaten path and it is destined to remain that way. For those seeking some jet set nightlife, St. Maarten and French sophistication are only twenty minutes away from Anquilla by ferry and for those in a hurry, just four quick minutes by air taxi.

Anguilla has no exchange controls, and interestingly, the U.S. Dollar circulates so freely in Aguilla that most residents keep two bank accounts, one for US$ and the other for EC$. (Eastern Caribbean Dollar, which is a common currency that is used on several Caribbean Islands.) We can open an account at an offshore bank in Anguilla with any of the worlds major currencies. The processes for opening a bank in Anguilla have been stiffened to include a charter that rates banks into three categories, or classes. Only the first two classes would be of much interest to most expats. The highest rating and theoretically the most solvent of banks are encompassed within what is called the unrestricted class. The other category is a restricted class; which includes banks that are prohibited from carrying out business within Anguilla, but may only do business offshore. The reader is on their own in dealing with Anguillan banks and other offshore services on the island. If a recommendation isn't in our fax-on-demand system its because we don't have complete information regarding a service or information regarding a banks solvency.*

Anguilla - Offshore and Online
URL: http://www.offshore.com.ai/taxhaven/
The following is text from the Anquilla WebPage listed above:

"Anguilla is a pure tax haven. There are no income taxes, no corporate taxes, no sales taxes, no value added taxes, etc. As the Internet grows, and more business is done over the Internet, the physical location of a business matters less and less. When looking for the best jurisdiction to locate your company in, don't just compare California and Washington, consider Anguilla. A zero-tax jurisdictions is hard to beat. Without a 50% tax burden your company's after tax earnings would be double, and the value of a growing company would be more than double."

Anguilla Home Page
URL: http://www.offshore.com.ai/anguilla/

Anguilla Internet Business Services is a branch of Offshore Information Services Ltd
URL: http://www.aibs.com.ai/
Anguilla Internet Business Services claims it can provide us with everything necessary to start and operate a business over the Internet from Anguilla. According to this WebSite, the fact that there is no taxation on Anquilla means that there are no tax returns to submit and almost no red tape and this fact makes Anguilla an ideal location for an Internet based company. They claim to provide a comprehensive Internet business package. From them, the client receives a complete corporate structure ready for business operation over the Internet. They claim that this includes all the attendant computer, accounting, administration, advertising, legal, management and other services necessary for carrying on international tax-free business. We have not investigated them further as of this writing. We intend to. As soon as we can determine what type of 'track record' they have we will pass this information along to readers via our fax-on-demand system. Until then, those readers who want to investigate on their own can contact **Anguilla Internet Business Services** at the following:
Phone: 809.497.3255 Fax: 809.497.2756 email: aibs@offshore.com.ai
P.O. Box 949 The Valley, Anguilla, British West Indies

* It should be noted that there are many international banks located in Caribbean tax havens that can transmit our money privately to a bank anywhere in the world, including Switzerland. It is entirely possible to use two banks, one in the Bahamas, Caymans or Anquilla where we keep a portion of our working funds and the other in Switzerland where we keep our investment funds and our savings.

An attorney practicing in Anquilla who we would recommend is **Ian Donaldson Mitchell**. He has a WebPage and is very knowledgeable on offshore matters. If it is our intention to form an offshore corporation in Anguilla, Mr. Mitchell would be someone to talk to.

Mitchells Chambers, Anguilla

Phone: 809.497.2391

Fax: 809.497.2050

email: mitchellm@candw.com.ai

URL: http://www.offshore.com.ai/mitchells/

We wish Anquilla would set up a Secretarial Service with a Mailing Service via Florida. It would sure be something many people could use.

INTERNATIONAL DIRECTORY OF BANKS

There is a complete **Directory of Swiss Banks** on the Internet. Banks are listed with city of their corporate headquarters; branches are only listed by request of the bank. Also available is a link to Swiss banks by Canton, Swiss banks with Internet connections, Banks in Liechtenstein, and Frequently Asked Questions about Swiss Banks. The page is a public service of a company called **SW Consulting**. The WebSite also has a number of related page links to: the Swiss stock exchange and to information on Finance and general information about Switzerland.

URL: http://www.swconsult.ch/chbanks/index.html

SW Consulting Home Page

is at **URL:** http://www.swconsult.ch

SW Consulting provides computer consulting services. Many of their clients are in the banking and financial community. They were founded in 1986 and have thus far developed a number of specialized computer programs and procedures for banks. They also have developed banking software packages which are in use by many of the Swiss banks and finance companies in office network environments.

They are very much involved with the Internet, believing it to be the beginning of a long-term change in the way people communicate. They believe that activities such as advertising and e-mail are examples of Internet Services which are at the forefront of this change because they do not jeopardize the security of the bank's mainframe computer system or the data it holds.

For more information about **SWConsulting SA**, contact them at info@swconsult.ch.

SW Consulting SA 1, chemin du Jura CH-1292 Chambésy Switzerland

Phone: (+41.22) 758.10.31 | Fax: (+41.22) 758.33.03

A listing on the Internet of 22 banks is available at:

BANKS - SOUTH AMERICA, CENTRAL AMERICA, & THE CARIBBEAN

URL: http://www.orcc.com/banks_sa.htm

There is a very good, very complete WebPage on **Banks of the World** at:

URL: http://www.wiso.gwdg.de/ifbg/bank_2.html

42

TAX HAVEN RESOURCES

The Offshore Tax Haven Reference Page

URL: http://www.nolimits.com/nolimits/offshore.html

This page provides links to hundreds of Offshore Tax Haven, Trust Account, Banking Secrecy and Financial Privacy information sources. The site provides the following links:

Tax Haven Services Tax Haven Money Making Opportunities A Guide to Tax Haven A Guide to Offshore Banks Offshore Investments Tax Haven Internet Services Tax Haven Magazine References Tax Haven Real Estate Tax Haven vacations Other Tax Haven and Privacy Links Tax Haven Books

TAX HAVEN BOOKS

Tax Haven Road Map - A basic book for starters.
Author: Richard Czerlau
Publisher: Uphill Publishing Ltd.
ISBN: 0-9698432-2-4

Take Your Money and Run
Author: Alex Doulis
Publisher: Uphill Publishing
ISBN: 0-9698432-0-8

Tax Havens
How to Bank, Invest, and Do Business Offshore and Tax Free
Author: Hoyt L. Barber
Publisher: McGraw Hill, Inc.
ISBN: 0-07-003659-4

Tax Havens
Author: Anthony S. Ginsberg
Publisher: New York Institute of Finance
ISBN: 0-13-886649-X

The Complete Guide to Offshore Money Havens
Author: Jerome Schneider
Publisher:
ISBN: 0-9-33560044

Harry Browne's Complete Guide to Swiss Banks
Author: Harry Browne
Publisher: McGraw-Hill Book Co.
ISBN: 0-07-008483-1

Using Offshore Havens for Privacy and Profits
Author: Adam Starchild
Publisher: Paladin Press
ISBN: 0-87634-767-X

Keep What You Earn:
Practical Strategies to Protect Your Assets from Taxes, Lawsuits and Financial Predators
Author: Terry Coxon
Published by Random House Trade
ISBN: 0812928288

TAX HAVEN CONSULTANTS

Terry Coxon
PRIVATE INVESTORS
625 2nd Street, Suite 102
Petaluma, California 94952
or mail: P.O. Box 2657
Petaluma, California 94953
phone: 707.778.1000 fax: 707.778.8804
email care of vkj@rpifs.com
note: Terry can advise on Swiss Banks and tax matters also. Minimum portfolio is one million dollars.

SWISS BANK CONSULTANTS

Camafin Trust AG
Postfach 1625
CH-8801 Thalwil-Zurich, Switzerland
Alte Landstrasse 147, CH-8800
Telephone: (001-411) 720-3131; Fax: 720-3141
Contacts: Bruno Brodbeck, Roger Badet
Minimum to open account: $50,000
Contact: Mr. Adrian Hartmann
Minimum to open account: $400,000

Weber Hartmann & Vrijhof Partners Ltd.
Zurichstrasse 1 lOB
CH-8134 Adliswil-Zurich, Switzerland
Telephone: (001-411) 709-1115; Fax: 709-1113
Contacts: Hans Weber, Robert Vrijhof
North American office:
555 West Georgia St., Suite 600
Vancouver, British Columbia,
Canada V6B 1Z5
Telephone: (604) 682-8622; Fax: 682-1329
Contact: Mr. Adrian Hartmann

US VIRGIN ISLANDS

While not a tax haven by any stretch of the imagination, the U.S. Virgin Islands does offer some unique possibilities. Lawrence W. Tuller* speaks highly of the potential both of Puerto Rico, which he calls the "best-kept secret in the Western Hemisphere," and of the U.S. Virgin Islands. (USVI) According to Tuller, for small and midsize businesses, the Virgin Islands offer more benefits and fewer headaches than many places in the Caribbean. Although an unincorporated territory of the United States, the USVI has retained its most-favored-nation status with Denmark, which owned the islands prior to 1917. This provides companies located in the USVI with a unique entrance to European Community markets duty free, or, in some cases, under preferential tariffs. The USVI also qualifies under the multilateral General System of Preference (GSP) from several countries, including Japan and Canada and may ship selected products duty free to those countries. But that's only the tip of the iceberg. U.S. direct investments in the USVI qualify for the following benefits: ✓ Section 936 financing ✓ Duty-free exports to the United States, Puerto Rico, and many Caribbean Basin countries ✓ Virtually tax-free income ✓ IRS foreign sales corporation status

There is information on the Internet for the **US Virgin Islands (USVI)** There is a page regarding business, taxes, tax incentives, and tax-free entities that is published on the Web by William L. Blum, a USVI tax and business attorney and a former counsel to the Governor of the USVI. He states in his WebSite that he is the author of several articles on USVI taxes and tax planning. Mr. Blum claims that he will provide free information on these subjects, including copies of articles and USVI laws and regulations. He states that he is also available to provide assistance in business, tax, and tax planning matters involving the U.S. Virgin Islands.
William L. Blum,Counsel Grunert Stout Bruch & Moore P.O. Box 1030 St. Thomas, V.I. 00804 Phone: 809.774.1320 [in St. Thomas] 718.802.1273 [in New York City] Fax: 809.774.7839 [in St. Thomas] 718.802.1760 [in New York City]
[We are not familiar with Mr. Blum so the listing of his name should not be considered an endorsement of his company.]

Additional information on the USVI Industrial Development Program can also be obtained directly from the USVI government as follows:
Industrial Development Commission 36C Strand Street - 2nd Floor Suite 2AB P.O. Box 3499, Christiansted St. Croix, <u>U.S. Virgin Islands</u> 00822 Phone: 809.773.6499 Fax: 809.773.7701

Additional information on USVI taxes can also be obtained directly from the Virgin Islands Bureau of Internal Revenue as follows: **US Virgin Island Bureau of Internal Revenue** 9601 Estate Thomas Charlotte Amalie St. Thomas, <u>U.S. Virgin Islands</u> 00802 Phone: 809.774.5865 Fax: 809.776.4037

Regarding business opportunities in the U.S, Virgin Islands there is a Home Page at **URL:** http://www.usvi.net/usvi/taxes.html

*Doing Business In Latin America And The Caribbean By Lawrence W. Tuller

SWISS BANKS

Here is a list of Swiss Banks recommended by Harry Browne in **Harry Browne's Special Reports. As** we have made fairly clear, Harry Browne's newsletter is the only investment newsletter which we are willing to recommend. He has written extensively on investments. In all, his first nine books sold over two million copies. Since 1974, he has been writing Harry Browne's Special Reports, a newsletter providing opinions on the economy, politics and investments. He is widely respected for his honest, down-to-earth investment advice. Over the years he has become one of America's better-known investment advisors. He has been a popular public speaker since the early 1960s. He has made appearances on the Today show, Wall Street Week, the Cable News Network (CNN), the Larry King show, the Financial News Network (FNN) and other national and local radio & TV shows. He just ran for President as the Libertarian Candidate

Anker Bank
Case postale 159
50, Avenue de la Gare
CH-1001 Lausanne, Switzerland
Telephone: (011-4121) 321-0707; Fax: 323-9767
Contacts: Mrs. Francine Misrahi,
Pierre-Andre Visinand
Minimum to open account: $5,000
Assets: SF 190 million
Liquidity: 57%
Anker Bank
P.O. Box 8022 Zürich
Switzerland
Tél: (+41 1) 224 65 65
Fax: (+41 1) 211 99 54
Telex: 812565 ank ch
Notes: Affiliated with Anker Finance SA, Geneva

Banca Unione di Credito
Bellariastrasse 82
Ch-8038 Zurich, Switzerland
Telephone: (011 -411) 482-6688; Fax: 482-2884
Contact: Hans Wihler, Heinz Heim, Mrs. Longo
Minimum to open account: $20,000
Assets: SF 2,012 million
Liquidity: 34%
Banca Unione di Credito
P.O. Box 6901 Lugano
Switzerland ·
Tél: (+41 91) 29 31 11
Fax: (+41 91) 22 70 09

NOTE: Some of the banks listed on this page and the next page have Caribbean branches. If we go to the library and look in a Bahamas telephone directory under the classification for banks we will find a large number of pages listing banks. Many of these banks are Swiss. We have found that most of the Swiss banks that have branches in the Caribbean prefer that we open our account through their branches located in Switzerland. Most of the Caribbean based Swiss Banks are commercial banks, many are not set up for merchant or private investor services.

ESCAPE FROM AMERICA

UeberseeBank
Limmatquai 2
CH-8024 Zurich, Switzerland
Telephone: (011-411) 267-5555; Fax: 252-2002
Contacts: Andri Gordon, Robert Lengacher,
Dan Schwab
Minimum to open account: $5,000
Assets: SF 500 million
Liquidity: 44%
Telex: 817125 ubz ch
Notes: Affiliated with American International Group, Inc., New York

Union Bancaire Privee
Bahnhofstrasse 20
CH-8022 Zurich, Switzerland
Telephone: (011-411) 219-6111; Fax: 211-3928
Contacts: Werner W. Schwarz, Peter Huber
Minimum to open account: $100,000
Assets: SF 11,182 million
Liquidity: 35%
Union Bancaire Privée
P.O. Box 1211 Genève 1 Switzerland
Tél: (+41 22) 819 21 11
 Fax: (+41 22) 819 22 00
Telex: 415423 ubp ch

ADVISORS
Camafin Trust AG
Postfach 1625
CH-8801 Thalwil-Zurich, Switzerland
Alte Landstrasse 147, CH-8800 Thalwil
Telephone: (001-411) 720-3131; Fax: 720-3141
Contacts: Bruno Brodbeck, Roger Badet
Minimum to open account: $50,000
Contact: Mr. Adrian Hartmann
Minimum to open account: $400,000

Weber Hartmann & Vrijhof Partners Ltd.
Zurichstrasse 1 1OB
CH-8134 Adliswil-Zurich, Switzerland
Telephone: (001-411) 709-1115; Fax: 709-1113
Contacts: Hans Weber, Robert Vrijhof
North American office:
555 West Georgia St., Suite 600
Vancouver, British Columbia, Canada V6B 1Z5
Telephone: (604) 682-8622; Fax: 682-1329
Contact: Mr. Adrian Hartmann

NOTE: Some of the banks listed on this page and the previous page have Caribbean branches. If we go to the library and look in a Bahamas telephone directory under the classification for banks we will find a large number of pages listing banks. Many of these banks are Swiss. We have found that most of the Swiss banks that have branches in the Caribbean prefer that we open our account through their branches located in Switzerland Most of the Caribbean based Swiss Banks are commercial banks, many are not set up for merchant or private investor services.

(Asset & Liquidity information is as of December 31, 1993)
The liquidity rating is a rough comparison of the assets a bank could turn into cash in a hurry versus the liabilities (such as demand deposits) for which bank customers could demand immediate payment. This tells us whether the bank could meet all its obligations if a banking crisis or other events caused most depositors to want to withdraw their money. A bank with a liquidity rating of 100% or higher should be able to meet all its obligations no matter what happens. The average Swiss bank has a liquidity rating usually in the range of 30%-40%.

Harry Browne Special Reports, Inc., P.O. Box 5586, Austin, Texas 78763
Phone: (800) 531-5142   (512) 453-7313   Fax: (512) 453-2015

HOW TO OPEN AN OFFSHORE BANK ACCOUNT

Opening a Swiss or Offshore Bank account is much the same as opening an account with any bank. The major difference is that for most of us our banking will be done by mail, by fax, by phone, or possibly by email. Bank business will very seldom be done in person. Any of the Swiss Banks just mentioned would be happy to send information and forms for opening an account with their bank.

SOAP BOX TIME: CONCERNING PRIVACY

We believe that privacy is the most fundamental of human rights,
because it is a psychic right.

We are born on this planet and we get to spend only so many years here and then we die.

Those years can be vital. They can be years spent learning and creating. Any one of us can create something that will benefit ourselves and humanity as a whole. There is not any question that such creativity is in our nature... every good thing that has advanced humanity is a result of some human's efforts. We are human. It is we who have done these valuable things for ourselves. It advances our evolution.

Certain things advance our creative efforts and certain things stifle those efforts.

Privacy is perhaps the greatest human value. With it we can aim at greatness. Without it we have nothing ...and I mean nothing. There is no greater psychological violation than a violation of our right to privacy. We believe that privacy is the most fundamental of human rights, because it is a psychic right. The right to privacy is even more profound a psychological necessity than our right to property. (Although one entails the other.)   There is not one thing more personal to a human being than our right to privacy. Once it's gone, the value entailed in our independent life disappears and we then become little more than slaves to whomever owns our privacy. It is as rude a violation as a pistol. No, it's ruder. Only savages live without privacy. Only savages disrespect our right to it.

The United States Government equates privacy with terrorism.

Well, they are not the same thing, are they? Privacy is not a terrorist act.*

According to Tax Haven Authority Terry Coxon, if we could take just one step to-wards insuring our privacy and to at least protect the privacy of our assets it would be to open a foreign bank account. However, if we do so, we are required to check a box on our U.S. tax return indicating whether we have a total of more than $10,000 in "foreign financial accounts."

According to Coxon, this leaves us three ways to use a foreign bank *lawfully* without reporting the existence of an account.

●We can keep an account with less than $10,000
●We can use a foreign bank to purchase investments that aren't reportable, [to be purchased in our behalf by the bank and taking care never to let the bank account balance exceed $10,000.]
●We can keep investments at a foreign bank that are not "financial accounts." Such as custodial accounts that hold precious metals or other valuables.

MAKING OUR OWN JUDGEMENTS

There are numerous books that explain how to open foreign bank accounts and many of these books include half their chapters debating the legality of this or that piece of legislation and the cleverness of this method or that method of getting our assets to a foreign bank. Some of these books talk endlessly regarding the problem of obeying or disobeying the law and these books give unsubtle tongue-in-cheek *hints* as to what the author is really implying.

STUPID STORY TIME

I had a lady friend who could always sense when I was in a dour mood. Whenever I started acting dour she would pounce on me and begin to wrestle me. No matter how much I asked her to stop she would continue until I was forced to defend myself. The moment I began to defend myself she would tell me that I wasn't allowed to use my full strength because I was a man and it wasn't fair. Inevitably she would keep it up until I started laughing helplessly at the absurdity of the situation. If I wasn't allowed to defend myself I couldn't win and if I defended myself I was a brute.

DECISIONS

Our relationship with the government regarding financial privacy is much like the game my lady friend played.

* It is instructive to note that in Italy and other civilized countries tax evasion is treated only as a misdemeanor, much like a parking ticket. What bizarre form of madness or mass hypnosis is it that allows the people of the United States to endure such a brutal travesty of justice as that perpetuated by the IRS and other government agencies? If we allow them to hand out felony jail terms and use a pistol to collect revenue money and to deny us our right to privacy in the process, then something is dreadfully wrong.

OPENING AN OFFSHORE BANK ACCOUNT

Opening a Swiss or Offshore Bank account is much the same as opening an account with any bank. The major difference is that for most of us our banking will be done by mail, by fax or by telephone and very seldom in person. (There is already 'online' offshore banking, but it is still not fully secure, nor is our opinion about it or any of the existing online banks.)   Any of the Swiss Banks just mentioned would be happy to send information and forms for opening an account with their bank.

We are required to report any export of currency or bearer instruments with a value of more than $10,000. Banks are required to report transfers of any amount over $10,000. There are however any number of ways to transfer funds to an Offshore Bank. The methods used depend on the amount of money being transferred. If our assets or portfolio are in the million dollar range then we strongly suggest contacting:
Terry Coxon
PRIVATE INVESTORS
625 2nd Street, Suite 102
Petaluma, California 94952
or mail: P.O. Box 2657 Petaluma, California 94953
phone: 707.778.1000 fax: 707.778.8804
email care of vkj@rpifs.com

Terry Coxon is the President of the **Permanent Portfolio Family of Funds** a mutual fund complex that manages over $280 million in assets. He was an advisor to Harry Browne, when Harry made his bid as the Libertarian candidate for President and he is the innovator of the **Passport Financial Protective Trust**, which is a low-cost asset protection trust system based in Bermuda. He is an investment advisor and consultant who has worked with Harry Browne for years. Terry also writes and speaks about offshore banking and investments. We highly recommend Terry Coxon.

The **Passport Financial Protective Trust** is a method devised by Terry that allows investors to place their finances offshore in a protective trust that is beyond lawsuits and confiscation by predators. As well as protecting our assets, the program facili-tates safety and control in the conveyance of inheritance. For those of us who are unsure about becoming full-fledged expatriates something should definitely be done to protect our assets and our privacy to whatever degree that we can. Not all of us want to divorce ourselves completely from America. If all of our assets are not removed from America what can we do to protect them? The Passport Financial Trust program would be an excellent way of increasing our protection from the unexpected. For information regarding this program contact:

Passport Financial, Inc.
P.O. Box 5586
Austin, Texas 78763
phone: 800.531.5142   or   512.453.7313
fax: 512.453.2015

ESCAPE FROM AMERICA

The following is directly quoted from an article by Terry that was published in the October 1994 issue of **Harry Browne's Special Reports.** The article is another reason we might be well advised to subscribe to the Special Reports and/or for those with larger portfolios to contact Terry.

No Trail
To approach an absolute assurance of privacy, you need to break the paper trail between you and the foreign bank by using actual cash at some point. For example, you could withdraw small amounts of cash from your bank account from time to time and buy cashier's checks or traveler's checks at a bank where you don't have an account.

Whether you'll want to will depend on how much secrecy is worth to you, and on how much money you intend eventually to send to a foreign bank. If you want to transfer $50,000 or $100,000 to a very secret foreign account, getting it there will be a chore, but it won't be impractical. But if you want to send, say, $1 million, you may decide that handling 200 cashier's checks is too much trouble.

Ironically, the institution that will most readily help you send small amounts privately to a foreign bank—enough to establish an account—is an agency of the U.S. Government. It's the U. S Post Office, where you can purchase money orders In amounts up $700 each without giving your name.

Once you have an account, a foreign bank will cooperate in almost any lawful plan to transmit money.

Cash Reports
If you want to use cash to break the paper trail between you and your foreign bank, be aware that a U.S. bank is required to report any withdrawal of cash that exceeds $10,000 or that is "unusually large." No one knows what "unusually large" means, so you should assume that any withdrawal over $5,000 will be reported. Also, don't abruptly begin making withdrawals of even $5,000. Start with small withdrawals, taking 6-12 months to let the withdrawal size grow to $5,000 or so.
   ~ ©Harry Browne Special Reports, Inc., P.O Box 5586, Austin, Texas 78763

Terry then goes on to discuss among other things how life insurance and annuities issued by foreign insurance companies have the same tax advantages as policies issued by U.S. companies, tax-free compounding of earnings and in the case of life insurance, tax-free payments to beneficiaries. However, Terry points out that a policy issued by a foreign company has the added advantage of being private, especially if we buy it in a country where financial privacy is the norm. Additionally, because an insurance policy isn't a "financial account," we can put as much money as we like into a foreign life insurance and annuities without mentioning the policies in our tax return.

Mr. Terry Coxon is a knowledgeable man. We would be well advised to get his new book: **Keep What You Earn:** Practical Strategies to Protect Your Assets from Taxes, Lawsuits and Financial Predators Published by Random House Trade
ISBN: 0812928288

NOTE: In the event that any bank moves in the direction of arranging independent agency insurance coverage of depositors accounts, or has in place a verifiable system of auditing; please contact us with information regarding your bank.

CHAPTER THREE

BUYING & OWNING
FOREIGN REAL ESTATE

> "Buying that ranch in Argentina today is going to
> make you look like a genius to your grandchildren."
>   -Doug Casey

HOW SAFE IS IT TO BUY & OWN FOREIGN REAL ESTATE?

For us to answer the question regarding the safety of foreign real estate we will need to consider and discuss the following:

- **Property rights**
- **Prevailing legal systems**
- **A nations record in fact versus its legal rhetoric**
- **Current trends within a country**
- **Past trends within a country**
- **The investment advice of those economic advisors who do recommend foreign real estate**
- **The monetary currency [paper money] in a nation and the existence of exchange controls**

Additionally, we need to believe that we know which way the world is headed.

Of course none of us knows for certain what the future holds. However we can make certain judgements based on the available facts. We can look at current technology and make rough estimates about future technology. We can look at current and past political and economic conditions and make rough guesses about future political and economic conditions. As an example; if current increases in human population continue with no interruption, it seems obvious that any nation that has surplus agriculture might fare better than one that is agriculturally poor. Of course we must keep in mind that this 'guess' is not an absolute prediction of the future, but only a guess. (Conjecture is a human form of guessing regarding the apparent outcome of what *appears* to be a 'probability' based on past performance.) Thus, by considering careful the possibilities of supply and demand today and what supply and demand will be like tomorrow we believe we are able to make pretty decent predictions regarding a nations potential. Another way to guess regarding a nations future, is that any nation worth considering must have begun to be doing better than it has been doing in the recent past; a nation whose trend is downwards, or consistently unpredictable makes life unpredictable for those who live there. Currency [paper money] convertibility is also an important factor, but a tricky one that we will need to discuss in uncomplicated terms.

PROPERTY RIGHTS

We would like to quote Ayn Rand regarding Property Rights. Her ability to recognize what was 'essential' remains her greatest legacy. Here is what she had to say about property rights:

> "Just as man can't exist without his body, so *no rights can exist without the right to translate one's rights into reality* — to think, to work *and to keep the results* — which means: the right to property. The modern mystics of muscle who offer you the fraudulent alternative of 'human rights' versus 'property rights,' as if one could exist without the other, are making a last, grotesque attempt to revive the doctrine of soul versus body. Only a ghost can exist without material property; only a slave can work with no right to the product of his effort. The doctrine that 'human rights' are superior to 'property rights' simply means that some human beings have the right to make property out of others; since the competent have nothing to gain from the incompetent, it means the right of the incompetent to own their betters and to use them as productive cattle. Whoever regards this as human and right, has no right to the title of "human.""

> — Ayn Rand   [emphasis added]

There is not one country (geographical area) on the face of the earth that is free of government control, (except maybe Italy). Governments by their very nature are the cause of most of the world's problems and as regards the issue at hand, they [governments] are the ones who expropriate property belonging to others. In a government controlled society, government has the power to tax, regulate, and confiscate just about anything it pleases. In the real world, thanks to governments, ownership is never an absolute, because ownership is not total, either by definition or in fact.

Does that mean we shouldn't venture forth from the shores of America?

SOAP BOX TIME

It means the exact opposite. We probably have more to worry about as regards real property expropriation within the United States in the near term than we do in most other civilized nations. It is arguable that we might have more 'laws' to protect us within the United States *vis a vis* expropriation than say Italy or France, but in Italy and France the practice of expropriation is considered repugnant, inhuman and unspeakable; while in the United States it is a means of crowd control, metaphorically speaking. Patriotic posturing and extraneous arguments pointing out the vast and superior quality and quantity of 'laws' in the United States 'in place' to protect us etcetera, etcetera; serve only to draw attention to and to clarify the fallacious illusion created by blind patriotism and government brainwashing. If they *'do'* expropriate our property in the United States for eminent domain, back taxes, or for any other reason; then the fact is: "they expropriate our property in the United States." Why equivocate? Whereas in Italy and France it is almost unheard of. In Italy, it must be remembered, they were incapable of having Sophia Loren serve a series of symbolic weekend jail terms for unpaid taxes, ...the Italian bureaucracy felt it was better to allow her to go free than to be stoned to death by the Italian people for jailing her. Where was a similar popular uprising in the United States when the IRS more or less murdered the American athlete and hero Joe Louis? It should be noted that Joe

Louis traveled the world entertaining GI's during World War II without monetary compensation; (because the GI's viewed him as a hero and his presence boosted moral.) The IRS agents who hounded him to the grave desecrated the spirit of this American legend, a man who defended America's honor as well as the boxing championship of the world against Nazi posturing and propaganda during an hour of American uncertainty and national need.

Is there anyone in the world today who would deny that Joe Louis unquestionably did what he did better than any other boxer in the world, both in the boxing ring and at the American Canteen? If no one denies his greatness, then why did the IRS murder him and why did no one protest? If owing the government some back taxes makes a hero into a criminal, what should we call those government employees who have run up a trillion dollar debt?

BACK TO BUSINESS

Putting it quite simply; it is an act of lucidity for an adult human to diversify assets so that some of them are located outside of the United States, (even if we choose not to be.) Of the investment advisors who have considered this issue most share the view[s] that: [1] exchange controls are eminent, [2] that weakness in the U.S. banking system increases the need to have hard assets abroad, or risk losing our assets, [3] the federal debt and the federal reserve policy have created an economic time bomb, [4] people's unpredictable and destructive reaction to a financial catastrophe in the United States may be worst than the catastrophe itself, [5] the dollar may soon be destroyed as a result of many of these very factors, [6] owning foreign real estate is a prudent, judicious and multi-faceted investment, [7] there is more opportunity abroad for ambitious Americans today than there is at home, [8] investments abroad in many places are dirt cheap, [9] most countries are untying the *statist* knot that has strangled them for decades while the United States seems headed in the opposite direction, [10] the ponderous regulations, increasingly expensive insurance requirements, potential liabilities, possible boycotts, and the growing proliferation of lawsuits in the United States are eliminating the incentive to excel, (11) confiscation and expropriation of our property is going to become more and more commonplace as government employees increasingly view us as 'national resources' whose property may be allocated in the "public interest," (12) government employees will create more and more confrontations with groups who oppose government oppression, thus creating a war-like atmosphere inside the borders of the United States, (13) exchange controls will happen suddenly and without warning, preventing those who have not yet expatriated some of their assets from doing so.

We will name a few of the investment theorists who hold some or all of these views, and some whose writings we admire so that the reader may refer to their individual writings and gain their differing perspectives. In alphabetical order, they are Larry Abraham, Harry Browne, Douglas Casey, Terry Coxon, Adrian Day, Jim Rogers, Harry Schultz, and John Train. Their view as regards the buying and ownership of foreign real estate stretches from the idea of buying a summer home in the Caribbean to the actual act of becoming a total expatriate and moving abroad; lock, stock and barrel.

ESCAPE FROM AMERICA

The obvious thinking about the summer home relies on the supposition that it is best to err on the side of caution. A summer home in the Caribbean, for instance, gives us [1] a refuge in the event that exchange controls are suddenly put in place without warning, [2] a place to escape to in the event of a total breakdown of the social order inside the United States, [3] allows speculation in a growing real estate market that may have more upside potential than the U.S. real estate market and [4] gives us a summer home even if nothing else comes to pass.

While I cannot dispute this clever wisdom, I am not in full agreement with it nor any other form of hesitation on the issue of expatriation. I believe that exchange controls are now inevitable. And more! However, realizing that we should avoid paranoia, that discussions of conspiracies are rank, and that there is much too much complexity to the modern world to pinpoint every subtle harbinger of doom; I will not include a manifesto of my own conjectures here that I cannot simply prove simply. I will just state clearly that the globalization of the economy has opened many opportunities abroad that didn't exist five years ago. If it's just as simple or possibly simpler to live and work abroad as it is inside of America and if the opportunities and life-style abroad are in many ways more dynamic then why the hesitation?

Of the above mentioned investment theorists, **Harry Browne** has lived abroad extensively in Europe and Canada. Browne provides thoughtful and careful advice regarding foreign investments on Swiss Banks, foreign currencies and on hard assets. He has published several books and publishes an investment newsletter. **Larry Abraham** now lives in Chile having left the United States completely. Abraham has published investment books and is the publisher of an investment newsletter. He warns of an American "brain drain" as a serious possibility coupled with an asset displacement due to "flight capital." **Douglas Casey** owns homes around the world and spends much of his time abroad; he is an authority on foreign investments, foreign real estate, and on mining and mining stocks worldwide. Casey provides some of the most innovative and daring suggestions regarding foreign real estate we are likely to find anywhere. Have a thoughtful and fun look at Casey's suggestions in his book *Crisis Investing for the Rest of the 90's.* **Jim Rogers** has spent considerable time abroad, owns land and assets abroad, and discusses quite passionately that the foreign cities he prefers are: Buenos Aires, Tokyo, Sydney, Bangkok, and Rome. Roger's became a sort of legend on Wall Street when he and George Soros founded the Quantum Fund, a Curaçao-based investment fund that was hugely successful. Roger's made himself $14 million dollars with this fund alone. Roger's gives a multitude of unique and innovative suggestions in his book *Investment Biker - Around the World with Jim Roger's.* Investment Biker is a great read and an eye opener concerning the lassitude in America today when compared with other countries. **Harry Schultz** was considered the original so-called *International Man*, having gone expatriate many years ago, he spent most of his life outside the United States living and working in Paris, Zurich, Copenhagen, and London. **John Train** has written numerous books on investing, his advice on money management is astute and thoughtful. In discussing the way to get rich in todays world, Train gives some fairly frank advice in his book, *The Craft of Investing.* He says that one of the best ways to get rich is to go abroad to a developing country and take some challenges, stating, among other things, that, "...If you are sufficiently clever and energetic enough to make the grade in a good law firm, you probably have what it takes to play a role in building up a developing country."

MORE THAN A TRIPLE PLAY

We believe that our purchasing foreign real estate can be viewed as more than a triple play. Consider these attributes: [1] It can appreciate more dynamically than U.S. real estate, [2] it can act as a safe haven in the event that things go awry, [3] it can be a summer home and [4] more in keeping with the theme of this book it can also be a dynamic place to live and the beginning of a new more fulfilling life.

HOW SIMPLE IS IT TO BUY FOREIGN REAL ESTATE?

How simple is it to buy foreign real estate? In many events it is as simple (or as difficult) as is for us to buy real estate in the United States. As in all things regarding investments, we need to do some homework. In this case some of the things we might consider researching are: a] the methods of holding land and ownership rights in the foreign country we choose, b] land use control, especially if we are seeking something beyond a residence, c] real estate financing, which is usually unavailable in countries with debased currencies, d] brokerage and attorney costs, methods and compensation practices, e] eminent domain practices and compensation, f] real property leasing practices, g] property prices and yield trends, h] methods of land description and document recording, i] construction costs, j] real estate investment characteristics, and k] the currency profile of the host nation. Finding the facts regarding these issues need not be as onerous as we might suspect. Just as in the United States we seek competent help and we ask intelligent questions. Foreign countries are not necessarily esoteric in their dealings with land ownership and there are competent honest individuals in every country of the world. The methods of land holding and ownership rights are generally the same from country to country, but the terms of ownership rights may be different and there may be distinctive characteristics associated with each ownership right. Most foreign countries have an **American Chamber of Commerce** that can be a great help in supplying the name of a reputable local attorney and the names of honest real estate agencies. In any event, the Chamber can supply the names of local law firms or real estate agencies that they themselves or other expatriates have had dealings with, even if the Chamber is unwilling or unable to give actual endorsement. The Chamber may also be willing to put us in touch with other Americans who have had dealings with a local attorney or agency. In the chapters on each individual featured country we have included the addresses, telephone and fax numbers of the American Chambers of Commerce located there. We have also included the names, addresses, telephone and fax numbers of real estate agencies in some countries, (without implying any endorsement of the agencies listed.) Real estate agencies can be of help in answering our questions if we care to fax them. They have an economic incentive to ingratiate themselves to our good wishes and are hence willing to spend some time and money faxing us back and answering our questions. Note that their answers can be at times helpful and at times misleading. If we ask what kind of clothing we should bring for a visit, or to send a color photograph of a particular property, or supply the name of a particular restaurant then they are going to be a real asset in answering our question. However they are also going to have a tendency to show us properties that are more expensive and 'gringo-oriented.' Consider the reply from an agency that supplies a list of residential properties all in the US$250,000 range along with color photographs of some lovely houses. This usually comes from a country where the Per Capita GDP (average income of the locals) is US$4,000 per year. Where are the locals living? Some rudimentary logic will tell us that if the locals can get by on $4,000 per year and live in fairly decent houses, then we should be able to find something for under U.S. $20,000; and the fact is that we usually can.

A good policy is to: [1] visit a country for a test visit before moving there, [2] move there only after the exploratory visit convinces us that we like the place and would really enjoy living there, [3] rent for a time in order to form a firm understanding and opinion of the country and [4] only purchase property after we have lived in the country for a year or so, can speak the language passably and we believe we have more or less learned the ropes. We will usually discover that the 'insiders' who have learned the ropes, know how to purchase local property for 25% of what the newcomer pays. That is how some local expatriates may go about making their living, by reselling subdivided local real estate to rich gringos who believe that all real estate should cost what it does in the USA. There is of course nothing dishonest about this, one of the rules of business is to sell something for more than we paid for it. So, as they say in Latin, *caveat emptor*; 'buyer beware.' If we don't have time to evaluate things we shouldn't buy! This is why we find fault with the idea of buying a 'summer house' in the Caribbean. We go there in a rush, we don't know the market, we pay an inflated price because all we've really seen of the country is the 'temples and the pagodas' and not the accurate cultural lay of the land. If we are smart we want to make absolutely sure that we are making a *pure play* in our real estate investment, not a whirlwind excursion-purchase of a souvenir. After a year of living in a new country we've also undergone some crucial personal acclimation — and we're more prepared to decide if we have found the right place for ourselves.

Robert Hopkins points out that the common first reaction to a new place is elation — the novelty of the situation, the feel of the tropical warmth, etcetera; but then culture shock sets in followed by self evaluation. This is the critical period and it requires acclimation and soul-searching on our part. If we hang-in, we discover that as we begin to participate in the new culture and begin to live our new life we move upwards towards a new happiness and probably a deeper understanding of ourselves in the process, ...but, it takes awhile. A year is a good amount of time to spend in a place before making any commitments. It is towards the end of the first year that we finally begin to acclimate to a new society; and it is by then that we finally begin to make strong decisions and commitments that are long lasting. This time period coincides nicely with the amount of time it will take us to understand the currency, the market conditions and the prices in our new country. Buying a home at that point in time will be just the thing to get us over the psychological hump and into a deeper sense of place, of purpose and of commitment and it will also be the point in time when we are more capable of making a pure play real estate investment as an *insider* and not like some dude on spring break.

PREVAILING LEGAL SYSTEMS & THE ART OF EXPROPRIATION

Our world has four basic legal systems and derivatives thereof; they are: [1] tribal law, [2] religious law, [3] civil code and [4] common law. Countries which we believe to be more advanced tend to use either civil code or common law. Common law is the system used in the United States and England. Civil code is the legal system used by such countries as Japan, France, West Germany and other Western European nations. Tribal law is still practiced in remote areas of the world and in Beverly Hills. Religious law is practiced by almost half of the world's population, in such countries as India, Saudi Arabia, Kuwait, Bahrain and in numerous other nations. (Religious law can and often does reappear in nations where the prevailing political system undergoes a breakdown — such as the breakdown that recently occurred in the Soviet Union. The areas most effected are those areas that have mixed ethnic populations such as we've recently witnessed in the former Yugoslavia. There are other Republics with mixed ethnicity such as Turkistan, Turkmenistan, Uzbekistan, Kyrgyzstan, Kazakhstan, Armenia, Azerbaijan and so on. These areas could easily see temporary resurgence of religious law as the local population seeks to regain its equilibrium by blaming its problems on someone else's religion.)

For the most part property rights in the Soviet Union are a mess of pottage; however republics such as Hungary, Czech & Slovak, Poland and other Eastern European republics make up what could easily be called one of the more exciting real estate markets for really great properties in today's Europe. Budapest and Prague are filled with classical stone buildings that were built when the republics had vast amounts of money. With the Soviet Union out of these republics, these cities are going to become *Living Museums*, (to repeat a colorful phrase that investment biker Jim Rogers used to describe them). Additionally, these cities are filled with culture, colleges, intelligent educated people, art, music, real food & real beer, plus a populace disgusted with the straightjacket of statism and bureaucracy. These places are open for business but in many cases lacking our technological know-how. They have recently experienced the specter of total expropriation from without and they did not like it. An apartment in Prague, or a farm house in Hungary can now be bought at bargain prices and these are historically rich and 'culturally' stable places that should be exciting places in which to live for a long, long time to come.

Expropriation has occurred in other places. It usually backfires. It causes flight capital and a decrease in foreign investment so it has declined in popularity among most despots. (Purely criminal governments are on the decline as prudent observers learn where and how their bread is buttered.) It remains continually difficult to know if all of the lessons have been learned and it also remains necessary to maintain eternal vigilance. Let's look at some major examples of past expropriations. The Colombian government in the 1980's took over the assets of a U.S. related affiliate of Occidental Petroleum. The president of Columbia justified the takeover on the basis of overdue taxes. Occidental Petroleum had agreed, (it was asserted,) that it would reinvest a portion of its earnings back into Colombian oil exploration. The Colombian government claiming that Occidental had not fulfilled it's obligation, took title to the company property, deducted US$50 million for back taxes and promised to turn over the residual funds based on the Colombian government's *government appraised* value of the property. Argentina took over the properties of foreign companies back in the 1970's with little if any compensation. It is worth noting that the Argentine government today is diversifying itself of government owned industries and attempting to place itself on solid economic footing. Also in the 1970's, Iran took over all the foreign-held company properties in Iran. Iran's revolution was an example of the recurrence of Religious Law resulting from the brutality of the Shan. Cuba under Castro expropriated the properties of foreign investors. The Cuban expropriations are rather complex. Cuba was being exploited prior to the Castro revolution by the American-backed dictator Fulgencio Batista. Batista had sold the birthright of the Cuban people out from under them; no contest to this. However, Castro has made a total mess of things; a subject we will address in greater detail in a later section. Several African nations have witnessed differing degrees of expropriation, leaving parts of Africa in shambles. Have the African nations made enough mistakes to turn things around without resorting to further expropriation? Perhaps. We'll look at some African nations and the opportunities there in further sections and discuss the possibilities.

Even though some of the world is improving by ridding itself of overt statism and despite the fact that criminal expropriation has been on an obvious decline outside of the United States, it is still too soon to make any definitive statements regarding this issue. It appears clear to us from observation and by way of good advice, that in all things it is better to err on the side of caution. But wherein lies caution? Is it cautious to repress all questions concerning the rapidly declining conditions within the United States and bury our heads in the sand until the night of the broken glass? Or is it cautious to reason out the facts from a multitude of facts and then carry out the best actions open to us even if they bear little resemblance to a comforting precedent?

What seems certain to us, is that regardless of either a good, bad or an ugly outcome to the world's current transitional tribulations; diversity by its plural nature increases our odds of surviving happily. It does so quite simply by increasing the number of possible alternatives that are open to us and our family. In todays global world it just makes plain good sense to hedge our bets; especially when it comes to real estate.

MAKING JUDGEMENTS

In each of the sections on the individual countries we try to evaluate each nation from a multitude of perspectives. When we look at a nations current policies we view them in conjunction with their historic and recent past. We try to separate the rhetoric from the actions and we examine current practices in relation to current rhetoric. We take a look at civil liberties, political freedom, crime, economic conditions, location, geography, natural resources, industry, poverty, military ambitions, infrastructure (such as telephone, internet access, mail service and shipping,) exchange controls and the degree of opportunity the subject country may provide us.

Not every country is for every person. We are all different, and we all have different needs, desires and values. Some of us like to take more risks than others and some of us are simply content with a safe crime-free haven where going to the opera is the big event of the week. We will look at many selected countries and try to decide which is the perfect one.

Perceptions of the world have changed noticeably as the world has become more global in its behavior. That is obvious or you would not be reading this book. Along with these perceptual changes there has been an unfortunate tendency to indiscriminately change the definition of words as if they were made of plastic and could be changed to suit the whim of the speaker. For that reason we have been careful when evaluating a country not to be swayed by catch-phrases such as: 'democracy,' 'capitalistic,' 'retirement haven' and so forth. These words in themselves tell us nothing about a country.

Simply saying that a nation is a democracy isn't saying a hell of a lot. At its best, democracy is a form of mob-rule, at its worst democracy is word used by government employee thugs to cover their complicity. ('we are not really robbing you, this is a democracy') Additionally, it does little to designate a country as being capitalist. The word 'capitalist' has lost both its precise and its colloquial meaning.* Thanks to the new-world artistry of double-speak the term can no longer be construed to imply that civil liberties or property rights are actually in place within a so-called 'capitalist' country.

The following terms are now used openly to describe a so-called capitalist nation: capitalist-statist, mixed-statist, capitalist-Leninist, mixed-capitalist, mixed-capitalist transitional, mixed-statist transitional, mixed-capitalist statist, and capitalist. The world's former bastion of communism, the Soviet Union is now a mixed-statist transitional on its way to being called a mixed-capitalist transitional. Add to this; that the closest thing to actual pure laissez-faire capitalism in the entire world, is the city of Hong Kong, which is being handed over [kicking and screaming] to China. Talk about irony! China is one of the world's worst slave-states. We should never allow ourselves to forget those mostly forgotten souls who are working in the slave-labor camps in China, Vietnam and in Myanmar [formerly known as Burma.] They are working within what is now called a mixed-statist economy, [or capitalist-Leninist to use the latest catch phrase.] When we purchase something made in one of these

---

* The word Capitalism describes an *economic system*, hence it is an *economic* term not a *political* term. To use the word as a description of a system that does not recognize property rights seems to be a contradiction in terms. Ayn Rand defined capitalism as a social system based on the recognition of individual rights, including property rights, in which all property is privately owned. By Rand's definition, Capitalism entails by it's nature a separation of State and Economy and precludes the use of force. According to the Austrian Economist Ludwig von Mises, Capitalism is: "An economic concept of civilization that is based on the *private ownership (and control) of the means of production.* Such an institutional situation permits and inevitably encourages the division of labor, economic calculation, capital accumulation, technological improvement and *voluntary* social cooperation of a market economy in which mass production is designed for the consumption of the sovereign masses. *Capitalism is the antithesis of statism, socialism and communism which are based on government ownership (or control) of the means of production.*" [emphasis added]

capitalist-Leninist countries, we can easily be purchasing something manufactured by a slave in a slave-labor camp working for a slave-master living in Rangoon, Beijing or in your own home town. The slave-masters are involved in the *capitalist system,* [i.e. they are profiting nicely from the sale of the items produced by their slaves and in turn buying themselves nice clothes, nice houses, sending their children to good schools, eating tasty expensive food and living the good life in general with their VCR's and Mercedez cars.] They have the 'Capitalist-Leninist' advantage of having resolved the problem of the minimum wage by sway of a dedicated constituency.

Everyone is now a capitalist, except maybe the Cubans and the North Koreans; (and I've heard that the Cubans were recently seen uptown Manhattan buying sunglasses and looking for tourist trade).

PAPER MONEY & CAPTURED MONEY

There are a few interrelated factors that apply to Exchange Controls, International Real Estate and to foreign currencies that are important for us to understand:

The purchasing power of a nations currency profoundly effects the *actual price* of that nation's property. Currency rates are cyclical and nations with high rates of inflation have weak currencies subject to periodic devaluations. **Immediately following a devaluation the price of commodities produced within that nation, (as well as it's real estate), becomes cheaper to buyers who have sound currencies and are capable of using those sound currencies to make their purchases. This buying opportunity will only exist for brief cyclical periods,** *from the moment of devaluation up until the time when the nations 'internal' prices are adjusted to compensate for the difference between the internal prices and those existing 'externally' to that nation.* **There is usually, but not always, a lag time between the moment of devaluation and the moment of adjustment. The lag time can be quite brief, however the differences in a strong currencies buying power within that lag time can sometimes be quite pronounced.**

Upon the inevitable upwards *price adjustment* to the external buying pressure the purchased property or commodity will then reflect its true internal value vis a vis its national currency once again. Example:

STUPID STORY TIME

A two hundred acre 'ranch property' in the imaginary Republic of Sabroso is worth US$100,000. The national currency of Sabroso is the Zapoloté. The official rate of exchange is Ten Zapoloté to the Dollar; (Z$10 = US$1). Hence, under normal circumstances it takes Z$1,000,000 [1 million Zapolotés] to purchase our two hundred acre ranch. Without warning, the Republic's Ministry of Economic Development and Finance announces a fifty percent devaluation of the Zapoloté. (The Minister-General himself, Raul Chappurito, is unavailable for comment; Senor Chappurito, his wife are eating dinner in Zürich and cannot be reached.) Internally, inside the Republic of Sabroso, little has changed. A housewife in the Capital City of Sâo

Donato goes shopping for groceries; there is no change in prices. Two tomatoes cost the same price on the day of the devaluation as they did the day before; a dozen eggs have not increased in price by as much as a single Zapoloté, even a pound of meat costs no more then it did a week ago. On the International Monetary Exchange however, things have changed. We can suddenly buy twice as many Zapolotés today for the our dollar than the number of Zapolotés we could buy the day before. We buy one million Zapolotés for US$50,000, (which would have cost us $100,000 just yesterday) then we fly to the Republic of Sabroso and for our US$50,000 (one million Zapolotés), we buy our two hundred acre ranch.

Ultimately the commodity (consumer) prices *within* the Republic of Sabroso will rise until they are in balance with the prices *outside* of the Republic. Ultimately our ranch will be worth two million Zapolotés, (or US$100,000) and two tomatoes will take twice as many Zapolotés to reach the kitchen. Such is the advantage of holding our money in a strong currency or in gold or silver, until such times as we can take advantage of a cyclical fluctuation.

We might well make the assertion that such a practice is mercenary. However, before we make such an assertion we should wonder if such an event has ever happened to us. The answer is a resounding Yes. The United States Dollar has undergone several devaluations. Those who were holding stronger currencies such as the Yen, or hard metal assets such as gold or silver were able to buy commodities and real estate inside the United States at bargain basement prices and did so! Welcome to the real world. Like it or not, this is the way of finance in a world of mixed economies; where government's exert control over not just the economy of a nation, but also over the ultimate value of a nations currency through an act of fiat. People who are in government service can unscrupulously take advantage of such a devaluation and profit handsomely at their citizens expense. However, this is not the place to discuss such issues; nor do I consider myself qualified to discuss them beyond a rudimentary level. See the resources section in the appendix.

We are not obligated to buy in this fashion, nor is it always to our advantage to do so. If we find a situation where there is a stable currency inside a stable nation; we may simply want to buy there because we like the place and we plan to spend part of, or the rest of, our life there regardless of cyclical fluctuations in property or monetary values. It may be crucial to point out that there are both practical and emotional reasons to purchase real estate. To many of us a family house is much more than just a home with a capital 'H'. While it is admittedly something personal that we make a part of ourselves our home is also a combination of other factors: a major investment, as well as a sort of savings program, tax shelter and a large part of our retirement insurance. Yet, it is important to realize that even though it fills these 'practical' investment criteria, it still remains very difficult for many of us to look at a house as something we simply buy and sell like a bushel of apples, or as we might buy and sell some stock in IBM. **It is an investment that we become psychologically attached to.** That fact changes it from just about every other form of investment. However, as we become expats we develop a global view, and because this view has a wider periphery, we are able to see what was once obscured by a narrower frame of reference. There are reasons to buy international real estate; good economic reasons that go beyond the emotional. **Owning foreign real estate takes us out of the dollar but keeps us in a form of real or hard assets.** In our imaginary scenario in the Republic of Sabroso, we purchased a swell property for fifty cents on the dollar. Now, what if that dollar should happen to fall? We'd have more Zapolotés to put on the wall? Well, yes, sort of. In our scenario we purchased a property for US$50,000 during a cyclical low in the Zapoloté. If the dollar should now fall by twenty percent, that increases the worth of our property in dollar purchasing power. [we can 'buy' more dollars] We now have a ranch worth US$125,000; each dollar has now fallen in value to .80¢ based on its former worth. We have in effect made US$75,000* simply by purchasing a ranch we wanted anyway. Do these things happen? Assuredly. So, another factor for us to consider in purchasing international real estate is a positive diversification of our assets out of the dollar.

This type of diversification has many positive attributes for the expat. Besides moving us out of the US Dollar (hence protecting us from a collapsing US economy) it also insulates us from potential foreign exchange control mandates that might be put in place by a panicked US government trying to shore up escaping assets. i.e. they'll want your bread. As we've discussed, US government employees are going to start looking around for someone to blame their mistakes on. Unlike Senor Chappurito they cannot all slip away to vacation in Zürich quite so easily. However, they are not our concern; our concern is to protect ourselves and our families from their fiscal idiocy. Real estate is difficult, if not impossible to repatriate, very much unlike money in a US bank account. [fully protected by the FDIC as it is]

We mentioned gold and silver and we also mentioned some other factors that should perhaps be addressed. Again, I do not consider myself qualified to discuss such things beyond a rudimentary level. I will say, that I believe that sound, cogent assets with intrinsic values are *usually*, if not always, preferable to the fiat ersatz creations of government employees. However, values are based on individual preference. In one of China's many dynasties the populace refused to accept the paper money, preferring the tangible assets of gold. That dynasties government employees in an act of utter desperation hit upon the brilliant idea of producing a money made from perfumed colored silk rather than paper. Of course, it didn't work, a piece of perfumed silk is never worth more than a piece of perfumed silk. Hitler had a better idea. Anyone who debased, speculated in, or undersold the Nazi German Mark was shot. What a concept!

---

* Actually not; because the US$125,000 is no longer worth US$125,000; it has a relative value. What has actually happened is that you have allowed yourself to double your buying power in one instance, (the utilization of a cyclical fluctuation in the Zapoloté) and prevented yourself from losing buying power in the second instance. (by holding an asset that was moved outside of the US Dollar) Value, in the fiscal sense of the concept of value, is relative to the existence of assets, and assets have *intrinsic* values. Concepts such as Deutschland Uber Alles have no relevance to fiscal values; they remain abstractions; and can only be upheld at the point of a gun. No one has to put a gun to our heads to make us accept a gold coin.

The issue of Exchange Controls is a simple issue with a simple solution: Avoid them. As pointed out in the section on Offshore Banking & Tax Havens there are many safe ways to own real estate anywhere in the world (including the United States). We can protect ourselves by the holding of title to any property within a jurisdiction that is different (safer or saner) than that of the jurisdiction where the property exists. We can hold title in the form of stocks in a corporation. We can hold title as a corporation. We can hold title by registering ownership through a third entity such as a bank or trust. It is probably safe to say that there are more than enough possible methods to hold title that we should be able to find a method to fit just about any situation. The important thing is to seek methods which are legal and which fully protect our privacy. We cannot overstress how crucial it is to protect our privacy regardless of any indoctrination to the contrary. **The right to privacy is not a crime.** There is absolutely nothing for which anyone should feel guilty in seeking to keep their own affairs private. It is also our right to protect the money we've earned from those who have not earned it. No one has a right to know our business. We can think of no reason that anyone needs to know who the principals are that own a property, a stock, or an offshore corporation. If the property taxes are paid on that property that should be the end of it. In the same regard, no one needs to know the name of the corporation or the individuals for whom a bank is holding title as long as the bank is maintaining the property and paying the property tax. If a corporation changes hands in a country or in a tax jurisdiction that is different from the jurisdiction in which the property exists that is the business of that jurisdiction. It simply isn't anyone else's business. Unless we are terrorists it should never be anyone's business who we are or what we own. Why should it be?

If we do decide to hold ownership of real property within a country that has exchange controls it is important to understand that we may have a difficult time repatriating our funds from the sale of that property. If we should ever decide to move to another country we will have the choice of keeping the property we've bought or selling it and reinvesting the funds inside that country. The latter is not a good option inside a country with a debased currency. However there may be instances and situations in which we may wish to hold ownership in such countries. We cannot offer any profound advice in such matters. The best advice we can give is not to break any laws especially when there are so many legitimate methods of doing business legally.

MOVING ON

Investment in specific properties will be mentioned to some degree in the sections on specific nations. There are certainly some great bargains out there, as there are always bargains for those willing to spend some time looking. Even though risk is a factor in price not every bargain out there entails risk. There are currently several low-risk places in the world where real estate prices are at bargain basement levels. Belize immediately comes to mind. Belize is an English-speaking country that's never been at war has no political corruption that we know of. It's geography is magnificent. It has the second longest barrier reef in the world, numerous islands and white sand beaches that are second to none. Real estate there is a steal!

Venezuela also has bargain real estate. Venezuela is actually the largest Caribbean nation in the world, with thousands of miles of white sand beaches. Venezuela is a country of striking beauty. It has immense ranch lands that are now being sold at bargain prices. With the largest lake in South America, Lake Maracaibo and the Orinoco River which is so immense it is a close rival in size to the Amazon River Venezuela is something to behold. It has almost 2,000 miles of white-sand beaches fringed with coconut palms all of which line the Caribbean coast. If there was ever a place and time to buy real estate it's right now in the Republic of Venezuela. We have heard of good arable land on the Orinoco River that is being offered for under $100 an acre.

On the opposite end of the risk spectrum we've heard of a 1,000 acre dairy farm being offered for $10,000 plus fifteen years back taxes in Mozambique. (The back taxes are said to be about $15,000.) Mozambique just went through a fifteen year civil war. How about a grant of 25,000 acres of cotton land? Someone just accepted it. He is going there, has his workers in place, (2,000 people willing to work for $10 per month) He expects to be making a profit immediately especially since he can import machinery, seed, and other needed materials duty free. Additionally, he was given a three-year tax holiday. The property will be worth between US$5 million to US$10 million dollars when Mozambique stabilizes.

It is probably important to remember that there is a cyclical fluctuation in the degree of risk we take in some of the world's furthest and most primitive backwaters, ...yes, cyclical risk. But cyclical risk has always been a part of human affairs, so it's no stranger really. Living in Los Angeles or San Francisco can be very dangerous. So risk is a matter of perception. There are relatively few people who spend any degree of time looking for first opportunities; most people wait until the opportunity is obvious and the price has gone up. Risk is a function of price but risk can certainly be a matter of perception.

Real risk, perceived risk and relative risk has flowed like a river through much of human history, slightly chaotic in nature and a little bit dangerous. But so are currency fluctuations and exchange controls as often as not. It must be remembered that even chaos follows a certain pattern as dynamic as planned obsolescence and as predictable as the lottery. Yet somebody has to win despite the risk of loss, so risk hasn't stopped the ticket buyers. Timing is like a lottery. War zones are transitory. After the war is like after the rain. If you are the first one in and the first buyer you stand to gain a considerable fortune for your courage. Unless the cease-fire is broken. And there are other risks. The only thing worst than getting shot is losing your money. Some who bought in Cuba after the Cuban revolution at rock-bottom prices are still holding their deeds. But the anticipation of the deed going good is still better than perfumed silk.

CHAPTER FOUR

PASSPORTS

"A Social Security number is not actually required for issuance of a passport, but Section 603E of the Internal Revenue Code of 1986 requires passport applicants to provide a Social Security number..."

EXCERPT FROM THE US DEPARTMENT OF STATE PASSPORT SERVICE CODE

There are three concepts all expats must understand. They are simple concepts but they make a great deal of difference to the relationship we have with governments. These concepts are called:

- **RESIDENCE**
- **DOMICILE**
- **CITIZENSHIP**

Residence is the country where we reside. Residency is usually defined and determined by the length of time we are in a country. In most countries, visits for ninety days or less do not cause us to be viewed as residents. The exact length of time that determines qualification for residence status varies from country to country.

Domicile is not the same thing as residence, nor is it necessarily determined by our country of residence. Domicile is a concept that entails the idea of permanence; which is the reason that we seek to have our tax jurisdiction domiciled in a tax-haven, while we have our physical bodies residing in another place altogether. This may seem complex, but it is not. View our relationship with governments as a paper relationship, and our relationship with reality as a physical relationship and the concept becomes a bit clearer. We want our paper relationship to remain domiciled, more or less permanently, in a low-tax or no-tax jurisdiction... this paper self, is our business self, our office self, our company self, our money-making self. It is what the governments of the world tax us on. If our business was actually a self, it would be considered to be residing in a tax-haven, far from our actual human body, while our human body, our actual self might be living in a nice country with brutal tax laws.

Citizenship is a relationship between a human being and a nation. Dual citizenship is possible among many nations, illegal among others. It is possible for us to have several passports and many people actually do. Those German-Jews who had more than one passport during Hitlers rise to power may have been committing a crime against Nazi-German law by having those passports. If so, they were called criminals. Many of those who did not have a second passport died as a result of not being able to escape Nazi Germany. For this reason, because of the untrustworthiness of governments and because a human being has a biogenetic as well as a psychological obligation to survive, a second passport is a rite of passage in every sense of the term. No expat should leave home without two.

There are several ways to obtain dual nationality, or more specifically; there are several ways to obtain a second passport. The simplest way is to purchase one. Purchase is the most expedient, because most countries require a five year residence minimum before they convey citizenship and a passport. There are exceptions to the five year minimum; Bolivia is one example. In Bolivia citizenship is granted after two years of residence, or after just one year if our spouse is Bolivian. There are other nations that convey citizenship in less than five years and circumstances within each nation that cause degrees of flexibility within the rules regarding residency. The goals of each expat is going to determine an individual course of action. There are a lot of countries and we predict there are going to be a lot of expats. This being so, we will give a general outline of the situation and a few recommendations.

GET A SECOND PASSPORT

Recommendation number one is to get a second passport. The simplest way, as we have stated is to purchase one outright. They range in price. A capital investment into Guatemala of 20,000 Quetzals (approximately $5,000) can cause the Guatemalan government to waive the five year period normally required for citizenship. The investment can be into real estate or industrial enterprise. This means we can have a cabin in Guatemala and a Guatemalan passport for a reasonable fee. The question then becomes one of degree. How good is the Guatemala passport when measured against other passports?

Any second passport is better than having only one passport. Generally speaking, the more power and sway a nation has, the more power and sway its passport has. The prices paid for passport vary from $5,000 to $750,000 depending on the place and circumstance. In each and every case, payment alone does not always produce an immediate passport. (governments love to play hard to get.) In some cases, payment is viewed (more or less) as a payoff for a passport and does not necessarily mean that the buyer ever intends to live in the country of issue. In other cases, the purchase is viewed as a rite of entrance; a method of separating the sheep from the goats. If we are rich enough to invest in a nation we are welcome to become citizens. In the simplest of scenarios, we plop down $5,000 and we pick up our passport. In the most complex, we make a payment (read: investment) of $750,000 and after three years of residency, we become good citizens with our own brand new passport.

Here is rough idea of what's out there:
- Canada; $250,000 and a three year wait.
- Belize; $44,000 at the time of writing. We suspect this price may soon change as well as the conditions regarding issuance. Currently, residence is not required, other than a visit to Belize once every five years. Our research on Belize causes us to predict a coming change in this policy.
- Bolivia; $20,000 to $25,000 without obligation of residency.
- Dominican Republic; $20,000 without obligation of residency.
- Mexico; unavailable at any price.
- Paraguay; any investment into 'real property' entitles an expat to a passport. Probably around $5,000 would do the deed. Citizenship also is granted to anyone who practices a science, art, or industry.

66

●Panama; gives instant naturalization to anyone who establishes themselves in agriculture, stock raising, the breeding of birds and other similar industries.

●Jamaica; has a number of schemes for the granting of passports. No residence is required for those who purchase a zero-coupon 10 year bond for $30,000 plus make a $50,000 investment into a development project. This sounds rather costly to us. St. Kitts and Nevis are also too expensive to consider. Many of the Caribbean Islands are pricing themselves out of the market; but than their landmass is limited.

●Mauritius; two years and 300,000 rupees.

●Australia; $500,000 plus two years residency.

●New Zealand works on a 'points system,' which is laid out in the section on New Zealand.

There are probably many 'smaller' countries that would be aminable to accepting an 'investment' to facilitate citizenship/passport goals. There is also the reverse twist of this; there are many smaller countries that are poor yet desire Honorary Consul representation by someone who is knowledgeable in different fields of expertise. It is quite legal for us to represent such countries. When such nations issues us a certificate attesting to our diplomatic status, the United States Passport office is *obliged* to issue us a black passport. A black passport is a diplomat status passport. The requirements could include being able to speak the language of the country we consul and/ or be able to perform some service to the issuing government (or to possibly have some connection with it's officials.) A variant of this is the outright purchase of representative status and the attainment of a "Lettre de Chancellerie" — a document indicating that we have been retained to perform services or consultation for the issuing government. Again, we gain a black diplomatic passport for our efforts. Such passports are very valuable and cause raised eyebrows, increased courtesy and quicker response time when presented at border crossings. If we really want to put on the dog, this is a very hip way of doing so. Bureaucrats and diplomats are obliged to respect each other...

Another very good way to attain a second passport, is by Right of Descent (through ancestry.) Ireland, France, Italy, Germany, Turkey, Israel, Hungary, Austria and the Netherlands, just to name a few countries, all have laws regarding the right of descent. Just about every country has some laws regarding the issuance of citizenship and a passport by right of descent. The laws however are very different from country to country. If we are of Irish descent, the chances are good that we can gain an Irish passport, just as is the case if we are Italian, or Turkish. To accomplish this goal, there are documents required, governmental hoops to jump through and some tediously slow paperwork to wade through, but the effort should more than pay for itself with an eventual bonafide legal second passport.

Another method of attaining a second passport is by forgery. Many books will mention this method, and then state that they do not recommend it. We will state the following as our enduring policy: Anything we can do to save our own life and that of our family, (along with the fruit of our labor) should be undertaken. If it is right for a CIA agent to use a forged document to murder innocent Guatemalan Indian women and children, then it sure as hell is right for us to use a forged document to help us and our children escape to safety. Anyone who disagrees with this is ignorant of the lessons history has to teach us, or they have blood on their hands and want more of it. That said; we will state that forgery should be the avenue of last resort. It is complex in its requirements and can create a paper-trail nightmare that can come back to haunt us. There are books on the subject, and there are tricks to it. With today's computer graphics and printing capabilities it is fairly simple to create some very sophisticated-looking documents. Anyone can easily change existing documents through scanning and rearrangement. Forgery and counterfeiting methods have become so widely accessible and so sophisticated that the governments of the world are having to totally rethink their policies on the production of paper money. It is seldom forgivable in the eyes of any government for any human being to commit those actions that are reserved for government employees. It's distracting.

Most forgery of identification involves the existence of a birth certificate of a person who died at a very young age. That is, most forged identification that is of an enduring quality, requires that the name of the individual on the identification is the name of an actual human being who was once alive. The process of creating a full 'life' and documentation for such an individual is tedious and laborious. The creation of such documents is hardly something anyone would do for a living. i.e. one could not purchase false I.D. based on such elaborate and precise convolutions any cheaper than one could purchase a second passport in most third world countries. This is the reason why most books will not cover the issue, because it is automatically suspected that the need for false I.D. is based on some sort of criminality. We need only think back on those German-Jews in Nazi Germany who were guilty of no crime.

Ironically, as the situation in Europe changes once again, the value and availability of passports changes yet again. Hungary for example, during the Communist era was a place where almost anyone would have given anything for a second passport other than Hungarian. Today, Hungary is the hot place to go to get a second passport for many people who are serious about getting into the Western European Community. As it is suspected that Hungary will be the first east-block nation to be accepted into the European Community, gaining a Hungarian Passport now ensures that the holders will be able to live anywhere in Europe upon Hungary's EC acceptance.

Similarly, for safety and personal security while traveling many Israeli Jews today would rather hold the dark green passport with the eagle on it issued from Germany, than be the holders of the light-blue passport with the Star of David. Germany automatically issues a passport to any Jew, or descendent thereof, whose family was criminally deprived of their German citizenship by the Nazi government. The world changes and the unpredictably of that change is an important factor in the need for a second passport.

We would be remiss if we failed to mention Garry Davis and his lifelong quest for a World Government of World Citizens. A 1992 book, *Passport to Freedom, A Guide for World Citizens*, (Seven Locks Press, Box 27, Cabin John, MD 20818) tells about Mr. Davis and his life long struggle to create a World Government. We would like to be able to say that Mr. Davis is simply ahead of his time, but while we applaud his admirable efforts we disagree with the basic premise. We would like to see one world without government, not one world government The distinction is a crucial one. That is not to imply that we cannot conceive of worthwhile governments, we can. We believe that the more limited a government is the better it is at creating liberty. This may be a difficult premise for many of us to understand and we would like to discuss it at length but space does not permit that. Two books on the subject are: *The Market for Liberty* By Morris and Linda Tannehill which may be available at **Laissez Faire Books** 938 Howard Street, Suite #202 San Francisco, CA 94103 Phone800.326.0996 or 415.541.9780 Fax: 415.541.0597 **email:** custsvc@LFB.org **URL:** http://www.lfb.org/ The other book is *For a New Liberty* by Murray N. Rothbard. Neither of these books have ISBN numbers that I can find. They are books written in the early 1970's, but they may still be available, either from Laissez Faire or from **Reason Magazine** whose address and phone number is in our Resource Section.

The problem we see with current governments is that they are brittle. They are not alive and they do not evolve. They have no goal. They will disagree, they will tell us about truth, justice and the American way,   ...with flags waving and trumpets blaring. Well, if they have a goal, what is it? Not; what is their policy to stave off disaster for the next twenty-four hours; but what is their goal? Where are they headed?

MOVING ON

As we have been bold enough to be making recommendations in this section we might as well make some final ones regarding the issue of passports. Each of us feels we know what works best for us. For some of us, it is the safety of living within a idyllic system and country such as New Zealand, having gone through the process of establishing our qualifying credentials and having the required points for acceptance. In such a scenario, we will have citizenship and a passport. New Zealand even allows a second passport and dual citizenship. In this way, we will be living within the country where we have our passport as a resident. This is truly safe, or at least it gives the impression of safety from this particular point in time and space.

In another scenario, we might have a second passport from the Dominican Republic and find ourselves living in Prague. In either case we have options, but the degree of safety we feel in both instances will be based upon our personal view of todays world and where the world will be tomorrow. While no one can predict the future; it is possible to be somewhat better prepared for a wider degree of possible futures through diversification than it would be if we placed all of our confidence in one passport and one outcome.

NEW COUNTRIES & THE ATLANTIS PROJECT

We believe that a new country based on the principals of market liberty is now inevitable. Just as some governments have learned that they can attract more revenue by establishing favorable tax status, so some nations will soon recognize that a totally free port will act to create enormous wealth and property. If there were an two hundred square mile area of the earth that had port facilities and a governmental system that ensured total market and civil liberty, hundreds of thousands of people would move there at once. The establishment of such a city would act as a magnet to those who want to be free of onerous government controls. Douglas Casey has worked on such a project and he has gotten fairly close to success a couple of times. We feel that the time is quickly approaching when a City-State or an entire nation will be totally free, a place where human liberty will actually exist, not just in rhetoric and slogan, but in actual fact.

In our Belize section we will mention the Atlantis Project. The Atlantis project is just such an attempt at building a new nation. As mentioned, we believe that a new nation is inevitably, but we are not sure how it will evolve. If such a free nation evolves out of an existing nation then being recognized by the United Nations will be a simple matter. Being recognized by other nations as a bonafide nation is important in insuring that our passport and our freedom is valid. The Atlantis Project involves the construction of a reef city and the creation of a City-State. The project is ambitious, hopeful and interesting, though we feel that it is perhaps poorly realized. We certainly don't want to be discouraging to the people who are working on the project and we wish them every success. They are now selling passports for the future City-State of Oceania. Sadly they probably aren't worth much as a second passport at this point in time. If the city of Oceania is ever completed and the Atlantis Project is fully realized, then I will have to eat my words. I will gladly eat this page of text in the city of Oceania. Nothing would make me happier. I doubt it will happen.

Oceania -- The Atlantis Project & Oceania Passports.
2656 Van Patten St. #23, Las Vegas, NV 89109
URL: http://www.oceania.org/

Text from the Oceania Home Page:" The Atlantis Project is dedicated to the goal of establishing a new country named Oceania. This country will be devoted to the value of freedom, and will first exist as a sea city in the Caribbean. As no collectivist nation is likely to sell us the land we need, we will build an island out of concrete and steel. At this point, the organization behind this new country, The Atlantis Project, is building the necessary financial resources to pay off past debts and to pay for the completed model of Oceania. Once this task is completed, The Atlantis Project will go into full gear and go well beyond its peak reached in early 1994 when it was covered by media across the U.S. and the world -- including the BBC, the Miami Herald, the Art Bell Show, Boating magazine, and Details magazine."

CHAPTER FIVE

TELECOMMUNICATIONS
COMPUTER TELEPHONY -- CALL BACK & THE
WORLD WIDE WEB

"...understanding what telephony is helps clarify why in a very short period of time it will not make any real difference where we live if we engage in certain types of work. If we can now purchase a splendid ranch in Belize or a spectacular condo in Bangkok for one tenth the price of what something similar might cost us in the United States, how long does the reader assume that it is going to take for other people to realize the very same thing?"

A USA DIALTONE IN BRAZIL

Computer Telephony. I said it wrong when I first read the word. The word is pronounced: [tell-ef-a-nee.] Computer lovers seem to like Byzantine language and acronyms. It is my belief that the stilted language is used to separate those of the high priesthood from us mortals of the congregation. However, humbled though we may be, we still wouldn't mind having a better understanding of what's going on in the world of technology. Yet, if we are only being presented a bunch of incomprehensible terms and symbols we often get stopped in our tracks before we ever get started. Technology is moving at an awesome pace and if some of us didn't get on the train when it was running slowly we sometimes feel hopelessly incapable of getting on it now that it is running so fast. What ultimately happens to us, is that even though there is a bunch of really good technology out there, we can't seem to be able to tell one piece of equipment from another or know what a new service really represents. If we go into a store to buy a computer, some pimply-faced young kid starts talking gibberish to us about DSP's, ISDN, Kbps, and how much RAM we think we need.

I'm not going to spend ten seconds trying to dazzle anyone with my acronyms and technological wisdom. My technological understanding of personal computers is impoverished. But I am now learning how to use one because the technology has finally reached the point, in my opinion, where it is getting pretty exciting. I will attempt in the section on personal liberties, to discuss my philosophical view of the computer and how I believe that it can increase our freedom from government controls; but I want to stress that I am not developing a libidinal attachment to the computer. It is a tool, one of many. Lets see if we can understand how it, and some of the other new technology can help us. Additionally, lets see if we can understand these new opportunities without becoming lost. I want the information in this section to be as clear and comprehensible as possible. I believe that the information in this section is crucial information for us if we want to make the best possible success out of our life as an expat.

CALLBACK

Callback is a relative new service being provided by a growing number of companies from different locations around the world. Before we describe what it is, lets take a look at what it provides. The following list describes just some of the services we can expect when we begin to use callback and the other related technologies:

✓ The ability to save between 50% to 80% on average for our international telephone calls and occasionally even more than that.

✓ The capacity to greatly increase our privacy by keeping our phone records and other aspects of our business totally private, as it should be.

✓ Worldwide access to a USA dial tone from whatever telephone we are using regardless of where in the world we are calling from or to.

✓ The ability to call USA toll-free 800 numbers from anywhere in the world, just as if we were still in America.

·✓ Automatic billing of all our telephone services to our offshore VISA or MasterCard with no USA billing record of our telephone business affairs open to scrutiny by anyone who's business should have nothing to do with our business.

✓ The ability to have for ourselves or our business a USA Area Coded phone line, including our own toll free 800 line that rings wherever we are in the world.

✓ Access to a new type of worldwide telephone card that accesses callback lines worldwide.

✓ The capacity to make telephone calls from foreign hotels (or American hotels for that matter) bypassing their high rate of billing, and bypassing their call blocking if need be.

As these words are being written, most of this service seems exotic and is fairly unknown. Within a year or so these services will become more and more a part of common global knowledge. More and more callback companies will enter the market. Services will improve, prices will drop, the global market will grow.

HOW DOES CALLBACK WORK?

State-subsidized telephone monopolies have had an incentive to suppress the knowledge of callback service. No, there is no conspiracy; although keeping the information regarding callback from becoming common knowledge probably is in the best business interest of state-subsidized telephone monopolies. In most countries, phone rates are structured so that long-distance international rates subsidize (or pay for) the rates of the local callers. That is just the way it has been, and it is good business on the part of the local carriers to maintain such a lopsided practice, even though it is a disadvantage to the international caller; which means us, the expats.

State-subsidized monopolies worldwide typically charge an artificially low rate for a local telephone hookup. The monopolies usually also charge the local telephone user a flat monthly rate, regardless of how long the local user talks in the local area. The person who installs a business line is sometimes charged a premium for installation. The international caller is always charged a premium by the local monopoly for long distance over the local caller. Many, if not most telephone companies charge approximately $15 per month for a telephone line in the home. This home line includes an unlimited number of local calls. Let us take a closer look at what this means:

In a thirty-one day month there are 44,640 minutes. (60 minutes times 24 hours, times 31 days) The local user receives that many minutes for $15 total. In Rio de Janerio, Brazil, a telephone call to Paris using the local monopoly would cost approximately $4 per minute. That works out to $178,560 per month. The $15 that buys 44,640 minutes of local time would buy less than four minutes of international telephone time. This practice makes it possible for the local monopolies to lose money on local calls, keep a happy constituency and allows them to keep the local inflation index low. Most monopolies are government owned.

Long distance calls do not cost much more for a telephone company then local calls. In some cases the local calls cost more. Yet, if the monopolies charged higher rates for local users the local users would complain long and loud. The business caller, the users of long distance, are less in number, therefore less vocal. How profitable is this practice for the monopolies?

Nippon Telephone & Telegraph, the Japanese telephone company, had a net profit of 103 billion yen between April and September of 1993. That is approximately US$1 billion in six months. More profit than any other company in Japan, $300 million more then the next contender. That figure represents NTT's *smallest* profit since it was privatized in 1986. A ten minute call from Japan to the United States using NTT would cost us $11.40, the very same telephone call using callback, the system we will be discussing in this section would only cost $4.80, a 50% savings. A ten minute telephone call from Rio to Paris using **Embratel**, the local Brazilian telephone system, would cost approximately $40.00, using callback the same ten minute call would cost approximately $10.00 a savings of 75%. The local monopoly in Brazil is running at a tidy profit and the service is not too great. There is every incentive for the astute expat to use callback.

WHAT IT IS

Let's take a look at what callback is and how callback functions. In order to gain a good understanding of what callback is and how it functions we need to take a brief look at some recent telephone history. Since the breakup of the **AT&T** monopoly in 1984 American telephone price rates have steadily declined until they are now the lowest rates in the world. (coupled with the most advanced service) **Sprint** and **MCI** forced **AT&T** to become competitive both in price and service. At about the same time, advances in fiber optics and microelectronics began reducing the price of information technology while simultaneously dramatically increasing the telephone users service options. The competitive war between the major service providers was fought by utilizing the ever increasing new technology, with each of the providers offering new and better service options to attract the customers of its competition. This happy battle resulted in a dramatic increase in the options available to the end user; which includes people like us.

Some of these new services include many things which we now take for granted such as caller ID, call waiting, call forwarding, call block, speed dialing, duplex ringing, repeat dialing and so on. Since 1984, rates have declined by almost 50%, making America one of, if not the most cost effective locations in the world in which to make a telephone call. If we are to become expats, we want to do so without having to give up any of the many benefits derived from technology and deregulation, regardless of where in the world those two attributes coexist. Callback is the means by which we can utilize the positive technological and deregulatory strides existing in one country without being physically stuck there, nor having to become subject to a state monopolized telephone system of another. (The issues regarding the morality or patriotic [ir]responsibility such actions might entail is an issue we will return to in just a moment.) Many countries have state-owned telephone monopolies and these monopolies are very high yielding cash cows that the state would have little or no incentive to open up to competition. For example, a ten minute telephone call from Rio de Janerio to Tokyo using the Brazilian state owned telephone system, **Embratel** costs $70.08. It would be difficult, if not impossible, for us, or anyone else, to run a business at those rates. Australia is only slightly better, but not by much. A ten minute telephone call from Sydney to New York would cost us $10.58; again thanks to prices set by a cash-cow monopoly. Amsterdam to Anchorage costs $31.61 for ten minutes of talk time. Singapore to Paris, $28.45, and so on. Needless to say these prices could be crippling to the expat trying to make a living by telecommunicating to the United States (or to anywhere else) on a daily basis. One 24 hour day on the telephone in Rio de Janerio would cost us over $10,000. ($70.08 for a ten minute call times six gives us a grand total of $420.48 per hour of talk time. If we multiply that figure for a 24 hour basis, it gives us a mere $10,091.52 per day paid to our friends at **Embratel**. Not too bad a yield, eh?) In one week we've purchased a new Mercedez Bentz for the local monopoly.

ENTER CALLBACK

Callback works rather simply, (if we ignore the technology involved in the process.) To use callback, we pick up our telephone in Rio de Janerio, dial a telephone number in the United States, we let the number at the location we are calling ring once, and then we hang up. What we have done is: we have placed a call to a computer located at a callback company in the United States. However, because we did not complete a telephone call to anyone we are not billed for the telephone call we made. So far, so simple, no? Next, the callback computer calls us back. (It is smart enough to recognize the number-signature of the telephone in Rio from which we called it and to call us back at that number automatically. It calls us back. Callback. Get it?) We pick up our telephone in Rio and the computer says, "Your call is connected." We now have an American USA dial tone. We can now call anyone, anywhere using this dial tone. Additionally, our dial tone is set up in a callback company that can and often does offer us lower rates than we would get even if we were still in the United States. This is due to the technology used by the callback company. Our ten minute call from Rio de Janerio to Tokyo now cost us $11.50 rather than $70.08, a 83.6% savings. If we were expats living in Amersdam, out ten minute call to Anchorage would cost us $5.50 rather than $31.61, a 82.6% savings. Sydney to New York: $3.94 rather than $10.58 (62.8% savings,) Singapore to Paris, $8.90 rather than $28.45 (68.7% savings.) It is, for all intents and purposes possible to use callback from every country in the world and it is also possible to sell this service to others inside some countries, either as a sales rep, a service provider, or in numerous other capacities. If we know anything about computers we can utilize our knowledge to provide this type of service in different capacities either as a rep for established American callback companies, or, given enough expertise, allow us to start our own callback company. [see resources] If we are not yet a computer wiz there are courses and videos that can ultimately make most of us a wiz if we so choose. However, the issue here is callback. We will discuss job opportunities in another section, or in one of the documents available through our fax-on-demand service.

Most callback companies require a minimum of approximately $25 per month. This is handled by way of a $25 monthly minimum billing for the service regardless of the amount of calls made. However, we are not billed for the first $25 worth of calls we make if we make more than the $25 minimum. If we have more than one telephone line there is usually a monthly minimum of $25 per line, however if we use one line for fax and the other for voice and we have exceeded the minimum of $50 on just one of those two lines then some companies will not bill additionally on the other line. There are now over a hundred callback companies and the services and prices are already beginning to become competitive. Additionally, some companies bill in six second increments, which is crucial for fax users, while other companies bill in larger second/interval increments, but have lower prices per minute. We will attempt to constantly analyze and evaluate the services provided by these companies and look for new companies offering newer and better services if and when they come available. It is our express intention that the reader will be able to readily and continuously contact us and to access our ongoing research from anywhere in the world through one of the access services we intend to make available. As new technology and opportunities come available we intend to have our finger on the pulse of it. Check the appendix to see what is available and to determine which of our access information pipelines works best for you.

Another service provided by callback is the 'follow me' 800 line and the USA toll free 800 line that rings outside of the United States. These services allow our customers to call us toll free no matter where we are; there is a slight difference between the two. The 'follow me' service is a rapidly programmable 800 number, that can follow us, much like call forwarding, and the callback USA 800 line while slightly less flexible, in that it takes a day or so to change the destination-program (which is done at the callback companies facility) is much less expensive in that it bills us the low cost callback rates for our toll free customer calls from the United States to our fixed location anywhere globally. The USA 800 line allows toll free calls to our customers from the United States to say, Brazil for example, at a cost to us of about $0.72 per minute, and our callback rate from Brazil back to the United States, using a callback service would be about $0.75 per minute. Fairly cost effective and competitive rates, especially when one considers that it cost about half as much to live in Brazil as it does in the United States. Not to mention the beaches, the samba, the good food, and so forth. Additionally, even though these rates are more then cost effective, we fully suspect that the rates for callback, and other high-tech telecommunication services will be dropping even further then they are now, and that this will occur not in a distant decade, but in the not too distant future.

Additionally, all the calls we have made 'outbound' using our callback service to call out globally, and all the calls whose payment obligation we assume from our 'inbound' service due to our 800 line client calls, are each and all written out fully on our billing with the length of the call and the numbers of both the caller and the called, including the country. What is more, the billing is consolidated, issued in one currency, and debited by our callback carrier directly from our VISA, MasterCard, or American Express Card. If we have an offshore ATM credit card drawn on an offshore bank as laid out in the section on offshore banks, we have taken a giant step to further insure our privacy, as is our right. To repeat: all our billing is private, consolidated, detailed, and precise; plus it is billed in one currency.

There is also a callback calling card. To use one of these cards in a foreign country, all we have to do is dial the local access number of the country we are in, use the card number to activate the service and place our call. Most countries already have local access numbers 'in place' within the host country which automatically accesses a USA dial tone without us having to dial the US ourself. No waiting, no prearranged automated callbacks as we might need with 'follow me' service; no reprogramming our callback location while we are traveling. These cards also bypass hotel blocking because the local telephone numbers that access the USA dial tone are routed as a local call out of the hotel PBX switchboard which doesn't recognize the call as anything other than a local call. Whereas, an overseas call to a computer is blocked by the PBX switchboard, which is programmed to recognize such a call, and a return call from a computer unless programmed to ask for us by name and room number is merely recieved by the switchboard and discarded. However, there is another trick for bypassing hotel PBX blocking repertoire. We can at our choosing, program a callback computer to call us at a hotel and ask for us by name and room number. This can be done as easily as programing the call-forwarding mode into our current domestic service. Most contact with the computer is done by punching in a couple of prompts using our touchtone phone.* While there is nothing especially complex about it, there is a certain James Bondish aspect of excitement and intrigue about constantly staying a step ahead of the monopolizers. Callback companies are inspired to keep their service-computers smarter then any telephone company computer that might be geared to spoil our fun.

TELEPHONY

There's that word again. [tell-ef-a-nee]. Telephony is the marriage of the telephone and the computer. The marriage was inevitable; anyone who has heard one fax machine electronically mate with another, could easily have suspected telepony was upon us. While love surprises us, this marriage may engender liberty.

As we write these lines, the hookup fees for a computer unto a telephone line, or Server, as they are called, cost approximately $20 per month for a standard line, and approximately $35 per month for an ISDN line. An ISDN line is a rather sophisticated telephone line that allows information to travel at greater rates of speed. While this is an admitted simplification, before we proceed, let's try to make some sense of the technology anyway. Simplified or not, its helpful to have a basic comprehension of what telephony represents in terms of the evolution of telecommunications technology. When we talk on a telephone, our voice vibrations move a diaphragm inside the telephone, which in turn moves a magnet inside the telephone. This magnet then generates electrical impulses which travel over a standard telephone line to another telephone whose magnet responds sympathetically to the electrical impulses, then transforms them back, via another diaphragm, into vibrations similar to those stimulated by our voice. These vibrations, of course, are then heard by our listener, as a rough, but discernible, audible approximation of our voice. This transmission is called an analog transmission, in that it travels in waves, much like the human voice.

In computers the process works slightly differently. Information in a computer is stored digitally, which means that it is stored in bits. Computers understand digital language. In order for one computer to talk to another over a telephone line, the information has to go from digital (bit) information to analog (wave) information

---

* There is a device called a 'tone dialer' which *imitates* those touch tone sounds which telephones use to 'talk' to other computers. It is available at Radio Shack. All expats will want one of these devices. Most, if not all foreign telephones do not use touch tone. Even if a foreign telephone appears to be touch tone, many times it is merely a rotary phone with a touch keypad. In order to 'access' and talk with most sophisticated computers a touch tone phone, or touch tone dialer device is required. As DSP voice recognition technology evolves touch tone telecommunication *may* become less crucial. But because of the very low cost for one of these 'parroting' devices, it's worth the insurance to have one even if we don't currently plan to use telephony. The tone dialer from Radio Shack code: 43-145 is priced at $16.99 as of this writing. A tone dialer with a 'memory' /code: 43-146 is $24.99

and move over an analog telephone line. When information from one computer reaches another computer, it must be transferred back into digital form in order for the receiving computer to make use of it. The computer chip which translates this information has made quantum leaps over the last year or so and this has opened up a whole new area of telecommunication technology, which as the chary reader may by now surmise, has been given the name: telephony, ...perhaps for lack of a better name.

ISDN is an acronym for Integrated Services Digital Network. ISDN is a type of line (and system,) that is now available which allows digital information to travel at a much greater rate of speed than a standard analog telephone line (or system.) These lines are not yet universally available. They are available in larger cities and in more heavily populated states within the United States. Their existence remains sketchy in most foreign countries. (By the time they are universally available they will be partially obsolete due to the fast-paced advance of satellite technology which will render them unnecessary to those who use satellite interconnections rather than cumbersome telephone lines.) Using an ISDN line we can now communicate anywhere in the world with an ISDN telephone hooked up to our personal computer.* If our monthly bill for our server hookup is currently $20, this means that we can now telephone anywhere in the world as often as we want and talk for as long as we want, for $20 a month. Period. Add to that video and we can now telephone anywhere in the world as often as we want, and talk for as long as we want, and see who we are talking to at the same time, all for $20 a month. This technology is now available. It can be purchased by anyone and used by anyone and the technology is improving on an almost daily basis.

How good is it? Its sketchy. The available ISDN telephones are relatively inexpensive, (under $100 as we write these lines,) but the technology is uneven. In order to talk to another person, they must have the same type of telephone we are using, and even then the sound quality is none too great. They require a more advanced personal computer to operate, (in the $2000 range as we write these lines,) and they require some expertise to operate. By the time your read these lines much of what is here written will have changed. The situation is improving rapidly. We predict, that

---

* As it is, much of what we were talking about regarding WebTelephones came into technological existence before we finished writing this book. There are now several Internet WebTelephones available. **Microsoft** included a telephone on its new Internet Explorer 3.0 Web Browser which can be shareware downloaded for free. There are already numerous software telephones that allow anything from voice to video. They do remain 'sketchy' as of this writing, but they are improving. Some of the ones we've tried are much like talking on CB radio. Few of them are full duplex. (i.e. only one voice at a time transmits and it 'blocks' incoming voice.) **ISDN** is still the *modus preferential*, in that it allows better voice, duplex capacity, and video. The almost incredible speed of technological development and consumer acceptance of this medium would be astounding if we didn't know a bit about human psychology. Humans love to communicate. Even if we have nothing to say, it seems that we still want to say it. We personally have had to disconnect our Web Phone from online access in order to continue writing. We receive as many as five calls per hour from around the world from people who we have never met but who just want to 'chat.' Psychologists and sociologists should be giving this phenomena some attention. It has no societal precedence we know of.

if you were to start planning to move to New Zealand as you read these lines, go to New Zealand, find property, buy it, move all of your belongings there and set up housekeeping, that by the time you were fully unpacked, gotten your dog out of quarantine and your children adjusted to a their new home, most of the technology for using computer telephones would be in place worldwide for global communications along with full video ability, and then some. We might include anything imaginable on to our screen while we are talking; blueprints, statistics, photos, films, live video of a third [or fourth] location, etcetera, etcetera, with each different image or data notation appearing within a separate window on the screen, or semi-imposed, all to hearts desire. The available technology will soon allow us, for all intents and purposes, to run a business from the center of the Australian outback or from an island in the middle of the Pacific Ocean; if that is our desire, and to call up any piece of information we might require at a moments notice.*

For example, in one obvious scenario, if we are talking to a client in Iowa; all the pertinent information about the client will appear on the screen next to a live conference video of our client so that we can be reviewing what we are talking about while we are doing the talking. We will be able to call up other information either by voice cues, mouse manipulation, or by keyboard commands. At this point, as with the ISDN telephone, the video available is still rather sketchy. The picture moves at a rate of four to 12 frames per second, resulting in herky-jerky movement, as we've heard it described. (Regular video, as seen on television, moves at a rate of 30 frames a second.) New specialized computer-chips called Digital Signal Processors, or DSP's, if you will forgive the acronym, are the chips we've mentioned that are making the telephony revolution possible. They accomplish this by being able to recognize audible sounds, signal transmissions and visual images. We have heard of these chips described as, being rather complex. For those of us who might view any computer-chip as being rather complex, this description is an understatement.

The DSP chip acts to transform sounds, signals, and images, into digital information that our computers can understand and process. They also play a role in transforming this information back into analog information which can then be communicated to us verbally, or transmitted in a number of different ways over an analog line. We might view DSP chips as translators between the computer world and the human world. Indeed, they can translate one human language into another, so that we can communicate, via computer, with someone who does not speak English, if English is our only language. They cannot translate literature, of course, because while they can recognize words and definitions, they do not grasp the human concept of meaning.

* This technological phenomena explains why now is the time to move abroad. That is to say, it clarifies why in a very short period of time it will not make any real difference where we live if we engage in certain types of global commerce. If we can now purchase a splendid ranch in Belize or a spectacular condo in Bangkok for one tenth the price of something similar in the United States, how long does the reader assume that it is going to take for other people to realize the same thing?

The greater our personal need for a computer to make our way as expats, the greater our need for an ISDN line could become. ...at least until satellite technology bypasses the telephone line and allows computers to transfer digital information directly to other computers by use of satellite dish antenna sitting on the deck of our sail boat.

The term telephony is also meant to include the use of the computer to transfer fax [facsimile] material from computer to computer, or from computer to fax machine and vice versa. This transfer, if it is between computers, and traveling over ISDN lines can move at fairly high speeds vis a vis traditional transmission speeds. This capacity allows the transfer of greater volumes of information at greater speeds at significantly reduced costs. Consider a twenty page document being sent by regular surface mail to Mozambique. As they say in the colloquial; good luck! The cost, a mere $7.00 to $10.00, plus envelope, plus paper, plus the time involved going to the post office, plus the pleasure of dealing with the US Post Office employees, plus the drive back in heavy traffic, plus the three to five week wait to see if we were lucky enough to have our package arrive in Mozambique, survive customs, and arrive at the desk of our recipient. The fax; from fax machine to fax machine, takes perhaps three minutes, costs maybe $3.00 to $5.00 in telephone billing, and is on the recipients desk as soon as the call is completed. Using telephony, the fax from computer to computer, reduces the transmission time even further, if such things are important, and if one is on the internet using e-mail, reduces the transmission cost to zero. (...which is not exactly true. Figure the costs thus: the cost of the electricity used to run our computer for three minutes, which is say .02¢ for lack of a more precise figure. The cost of three minutes of internet access, @$20.00 per month divided by 44,640 minutes is .00004¢ per minute times 3 minutes equals, .001¢ plus the cost of the paper to down load the information in Mozambique, which we can put at perhaps .03¢, plus our recipients electricity and internet costs of .021¢, gives us a grand total of .072¢, not even a dime for the total transfer of data. And because we exaggerated some figures, the cost is probably even less.) No drive to the post office, no hassles, just sitting in the deck chair on our boat drinking a cup of coffee and using some of that good old telephony. [tell-ef-a-nee]

There are no requirements to becoming an expat. We don't have to stay in touch with the United States, we don't even have to own a telephone. We can find some idyllic retreat and let the world go about its chaotic business without us; it isn't our responsibility to reach out with the latest advanced telecommunication equipment and add to the global turmoil. Our life is our own, and there is much to be said for solitude, privacy, and inner peace. This section has talked about what is available, but it isn't a formula; it is just one of the many choices available in todays world. We make our choices based on our inner motivations; but it helps to know the options, for without any choices we would not be able to have any values. One set of options does not a reality make. Indeed, a single option is a contradiction in terms.

If we make it our choice to set up a home office abroad, in many cases it is best to bring our equipment with us. This is especially true if we are going to a so-called third world country where high-tech might mean something far different to what we are used to. With our own high-tech equipment in hand we stand a very good chance of making a very good living wherever we choose to go in the third world. Most countries will allow the duty-free import of our household effects and whatever equipment deemed necessary to run our business. This is especially true when we make it plain that our aim is to provide jobs for the people in our new country. Sometimes there is a import fee for some commodity or another, such as automobiles, sailboats or obvious luxury items, sometimes not, and the situation changes from country to country; (and occasionally from port to port within a country,) although the best destinations are consistent in their port authority, just as they are in their exchange controls. This is not to say that we can't make a great living in a country with poor or corrupt port authorities, and perhaps even with exchange controls in place. My gut feeling tells me that if a country will rob us at the door, they will probably rob us in the living room and the dining room too. However, such countries are quite suitable to the seasoned expat who is looking for adventure and high yields. Relative risk is a function of price, absolute risk is a primary question. If we choose such countries, it is best that we are single, can move fast, and know at least three of the local dances. If not, life insurance through a Swiss Bank could be a definite asset.

MORALITY, PATRIOTIC [ir]RESPONSIBILITY
& THE GLOBAL EVOLUTION OF LIBERTY

From this point onwards in time, the nations of the world are going to have to bid on the talents of the best and smartest human beings in order to attract them. Nations, and their governments, can adopt one of two policies. They can move towards statism, endlessly increasing the degree of government intervention in our lives. Or, they can move towards greater degrees of individual liberty, decreasing government controls and deregulating the free flow of information, energy, and human action. Let's take a brief look at what each of these choices entails for the nations who pursue one or the other direction.

Already 250,000 people per year are leaving the United States. These are not poor and helpless immigrants; these are the best and the brightest. The United States has three basic choices in this matter:

1) It can improve its posture.

Over the last two decades America has been going straight downhill entirely as a result of steadily increasing governmental control and intervention into the economy and human action. During that period of time the standard of living has not improved one iota. Average real wages in the United States have not gone up during this period because so much of our money that is being taken away from us by the government goes into nonproductive uses. This policy has also acted to create the burgeoning debt. Why? How? Because most of the government programs are economically foolhardy and ill-planned. No business could run like that. If a business cannot, a government cannot. Let's make this clear: the government's plans cannot work because they are ill-conceived plans. The plans and policies are unworkable. Or, to explain the U.S. Government's current policy in highly complex terms: a.] It does not work. b.] It cannot work. c.] It will never work. Those are the A, B, C's. And this fact must be faced or repressed. Continued pursuit of them, as if it were possible to trick reality, has led to an unimpeded two decade decline in the American dollar as a viable currency. The dollar has been ruined by the people who run the United States government. There is no future in the United States for any worthwhile young person with a brain. Only a fool would believe otherwise. The best and the brightest Americans are going to leave. Period. If you who are reading these words are a politician you must face this fact. You can rule over a welfare state filled with incompetents, or you can correct the situation by reducing the size of government and eliminating the endless tangle of regulations you have used to destroy American Free Enterprise. You can do this only if you can kick your habit and can get off of the backs of the American people and if you can give us back our freedom, (and if you can quit taxing us to death in the process.) It's tough to admit you're a junky. You may believe that you don't have to. You may believe that you can ride us to death like we are well-trained fools. But you'll only end up with the fools. Those young people who are competent will leave. They'll go to where they find more liberty and then you can try to run your greater-fools game without them and without their brains.

2) The second alternative is for you, employees of the US Government to imprison the competent.

You can put a gun to their collective head. Stop emigration. Place exchange controls on their bank accounts. ...and declare martial law. This is the most expedient and it goes along with your traditional policy of burying your head in the sand and blaming the citizens for your rotten habits. (Admittedly, there is no better way to have law, order and discipline than by declaring martial law.) You can include censorship, armed repression, (especially of anyone who suspects you of having sold-out America,) you can include curfews for the physically abled and lobotomies for everyone with an IQ above sixty-five.

3) Or, the United States Government can continue its decline to zero.

It can ignore the lessons of statism around the world and become a has-been nation like so many nations before it. This is not without precedent. Few borders in history have stood more than a hundred years. There isn't any reason in the entire universe why America is immune to what has befallen every nation since the dawn of human history. Is there? It's different this time because its us? It's never different this time. Never.

What has changed that allows all this exodus? Thirty years ago this would have been unthinkable, even given the massive degree of governmental vandalism perpetuated upon the American people. The American of a few decades ago, might have stood still and taken it on the chin before going to greener pasture. Why won't today's intelligent Americans simply sit back and allow a runaway government to exert greater and greater degrees of control over every aspect of the knowable universe? Using us as cannon fodder for a Viet Nam wouldn't work today, why is that?

Many reasons. The end of the cold war has given us a different focus of the world. ✓ The advances in personal computers and in telecommunications that we've just discussed as tools of commerce also prevent any government from lying to us; and governments are famous for lying to human beings. ✓ The absolute failure and collapse of communism has been perceived as a wake-up call by a good many nations as to the inherent dangers of statism and to the economic perils of heavy-handed government control. ✓ Global trade is booming and becoming the global modus operandi of advanced nations, with a concomitant acknowledgment by most governments of its deregulatory requirements and of the need for a fair and open market accessible to the largest number of free people operating with the greatest degree of latitude. ✓ The recognition by many nations that while they have a multitude of natural resources, because of decades of mental suffocation under statism, that the knowledgeable, capable people who can make things happen are sorely lacking. ✓ The creation of the World Wide Web allows human beings to communicate with human beings globally for the first time in human history, totally without the intervention (and interpretation) of government employees. (i.e. no border checks, no radio jamming, no censored telephone lines, no controlling government monopoly of the technology or its evolution, no propaganda credibility, no nationality.)

THE INTERNET & THE END OF THE NATION-STATE

If any government, regardless of its size and power, attempts to stop the free exchange of information and ideas which is now taking place on the web, here is what they will need to confront: They will need to try to stop the WebTelephone, email, facsimile and video, because each can and will bypass all the state-subsidized telephone monopolies of the world, (thus allowing free communication between human beings globally.) They will need to prevent any and all advances in telecommunication globally. (Perhaps by killing people with IQ's greater than the IQ's of government employees. I suspect an IQ of 45 and above would suffice.) They must be willing to shoot down the communications satellite of any nation that attempts to give access to human beings using the Web. They must find some method of jamming the Web to prevent the free flow of information between one free human being and another. They must be capable of preventing any technology which bypasses their jamming techniques. They must have better brains than the people who want to be free of them and their repression. They must be able to keep this war going indefinitely, because technology will wage a war of attrition against them; and the moment they hesitate for an instant, thinking human beings globally, who break free of their chains will be in immediate communication with other human beings. (unraveling chains quicker then governments can bind them.)

Have we answered the question of morality and partriotic [ir]responsibilty? Yes, we have. We are humans. Our obligation is to liberty and human evolution. We deserve to be free of repression and idiocy. Nations around the world are already vying for the best and the brightest. We have more than merely an incentive to gain greater liberty for ourselves and our families, we also have an obligation to force the nations of the world to bid for our service just as if they were companies bidding for the best employees. In no other way that I can think of can we force the governments of the world to recognize that certain codes of morality and ethics attract the best and the brightest. And that repression, oppressive regulations, and runaway taxation is not an attractive way to run a company. (or attract good people.) A company (or government) that pursues an irresponsible fiscal course will go broke. Why? Because reality dictates all outcomes and not a government or a companies good wishes, or it's emergency legislation. Such companies (or governments) that are foolish do not deserve our blood to keep them going with their chain-letter economic schemes. To view governments as companies, makes obvious that any entity which placates massive blocks of constituency [call them stockholders] through subterfuge, malfunctioning giveaway programs, or theft, just to convey a false impression in the hope of gaining stockholder [or constituent] votes and investors, (or loyal field-mice) is a company that is going to end up with damn few viable long term investors or employees [citizens] willing to put up with being continually robbed and hoodwinked.

We are free at last.

WRITE IF YOU GET WORK

Do the employees of the United States government want to try to enslave us by preventing emigration and using us for slave labor?

Probably not in those terms. But, they may try just about anything if they are sufficiently panicked. Including shutting the exit doors.

Is there a better way?

To straighten out the mess they have created, the employees of the US Government have only so many options if they hope to attract back their customers [intelligent & productive citizens.]

First, they must face the fact that reality cannot be tricked. A government has to obey the rules of reality just like everything else in the universe. Simply calling something The United States of America does not remove what you have named from the laws of the universe. Could a company be run with the policies that are used by the employees of the US Government?

Let's find out.

A company on the road to ruin usually has four basic options:

1) It can change it's policies by eliminating all nonproductive programs from the companies business,

2) It can be more disciplined in it's cash outlays so as not to exceed incoming revenues,

3) It can borrow to cover it's deficits, or,

4) It can print more stock to increase it's existing revenue base. [in the governments case, this means printing more money.]

Once a company has exhausted these options without improvement, then numbers one and two must be repeated with increased efficacy.

In the event a company is still on the road to bankruptcy, then it is left only with number one.

Somewhere, somehow, a company [or a nation] on the road to ruin is simply not producing anything that real customers want. ...and if real customers [citizens, human beings, families, workers,] don't want it, then why the hell is it being produced?

WEB PAGE JURISDICTION

URL: http://online.offshore.com.ai/services.html

In subsequent issues of this book we hope to be able to address the issue of virtual jurisdiction. At this point in time the concept is much too complex for us to include in this edition. But we certainly do find it an interesting issue. Take a look at the above WebSite.

LATIN AMERICA
& THE CARIBBEAN

"History is not evidence against the future."

Ha llegado el tiempo del amanecer, de que se termine la obra y que aparezcan los que nos han de sustentar y nutrir, los hijos esclarecidos, los vasallos civilizados, que aparezca el hombre, la humanidad, sobre la superficie de la tierra."*

"a carioca? ...a carioca is someone who came to Rio and stayed."
-Ze

If we include the Caribbean Basin when we talk about Latin America we are truly abstracting an area that covers a lot of ground and of water. It has always seemed to us the freshest, youngest, and most exciting area of the world. The reader will notice that we have dedicated a disproportionate amount of book space to the section on Latin America; it being by far the biggest section of the book. This uneven dedication to one section is not merely personal preference, although personal preference did have much to do with it. We believe that expat opportunity is greater in Latin America than it is in any other section of the world. Other places may be easier to move to, deal with, and set up a new life in; but we cannot think of any place where the opportunities are so tremendous for expatriate living. If we just singled out the country of Argentina and made comparisons to other world areas we believe that a pertinent and explanatory point can prove our assertion. Argentina has a total area of 1,073,115 square miles. This is an area greater than Italy, Switzerland, France, Germany, Spain, Portugal, Belgium, and the Netherlands combined. Argentina has a population of 32,646,000 while Italy alone has a population of almost double that figure. If we overlaid Argentina and Western Europe and compared agriculture potential, and existing mineral resources, Argentina would come away the winner. Because Argentina is singular and young it cannot compare with Western Europes cultural history and diversity, though it is certainly not devoid of culture. In terms of environmental diversity, Argentina is again a strong and unpolluted contender; having an alps area that compares with the Swiss Alps, a Pampas that is incomparable, an Arctic region, a desert region, and a 3,000 mile coast line. Argentina seems like a good bet to us.

Additionally, if we include Chile, Uruguay, and Brazil into our equation and place them along side Argentina when we make a comparison with other areas of the world, then the betting stops. There is enough in these four countries for anyone. There is simply no other area of the world which we can overlay unto this region and even come close in terms of future potential.

* "The time has come for dawn, for work to be completed, for those who nourish and sustain us to appear, the enlightened sons, the civilized people; the time has come for the appearance of humanity on the surface of the Earth." - POP WU

People talk of China as being a major player in the coming millennium. They can't even feed themselves. How anyone can even discuss China as anything other than a slave state is beyond us. The potential of China is thought to lie in manufacturing. If we believed that the future of the human being was to be an ant in an ant farm manufacturing pieces of phantom to sell to other ants then perhaps China is the world's future mover & shaker. Our guess is that China has had its last hurrah and they are going to subsist, or perish, but nothing better. We have heard that they are clever people. Do clever people breed themselves into a corner, kill their children for seeking political freedom and suppress innovative thinking? China is a place to escape from. Latin America is an area to escape to. History, including that of China's illustrious past is not evidence for or against the future.

Many readers might point out that there are numerous people from Latin America who seek to escape to America. As we've mentioned elsewhere, the world has changed. There are currently two migratory trends in action: immigration, and emigration. Those who immigrate to America from Latin America are seeking jobs which most of us wouldn't want. Those who emigrate to Latin America from the U.S., are seeking jobs (and life-styles) that many Latin Americans cannot attain or accomplish due to a lack of education, capital, or understanding. (Although that is changing.) The potential in Latin America for a bright young American couple is many times greater than the potential in the USA for the same couple. Additionally, the environment in much of Latin America is better; more pristine, less crowded and many times more affordable. Latin America is upward bound. America has had it and is on its way to joining China as one of the world's most heavily armed slave states.

We'd like to express to the reader that despite what we are saying, we don't consider ourselves doom-sayers or anti-American and we aren't predicting the end of the world. We are not talking about bible predictions, nor Nostrodomus, nor signs in the zodiac. Our intention is merely to point out the irrefutable historical fact that nations rise and nations fall. **All nations.** At this very moment, the bells are tolling loudly; but the clues as to whom they toll for are not in the zodiac, they reside in an understanding of the unstoppable change to globalism and in the unnegotiable human need for personal liberty. When these two factors are fully faced and are then used as the equation to understand todays world, they can act as navigational tools which allow us to design a chart for glimpsing the world of tomorrow.

For those of us who are looking towards expatriation and who have some sort of understanding of the wide range of possibilities that are everywhere opening up in todays world, the countries of Latin America and the Caribbean truly offer something for every pursuit.

● **Puerto Rico**, the **U.S. Virgin Islands**, the **Eastern Caribbean** Island states and **Mexico's** maquiladora free trade zones offer excellent places for those without huge amounts of capital or international experience to get started in the global market.

● Those of us looking for enhanced access to the European market place, might consider doing business in the **Dominican Republic, Costa Rica, Jamaica** and **Panama**; as these areas have preferential trade agreements with Europe. In addition these areas have excellent skilled workers and wage levels that allow expatriates to set up small companies that are much more competitive than their U.S. counterparts could ever be.

● The offshore financial services and tax-haven benefits of the **Cayman Islands**, the **Bahamas**, as well as other Caribbean Islands and the nation of Panama are world renown. These service centers have recently been made available in other Latin American and Caribbean nations, including **Belize** and **Uruguay**.

● The country of **Argentina**, which we mentioned above, is poised to become one of the great nations of the world by any standard in the opening part of the coming millennium.

● **Chile** is not waiting for the coming millennium and is already advancing faster than the U.S. in many areas.

● **Belize** has become an expat destination offering excellent potential and a pristine environment.

● Several Central American countries offer excellent real estate potential, as does **Venezuela**.

● **Columbia** and **Equador** are sleepers with tremendous opportunity for the experienced expat.

● There's **Paraguay**, with excellent real estate prices, **Peru** and **Bolivia** with difficult logistics and potential risks but with excellent potential rewards.

● There's **Dominica** the tiny pristine island in the Lesser Antilles that may be the Caribbean's best investment, there's **Mexico**, there's **Costa Rica**, and there's no end of other countries, islands and pristine hideaways in this vast and mostly unspoiled region of the world. In addition to all that, there is also **Brazil**; one of the most exciting countries on the face of the earth and one that could constitute an entire book in itself.

Having said all this, we obviously cannot claim that this section is all inclusive. We began to realize soon after we started writing this book the enormity of our task. The entire world does not fit in a book. Latin America does not fit in a book. One small island in the Caribbean does not fit in a book. The single city of Rio de Janerio does not fit in a book. If we continued to write all of what we wanted to write, we would have never finished this book.

What to do? We chose to do what we could as good as we could. If we could not include it all, then we would choose to concentrate on and include what we believed was most crucial. But what to do with the leftover facts? What to do with the facts that changed after the book went to press, or those facts that seemed to be changing even as we wrote? The Fax-On-Demand seemed the only system that offered a solution to these questions. But knowing that this was a possible objective did not mean that we allowed ourselves to skimp on what we are here presenting. The reader may view this book and this section as an introduction to the subject. But it is certainly as full an introduction as we are capable of making in one volume.

In addition to those countries we have concentrated on there are numerous other countries we would eventually like to more fully analyze. There are some real opportunities out there. **Guatemala**, which we personally have always viewed as a problematic expatriate destination, has recently come to our attention as having some very good real estate opportunities. Additionally, Guatemala may have reached the point where things simply can not get any worst. (Although we have sadly learned not to underestimate the capacity of absolutely inhuman brutality from those who have been sufficiently trained and supplied by the C.I.A.)

In terms of real estate opportunities and having reached the bottom of the barrel, much of the same could be said about Guatemala's neighbor, **Honduras**. **El Salvador** has also probably bottomed out and may be on its way to a turn around. **Nicaragua**, may be a good bet as investors begin to find **Costa Rica** too overpriced and problematic.

Much of the Caribbean is overpriced, but there are still numerous bargains for those who know where and how to look. **Mexico** is a like a field of opportunity filled with land mines. We love Mexico. It is an incredibly beautiful country with a rich culture and some of the best food on the planet. Living ones life there is a pleasure. Everything about it is wonderful, especially the people who I love more than any other. Mexico was the first foreign county I ever visited and lived in. I have a daughter who is half Mexican, a son-in-law who is Mexican, twin granddaughters who are Mexican. So, I am under the impression that I know something about Mexico. I am probably wrong, but it's my book so I will tell you my opinion anyway. In Mexico nothing is ever as it seems. In Mexico, nothing is predictable until it happens. And in Mexico, it usually happens when we are least prepared for it to happen and often when we can't do anything to prevent it from happening. In Mexico you must be very careful. Very, very careful.

With that said, it must be pointed out that much the same could be said in varying degrees about many parts of Latin America. Darwin's theories are at work in the world, and the law of natural selection prevails in Latin America. North Americans to a good degree have been coddled and protected and are to some degree unprepared for independence and self responsibility. It is difficult, if not impossible, to starve in the United States. Hell, even if we try to starve ourselves to death in the United States some government agency comes and force-feeds us. This is not true in Latin America. Much has improved in Latin America over the last decade and a half, but living in Latin America is not for fools. If we are liberals we might find our politics challenged, and if we persist on forcing our view we might find ourselves being dropped out of a helicopter into the ocean. If we are feminists or if our wife's are feminists, we must remember that most Latin American countries are not bastions of feminism. What is more important to remember, is that they may not be bastions of feminism tomorrow; and the chances are they may never ever be bastions of feminism, nor even sympathizers of feminism. In fact, the prognosis is that Latin America will probably remain hostile to feminism forever. It is the nature of the beast. By the same token it is, in our opinion a better place to raise children than the United States. Rape is almost unheard of in Argentina, Chile and in Uruguay. In much of Latin America, the very concept of child rape is repugnant, and children can and do play in a city park in Buenos Aires at two in the morning on a warm summer night with full impunity just as they once did in America. In Argentina boys grow up with a full understanding of what it means to be a boy and a man. If. you don't know what that means, or you have questions about it, then Latin American may not be for you. If you prefer that your son does not grow up with an under standing of what those concepts mean, then you should not bring your son to Latin America, you should raise him in America where he will learn that such concepts are meaningless. We are not asked to like the conditions of Latin America, nor are we required to go. If we go, we go because we are seeking something we no longer have in the United States. The best personal advice I can convey is not to bring our dreary shit with us when we go. America is a has-been nation and most of its social ideas are weak and declasse. The social ideas of the United States are no better than the social ideas of Rome's when Rome was falling head-first into decadence and decline. (for many of the same reasons) If you disagree with the social climate in Latin America, stay home, because home is where the hearts on fire.

Some social attitudes in Latin America are admittedly repugnant. There is tremendous social injustice, ranging from a lack of press freedom to poor judicial representation. There were numerous cases of rape and other acts of barbarity reported that are related and therefore 'excused' because they were aspects of the so-called dirty war. War is not an excuse for barbarism, nor is there usually much excuse for war, especially the absurd social wars that existed in Latin America until recently. These situations have improved and continue to improve. Even so, if it is our intent to go to Latin America and challenge the power structure we would be well advised to stay home. These people can be quite brutal when they are challenged.* There is change, but is of a different order than the order we may be accustomed to in the United States. Things in Latin America are evolving, but not in the same direction as they are evolving in the United States. We expect a more solid type of evolution, towards a type of society that has both feet on the ground and is more concerned with traditional family values and lifestyle. In Latin America, they don't think much of American family values; they view the American male as a weak coward, and the American female as a spoiled snot. To assume that other nations are following the United States is wishful thinking. In a few years many of the nations of Latin America will have seized the lead and will be setting the directions of the future. When strength of character, the capacity to innovate and independence are nipped in the bud as they have been in the United States, then nations with the spunk will snatch the prize.

*Unlike Janet Reno who 'saved the children' by roasting them alive.

We believe **Belize** is the best nation to open this section. It is an absolutely wonderful nation. It is an English-speaking nation and a place that Americans as a whole will find it easier to 'fit-in' than they might in a more Latino nation. However, with that said, it should be pointed out that Belize is 33% mestizo and these mestizos speak Spanish. They are not Mexican. They are Belizian. Belize is a polyglot society and a peaceful one. Never a war. No serious problems. The second biggest barrier reef in the world. Marvelous real estate, ...but we're getting ahead of ourselves. Let's go to Belize.

CHAPTER SEVEN

BELIZE

*"If the world had any ends, [Belize] would certainly be one of them.
It is not on the way from anywhere to anywhere else. It has no strategic value.
It is all but uninhabited."*

-Aldous Huxley

Huxley would be surprised by today's world. If he were suddenly transported here tomorrow, he might be on his way to Belize the day after. Perhaps for the very reasons he stated but with a different value placed on them. Belize is terrific! Belize is like nowhere else in the entire world and there is nothing with which to compare it. It is as Huxley called it, exactly and to the letter. Ah, but what he said yesterday sounds so great today.

Belize is everything Costa Rica is purported to be. For people looking for a young unspoiled nation, Belize has to be one of the choicest expatriate destinations imaginable. The language is English. The people are friendly. The government is an absolute anomaly for Central America. It is a true democracy, operating under the parliamentary system it adopted from Great Britain (which until 1981 upheld Belize in colonial status.) There is absolute freedom of the press. Little, if any serious corruption. An intelligent attitude towards business and an absolutely astounding respect for ecology. It is in our opinion a world leader in its efforts to create a balance between tourism and sound principals of ecology. There are few countries towards whom we feel a greater degree of respect. Its tiny population is numerically less than many of the world's cities. (Note that while the country of El Salvador consists of approximately the same land area as Belize, El Salvador contains thirty times as many people; with an overall population of almost six million people compared with Belize's 200,000.) Yet despite its small population Belize manages to attract the worlds attention for its modern attitudes, stable government and respectful treatment of its indigenous peoples.

Good telecommunications, a great environment, real estate prices that are significantly lower than that of Costa Rica, the best diving in the world, the second biggest barrier reef in the world, a growing offshore tax haven sector, offshore corporate services, developing offshore banking practices, a soon to be established free trade zone, an international airport, a free trade zone at the border-city of Chetumal, close proximity to Cancun, an archeological storehouse of Mayan Ruins (some still not totally explored), a polyglot culture that lives in harmony, proximity to Mexico and the United States, (the fact that we can actually drive from Belize to the United States has some positive values,) a series of Cayes (islands) some of which are available for purchase at prices that are so reasonable they make you want to pack your bags and catch the next plane. It is difficult to think of a better destination for the expatriate seeking a new home in an unspoiled land.

SCHOOLS EDUCATION & DIVERSITY

The quality and availability of public education in Belize compares favorably with most other nations in Central America. Primary school is compulsory and free. The *official* literacy rate is 90 percent, however the Ministry of Education acknowledges it is probably closer to 70 percent. Education receives the largest share of the national budget and the government is intent on further improvements.* It is significant to note that the cover of my Belize telephone directory contains twenty-six color photographs and all of them are of the children of Belize. These children have smiles on their face that one no longer sees on the faces of American children, yet they are members of one of the most diverse social mixtures in the world - culturally, ethnically and linguistically. Belize is made up of mestizo's (who speak Spanish as well as English), a large colony of Mennonites who speak German as well as English and Spanish, a number of Chinese, East Indians, Caribbean Creoles, Garifuna (a mixture of Caribbean-African and Carib Indian,) with their own very unique culture and language, Mayans, (who in the combined countries of Belize, Mexico, Guatemala, Honduras and portions of most of the other countries of Central America, make up perhaps the largest indigenous native culture in the entire world,) refugees from other Central American countries and a spattering of every other race imaginable including a growing expat population.

While Belize is making strides towards improving its educational system there is some room for improvement. There is a shortage of qualified teachers. Qualified educators take notice! While the wages would not be as good in Belize as they would be in Boston; teaching school in Belize would be an interesting challenge. Additionally, we would have the pleasure of making a difference in the growth of a developing nation rather than growing fat developing tenure.

"If you are sufficiently clever and energetic enough to make the grade in a good law firm, you probably have what it takes to play a role in building up a developing country." — **John Train**

TOURISM & ECOTOURISM

Belize with its population of 200,000 plays host to over 150,000 tourists every year. The money-making possibilities in the tourist industry, especially in ecotourism, is immense. Those expats already having made the move to Belize have opened, among other things; resort restaurants, low-key hotels, bread & breakfast inns, diving schools and a score of other businesses, most of which sound a great deal more interesting than what we might imagine them to be doing in the United States. We believe that the level of comparative opportunity in Belize when compared to the level of opportunity in the USA is disproportionately in favor of Belize. For the able.

Belize is such a tremendous storehouse of raw beauty that more than one expat has compared going to Belize like stepping backwards in time. Its barrier reef is 185 miles in length making it the second largest barrier reef in the world after Australia's Great Barrier Reef. Its coral and marine life is said to be unequaled in the northern

* Last year China spent ten times as much on military expenditures than it did on education.

94

hemisphere and within the unpolluted water of this reef lie well over 200 cayes, (or islands; the word is pronounced: key or keys.) If we've ever dreamed of owning an island and who among us hasn't, and if we are not yet multi-millionaires, and many of us are not, then Belize may easily be our very best and final chance to become island owners. Here are the prices of some of the islands (and on-island properties) for sale in Belize as of this writing:

● 5 Acres island near Belize City. $50,000 cash for quick sale.

● Beautiful medium sized island located some 13 miles east of Placencia Peninsula in southern Belize. White sandy beaches, coconut trees, excellent swimming, fishing and diving. $66,000. Terms available

● 84.5 acres on island located 30 miles southeast of Belize City. Many coconut trees, white sand beaches, good fishing area. Has great potential for development. $400,000. Write for more information.

● New resort development located 34 air miles ESE of Belize City. The famous Blue Hole with its fantastic diving is to the north and the lovely Half Moon caye with its protected red-footed Booby nesting colony to the east. A number of building lots offered from $6,050 and up.

These are real prices. They are not made up. For less than half of the price of home in the smog-filled suburbs we can buy a 5 acre island inside a coral reef. As Emory King, one of Belize's more famous citizens is fond of saying, you can't starve in Belize. Meaning, that in Belize it is literally possible to live off the land and sea without starving. But before we rush off we should take careful note that Belize wants citizens of good character who are going to add something to the country; they are quite understandably not looking for 'pure-play' back-to-nature-enthusiasts who want to live off the wilderness. Recalling such folks from the 60's, we have to admit that despite their rhetoric and posturing, they inevitably were responsible for more small-scale ecological vandalism than some of their less naturalistic neighbors.

Purchasing property in some foreign countries can be a nightmare, not so Belize. Land is privately owned and held Freehold. Rural property taxes are assessed at 1% of the lands market value for undeveloped land, while developed land in the City is generally runs anywhere from 3% to 8%. There is a land transfer tax of 8% for foreigners and for corporations that are foreign controlled. If you are Belizean, or if you become a Belizean citizen the transfer tax is 5%. Fees for attorneys are about 2% of the sale price. Purchasing land in Belize is a rather simple process without some of the difficulties and/or outright restrictions against foreign ownership we may experience in some foreign countries.

While it might go without saying that we should visit Belize and spend some time there before buying anything, we will say it anyway. We would like to assume that no one capable of using rudimentary logic would purchase land sight-unseen. If we are dumb enough to even consider a purchase of unseen land we should assume that we are probably too dumb to consider being an expatriate. For an American expatriate to discover opportunity in Third World countries requires that the American have a rudimentary intelligence and the capacity to call forth skills that are innovative by Third World standards but commonplace in America. There is no safety net beneath us in Third World countries and often no laws to protect idiots. While the prospect for rewards is far greater and the costs much lower for the prudent, it should be noted that the law of natural selection is alive and well in the Third World. If we would even consider purchasing land we've seen only in the bright color photographs of a glossy sales brochure, then we would be doing ourself a tremendous favor by staying in America.

According to reliable sources, conventional building costs in Belize run from $30 to $60 a square foot. We have asked several people why we don't see any adobe construction in Belize, but no has given us a satisfactory answer. There certainly is adobe in Quintana Roo and Campeche, two Mexican States which border Belize. Yucatan, which is in close proximity to Belize also has adobe construction. In fact, all of Central America seems to have adobe construction except Belize. Its construction tends towards ramshackled Caribbean; which is colorful and colonial yet costly compared to adobe. How many unemployed Belizeans would jump at the chance to start producing our adobe blocks we cannot say; but we can recommend several books on adobe construction and we believe that instruction in the art of adobe construction is taught in the American South-West around New Mexico and Arizona. If we are not mistaken, Belize does not have the ponderous building codes which add 40% on the dollar to U.S. construction costs; add to this scenario that Mexican Ceramic Tile and other highly artistic construction materials are in very close proximity.

We cannot but believe that Belize would be more than a bit happy with an increase in American retirees coming to Belize; perhaps even to the degree of initiating a program along the lines of Costa Rica's now defunct Pensionado program. While Belize lacks the sophisticated European-like ambience available in San José, there are other attractions that retirees might find of value. The fishing is great, the diving is great, land costs are lower and the language is English. As we've already stated, the government of Belize is a refreshing anomaly in Central America. There is no question for us, that we would feel many times more confident in dealing with the government officials of Belize that their counterparts in most countries. There is something to be said for knowing that what we have been told by a government isn't subject to change when its suddenly time for the mordita. We have no wish to single out or to disparage Costa Rica, which is a charming country. However the fact is that Costa Rica lured a number of retirees to Costa Rica with its pensionado program, which the government of Costa Rica has now decided to rescind. We will deal with these issues in the section on Costa Rica. We will add at this time however that while we don't believe that it is fair to single out Costa Rica, which is in so many ways a wonderful country filled with wonderful people; our confidence in the government of Costa Rica simply does not match the degree of confidence we have in the government of Belize. To clarify matters fully, we will state that we would prefer to deal with government officials in Belize than their U.S. counterparts. While the Belizean government is not a swift-moving highly efficient government like say Switzerland, the officials there with whom we have dealt have treated us with courtesy and a level of human dignity that hasn't been seen in America since the time of Thomas Jefferson.

Will American retirees buy it? It's questionable. Perhaps not suddenly and not to the degree that they have taken to Costa Rica, but we wouldn't rule out researching the creation of a nice modern adobe retirement village with ecology and nature as its selling point. Or at the very least doing some market research regarding its feasibility. Things have changed for retirees just as they have for everyone else. Who can deny that today's retired Americans are not like the retired Americans of yesteryear. It is obvious that they no longer fit the bathetic image we hold in our mind of the retired. That the retired have begun to change their world-view as well as their view of themselves should come as no surprise, yet what they do surprises us. They no longer seem quite willing to step aside and die, either metaphorically or in corporal fact. They are not content to simply live longer healthier lives, they are beginning to show up at sporting events not as spectators but as participants. Activities that were once reserved for the under thirty are now open game to the under seventy. (Soon perhaps the under 150?) Who today is startled by a seventy year old running a marathon? How far in the future is the *eco-retirement village*, with sailing, skin diving, competitive sporting events and a challenging lifestyle?

While petty crime is an existing but very minor problem in Belize there is almost no violent crime. One may have to deal with petty theft and vandalism occasionally in Belize City itself, but murder anywhere in Belize including Belize City, is almost unheard of; the people of Belize are extremely friendly and the country as a whole is very safe place to be. They have never had a violent revolution and they have never been at war. Belize has only about 750 soldiers. They are members of what is called the Belize Defense Force (BDF) and are a merger of the Police Special Forces and the Belize Volunteer Guard. Their main work has been in preventing the movement of drugs through Belize. There have been some problems with refugees from Central America, both drug related and wage related. And there have been the usual accusations by refugees from other Central American countries that they were mistreated in Belize by Belizean Security forces. There are also reports that these refugees are often underpaid by Belizean employers. These same accusations and words could be made and substantiated every day of the week against American police and American employers by Central American refugees living inside the U.S.A. We are aware of it, we don't like it, and it will probably continue forever in one form or another.

It is said that both Great Britain and the United States are committed to the defense of Belize. Guatemala has a [nonviolent] border dispute with Belize. Although heavily armed by your tax dollars, Guatemala is much too busy decimating its Mayan population to be much of a threat to Belize. Until recently Great Britain kept a couple of divisions of Goerkas on the Belize-Guatemala border. But after years of reluctance on the part of the Guatemalan army to engage them the Goerkas were withdrawn. They could be returned if the situation warranted it. The Guatemalan army was trained by the CIA to kill unarmed Mayan women and children and the consensus among real soldiers is that entire Guatemalan army would be no match for two divisions of Goerka.

There is now much too much American civilian and tourist presence in Belize for the US to allow any incursions by Guatemala. The U.S. Government now contributes to and supports the sovereign rights and defense of Belize, as does Great Britain. Great

Britain would act swiftly and decisively in the event of any military incursion into Belize, even in the event that United States Government should abandon Belize as they did Taiwan and South Vietnam.

Which brings us to hurricanes. Belize has them, but so does Florida, some of the continental US East coast, much of the gulf coast, all of the Caribbean and parts of Mexico. Costal construction at sea-level in Belize reflects hurricane concern. Many of the structures are on stilts, posts, or pillars and open underneath. The sea evidently can come into low-lying areas as winds agitate the shallow waters inside the reef.

We'd like to digress for a moment and do some speculation of a rather fantastic nature. The more serious taciturn reader is asked to either indulge us or to skip ahead to calmer ground. The Atlantis Project an organization mentioned in the passport section has designed a city that can be built upon [and within] ocean reefs. We have seen the architectural design for this project and a rather impressive scale-model of this very intriguing city which is said to be capable of withstanding any type of sea. We were impressed. The intention of the Atlantis Project is to create a free market City-State like Hong Kong where free-trade and free markets could exist. As farfetched as it sounds, the Government of Belize would be well disposed to at least consider such an idea. There is no reason why such a plan could not be initiated giving a portion of the reef over to creating a reef city built partially undersea. The Belizean Government could ask that it be done in a way that benefited the country without damaging the ecology. The rent paid to Belize for use of the reef could be astronomical. The fee could be attached to the price of gold or some other index so that the Belizeans would always be assured of achieving a consistent and worthwhile yield. Conjecturally, the free-market 'reef nation' would have a stable host country that would not intervene in their free market activities, a one hundred year lease with comprehensive and guaranteed rights of renewal. Belize's position as an ecotourist haven would be insured by an income that would be significant while their agricultural exports would have a ready market right on their reef.

We can anticipate that there would be much opposition to such an idea. It is easy to claim that a reef city might cause ecological or reef damage. We all know that there would be an abundance (or overabundance) of voices telling us why we should not or cannot achieve a project such as the Atlantis Project. Our belief is that it is the dynamic quality of an idea which really frightens some people.

Most of the voiced concerns are really smoke screens. Opposing such a project on ecological grounds is much like saying that as a species we don't have the brains to plan or do anything right. Obviously a reef city might cause ecological damage. Overpopulation is causing more damage than all other forms of ecological vandalism combined, yet we hear very few of even the most vocal of environmentalists offering to commit suicide to improve things. In many cases their departure would be a vast improvement. Why should innovation always be the first thing to be thrown out the window in times of uneasiness? We can't help believing that problems reside not so much in radical innovation as they do in inflexible thinking. Human beings by their nature are problem solvers. If we are afraid of problems the best solution is to create governments which will protect us from everything including our freedom. On the other hand perhaps many of us will soon deserve to be free of governments, or capable of using limited governments. There is also the possibility of having a living [dissipative] government. Meaning: a government that responds to creative situations with creative thinking. Creative thinking would create a government that evolves as the world evolves, shedding outdated ideas as it progresses. If anything has stopped America, it is the stifling rigid thinking of its government leaders. Washington D.C. is run by people who believe that the programs that failed yesterday will somehow work tomorrow. It is not a lack of new ideas we are talking about, but a lack of any ideas. That is precisely what has left the U.S. government idling by the side of the road, unable to keep up with the evolution of it's own citizens.

Reef cities are not a problem.

Rigid thinking is. The brain needs to be supple in order to function and humans need brains in order to evolve. The human ascent has been the most consistent upwards trend of the last 10,000 years; it is as they say, a good bet. We are not doing so badly really, and those who say we are may represent our own built-in societal feed back system. Perhaps its thanks to them and their sparkling wit, that we don't progress too fast and outrun ourselves. They will probably be unable to stop the trend towards globalism, as will the repressive governments of the world. (though they will try) The new expatriate, free from the bounds of nationalism, is going to be a part of the first human generation to know the wings of extraordinary global liberty. Our choices may range from raising sustainable orchard products in Jamaica to running an Irish Pub in Dublin; (and could conceivably include living in a reef city named Cousteau off the coast of Belize.) Regardless of the path chosen the real pursuit is the pursuit of global liberty and the evolution of our species. It is easy to poo-poo this as being too idealistic, too lush and green. We are usually told to lower our sights and hang our heads as if we are a loser species that has been trained to avoid enthusiasm. Evolve? Freedom from government? Everyone seems to tell us why not. But if not now; when? When the hell can we be free to progress? When can we shed the rotten stinking murderous governments that brainfeed our children with polluted subliminal crap? We are surely smart enough to govern ourselves better than they have governed us. Their record stinks! For many of us, their time is up.

We know that much of what we have been saying sounds like a digression and perhaps it is. But with the end of the Nation-state and the advent of evolving globalism we feel that dynamite should be inserted into the roadblocks caused by historic attitudes. We view the new expatriate as an evolutionary human. A global human. If we are going to shed outdated governments and repressive governmental concepts we are obligated to shed outdated perspectives. Failing that, we will simply re-create more bad governments to take the place of those from which we've evolved.

Does this mean we believe that a reef city will be built in Belize water? Well, why not? The probability is that somewhere in the world a reef city will be built some day. If those with the courage and the capacity to build an Atlantis Project should succeed we would like to put in our reservations right now for the first condominium to come available with an underwater ocean view.

A good many of the expats who go to Belize, go there for the laid-back ambience. Some of those who have gone there for that reason would be appalled by our idea of a reef city. We commiserate. It is that-laid back comfort of any area that hasn't been mindlessly developed that makes countries like Belize so special. To state our position clearly, we could say that there is only one thing we dislike more than uncontrolled mindless growth and that is mindlessness itself.

THE CAYES

Belize is famous for its Cayes; (the word is pronounced *'keys'* and means "islands,") and they seem to be everyone's destination. They are the place where the *cognoscente* expats seem to go and to play, and where many end up living. Belize has over 200 cayes, and as unbelievable as it may seem to us, most of them are uninhabited by humans. Many are nesting sites for sea turtles and ocean-going birds and apart from an occasionally human visitor, they remain stunning and unpolluted little jewels of bright green mangrove with palm studded white sand beaches. What it is even more interesting is the fact that they are inside the barrier reef in crystal blue-green waters calmed and protected from the outer sea by the barrier that the reef creates. Nothing else in the Caribbean even comes close to this reef system; nothing. A scuba diver could spend a lifetime, or a dozen lifetimes exploring these waters and never have a boring dive, nor ever even have to make the same dive twice. Almost 250 species of fish live amidst the dozens of different corals of which the reef is composed.

There is a caye within the reef waters that has a town on it of sorts and it is an unusual place where for reasons we'll explain many expats seem to go and end up staying. Staying perhaps, because once they visit the place and see it with their hearts, they find themselves unable to ever leave it. This expat island is a place called Ambergris Caye, and it is a very, very laidback place that is said to still have a touch of Joseph Conrad to it. On this 25 mile long caye there is, as we've said, a town of sorts, that goes by the name San Pedro. It is probably safe to say that San Pedro is absolutely unlike any other town on the face of the earth. In San Pedro, while no one is the least surprised that the mayor goes barefoot they would be surprised if the mayor showed up in shoes. It certainly fits perfectly Huxley's allegation regarding Belize in general; that, "...it is not on the way from anywhere to anywhere else." San Pedro and Ambergris Caye is a place fit only for a certain breed of people, people who destain the overdeveloped and admire the rawer beauties. San Pedro and Ambergris Caye are definitely not upscale. In fact, it is the sort of place that puts the word quaint on trial, or more precisely, makes the word sound like something a dude would use. But if we've been wanting to go back in time fifty years to a day when there was much to life that was very agreeable, San Pedro is the perfect place to launch our boat from.

If on the other hand if we are looking for a place to launch a 'rapid development' in that moochy style that has totally decimated the tranquility of many parts of the Caribbean, we probably won't receive much of a welcome from the San Pedro locals. (What is quite surprising, is that the Government of Belize is also eco-smart.) We won't argue with them. It has become pretty much a part of common knowledge that the end result of most upscale developments, especially those done with very high capitalization, has been a brutal decimation of those attributes which make a distant land like Belize more vacation-worthy than say, the Marriot near our hometown's center. We find ourself wondering why someone from Chicago or L.A. should wish to visit a resort in the Caribbean that looks like a Beverly Hills stage set. The fact is, that many do and many are satisfied, or if not satisfied, at least uncomprehending of what it is that they didn't see.

What they didn't see still exists in places like Belize, Dominica, portions of the Dominican Republic and several other spots that we'll discuss. These questions and issues of development have not been lost on the people of Belize and this includes both those who were born in Belize and those expats who have moved to Belize specifically for its natural environment. While there isn't an absolute consensus, it seems that many if not most Belizeans are learning through actual experience that an incredible number of tourists will visit and spend dollars to see the real world rather than go elsewhere to see a Hollywood version of the real world. Why change what is agreeable if what is agreeable earns us a living? Of course it is more complex than this and not everyone in Belize is making a great living. Predictably, there are some voices in Belize calling out for development. We suspect that the best method of encouraging the preservation of Belize is to create a workable system that respects sustainable ecological capitalism (eco-capitalism) and provides a good standard of living for Belizeans at the same time. If the system works and there is no reason why it shouldn't, Belize could act as an example to the rest of the world.

TALKING WITH AN AMERICAN EXPAT IN BELIZE

We have talked with a lot of expats from around the world. Additionally, we have given a great deal of thought as to what the future will be like. To our way of thinking, these two issues are strongly interrelated. Expatriates who assist in the development of distant geographical areas are going to have a major impact It is safe to say that no one can predict the future, at least with any degree of accuracy. The future is created by the desires of every human being who is alive as they each in their own way pursue their own goals. Of course, each and every expat we've talked to also has their own personal goals and desires. Most expats seem to want less governmental control over their lives. We've often assumed that the desire to be free from the repressive social and governmental atmosphere presently permeating America was the main stimulus underlying the desire to emigrate. While that may indeed be the underlying cause, it is safe to say that most expatriates have not really given any deep thought to the issue. Many, if not most, seem to just enjoy living in a new country without questioning the reasons why. The expats we've talked to from Belize seem to like Belize because they like its openness. Belize is indeed a laidback country. But admitting that it is laidback does not imply that expats in Belize have not registered some strong financial success. We know of several who have done extremely well. One expat who lives in Belize is Lester Langdon. He has lived in Belize for almost two decades. We thought it would be interesting and instructive to ask questions of an expat who has been in Belize for such a long time. We got a chance to talk with Mr. Langdon. What follows is what he had to say about Belize.

Q We appreciate your taking the time to answer our questions. First, tell us a little about your national origins and tell us how long you have been in Belize.

B I am a US citizen from the pacific northwest and have been living in Belize for 15 years. I now also have Belize citizenship, which makes me a dual citizen.

Q We've been told that you have several different businesses going, how many different businesses do you operate in Belize?

A I operate with Belize Real Estate which has three branches. The principle offices are in San Pedro, Ambergris Caye, and Belize City. I also have an investment company called INT, Inc., which deals in offshore accounts, and a citrus grove operation called Cotton Tree Limited, as well as being involved in several partnerships that do real estate development. One of my partnerships is also involved in importing.

Q You're obviously involved in Belize for the long term, which seems encouraging to us; tell us has tourism overtaken agriculture in Belize?

A Agriculture is still number one, but tourism is swiftly gaining on it and may soon exceed it in terms of gross national product.

Q Belize is said to have high port charges, is this because there is no deep water port, and if this is actually so, what can future entrepreneurs do to reduce their shipping costs?

A At this time I can't say what might be done; there is a Port Board, whose members might be willing to discuss this matter.

Q What is the future of aquaculture in Belize, and what would you recommend to someone interested in coming to Belize and entering that area?

A Aquaculture is large in Belize in the shrimp business at this time. There is room for more. The other types of aquacultural have not been developed at this time.

Q We've heard a rumor that magosteen, (an exotic fruit from Indonesia,) has tremendous market potential, and that growing them here in Belize would generate $20,000 per acre. While we believe this to be hyperbole; what in your opinion could do well as an exotic or unusual agriculture crop in the Belizean climate? Additionally, tell us what one would face in getting a crop to market?

A I haven't heard the rumor about the mangosteen, it sounds great, get me more information and I'll raise them myself. As to the logistics of getting a crop to market, it would depend on the crop and its perishability, what its shelf life would be, and what US laws would pertain to it, if that is where you would be shipping it.

Q What would you recommend to someone wanting to start a business in Belize? What fields do you believe have the best potential?

A Businesses relating to the tourist industry and citrus farming are the easiest and perhaps the surest businesses to get into in Belize. What is needed are canneries of all sorts, and a citrus concentrate facility. Skilled mechanics of any type will do extremely well here, from truck and auto mechanics to those who know how to work on marine engines. They would be busy full time.

Q Where are property values headed in Belize? What areas of Belize do you feel have the most exciting potential? What cautions would you point out to someone unfamiliar with Belize when purchasing Belizean real estate?

A Property values are rising about 15% a year. There was a decline in beach front property in 1990 which is gradually coming up again. At the moment Ambergris Caye is the biggest potential in beach front, the Cayo area in the eco-tourism field is big, however the rest of the country is gradually catching up along side of the top areas. People intending to buy real estate in Belize should deal with qualified people. Also, the best lawyers are needed. A qualified Realtor will explain the ins and outs of buying real estate here, and will also save you money.

Q What would you say to someone interested in moving to Belize and entering into a business?

A Visit.

Q Would you be willing to talk to expats interested in opening a business in Belize?

A Definitely. They should also consider spending some time in a charter airplane to see the various parts of the country. That would be money well spent. I'd be willing to give advise based on what I know. Also, as I say, talking to an attorney is very important. That much is just like the US. In Belize the pace is generally slower and you'd probably live longer as a result, but you still have to do business in an circumspect way. As I say, I've been here for 15 years, and I've seen what makes Americans successful and what makes them fail. Definitely visitors are welcome to stop by and see me when in Belize. Probably its best to call ahead, especially if you have something specific in mind. Our offices can also supply a listing of available properties from one end of Belize to the other. Phone or fax ahead. Its best to have a passport when visiting. Anyone wishing to stay in Belize, can get residency, which is between citizenship and being a foreigner; this prevents you from having to get your passport stamped each month, and you are generally treated with more respect. After three years of residency, you are entitled to citizenship; however it can be purchased sooner, if that is a necessity.

GETTING IN / STAYING IN

Visiting Belize is easy. American citizens need a passport but no visa or tourist card for stays up to thirty days. To extend your stay beyond thirty days go to the Immigration Office (tel, 02-77273) in Belize City (115 Barrack Rd.) or to a police station in one of the major towns. An extension costs BZ$5. You must leave the country every three months for one night. The shopping and nightlife in Chetumal just across the border into Mexico provides for a day of entertainment and a pleasant nights stay. If you move to Belize just to live, getting a residence standing takes about 6 months to a year and costs about US$300. To work in Belize you need a work permit. We have recently received information that states: Belize has a new Residency Program to go along with the old one. We are not sure how to interpret this statement and we're not sure anyone else does either. We must remember that Belize has only two hundred thousand people. Its government has to operate within a very limited budget. It does a fine job, better then many American States with ten times the population and ten times the budget. Nonetheless, we have found that there are some contradictions in interpreting what the final word is on some regulations. The new 'Residency Program'; if our understanding of it is correct, states that residency can be granted to persons who are professional and skilled, and 'whose expertise is generally identified to be in demand in Belize'. Probably, if we an MD, or we're school teachers, or other professional we are going to experience less trouble gaining a work permit and/or Residency. Retirees, who wish to reside permanently in Belize are also welcome; providing they can demonstrate they receive regular remittances from abroad, and/or retirees who have transferred their savings into the banking system of Belize. How much of their savings? It doesn't say. We would suspect that a minimum amount would suffice, enough to demonstrate a seriousness about living in Belize for some time, although possibly the purchase of property would also suffice. Third; there is a special category. This special category allows an investor to dispense with much of the waiting game by investing US$25,000 (or its hard equivalent) into Belize in "a productive area". To quote one interpretation: "Applicants in this category would be initially issued a provisional permit, facilitating temporary residence, up to six months, enabling their investment plans to be implemented and for their investment to be verified." Our interpretation of this is rather straight forward. In order to facilitate the process for investors, or for people wishing to engage in business; they are asked to simply dish up US$25,000 of their grubstake, as 'earnest money' to demonstrate that they are a serious player. A reasonable request! The money is then used by the new resident-investor for the business they intend to start anyway. What the government of Belize will take into consideration in this situation is the geographical location, the type of activity, its economic impact and how much, if any, employment it will generate for Belizeans. Nothing unreasonable there.

We can bring in our furniture, personal effects and other items duty free. However, items like our car, television, or boat, etc., are subject to a duty fee, which can run anywhere from 20% up to 70%. If we go into business we will probably first want to form a Belize or other offshore Corporation. (See section on offshore banking and investment) Once our corporation is formed we can get a duty free concession to bring in those things required to run our business. We have not been able to determine if this duty free concession applies only to Belize Corporations or to any and all

Corporations. If it should apply only to Belize Corporations one course of action would be to form two Corporations; one to use for bringing in our goods duty free and the other to operate offshore. (This may be necessary if our business includes selling anything within Belize jurisdiction in order to use the best tax jurisdiction.) If our business generates all of its monies from outside of Belize we suspect that a Belize Corporation might be enough. Belize has offshore financial services: and we can form what is called an International Business Corporation (IBC) in Belize, that is totally exempt (in Belize) from all forms of income tax within Belize. They are also exempt from tax in Belize in respect of dividends and other distributions, capital gains, interest, rents and so forth. Additionally, they are exempt from all forms of gift and inheritance taxes and as stated, from stamp duties. According to the Belize Bank, one of the larger Belizean banks in Belize, the Belize IBC can be formed in about an hour and a half. The one restriction on the Belize IBC is that we cannot engage in activities that produce income from within Belize. We would need to form a second offshore corporation if we also wanted to produce income from within Belize. Such labyrinthine maneuvers are probably something best suited when designed by a bonafide attorney who has experience in such matters and is capable of guiding our financial ship through such tricky waters.

RESOURCES FOR BELIZE

PERMANENT RESIDENCE: [note that we list two addresses and sets of telephone numbers for permanent residence; gained from two different sources, however one may be for retirees and one for other categories of immigrant, so we decided to list both.] Contact: **Immigration Department**; part of the **Ministry of Home Affairs**. In Belmopan, Telephone 08-22423, (if calling from the United States, we would dial 011-501-8-22423) Note that 501 is the country code when calling Belize from outside of the country, and that the 0 is dropped from the city code, which for Belmopan is 8. The city code for Belize City is 2. The fax number for the Immigration department in Belmopan is 08-22662. The immigration office in Belize City is 02-77237.

RETIREES: For those who wish to retire and live in Belize; we were informed by the Government of Belize to contact the Director of Immigration & Nationality Department, Belmopan, Cayo District. Belize, Central America. Telephone: [from the USA] 011-501-8-22611 FAX: 011-501-8-22662

SHIPPING OUR GOODS: In order to ship our belongings into Belize contact: Comptroller of Customs, Customs Department P.O. Box 146 Belize City, Belize Central America Telephone: [from USA] 011-501-2-77405 FAX: 011-501-2-77091

PETS: If we wish to bring pets, we will need a health certificate from a certified Veterinary Clinic.

EMPLOYMENT: If we wish to seek information regarding employment in Belize, we need to get in touch with: **Director of Labour Department** Belize City, Belize, Central America Telephone: 2-44891 We would also contact this department for Labor Permits. Belmopan also has a Labor Department; telephone 08-22323.

AGRICULTURE: If we are planning to invest in agriculture or land used for agriculture, we should contact: **Chief Agricultural Officer, Agriculture Department Ministry of Natural Resources**, Belmopan, Cayo District, <u>Belize</u>, Central America Telephone: 02-77492

CAVEAT: In researching and contacting foreign countries we have learned that no telephone number is etched in stone. [perhaps in funny-putty] It is one thing to find that a telephone number has been changed, but we have found entire telephone systems changed. Most systems where they have five numbers like in Belize are going to a seven number system (like that of the United States and most other Western Countries.) So, what happens is that one bright sunny day when we try to telephone our friend in Helsinki or Milan and we find that we don't have a clue as to how to go about it. Worst, if the country we are trying to call is Third World and the language is one we cannot speak, we must be prepared to jump through some hoops to get each and every telephone number we want to call within that country. This is simplified with multi-language information centers such as the ones they have with MCI, AT&T, and other long distance carriers, but it is not guaranteed.* Once we were trying to call a University in Sri Lanka. There was no way to even get close to the number. The existence of the University couldn't even be attested. To overcome some of these problems we have taken to getting the telephone directories of some cities in some countries. Our telephone directory for Belize is wonderful. We have the entire country, (128 pages total,) in one directory. As long as Belize doesn't go to a seven digit system we can more or less contact who we need to contact. Facing a similar problem when trying to contact people in Rio de Janerio we opted for buying the Rio Directory. Our source for directories informed us that for some reason they simply could not obtain a Rio de Janerio Directory. Frustrated, we contacted the Brazilian Consulate in San Francisco, California. The information officer at the consulate in a desperate voice told us that if we did find a Rio telephone directory to please contact the Consulate at once; they didn't have a Rio directory themselves and they didn't know anyone did. In fact, they said, to the extent of their knowledge no one has had the courage to try to print a Rio directory in over a decade. Ah, Rio.

Almost every single one of the telephone numbers listed above for Belize we know to be currently working numbers as we write these lines. And, as we've indicated, Belize seems to be quite the rock of stability with not even the slightest signs that its course might soon go astray. Nonetheless, we will be looking for reader updates and experiences. It should also be pointed out, that in the duration of time that has passed while we worked on this book a vast quantity of resources have opened up on

* Australia has a telephone Interpreter Service: This is an extremely successful free service to migrants or to anyone whose first language is other than English. For the cost of a local call, a person can telephone into the service which has skilled translators available in more than 100 different languages. This is a very valuable help to all new arrivals to organize their new life there. (As I say in the section on Australia, even though this is a 'government sponsored' concept paid for by tax payers, I admit that I actually like this idea. But I'd also like to see *Jazz* and *Bossa Nova* subsidized, so maybe my ideas of what constitutes a good government handout wouldn't fill a constituency.)

the Internet that list telephone numbers worldwide. We will miss the sometimes interesting graphics that were in some of the directories and the 'sense of place' we often gained from looking at them. However we have to recognize even though we will still need such directories to some extent, at least in the near-future; much like the beloved Long Playing Record (LP) with it's wonderful graphic-covered jacket, the telephone directory is now an endangered species.*

REAL ESTATE COMPANY RESOURCES

As the reader knows, it is not our policy to recommend any of the private businesses we list as resources. With Belize we have inadvertently made an exception in that we interviewed an expat who is also the owner of one of the largest real estate companies in Belize. Our interview is not an endorsement. We nonetheless must state that we have the highest regard for Lestor Langdon and believe that the reader will be well-served to contact him in seeking property in Belize. Additionally, there are other real estate companies in Belize.

REAL ESTATE COMPANIES IN BELIZE:
  •
- Belize Business Consulting Services, P.O. Box 407, Belize City, tel. 501-2-30012,   fax 501-2-31048
- Belize Land Consultants, Ltd., P.O. Box 35, Corozal Town, tel. 501-4-23195, fax 501-4-23396
- Bella Vista Group, 63 Bella Vista, Belize City, tel. 501-2- 44711, fax 501-2-32895
- Caye & Country Real Estate Ltd., P.O. Box 2231, Belize City, tel. 501-2-35308, fax 501-2-32770
- Langdon Supply Limited, P.O. Box 15, San Pedro, tel. 501-2- 62147, fax 501-2-62245 (affiliated   with Belize Real Estate)
- Maya Landings at Moho Caye, Belize City, tel. 501-2-33075
- Playa de Piratas Properties, Placencia, tel. 501-6-23180, fax 501-2-23203
- Scheffer Real Estate, 24 Gabourel Lane, Belize City, 501-2- 34285
- Southwind Properties, P.O. Box 1, San Pedro, tel. 501-2-62005, fax 501-2-62331
- Sovereign Real Estate, 39A 4th Avenue, Corozal Town, Belize, tel. 501-4-23160, fax 501-4-23157
- The Windstar Agency, P.O. Box 33, San Pedro, Belize, tel. 501- 2-62525, fax 501-2-62497
- Toledo Real Estate & Assoc., P.O. Box 73, Punta Gorda, tel. 501-7-22470, fax 501-7-22199
- W. Ford Young Real Estate, Ltd., P.O. Box 354, Belize City, tel. 501-2-31022, fax 501-2-31023 (affiliated with Belize Real Estate)

*Those who make the assertion that they will never buy a computer and that my assertion is misguided, will be delighted to learn that there is already a design for a telephone that has a built-in computer directory access that 'pulls-up' any telephone number in the world by keying in the appropriate name. Voice prompt query capacity will quickly follow for those with stubborn pocket books.

BELIZE FIRST MAGAZINE

Belize First is intended to be a guide to travel and life in Belize and the rest of the Caribbean Coast of Central America and Mexico. They publish the leading travel writers and reporters covering the region (They claim that they pay more for articles than the Chicago Tribune!) Belize First presents candid, independent views..
Regular features include:

●Latest news from Belize and the Caribbean Coast
●Candid critiques of hotels and lodges from readers (who get a free pound of fresh-roasted Central American coffee when their reviews are printed)
●Living, working and retiring in Belize and other English-speaking areas of the Caribbean Coast Buying land or a house in Belize
●Eco-traveling in the rain forests and bush of Belize
●Diving and snorkeling on Belize's atolls and barrier reef
●Visiting Mayan sites in Belize, Honduras, Guatemala and Mexico
They published quarterly, with a fifth "Best of the Caribbean Coast" book-format issue, in Asheville, North Carolina, by Equator Travel Publications, Inc., 280Z Beaverdam Road, Candler, NC 28715 USA. Fax 704-667-1717. Lan Sluder, Editor and Publisher
E-mail address: 74763.2254@compuserve.com.
URL: http://www.zine.net/belize/index.shtml
Mail subscription rates for the full paper edition with maps, photos and 10 to 20 in-depth articles every issue: US$29 a year in the U.S., Belize, Canada and Mexico, US$39 a year in other countries. Free catalog of books, maps and other hard-to-get information on Belize and the Caribbean Coast also available.

The Belize Chamber of Commerce and Industry is located at:
63 Regent Street, P. O. Box 291
Belize City, Belize
Central America
(501) 2-73148 fax (501) 2-74984
Note: They have a limited budget. Belize is a small country. If we want information & help, we can expect to pay for it.

EMBASSY OF BELIZE
2535 Massachusetts Avenue, N.W.
Washington, D.C. 20008
(202) 332-9636
(202) 332-6888

TELEPHONE DIRECTORY ON THE WEB FOR FOREIGN COUNTRIES:
(We told you about it and here it is... not yet hooked to your telephone, but coming to telephone near you.)
URL: http://www.contractjobs.com/tel/ [This URL is a multi-nation telephone directory]

SELECTED TELEPHONE NUMBERS IN BELIZE

Atlantic Bank Ltd
Freetown Road
Belize City, Belize
Tel. 2-34123 Fax 2-32090
Contact: Sandra Bedran

Barclays Bank
21 Albert Street
Belize City, Belize
Tel 2-77211, 2-77054 Fax 2-78572
Contact:Tilvan King

Belize Employment Agency
The Commercial Center, Booth 35, P. O. Box 1363
Belize City, Belize
Tel 2-71771 Fax
Contact: Richard Batchelor

Caribbean Shipping Agency
115 Albert Street, P. O. Box 352
Belize City, Belize
Tel 2-77396, 2-73015 Fax 2-77681
Contact: Stanley Longsworth

Corozal Free Zone Development Ltd.
Park Street South
Corozal Town, Belize
Tel 4-22165, 4-22166 Fax 2-22108
Contact: Michael Arnold

FIND MORE NUMBERS FOR BELIZE ON THE INTERNET AT:
URL: http://www.belize.org/bcci/member.htm

Ambergris Caye has it's own newspaper. **The San Pedro Sun** and they have a USA
address:
c/o Advantage Information Management
3762 West 11th, Suite 501
Eugene OR 97402
FAX for information to their US office at: 541-344-7944.
email:sanpdrosun@btl.net,amcneill@ambergriscaye.com
They have a web site with some information on internet access on the caye, try them
at:
URL: http://www.ambergriscaye.com/ or: http://www.ambergriscaye.com/pages/
endorse.html

Maya Airways
Belize Municipal Airport, P. O. Box 458
Belize City, Belize
Tel 2-35794, 2-35795 Fax 2-30585
E-mail: mayair@btl.net
Contact: Pablo Espat
Providing domestic air services. Both scheduled and chartered airline service in and around Belize.

Radisson Fort George Hotel
2 Marine Parade; P.O. Box 321
Belize City, Belize
Tel 2-77400, 2-31234 Fax 2-30276, 2-73820
Contact: Steve Maestre

Tropic Air San Pedro
Ambergris Caye, Belize
Tel 22-2012 Fax 26-2338
Contact: Ramon Cervant
TROPIC AIR is the Belize Airline
P. O. Box 20 San Pedro, Belize
US & Canada 24-hour Reservation Hotline (800) 422-3435
In Belize Tel 501-26-2012 Fax 501-26-2338
Corozal Town 04-22725
Int'l Airport (Belize City) 025-2302
Municipal Airport (Belize City) 02-45671 Punta Gorda 07-22008 San Pedro 026-2012

UNOFFICIAL NOTES REGARDING GETTING IN & STAYING IN
[Information found on the Internet]

RESIDENCY: Some people stay in Belize for years simply by renewing their 30-day entrance permit. That requires either leaving or reentering the country every 30 days (even if just across the border at Chetumal to do some shopping), or paying the immigration office US$12.50 per month (it can be paid in a six-month lump sum) for permit renewals. However, if you are a citizen of the U.S, Canada or some other countries, official permanent-resident status is possible. You retain your present citizenship and have most rights of Belizean citizens except the right to vote and serve in the army. It is somewhat easier and faster to obtain residency status if you are retired. Those not retired generally must live in Belize for one year before applying (you can leave only for medical treatment of no more than two weeks' duration). However, if you invest at least US$25,000 in Belize in a "productive area" you may be granted a provisional residency permit for up to six months so that the investment can be implemented pending permanent residence status. Note: Application for permanent residency by citizens of Central American and some other countries involves a different procedure.

RESIDENCY FOR RETIREES: A recently revised policy on permanent residency allows retirees to apply immediately upon entering Belize. As a retiree, if you relocate to Belize and can show evidence of a fixed monthly income of at least US$750 for single persons or US$1,000 for couples, or show savings equal to US$27,000 for singles and US$36,000 for couples (which you must deposit in a Belize bank), you can quickly get a permanent residency permit. The income/savings requirement are somewhat flexible, and each case may be handled on an individual basis. You are issued a provisional permit good for six months' residency while your application is being processed. In addition to the above requirements, you must have a valid passport, have a medical exam including HIV test, and make a deposit of US$300 per adult (refundable three years after residency is granted) plus an application fee of US$50 per adult.

REQUIREMENTS FOR IMMIGRATION & CITIZENSHIP: Belize "welcomes immigrants who are in a position to go there and establish themselves without government assistance for ... agricultural purposes, either on a small holding or a plantation basis, industrial development or sponsored employment by established commercial organizations" says the Belize Immigration and Nationality Service. Immigrants must have a medical exam, provide a police reports, and show evidence that funds are available to finance the proposed business. The government now offers an Economic Passport program, requiring an investment of US$25,000 ($50,000 per family, with children over 18 paying an additional $15,000), plus a deposit of US$50,000. A scandal developed recently involving the alleged sale of immigration papers to Taiwanese. Responsibility for immigration has been transferred to the Foreign Affairs Ministry.

PURCHASING PROPERTY: Non-Belizeans can buy property in Belize. Purchases of 10 acres or less in a rural area or 1/2 acre or less within city limits require no special approval. There is a land transfer tax of 10% for non-Belizeans and 5% for Belizeans, typically paid by the purchaser. Attorneys fees and other closing costs runs to several percent of the sales prices. Property taxes are 1 to 1.5% of value annually, higher in cities. Most tax bills are nominal, especially by U.S. and Canadian standards. Work with a knowledgeable attorney or other adviser in Belize to assure that title and other papers are sound. Citizens and those officially resident in Belize for at least three years can lease land from the government for a few dollars a year. Once land is cleared and a residence is built, the land can be bought from the government for under US$500. Local financing for non-Belizeans is difficult to obtain, and interest rates are higher than in the U.S. and Canada. Owner financing is sometimes available, especially on land purchases, with 10-10-10 being about the best available ~ 10% down, 10% interest rate, paid over 10 years.

REAL ESTATE PRICES: Raw land still is cheap in Belize, especially in rural areas. In large tracts, it often goes for only a few dollars an acre, $100 to $1,500 an acre in smaller tracts. Surveying costs may exceed the purchase price. Waterfront land has risen in price considerably in recent years, and is now US$1,000 a front foot, or more, on Ambergris and some other areas. North American-style houses are priced only a little lower than similar properties in, say, Florida, but Belizean-style homes can be inexpensive to buy or rent. Building prices vary, labor is cheap but slow, and imported materials prices are high. A North American-style home can be built for US$30 to $65 a square foot, depending on the level of finish and the amount of time you personally spend supervising construction.

TAXES: Generally, non-Belizeans in Belize pay tax only on income derived in Belize. The progressive income tax maxes out at 45% for individuals, 35% for corporations. A Value Added Tax (VAT) of 15% has been in effect since April 1996. This is supposed to replace some import taxes and the gross receipts tax of 1 to 2%. Even with this national sales tax, import taxes remain high ~ from 25 to 88% on cars and trucks, for example. Happily, some items are "zero rated" for VAT. These include basic food items, medical and dental services, hotel rooms, books, and some home appliances. Very small businesses ~ those grossing less than US$50,000 ~ aren't required to register as VAT traders and therefore do not collect VAT from customers (although as tiny businesses their prices may be higher than VAT traders). There are no capital gains or inheritance taxes in Belize.

WORKING IN BELIZE: Possible but difficult for most. Unemployment is officially 12% in Belize and the effective rate is higher. Although Belize badly needs skilled workers, since tens of thousands of the best-educated Belizeans have emigrated to the U.S., permits for work in many fields, including tourism, are difficult to get (unless you are investing), and professionals such as physicians also find it difficult to get a license to practice. The official procedure to obtain a one-year work permit is that you must fill out an application and bring it in person (if working for another, the employer must also appear), along with passport and three passport-size photos, to the Department of Labor in Belmopan. Annual fee for the permit ranges from US$2.50 for farm workers to US$300 for professionals. Applications by those

112

investing in Belize in businesses that will employ Belizeans are most likely to be approved.

INVESTMENT OPPORTUNITIES: 100% foreign ownership of Belize companies is permitted, although the government encourages Belizean participation. Tax abatements and holidays are available. Investment is especially sought in agriculture. Products must be exportable, as the home market is small. There are also opportunities in tourism. The International Business Company (IBC) Act of 1990, the Trust Act of 1992, and the Offshore Banking Act of 1996 were passed, in part, to increase foreign investment in Belize. These laws protect investments in Belize from appropriation or taxation. IBCs do not pay income taxes and do not file income or dividend statements with Belize or other governments. Shareholders are not identified.

OFFSHORE BANKING: The Offshore Bank Act of 1996 is designed to move Belize into the ranks of other offshore banking havens such as the Cayman Islands and Panama. Whether that will come about is still very much up in the air. Offshore banks chartered in Belize pay no taxes in Belize and can take deposits from the public, make loans, conduct stock brokerage, offer credit cards, and have other traditional banking functions. Minimum capital for a "Class A" bank allowed to operate without restrictions is US$500,000; minimum for a "Class B" bank, which cannot solicit funds from the public, is US$200,000. Offshore banks in Belize need have only one stockholder. The bank must maintain a registered office in Belize and have at least two Belizeans on the board of directors. Companies in Belize offer these services as part of a package. It typically takes about three months to secure a banking license from the Belize Central Bank and to put together documentation.

TYPES OF INVESTMENT: Most foreign investment in Belize has gone into agriculture and, in recent years, tourism. There still are opportunities for investment in those areas, as well as in manufacturing and perhaps in services oriented to the international market. Investments of any type have to focus on international export, since the home market is so small. Traditionally, sugar cane, bananas, and large citrus plantings have dominated the agricultural sector in Belize. More specialized types of agri- and aquaculture such as shrimp farming may become more important in the future. Most tourism investment has been in the form of small resorts and lodges. In many cases, these small operations have not been able to develop the type of international marketing relationships which would let them achieve high occupancies and solid profitability. Average hotel occupancy in Belize is in the low 30-percent range, about one-half that of profitable hotels in the U.S.

MEDICAL CARE: Belize is a developing country and cannot afford the high standards of medical care available to many, though not all in North America and Europe. Low-cost or free public care is offered at the new Karl Heusner Memorial Hospital in Belize City, in district hospitals in Orange Walk, Corozal, Punta Gorda, Belmopan, and San Ignacio, and in health clinics and centers in several towns and villages around the country. The quality of care appears to vary widely. In some cases, it is good, while in others health care professionals lack the equipment or training to handle some health care problems. There also are a number of physicians, dentists, and clinics offering private care at costs lower than in the U.S. Most of these are in Belize City. Those who can afford it often go to Guatemala, Mexico, or the U.S. for diagnosis and treatment of heart disease, cancer, and other health concerns requiring state-of-the-art care.

COST OF LIVING: Belize can be surprisingly expensive, especially if you try to live in a U.S. style. Because so much is imported, the Belizean market is small and inefficient, and import and VAT taxes are high, many items purchased in Belize, such as appliances, cars and supermarket items, cost twice what they would in the U.S. There are no Wal-Marts or McDonald'ses in Belize. Still, if you live closer to the Belizean style, and eat Belizean food, it can be affordable, especially outside Ambergris Caye and Belize City.

FOR MORE INFORMATION: In addition to *Belize First Magazine*, two small books are starting points for living and investing in Belize: *Belize Retirement Guide* by Bill and Claire Gray, US$19.95, and *Guide to Business, Investment and Retirement*, by George W. Rea, $25. Both are available from **Equator**, 280 Beaverdam Road, Candler, NC 28715. Shipping and handling in North America is US$3.50 for the first item and $2 for each additional item. Bill and Claire Gray, who live in Corozal, also conduct annual "Belize retirement tours" for those interested in retiring in Belize. For facts on investing, contact the **Ministry of Economic Development,** P.O. Box 42, Belmopan, Belize, C.A., or **Embassy of Belize**, 2535 Massachusetts Ave. NW, Washington, DC 20008. For residency matters, contact **Immigration and Nationality, Ministry of Foreign Affairs**, Belmopan, Belize, C.A.

US STATE DEPARTMENT TRAVEL SAFETY INFORMATION

BELIZE - CONSULAR INFORMATION SHEET

COUNTRY DESCRIPTION: Belize is a developing country. Its tourism facilities vary in quality.

ENTRY REQUIREMENTS: Information on entry requirements may be obtained from the Embassy of Belize at 2535 Massachusetts Avenue, N.W., Washington, D.C. 20008, tel: (202) 332-9636, the Belizean Consulate in Miami, or the Belizean Mission to the U.N. in New York.

MEDICAL FACILITIES: Medical care is limited. Doctors and hospitals often expect immediate cash payment for health services. U.S. medical insurance is not always valid outside the United States. In some cases supplemental medical insurance with specific overseas and medical evacuation coverage has proved useful. For additional health information, travelers can contact the Centers for Disease Control and Prevention's international travelers' hotline at (404) 332-4559.

CRIME INFORMATION: Crime, including robbery and mugging, continues to be a problem. Travelers who keep valuables out of sight, do not wear jewelry, and travel in groups during daylight hours minimize the risk of being targeted. Individuals may contact the Belizean tourist police as well as regular law enforcement officials for assistance. The loss or theft of a U.S. passport abroad should be reported immediately to the local police and the nearest U.S. embassy or consulate. Useful information on guarding valuables and protecting personal security while traveling abroad is provided in the Department of State Pamphlet, "A Safe Trip Abroad." This publication, as well as others such as "Tips for Travelers to Central and South America," are available from the Superintendent of Documents, U.S. Government Printing Office, Washington D.C. 20402.

DRUG PENALTIES: U.S. citizens are subject to the laws of the country in which they are traveling. Penalties in Belize for possession and trafficking in drugs are strict, and convicted offenders can expect jail sentences and fines.

AVIATION OVERSIGHT: In August 1991, the U.S. Federal Aviation Administration assessed Belize as not providing oversight in compliance with international aviation safety standards for Belizean carrier operations. Belize presently has no national air carriers operating flights to the United States. Commercial passenger service between Belize and the United States is conducted by carriers from countries which meet international safety standards. For further information, travelers may contact the Department of Transportation at 1-800-322-7873.

REGISTRATION/ EMBASSY LOCATION: U.S. citizens may register at the Consular Section of the U.S. Embassy in Belize City and obtain updated information on travel and security within Belize. The U.S. Embassy in Belize is located at the intersection of Gabourel Lane and Hutson Street in Belize City; telephone (501-2)77161.

FACTS AT A GLANCE (STATISTICS ON BELIZE)

LOCAL NAME: Belice, Origins of name disputed.
TIME ZONE: GMT-6
AREA: 8,864 sq. mi. (almost exactly the same size as El Salvador)
STATUS: Independent state within the Commonwealth
DATE OF INDEPENDENCE: 1981
POPULATION: Figures range from 200,000 to 230,000 (1996 est)
CAPITAL: Belmopan (population: 4,000) Belmopan like **Brasília** and **Canberra***
is an artificially located capital. Set inland because of the hurricane potential along
the coast. Belmopan has never quite caught on as either a city or a Capital.   Most
workers in the Capital commute daily to and from Belize City or San Ignacio rather
than live in Belmopan. Belize City is the urban, social and spiritual center of Belize.
BELIZE CITY POPULATION: 60,000
LANGUAGES: English (official), Spanish, Garifuna, Maya, German [Mennonites]
ETHNIC GROUPS: Creole (40%), mestizo (33%), Mayan (9.5%) Carib (8%)
RELIGIONS: Roman Catholic (62%), Protestant (30%), Though we searched
everything we could lay our hands on for some strange reason we were unable to find
any accurate statistic for the number of Mennonite in Belize.
PHYSICAL FEATURES: Though located in Central American, Belize is also
considered a Caribbean Nation, possibly because of the number of islands located
within its coastal waters. There are extensive costal plains which are swampy in the
North, and fertile in the South; the major mountain chain, the Maya Mountains
extend almost to the East coast, rising at their highest point to 3,674 feet at Victoria
Peak. The major river, Belize River, flows West to East. The inner costal waters are
protected by world's second longest barrier reef. Numerous islands, called 'cayes'
[pronounced: 'keys' in the local idiom,] exist within these reef protected waters.
CLIMATE: Generally sub-tropical, but tempered by trade winds. Average annual
temperature 75° F (Jan), 81°F (Jul); variable rainfall; average annual rainfall 51
inches in the North and 175 inches in the South. Hurricanes can and do occur in
season.
CURRENCY: 1 Belize Dollar (Bz$) = .50¢ U.S. as of this writing.
ECONOMY: Belize has what is called a developing free-market economy. This
economy is based on agriculture, some forest products, and a swiftly developing tourist industry based on 'eco-tourism'. The tourism industry has created spin-off industries in construction and the service sector.
GDP: $550 million (1993 est)
GDP PER CAPITA: $2,700 (1993 est)
FOREIGN DEBT: $140 million; (lowest foreign debt in Central America) There is
a low ratio of debt to GDP. Also low ratio of debt to export income.

FREEDOM HOUSE RATING:
Political Rights: ① **Civil Liberties:** ①
Note that no other country in Central America has such an exemplary record regard-
ing civil liberties and political rights as does Belize. This is commendable!

* St. Petersburg and Washington D.C. also fall into this league.

WWW, TELEPHONY & TELECOMMUNICATIONS:

Belize is connected and has some WebSites of note; the Nation of Belize maintains one at: http://www.belize.org/main.html Unfortunately, going online in Belize is currently being crippled by the local telephone monopoly, **Belize Telecommunications Limited (BTL)**, which is somewhere back in the last century mentally. They are trying to keep independent Internet Service Providers from 'competing' with them. This will be remedied one way or the other. **Hugues Satellite Dishes** that will connect anyone, anywhere, to everything are only a year or two away. BTL will cut their own throat, (and that of the entire Nation,) if they don't get someone to explain the facts of global economics and techno-reality to them. Once the government is brought to understand that free access to Internet Service Providers spells future success or failure to Belize; it is hopeful that the situation will be remedied internally. It is simply not possible to move effectively into phase two of Internet development without a proliferation of commercial Web Servers offering products and services to local customers. As Mary J. Cronin defines it: "For any country this phase [phase two] is a prerequisite to having a critical mass of buyers and sellers participating in global electronic commerce." In her book, *Global Advantage on the Internet*, Ms. Cronin states that the advent of having multiple server-providers indicates the foundation of an electronic marketplace phase.*

In any event, the technology to go around BTL is at hand.** Those with the skill and telephony technological know-how will simply move into the vacuum created by BTL and make a fortune by providing Internet Connection Service at a realistic rate. We suggest that the concept of Remote Access Transmission Providers (RAT) will be a tremendous market for those who provide it. Just imagine how nice it would be to set a small antennae on one's desk that put one into the internet. How about $30 a month from 10 million subscribers? Let's see, that works out to....

* For an explanation of this concept please refer to *Global Advantage on the Internet* by Mary J. Cronin. See Resources in the Appendix.

**Indeed, if I was to live in Belize and wanted to maintain a WebSite, I would simply 'hang' my WebSite Pages in a different *'Server Jurisdiction,'* [to coin a phrase.] I would use BTL to access the internet if I had to, but the larger portion of my internet business would be operated out of a different jurisdiction. That way I would be insured of having the going market Web Hosting rates and uninterrupted service. Where we hang our WebPage may soon be where we have our jurisdictional presence and that may have little or nothing to do with where we have domicile. While this presents interesting questions, the point here is BTL and their monopoly. BTL in this circumstance would not have my business. If there is no positive reason to hang my WebPage with BTL, I would simply go to a jurisdiction which Hosted my Web Page, insured my right to electronic commerce privacy and did so at a fair market price.

CHAPTER EIGHT

BRAZIL

"There won't be equality in the world until everyone gets to live in Ipanema"
-Antonio Carlos Jobim

Brazil: An enigma.

We have often heard divers who dive for the first time describe the world within the ocean as "another world." We lived there for awhile in Rio. That's what we would use to describe it. It is another world. ...and not the Third World, as users of 'catch phrases' might describe it. Catch phrases are out when we want to describe Brazil. If you want to experience life on another planet that moves to a different rhythm, go to Brazil. You don't necessarily have to go as an expat, just go.

We had a friend from Greece who worked in a Greek restaurant in the United States. It was a good restaurant and he was an interesting and pleasant friend and we spent many hours drinking Greek beer and talking about the world. I spoke often to him about Brazil and about Rio. One day he decided to go there for a vacation. When he returned I of course wanted to hear about his trip.

He'd been robbed. Someone in Rio had taken his wallet when he was on the beach. He'd met a girl and fallen in love. He twisted his ankle playing volley ball. He'd gotten a first degree sunburn. He was in a taxi cab that got in a wreck on the way to the airport and missed his plane home. It took him three days to straighten everything out, he had to wire the U.S. for more money. And he was moving to Rio.

Ah, Rio

NAMES: Conventional long form: Federative Republic of Brazil, (Republica Federativa do Brazil), Short form: Brazil, (Brasil)

TIME ZONES: GMT-3 (E); GMT-4 (mid-W); GMT-5 (W)e Time: Three hours behind GMT in the east, north-east, south and south-east; four hours behind GMT in the west; and five hours behind GMT in the far west.

AREA: 3,285,618 sq.mi.

STATUS: Republic

DATE OF INDEPENDENCE: 1822

POPULATION: 158,739,257 (July 1994 est.) 160,737,489 (July 1995 est) population growth rate: 1.22%Population: 158,739,257 (July 1994 est.)

Population growth rate: 1.28% (1994 est.)

Birth rate: 21.48 births/1,000 population (1994 est.)

Death rate: 8.63 deaths/1,000 population (1994 est.)

Net migration rate: 0 migrant(s)/1,000 population (1994 est.)

Infant mortality rate: 59.5 deaths/1,000 live births (1994 est.)

LIFE EXPECTANCY AT BIRTH:

- total population 62.25 years
- male 57.41 years
- female 67.32 years (1994 est.)
- Total fertility rate: 2.44 children born/woman (1994 est.)

CAPITAL: Brasilia

LANGUAGES: Official: Portuguese.   Spanish is not the language of Brazil, however it is widely spoken, as well as what is called 'Brasilero,' which is a combination of Spanish-Portuguese.   This is especially true along the borders of the surrounding Spanish speaking nations.   We have noticed that for some strange reason, Brazilians have a great facility with language regardless of its origins.   They tend to speak languages slowly and quietly and are exceptionally even-tempered; whether this has anything to do with their capacity with other languages, or if the talent results from being a multi-racial society we cannot say.   English is spoken fairly widely, especially in the more cosmopolitan cities.   There are areas of the country where German is spoken fluently, as is French, and even some of the Slavic languages, including Russian.

ETHNIC GROUPS: Describing the ethnic mix of Brazil would be a difficult task. There is no simple division between races. Brazilians tendency towards racial innermingling has created a racially homogenous society. Brazilians also tend to be quite proud of their racial tolerance; statements such as, 'In Brazil, we are all black.' coming from someone with fair skin, blond hair and blue eyes, or a Japanese-Brazilian saying with obvious national pride, 'In Brazil only my face is Japanese.' Yet, in these platitudes just as in everything else, Brazil tends to be a nation of paradoxical extremes. For despite these assertions of tolerance, which we know are made in good faith, there is a measurable degree of de facto racism in Brazil. Brazil's type of racism is a racism based more on economics perhaps then one of social attitude, but it is an existent factor nonetheless. After all, while attitude is an important commodity, it's hard to take it to the bank. Blacks seem to end up on the bottom of the economic pile in Brazil, just as they do almost everywhere else, and of the Brazilian street children 'disappeared' by the military police, almost 80% are black.

If it is at all possible to place these gruesome statistics aside, nowhere else will the expat encounter such a degree of social tolerance as one finds in Brazil. Brazil is not something one can define from the outside as one can a barrel of apples. If humans live in an unpredictable universe, Brazil is at the center of it's vortex. If some sort of psychological guideline would be helpful, we might say that anyone who is intolerant of other races should not go to Brazil; but we won't say it. Instead, what we will say, is that if anyone wants to get over their racial intolerance Brazil would be the best place to start. Official statistics claim that Brazil is 55% white, 38% mixed, and 6% black. Anyone wanting a comprehensive understanding of the Brazilian view of race must absolutely see the Brazilian film *Gaijin*, a film made by Tizuka Yamasaki, a second generation Japanese-Brazilian woman about her immigrant maternal grandmothers adjustment to life in Brazil. The film is remarkably good, quite poignant, and totally unforgettable.

RELIGIONS: Statistics claim the Brazil is 89% Catholic. Again, this is misleading. African Spiritualism permeates the entire society at every level. The Catholic Church in desperation unofficially allows the practices as long all the African gods and goddesses are given the names of Saints. So, Iemanjá, or Yemanja; [pronounced ee-mahn-jaH], a goddess who lives in the sea, can be called the Virgin Mary and everything becomes suddenly kosher because Catholicism is officially being practiced. The several different sects of African Spiritualism practiced in Brazil, for the most part, are all somewhat loosely interrelated, much as differing forms of Christianity are more or less interrelated. The practicing of these Spiritualistic religions has become very chic in Brazilian high society, and everywhere we go in Brazil at every stratum, there are signs of some aspect of these beliefs; in images, habits, rituals, superstitions, and artifact.

PHYSICAL FEATURES: Brazil is a large country, the fifth biggest in the world. It is mostly tropical, especially in the north. The south of Brazil can be temperate at times, but not in the extreme. There is, we believe only one place in Brazil where it ever snows; a place in the mountains of Santa Catarina near Sao Joaquim. There are few high mountains, what mountain ranges there are, are mostly along the coast pressed against the sea; inland Brazil tends to be flat with low hills. Brazil's highest point is Pico da Neblina at 9,888 feet. Brazil is filled with a storehouse of natural wonders. A dozen books could not contain a full description of Brazils natural bounty. Its rainforest is so immense that it must be crossed over in a plane to be fully comprehended, and even then it is like crossing over an ocean and trying to comprehend the sea. The mouth of the Amazon River is over 200 miles across, a stretch so broad, that an island the size of Switzerland could easily be placed in its center and not be visible from the rivers shores. There are eight major river systems 30,000 miles of which are navigable. Brazil's vastness is difficult to place in perspective. With almost two million miles of highway, major portions of Brazil still remain loosely connected, if not entirely remote. In the south the Iguassa Falls easily rival and completely dwarf Niagra. On the southern Atlantic coast there are modern cities filled with Germans, Russians, and Italians. In the rich Santa Catarina farm land everything grows; from wine grapes to coffee. In the east is the architectural wonder of Brasilia, the wildwest-type frontier towns and the Pantanal. In the west, from Rio Grade do Sol to Bahia are numerous modern cities, some whose populations top 10 million. ...and in the north, is the Mata: (or forest,) which is the known to the world as the Jungle Amazon.

ECONOMY

"Statistics are like bikinis; they show what is impressive
and hide what is essential."

CIA WORLD FACT BOOK OVERVIEW: The economy, with large agrarian, mining, and manufacturing sectors, entered the 1990s with declining real growth, runaway inflation, an unserviceable foreign debt of $122 billion, and a lack of policy direction. In addition, the economy remained highly regulated, inward-looking, and protected by substantial trade and investment barriers. Ownership of major industrial and mining facilities is divided among private interests - including several multinationals - and the government. Most large agricultural holdings are private, with the government channeling financing to this sector. Conflicts between large landholders and landless peasants have produced intermittent violence. The COLLOR government, which assumed office in March 1990, launched an ambitious reform program that sought to modernize and reinvigorate the economy by stabilizing prices, deregulating the economy, and opening it to i n creased foreign competition. The government also obtained an IMF standby loan in January 1992 and reached agreements with commercial bankers on the repayment of interest arrears and on the reduction of debt and debt service payments. Galloping inflation (the rate doubled in 1992 and by March 1994 had risen to 42% per month) continues to undermine economic stability. Itamar FRANCO, who assumed the presidency following President COLLOR'S resignation in December 1992, was out of step with COLLOR'S reform agenda; initiatives to redress fiscal problems, privatize state enterprises, and liberalize trade and investment policies are gaining momentum under the new administration of Fernando Henrique Cardoso. Brazil's natural resources remain a major, long-term economic strength. Inflation in 1995 is forecasted to be around 30%.

SELECTED STATISTICS ON THE ECONOMY

GDP: $785 billion (1993 est) $886.3 billion (1994 est) growth rate: 5.3% (1994 est)
National product: GDP - purchasing power equivalent - $785 billion (1993 est.)
National product real growth rate: 5% (1993)
National product per capita: $5,000 (1993 est.)
Inflation rate (consumer prices):30% (1995 est)
Unemployment rate: 4.9% (1993)
EXPORTS: $38.8 billion (f.o.b. 1993) commodities iron ore, soybean bran, orange juice, footwear, coffee, motor vehicle parts /Trading partners EC 27.6%, Latin America 21.8%, US 17.4%, Japan 6.3% (1993)
IMPORTS: $25.7 billion (f.o.b. 1993) commodities crude oil, capital goods, chemical products, foodstuffs, coal /Trading partners US 23.3%, EC 22.5%, Middle East 13.0%, Latin America 11.8%, Japan 6.5% (1993)
External debt: $119 billion (1993)
Industrial production: growth rate 9.5% (1993); accounts for 39% of GDP

Electricity: capacity 63,765,000 kW production 242.184 billion kWh consumption per capita 1,531 kWh

Telecommunications: good system; extensive microwave radio relay facilities; 9.86 million telephones; broadcast stations - 1, 223 AM, no FM, 112 TV, 151 shortwave; 3 coaxial submarine cables, 3 Atlantic Ocean INTELSAT earth stations and 64 domestic satellite earth stations.

CURRENCY: For many years the currency in Brazil was called the Cruzerio, and after that, the Cruz; today the name has undergone yet another incarnation, and has been born again as the Real, which means 'real' as it does in English. Perhaps this is a bit of Brazilian humor, it is certainly laughable. Of course, the word real, could also be interpreted as 'royal,' which is perhaps an even better name for the money. I almost prefer royal to real.EXCHANGE: 1.00 US Dollar = 1.011 Brazilian Real On 09/08/96

ECONOMY COMMENTS: Brazil is one of those countries like Mexico and Argentina which are so rich in natural resources that poverty seems incomprehensible. Brazil has wretched poverty. In every way shape and form Brazil is a country of contrast and nowhere is that more apparent than in its unequal distribution of wealth. Brazil is grossly mismanaged and it makes any sort of commerce extremely complicated. The Brazilian government is almost on a par with the government of Italy for screwing things up. It is a mess. But nowhere else in the entire world is there so much raw opportunity as there is in Brazil. Comment: Another figure we have see for the GDP per head is $5,580 (1994 est) We doubt in the extreme that this figure is even remotely accurate, but it is surprising close to the CIA statistic. One Brazilian economic minister claimed that statistics are like bikinis; they show what is impressive and hide what is essential. Remember that when you get to Ipanema.

RELATIVE COSTS:
●cheap meal: US$2
●restaurant meal: US$6
●cheap room: US$5
●mid-range hotel room: US$20

STUPID STORY TIME

We recall staying in a hotel room in the Flamengo district of Rio de Janeiro for $7 per day. The room was air-conditioned, had room service, a private bath, included a breakfast and was one block from the beach. We used to eat a nice pasta dish with fresh mussels in a wonderful restaurant close to the hotel and just across the avenue from Flamengo Beach. They had a decent white wine for a dollar or so a bottle and we remember that the dinner and the wine was under $5. You could look out on Avenita Atlântica from the glassed-in patio of the restaurant and watch the evening with the cars and the people and the lights from Sugarloaf shining on the Bay of Botafogo. We wish we were there right now.

American Chamber of Commerce for Brazil - Sao Paulo
Rua Alexandre Dumas 1976
04717 Sao Paulo, SP, Brazil
Phone: (5511) 246-9199
Fax: (5511) 246-9080 email: puharre@amcham.com.br

Investing in Brazil

The **American Chamber of Commerce- São Paulo** provides a series of information bulletins on how to do business in Brazil: The booklets provide initial information about several aspects of initiating business operations in Brazil. Each contains about 16 pages and all are essential tools for any American company planning to invest in Brazil.

- How to Buy A Company in Brazil
- How to Locate Your Office in Brazil
- How to Set Up Your Company in Brazil
- How to Remunerate Your Employees in Brazil
- How to Move Your Family to Brazil
- How to Choose your Office in Brazil
- How to get a Visa in Brazil
- How to Search for Management Talent in Brazil

Upcoming editions will be on how to register your brand name, how to trade your product or service and other relevant themes: Prices: are in listed in *Real*, contact the Chamber for further details.
Members: R$ 5,00 Non-members: R$ 10,00 International: R$ 15,00

There is also a series called ABLIB. The next in the ABLIB series is specially directed towards assisting international investors to identify non-conventional locations for businesses. With the improvement of the national transportation and telecommunication systems, many towns in Brazil now offer advantageous infrastructure, resources and locations that deserve some attention.
Titles available now: ✦ The Mogi region ✦ Jundiaí These two areas are well located, providing easy access to the largest markets in Brazil; the metropolitan region of São Paulo and the interior of the state of São Pauo.For more information, please contact Mrs. Daniele Puharré at 55 11 246-9199, or send e-mail to: puharre@amcham.com.br

American Chamber of Commerce for Brazil - Rio de Janeiro
C.P. 916, Praca Pio X-15, 5th Floor
20040 Rio de Janeiro, RJ Brazil
Phone: (5521) 203 2477
Fax: (5521) 263 447

FREEDOM HOUSE RATING:

Political Rights: ② Civil Liberties: ④

Brazil's constitution guarantees freedoms of religion and expression and the right to organize political and civil organizations. However, a nationwide breakdown in police discipline and escalating criminal violence — much of it fueled by the drug trade — have created a climate of lawlessness and generalized insecurity in which human rights in Brazil are violated in the name of expediency. In the regional areas, the local police tend to be corrupt, while on a national level, the military police tend to be brutal in an attempt to mediate the corruption. This said, it should be pointed out that because Brazil is such a vast country, one could live there for a lifetime without ever seeing any signs of a problem, (much as one could live ones total life in Arizona without ever experiencing anything like the riots in Los Angeles, the violence in New York City, or the drug problems of Cleveland.) Tourists have a tendency to go to the very areas where the problems exist, just as the press seems to concentrate on them because they are newsworthy. That is not to deny that problems exist. But as is usually the case, our strongest opinions seem to be formed by the most graphic of impressions and seldom by an equal accounting. Brazilian parents love their children as much, if not more, than their counterparts in most other parts of the world. The homeless children are a by-product of poverty, and the poverty is a by-product of government corruption. That these factors should lead to despair is not surprising, and that the despair should lead to violence is predictable. Human beings are not yet very good at long-range thinking, because we have never been called upon to think long range in our entire evolution. We can learn — given enough time. It should be noted, that fifty percent of the population of Brazil is under the age of twenty. (In Brazil there is a common saying; '...half to the people in Brazil are under the age of twenty, and half of them are pregnant.' We would like to add a comment to this self-deprecating Brazilian humor but we'll wait until we can do it in Portuguese.)

WWW, TELEPHONY & TELECOMMUNICATIONS:

Brazil leads South America with network size. (and in our opinion, in all of South America, only Chile rivals Brazil in terms of Web Site sophistication; the Brazilian genius for things artistic is quite apparent on the Brazilian Web Sites we've seen.)* As of May 1995, Brazil had 165 Internet-connected networks. This figure represents an increase of 96% from the previous year. Whether this rate of growth can continue is debatable — while growth rate in the United States is almost continuously exponential, the U.S. has a more affluent middle class then Brazil, and affluence would seem to be a determining factor to PC home use. How far growth can continue without prolific home use is a variable we have no way calculating. There is a tremendous amount of commerce in Brazil and already a large number of Access Providers have moved into position. The Web Sites we have seen show a high degree of sophistication and creativity, many of them being products of Universities. Thus far most Web Pages are emphasizing technology and finance aimed at the international market with few products or services aimed at the local market. We should

---

* Since writing these lines, the countries of Argentina and Uruguay have made us eat our words. They have terrific Web Sites! There are some amazing things being done with the Internet in South America.

also make the reader aware, that a government subsidized monopoly called **Embratel** manages all Internet access services, and that Embratel is a subsidary of **Telebras**, which is Brazil's only telephone company. (see the section on WWW, Telephony, & Telecommunications.) Whether or not this is an ominous caveat, we cannot say. It certainly is something that should be kept in mind by individual expats and companies that are planning on moving into the Brazilian market.

BEHIND THE SCENES ON THE INTERNET:

If you want to get into the list of brol/ links and into the index try:

URL: http://www.ultranet.com/~brol/links/

This site will get you into every worthwhile site concerning Brazil. It's an index site used by the people who set up the sites and links. By going directly to the index site we avoid all the graphics, the advertisements and the multimedia time-takers. The following list gives the reader just the barest indication of what the site contains. Each of the links listed below leads to numerous sites. For instance, by clicking on the site

>/business-eco.html< we are lead to a page that links to a dozen or so very relevant sites relating to Brazilian business. These dozen sites each lead to a dozen sites, and so forth. This one *hit* leads us to a hundred or more good sites relating to Brazil. Go to: http://www.ultranet.com/~brol/links/ and check out the action.

- Parent Directory
- anuncio.html
- arts_entert.html
- beaches.html
- blank.html
- business_eco.html
- culture.html
- education.html
- environment.html
- food_drink.html
- govmt_polit.html
- internet_direct.html
- news_mag.html
- pictures.html
- places.html
- places_pict.html
- science_tech.html
- sports.html
- travel.html
- travel_links.html

THE PRISONERS OF HOPE

> *...and the riverbank talks*
> *of the waters of March*
> *It's the promise of life.*
> *It's the joy in your heart.*
> **-Antonio Carlos Jobim** *"The Waters of March"*

Antonio Carlos Jobim lived a perfect life. We believe that. His universal influence on music is one of Brazil's greatest legacies.

It might be said that to understand Jobim is to understand Brazil. He lead with his heart. He was an incurable romantic, a brilliant composer, a lyricist of great subtlety and a musician with a perfect sense of pitch. He loved life and he enjoyed living it. He often said that happiness is the child of pain, and he had within his music a happy sadness that is difficult to describe. Brazil also has this happy sadness. Of all the countries in the world, none has such a high degree of promise as does Brazil, and nowhere else is there a country for which the great promise seems so continuously elusive. Brazilians are a fun loving people with a dual nature. They are times like children, at other times they seem to perceive lives illusions better than the rest of us. They have in Brazil's natural resources an immense bounty which they have wisely chosen to keep to themselves, but which thus far has been totally misappropriated and grossly mismanaged by one corrupt government after another. They have in their own person an incredibly creative populace whose hands are eternally tied by a burgeoning bureaucracy. The decentralized government, is totally out of touch with itself. Nothing in Brazil moves forward without an overwhelming volume of bureaucratic paper work. The number of bureaucratic offices and conflicting laws we are required to attend to in order to procure the simplest of permits acts as a thorough impedance, if not an absolute barrier to any sort of progress. Yet written across the face of Brazil's flag are the words; 'Order and Progress,' as if life itself were playing some sort of cosmic joke. As we've mentioned, the currency is now called the *Real*, [pronounced: Rhee-EL,] a word which more or less means: 'real' or 'actual' as it does in English, but can also mean 'Royal.' To fully grasp the depths of this most humorous of jokes, consider that while world price levels multiplied 244,000 times all over the globe during the years of our worst inflation, in Brazil prices multiplied 29 million times! That someone could give the name 'real,' to any currency that has lost its value to such a grand extent is either an out and out act of absurdest humor, or it is an attempted insult aimed at the intelligence of the Brazilian people. We believe that it surely must be the former. While we met many fun-loving people in Brazil, we don't remember meeting too many fools.

Brazil is a very rich country. It is often said that people from the Brazilian State of Minas Gerais [pronounced: Me-nas Jher-eyez,] will not pick up a piece of gold, because their pockets are too filled with diamonds. Of course this is an exaggeration, but we have been to Minas Gerias, and we admit to seeing a warehouse filled with gemstones piled upon rows of tables. Our estimate is that there must have been several hundred thousand gemstones in that room, and that is not an exaggeration.

If Brazil is not the worlds richest country, it is certainly very close. Yet, Brazil has some of the most abject poverty in the world. By the same token, every person we've ever spoken with in Brazil was friendly, enthusiastic, and joyful; even the poorest of people. How can this be?

What is it about Brazil and the Brazilians that makes Brazil so different from the rest of the world? We believe it is the very strong and passionate belief that Brazilians have in Brazil as a country and in themselves as a people. Brazilians are truly proud of Brazil in a way that is exceedingly rare in this modern world of worldly disillusionment. We believe that their uncommon hope in the face of adversity and their world famous love of happiness stem from their national pride. Their love is both admirable and sad. Admirable because of the strength it bestows them and sad because their hope has deceived them. In the final accounting many Brazilians have nothing beyond their hope. It is what sustains them in the face of inequality, injustice and corruption. They endure their misfortunes heroically, (even the poorest among them) with remarkable good cheer and an unending optimism for Brazil's future. They are Brazilians after all and they are unlike anyone we have ever met. They remain free in their hearts because of their pride in Brazil and the hope that pride gives them. They are the prisoners of hope.

IS BRAZIL A PLACE FOR EXPATS?

There is a <u>great deal</u> of opportunity in Brazil. Whether we choose to trade *'into'* or trade *'out of'* Brazil, there are fortunes to be made. Additionally, if we are able to run the bureaucratic gauntlet of paperwork and regulations, operating a business inside of Brazil can be enormously profitable. It is a tricky game however, and the rules would take us some time to learn. The constantly declining value of the currency is in itself a minefield that requires a specific logistic formula to transverse. And the problem of the currency is ongoing. Brazil is a country that absolutely requires an adequate amount of time for us to gain our bearings. Trading into Brazil is possibly an easier route than working inside of Brazil, but we certainly cannot say that with any confidence. We have compiled a storehouse of information about foreign trade; please check our fax-on-demand system to access this information.

Briefly we can recommend the following markets for the reader to consider:

● **Information Technology:** Brazil is the largest market in South America for Information Technology equipment (IT). The market has been repressed for decades by a policy that restricted the importation of computers and other IT equipment. Brazils IT market exceeded $11 billion in 1993 and has grown by a 9-10 percent annual rate over the past several years. International Data Corporation predicts Brazilian IT market growth at 13 percent for the period 1992 to 1997. If Brazil can stabilize itself, the market could even surpass this rate of growth, if such a thing is imaginable. Because Brazil cannot possibly compete in global markets without the development and growth of this sector, it is imperative that Brazil move quickly to increase facility and decrease barriers to all forms of commerce, including its labyrinthine bureaucracy. Whether this will happen is purely conjectural, but the market, even in its present state, offers immense opportunity. US exports [into Brazil] of

IT equipment and components, totaling $985 million in 1993, have been growing at an annual rate of almost 14 percent. (And even these numbers are understated, because of the large number of products that enter the country of Brazil illegally.) In Brazil, products from the United States have a reputation for quality, durability and state-of-the-art technology that makes them very attractive to purchasers. However the Asian suppliers are moving into the marketplace very aggressively with lower-priced products and underselling the American suppliers.

We suggest, to those with the knowhow that they should consider going to Brazil and investigate opening a facility to assemble [from imported components,] using Brazilian labor and developing their own Brazilian label. We would make very sure that we lined up all our bureaucratic ducks before we made any financial commitments. We believe that Brazil would be foolish not to be fully receptive to such a program and well might find some way to bypass import tariffs on unassembled components. With success, it might be possible to eventually move into component production. With an untapped market of 150 million people, the footwork and homework required to investigate such a program has to be well worth the effort. The present alternative is to concentrate on high-end market segments which is too restrictive, especially since we view Brazil as having a smaller middle-class with less money to spend. IT is after all an American innovation. If Asia manufacturers can produce IT products at low prices, so can smart American expats.

● **Telecommunications:** Brazil actually has a lower teledensity than other emerging markets, including India, China, Indonesia and Turkey. The number of telephone lines per hundred people in Brazil is 6.8 with a total of 10.3 million lines in service. While import tariffs are coming down on telecommunications products, it seems slightly absurd that there should be any tariffs at all on products that Brazil so desperately needs. As usual where a burgeoning leviathan government exists, one hand is blindly fighting the other to the detriment of the common citizen. If *we* need medicine and *we* charge *you* to give it to *us,* we are playing against ourselves. Telebras has recently stated that it is encouraging the offer of joint ventures. We aren't excited. They should simply get the hell out of the way. They are bumblers and the source of much of Brazils telecommunications problems, their continued existence as a government subsidized monopoly prevents real solutions. The Brazilian Congress is currently considering private sector participation in telcom services. While we are not entire sure how to interpret that statement, we applaud the direction of intent. If the usual payoffs, bribes and corruption abate, there is hope for an open-market telecommunications system for Brazil. Where communication is free of government coercion is precisely where people with brains will want to be. Prosperity follows.

There is enormous potential in Brazil for anyone having knowledge in telecommunications-technology. In order for the country to modernize its governmental and economic structures, it must upgrade its communications services. If the government doesn't tie the hands of everyone who tries to improve the situation they may even improve their own situation. Do we expect such far-sightedness on the part of the Brazilian bureaucracy? Yes, we do. The Brazilian bureaucracy, while slave to an antiquated Portuguese system that is inoperable, is made up of some very bright people. The younger people coming into political office in Brazil are actually more tired of governmental corruption than are the people of the United States. There are innumerable bright young people who can make a difference in Brazils future. Like the people of Brazil, we are hopeful.

Other fields that have good potential include:

- Healthcare Technology
- Environmental Technology
- Transportation
- Aerospace
- Infrastructure
- Energy
- Financial Services
- Education supplies and equipment
- Tourism-related products
- Printing and graphic arts equipment (desktop publishing?)
- Organic chemicals
- Aircraft and aircraft parts (ultralights ?)
- Machine tools

Brazil does not have a Free Trade Zone of any significance. The only one we know of is in Manaus in the state of Amazonas. It isn't very impressive. Another, possibly more sensible access to Brazils markets might be through another country, such as Uruguay. [See the section on Uruguay] The reader is advised to research the possibility of using **MERCOSUR**, [see the references made to MERCOSUR, the Common Market agreement between Argentina, Uruguay, Paraguay, and Brazil,] as a method of accessing Brazil from a nearby country. We suspect that Uruguay's or even Paraguay's bureaucracy might be less cumbersome than that of Brazils.

As to operating a small business inside of Brazil, the bureaucracy would be the biggest stumbling block to success, followed by the specific peculiarities that are particular to Brazil itself. Brazil is somewhat like America, Australia, and Canada, in that they are all multi-racial societies. This diversity in Brazil is rendered quite interesting by the tonalities given to it by the Portuguese language and culture. Brazil changes with location. The south of Brazil is very different culturally from the north, much as the south of the United States used to be quite different from the north before television destroyed America's distinguishing regional characteristics. These differences [within Brazil,] must be understood prior to any domestic commercial undertaking.

ON THE GROUND IN BRAZIL

"I go to sleep to the music of doorway guitar and awake to the sounds of roosters, parrots and church bells...In the garden a macaw is going crazy" **--Richard Alleman**

Brazil is an exciting place and it has a large selection of wonderful cities and natural settings to choose from, each as different in culture as they are in location. Many of the cities in Brazil do not have the gruesome problems of Rio or Sao Paulo, and some of the cities are environmentally spectacular. Several that might be considered, include **Florianópolis**, **Porto Alegre** and some of the other costal cities in the south. **Recife** and **Olinda** in the north, and possibly even **Brasilia** in the east. Of course in a country the size of Brazil it would be impossible to name or know each and every interesting place. (Although we are working on it.) One very interesting city is **Curitiba**, the Capital of the state of **Paraná** in the south of Brazil. Curitiba is said to be the most ecologically balanced city in the world. With almost two million people, Curtiba has managed to avoid many of the problems that have plagued most of the worlds cities. This has been accomplished through innovations in the areas of transportation, housing and land use; but it also includes garbage-recycling and some environmental concepts no other city has considered. Curtiba has planted over 1.5 million trees within the city itself while drastically decreasing automobile use within the city at the very same time through an absolutely ingenious transportation system. The net result is excellent air quality. To accomplish the decrease in automobile use they developed a system that allows buses to run as quickly and efficiently as subways; a system which must be seen to be fully appreciated. There are fifty square meters of green area (park or plaza) for each citizen. Their zoo is a world famous zoo designed as a wild habitat that exists within the parameters of the city itself. The green belts which are everywhere crisscross the spider web of transit lines that interconnects the entire city in a system of: fast lane, slow lane, two way, low speed, bus line, and multiple parallel streets, with bike paths, jogging paths, rivers and streams. Fast, articulated buses run at twenty second intervals on a two way exclusive lane that allows such rapid efficient transportation that using a car would be ridiculous. The tandem style buses have 300 passenger capacity. These vehicles stop at attractive steel and acrylic tube stations which are built equilevel with the buses and designed to fit their doors. Fare is collected at the tube stations turnstiles, thus facilitating boarding. The system is so effective that ridership increased by 28 percent in the first year of its inauguration. The use of auto fuel in Curtiba is less per capita than any other Brazilian city despite the fact that it has more cars per capita. Pedestrians can shop 24 hours a day in crime-free parks and plazas and bike everywhere on more than 75 miles of bike paths that criss-cross the city. The parks and plazas are filled with everything; art, shopping, sculpture, free classes in trades, theaters, concerts, opera and samba. Over 100 tons of the cities trash is recycled each day; even the poor are involved; trash can be traded for transportation, recyclable material for groceries. Old buses are used as mobile classrooms that go to the poorer neighborhoods and teach hair styling, typing, plumbing and other trades. The city recycles enough paper to save 1,200 trees a day. The children of Curtiba are the best and biggest contributors to the various programs and create objects out of recycled material as research projects. Curtiba is said to have one of the best Universities in the Brazil. We feel that Curtiba gives us a much more accurate perception as to what Brazil is really all about, once we depart from the sensationalism of the media hype.

In the adjoining state of **Santa Catarina** are some German towns and cities that are very rich in Germanic-Brazilian culture. The city of **Blumenau**, a city of 200,000, has an annual Oktoberfest that draws over a million people every year from around the world to join in the celebration. Blumenau, despite its small size has an almost world-class orchestra under the direction of Norton Morozowicz. The island city of **Florinanapolis** is the Capital city of Santa Catarina. It is astoundingly beautiful, has a low crime rate, top rated universities and an excellent economy. It is where many Argentines go to vacation. Anyone considering Brazil as an expat destination should start in Florinanapolis, Curtiba, or Blumenau and not in Rio.

In the north there is a city called **Recife** (meaning: reef.) Recife is considered the Venice of Brazil and it is absolutely a must-see city. Attached to Recife is a city called **Olinda**. Olinda is not merely a national treasure, it is an international trea-sure. Along Olinda's 400 year old cobblestone streets sit some of the most magnifi-cent architecture imaginable. Olinda is Brazil's former capital and is one of the best preserved colonial cities in the world. It is recognized by the United Nations as an international historic city. Olinda is elevated and overlooks Recife and the Atlantic Ocean. The main historical district is concentrated on its winding cobblestone streets in the upper-most section of town. Olinda is not however a lifeless museum of the past, it is very much a living city with a dynamic cultural scene that is totally alive and kicking, Its beautiful enclave of preserved colonial buildings is populated by artists, students and bohemians. Find some real estate here and you'll own part of a treasure. Churches, museums, art galleries and convents vie with outdoor restaurants and craft markets, attracting locals and tourists alike. Carnival in Olinda is a mega affair, the historic setting and party-animal residents providing an intimacy and sense of security that other Carnivals lack. The May 1988 issue of *Conde Nast's Traveler* had a front cover feature article on Recife and Olinda. It may be possible to find the back issue of Traveler that has the story at a public library. The reader is advised to check it out.

Another spot worth checking out is **Jericoacoara**. Jericoacoara is the latest remote-and-primitive 'in' beach to become popular among backpackers and hipper Brazil-ians. Situated on the **Ceará** coast, north-west of Fortaleza, it's a rough little fishing village where dozens of palms drowning in sand dunes face jangadas (sailboats) stuck on a broad grey beach. It's very hard to get there so you might as well stay a while. Pigs, goats, sheep, horses, burros and dogs roam the sandy streets at will. You can boogie at the forró held every evening - just follow the music. You can also climb the sand dunes, hitch a ride on a jangada, or walk to Pedra Furada, a rock three km east along the beach. You can also hire horses and gallop 18 km westward along the beach to the still smaller town of Mangue Seco.

Earlier we mentioned the **Pantanal**. The Amazon may have all the fame and glory, but the Pantanal is a far better place to see wildlife. This vast area of wetlands, about half the size of France, lies in the far west of Brazil and extends into the border regions of Bolivia and Paraguay. Birds are the most frequently seen wildlife, but the Pantanal is also a sanctuary for giant river otters, anacondas, iguanas, jaguars, cougars, crocodiles, deer and anteaters. The area has few people and no towns, and access is via the Transpantaneira road which ends at the one-hotel hamlet of **Porto Jofre**. Boat tours are available from the port city of Rio Paraguai on the Bolivian border, but be cautious as the town has a reputation for gun-running, drug traffic and poaching.

But, we recognize that we are diverging from the intent of this book. This is not a tourist guide. To read about Brazil is an act made doubly simple by the number of fine books available. We will list a number of Brazilian guides and contacts in our resource section. It should be sufficient for us to state that we could never be bored in Brazil. It is impossible. Brazil has miles of untouched beaches, the Amazon River and Jungle, the Pantanal, Cities that are astounding, a tremendous diversity of culture so rich as to rival that of any country in the world, excellent farm land, excellent resources, a wonderful populace as varied as it is possible to imagine, and music which is totally unlike anything anywhere else. Being in Brazil is like being fully alive. We like Brazil and we will always like Brazil. It swings.

REAL ESTATE IN BRAZIL

We believe that Brazilian Real Estate is quite often available at bargain prices. The technique for purchasing Real Estate in Brazil is based on timing and a comprehension of currencies. Please check our fax-on-demand system for updated information on Real Estate conditions and currency fluctuations. Any information placed in this book regarding Brazilian Real Estate would be a disservice to the reader because of Brazil's constant battle with inflation and currency debasement. To fully comprehend what we are saying, it is necessary for the reader to recognize that when Brazilian prices multiplied 29 million times during the heaviest years of inflation what really happened was not an actual increase in price but a debasement of currency. What this would mean for us is more fully explained in the chapter on Real Estate, but in summary: we believe that there is a cycylical window of opportunity that occurs as currencies fluctuate in value vis a vis commodities. In the best of all scenarios, we can imagine ourselves purchasing a 29 million dollar property for one dollar. Will this actually occur? It is pretty unlikely. But it is the basic premise of our window of purchasing-opportunity theory.

Brazil's Real Estate, like Brazil itself is magnificent! Our advice about spending at least one year in any new country prior to purchasing Real Estate applies equally, if not more so, to Brazil. It goes without saying that any Real Estate purchased in Brazil must be done only after full consultation with a reputable attorney.

GETTING IN / STAYING IN

Please note that the information beginning on this page and continuing through page 139 is copied pretty much verbatim from the Consulate WebSite listed below. While some of it is incomprehensible government gibberish, we felt that it was valuable enough to include in this section.

Consulate General of Brazil in San Francisco
300 Montgomery Street, Suite 1160
San Francisco, CA 94104
Tel: (415) 981-8170   ext. 116
Fax: (415) 981-3628
email: brazil@crl.com
URL: http://www.crl.com/~brazil/index.htm

BUSINESS VISA

1. A Passport valid for a minimum of six months from the date of intended arrival in Brazil.
2. Two visa application forms provided by this Consulate, filled out, dated and signed by the applicant. Please type or print legibly.
3. Two passport photos size 2"x2". Snapshots are not accepted.
4. Letter (on letterhead) from the applicant's employer, addressed to the Brazilian Consulate General, stating the employee's name and title, how long he/she has worked for the company, the nature of business that he/she will be conducting while in the country, and the duration of stay. The company must also state that it will take full financial responsibility for the applicant while in Brazil.
5. If the applicant is self-employed, an additional letter will be required from his/her bank, containing financial references.
6. The Visa fee is US$ 60.00. There is and additional US$10.00 fee for visa requests not made in person by the applicant. Personal checks are not accepted.
7. This Consulate does not process visas by mail or courier service. We suggest that you come in person or use a visa service. We ask for two working days to process a visa.
8. The Business visa is good for multiple entries, for the duration of the visa. Each stay, however, may not exceed 90 days, unless extended by immigration authorities in Brazil.
9. The Brazilian Consulate General in San Francisco has jurisdiction over the States of Oregon, Washington, Alaska, as well as, over Northern California. Unless presented personally by the applicants, this Consulate will not process requests for business visas for employees of companies outside its jurisdiction.

The Brazilian Consulate General's working hours are from 9 to 5, from Monday through Friday. We are open to the public from 9:30 AM to 3:00 PM.

PERMANENT VISAS

Spouses and Minor Children of Brazilian Citizens

Foreign spouses of Brazilian citizens must present the following documents to this Consulate:

1. A letter addressed to the Brazilian Consul General stating that your spouse is a Brazilian citizen and that both of you wish to reside permanently in Brazil.

2. Marriage certificate: •if the wedding was performed in Brazil, make sure to enclose a certified copy (cópia autenticada) of the marriage certificate. •if the wedding was performed outside of Brazil, the marriage certificate must be registered at the Brazilian Consulate under whose jurisdiction it took place. •marriage certificates will be registered at the Brazilian Consulate General in San Francisco if performed in Northern California or in the States of Washington, Oregon or Alaska.

3. Passports •two copies of all pages of the applicant's passport. One of the copies must be authenticated by a Notary Public or, alternatively, at this Consulate General. Please note that there is a fee of US$5.00 per page to have copies certified at this Consulate •two copies of the Brazilian spouse's passport, following the same procedure as above for certified copies. •once the visa is approved, it will be necessary to present the original passport of the foreign spouse.

4. Birth certificate •two copies of the applicant's birth certificate, one of which must be legalized at the Brazilian Consulate under whose jurisdiction it was issued. •two certified copies of the Brazilian spouse birth certificate (cópia autenticada).

5. Identification Applicant: Two certified copies of a driver's license, one of which must be legalized at this Consulate.

Brazilian spouse: Original and two photocopies of Cédula de Identidade, Título de eleitor, Cartão de Identificação do Contribuinte (CIC), Certificado de Alistamento Militar (Brazilian husbands)

6. Proof of residence and of no-criminal records

Both the applicant and the Brazilian spouse must present one copy of a no-criminal record, which must be obtained from the police department at their place of residence and subsequently legalized at this Consulate.

Applicants must also show a proof that they have been living in their present address which must be in the jurisdiction of this Consulate General, for at least one year.

7. Proof of financial status/ Compromisso de manutenção/ Declaração de não contribuinte

The Brazilian spouse will also be required to present to this Consulate:

•documentation proving that he/she has sufficient means to support his/her family in Brazil (checking or savings bank accounts; proof of ownership of properties in Brazil, etc.) ; •a document, signed before a Notary Public or at this Consulate General, stating that he/she has the means to support his/her family in the Brazil. •if the Brazilian spouse is already in Brazil, please forward the original of a document called "ESCRITURA DE COMPROMISSO DE MANUTENÇÃO", drawn up before a Brazilian "Tabelião" (Notary Public), also stating that he/she will be financially responsible for his/her spouse (and children if there are any). •applicants must present a written job offer (PROMESSA DE EMPREGO) to either one of the spouses from a Brazilian company, drawn up before a Brazilian cartório. (Please, send the original). •a copy of his/her Brazilian income tax declaration for the previous fiscal year.

Brazilian citizens who did not file their income tax return with the Brazilian authorities during the previous fiscal year must sign a document attesting to this fact before a Notary Public or at this Consulate General.

NOTES: APPLICANTS WILL BE ADVISED OF THE TOTAL AMOUNT OF THE CONSULAR FEES CHARGED FOR THE LEGALIZATION OF THEIR DOCUMENTS, AFTER PRESENTING THEM TO THE CONSULAR OFFICER. ALL THE AFOREMENTIONED DOCUMENTS WILL BE FORWARDED TO THE BRAZILIAN AUTHORITIES FOR CONSIDERATION. CANDIDATES SHOULD BE PREPARED FOR A WAITING PERIOD OF AT LEAST 8 WEEKS BEFORE WE CAN ADVISE THEM IF THE VISA HAS BEEN GRANTED.

RETIRED PERSONS VISA

Retired individuals, age 60 or over, (and their families) who receive a minimum of US$ 2,000 per month in retirement benefits - which are required to be transferred each month to a bank in Brazil - may apply for a permanent visa. If there are more than 3 family members, US$ 2,000 per month must be added for each person. Please contact the Brazilian Consulate for more information.

WORK VISA

In accordance to Brazilian immigration regulations, foreigners who wish to work in Brazil must first secure a contract with a Brazilian company or with an educational institution, which will then place a formal request to the Immigration authorities at the Ministry of Labor (specifically, the Coordenação de Imigração), for the visa, known as "Temporary Visa V".

Once the visa is approved, this Consulate General will forward to the applicant instructions regarding the issuance of their visas.

In order to obtain information on jobs abroad, we suggest that candidates consult the following sources for jobs overseas: •Almanac for International Jobs and Careers, by Ron and Cary Krannich, 1994, Impact Publications. •American Jobs Abroad, by Victoria Harlow and Edward Knappmann, 1994, Visible Ink Press. •Magazine Transitions abroad, published every other month, can be ordered by calling (800) 293-0373

THIS CONSULATE GENERAL DOES NOT HAVE INFORMATION ON AVAILABILITY OF JOBS OR ON RELOCATION IN BRAZIL. IN ORDER TO OBTAIN SUCH INFORMATION, THE CANDIDATES SHOULD CONTACT THE BRAZILIAN COMPANY WHICH IS INTERESTED IN HIRING THEM.

These are the categories most likely to get permanent residence:•Industrialists and businessmen willing to invest US$ 200,000 in Brazil. The investment project will have to be approved by the CNI. •Individuals who have a work contract for at least 3 years, by an employer which is a Brazilian or a foreign company established in Brazil. The petition will have to be submitted to the Brazilian Labor Department: SIMIG - Secretaria de Imigração - Ministério do Trabalho - Esplanada dos Ministérios, Bloco F, 8 andar -- 70059 Brasília, DF Brazil telephone: (061) 226-2555 and 225-6842. •Individuals with post-graduate degrees and professionals with certification in highly specialized field which are in demand in Brazil at the time the application is submitted. A work contract maybe required.

STUDENT VISA

Requirement for a Student Visa
1. A passport, which must be valid for at least six months. 2. Three visa application forms (provided by this Consulate), filled out in type or print, dated and signed by the applicant.
3. Three photographs (2"x3"), front view.
4. Copy of the enrollment document at a Brazilian institution or of a letter conferring the applicant a grant to study in Brazil. Please indicate the length of the intended stay in Brazil.
5. Applicants under 18 years of age are required to present a notarized letter from both parents authorizing them to travel to Brazil unaccompanied.
6. Applicants over 18 years of age must also present a no-criminal record (validity: 90 days) to be obtained at the local police department.
7. Both the parent's consent letter and the no-criminal record must be authenticated at this Consulate. There is a consular fee of US$20.00 per document.
8. Proof of residence in the jurisdiction of this Consulate for at least one year.
9. A US$40.00 visa fee (please, no personal checks).

Notes: a) The issuance of the visa requires five working days. b) Bearers must enter Brazil no later than 90 days from the date the visa was issued. c) Upon arrival in Brazil bearers of a student visa whose stay exceeds 90 days must register with the Brazilian Federal Police (Delegacia de Estrangeiros).

VISAS -- CULTURAL

Temporary visas for Brazil may be granted to:
A - Students or professors, invited to participate in conferences, workshops, seminars, or who are members of a cultural or scientific mission. In order to qualify for such a visa they should not receive payment from a Brazilian source, with the exception of a traveling expense allowance.
B - University students attending extension courses or Master's and Ph.D. degrees programs in Brazil.
C - Trainees working in a company's Brazilian branch office, provided their salaries are paid outside of Brazil.
D - Volunteers working for charity institutions, churches or other similar activities. In order to qualify for such a visa, as in item a, above, they should not receive payment from a Brazilian source, with the exception of a traveling expense allowance.

STUDENT VISA

Requirement for a Student Visa

1. A passport, which must be valid for at least six months. 2. Three visa application forms (provided by this Consulate), filled out in type or print, dated and signed by the applicant.

3. Three photographs (2"x3"), front view.

4. Copy of the enrollment document at a Brazilian institution or of a letter conferring the applicant a grant to study in Brazil. Please indicate the length of the intended stay in Brazil.

5. Applicants under 18 years of age are required to present a notarized letter from both parents authorizing them to travel to Brazil unaccompanied.

6. Applicants over 18 years of age must also present a no-criminal record (validity: 90 days) to be obtained at the local police department.

7. Both the parent's consent letter and the no-criminal record must be authenticated at this Consulate. There is a consular fee of US$20.00 per document.

8. Proof of residence in the jurisdiction of this Consulate for at least one year.

9. A US$40.00 visa fee (please, no personal checks).

Notes: a) The issuance of the visa requires five working days. b) Bearers must enter Brazil no later than 90 days from the date the visa was issued. c) Upon arrival in Brazil bearers of a student visa whose stay exceeds 90 days must register with the Brazilian Federal Police (Delegacia de Estrangeiros).

VISAS -- CULTURAL

Temporary visas for Brazil may be granted to:

A - Students or professors, invited to participate in conferences, workshops, seminars, or who are members of a cultural or scientific mission. In order to qualify for such a visa they should not receive payment from a Brazilian source, with the exception of a traveling expense allowance.

B - University students attending extension courses or Master's and Ph.D. degrees programs in Brazil.

C - Trainees working in a company's Brazilian branch office, provided their salaries are paid outside of Brazil.

D - Volunteers working for charity institutions, churches or other similar activities. In order to qualify for such a visa, as in item a, above, they should not receive payment from a Brazilian source, with the exception of a traveling expense allowance.

TOURIST VISA

Requirements for Tourist Visa.

1. Passport, valid for at least six months from the date of intended arrival in Brazil.

2. One visa application form provided by this Consulate, typed or printed, dated and signed by the applicant. Parents should fill out and sign applications for their own children who are minors.

3. One passport photograph, size 2"x2", either black and white or color, front view. Snapshots are not accepted.

4. A round trip ticket or a statement from a travel agency, addressed to the Brazilian Consulate, containing the name of passenger, itinerary, flight number and arrival/departure dates.

5. Proof that the applicant has sufficient means to support him/herself during his/her stay in Brazil (e.g. a valid credit card, traveller's checks, or a bank statement).

6. Proof that the applicant is currently employed.

7. For minors under 18 years of age traveling alone, a notarized letter of authorization signed by both parents is required. If the minor is traveling with only one parent, the other parent must write a notarized authorization granting his/her spouse permission to take the child with him or her. There is a US$20.00 fee for the legalization of either authorization.

8. A Certificate of vaccination against polio is required for children between ages of three months and six years. If the child cannot be inoculated, a notarized letter from the child's physician will be required.

9. Visa fees are waived for holders of US passports. As the requirements vary for each country, please ask for instructions if you are not a US citizen.

10. The Consular Officers will only receive applications from candidates who are able to comply with the above requirements. We request your cooperation on that matter.

NOTES:

A) Tourists must enter Brazil within 90 days of issuance of the visa. Please, do not apply for a visa earlier than one month before your planned departure.

B) Initially, the tourist visa is valid for a 90 day stay in Brazil. Applicants who wish to remain in the country for 90 additional days should request an extension at the local Brazilian Police Department (Delegacia de Estrangeiros). Tourist visas, although valid for a total of five years, allow for a maximum stay of 180 days per calendar year in Brazil.

Please, remember that bearers of tourist visas should not engage in gainful employment.

C) This Consulate does not process visas by mail or courier service. We suggest that you come in person or use a visa service. We request two working days to process the visa.

D) The Brazilian Consulate General in San Francisco has jurisdiction over Northern California and the States of Oregon, Washington, and Alaska.

E) Unless presented in person, this Consulate does not process tourist visas of applicants residing ouside our jurisdiction.

WEB SITE OF THE CONSULATE GENERAL OF BRAZIL IN SAN FRANCISCO:
URL: http://www.crl.com/~brazil/index.htm

Consulate General of Brazil in San Francisco
300 Montgomery Street, Suite 1160
San Francisco, CA 94104
Tel: (415) 981-8170
Fax: (415) 981-3628
email at: brazil@crl.com

Note that the list below is a list of available online Consulate information at:
URL: http://www.crl.com/~brazil/secom.htm

- **Departamento de Promoção Comercial do Ministério das Relações Exteriores**
- **Investment Opportunities**
- **Exporters Register**
- **Calendar of Events**
- **Services Companies Search**
- **Company Formation in Brazil**
- **Trade Points**
- **Mercosul**
- **Special Service Codes**
- **The Harmonized System**
- **Focal Points**
- **Trade Promotion Bureaus**
- **Ministério da Fazenda (The Treasury)**
- **The Trade Promotion Bureau at the Consulate General In San Francisco**
- **The SIPRI Program**
- **Business Visas**
- **The Economy**
- **Brazil as an Emerging Market**
- **Banks and other Financial Institutions**
- **Information at the US Department of Commerce**
- **The "Real" Plan (The Economic Stabilization Program)**
- **Privatization •An Assessment of the "Real" Plan (March 1995)**
- **Reducing the "Brazil Cost"**
- **MERCOSUL**
- **Doing Business with Brazil**
- **A Guide for the Foreign Investor**
- **Public Sevice Concessions**
- **Foreign Trade Information System**
- **Environmental Law and Business Opportunities**
- **Extractive Industries in the Amazon**
- **GATT**
- **NAFTA**
- **IBGE - Instituto Brasileiro de Geografia e Estatística.**
- **PBD - Programa Brasileiro do Design**
- **The São Paulo Stock Exchange**
- **The Rio de Janeiro Stock Exchange**
- **The Commodities Market**

US STATE DEPARTMENT TRAVEL INFORMATION

COUNTRY DISCRIPTION: Brazil has a developing economy. Facilities for tourism are good in the major cities, but vary in quality in remote areas.

ENTRY REQUIREMENTS: A passport and visa are required. Brazilian visas must be obtained in advance as immigration authorities will not allow entry into Brazil without a valid visa. Minors (under 18) traveling alone, with one parent or with a third party must present written authorization by the absent parent(s) or legal guardian, specifically granting permission to travel alone, with one parent or with a third party. This authorization must be notarized, authenticated by the Brazilian embassy or nearest consulate, and translated into Portuguese. For current information concerning entry and customs requirements for Brazil, travelers may contact the Brazilian Embassy at 3009 Whitehaven St., N.W., Washington, D.C. 20008, Tel: (202) 745-2828 or the nearest consulate in Los Angeles, San Francisco, Boston, Houston, Miami, New York, Chicago or San Juan.

MEDICAL FACILITIES: Medical care varies in quality, particularly in remote areas. Doctors and hospitals often expect immediate cash payment for health services. U.S. medical insurance is not always valid outside the United States. Medicare/Medicaid do not provide payment of medical services outside the United States. In some cases, medical insurance with specific overseas and medical evacuation coverage has proven useful. For additional health information, travelers may contact the Centers for Disease Control and Prevention's international travelers hotline at (404) 332-4559.

CRIME INFORMATION: The incidence of crime against tourists tends to be greater in areas surrounding hotels, discotheques, bars, nightclubs and other similar establishments that cater to visitors, especially at dusk and during the evening hours. Kidnappings of wealthy residents and carjackings of luxury and four-wheel-drive vehicles are increasing. Several Brazilian cities have established specialized tourist police units to patrol areas frequented by tourists.

Rio de Janeiro, Brazil's most popular tourist destination, understandably experiences a proportionately high amount of crime against tourists. While still very serious, the rate of crime has lessened somewhat due to the deployment of tourist police units in 1992. Crime against U.S. citizen tourists generally takes the form of street thefts and robberies adjacent to the main beach areas of Rio.

Sao Paulo has noted a recent increase in street crime where guns are involved. This has occurred especially in the downtown areas. Additionally, Sao Paulo has reported thefts at its international airport (Guarulhos) involving carry-on luggage or briefcases which had been set down, sometimes for a moment. Arriving and departing travelers should be especially vigilant and take the necessary precautions at this and other Brazilian airports.

The loss or theft of a U.S. passport abroad should be reported immediately to the local police and the nearest U.S. Embassy or Consulate. Useful information on guarding valuables and protecting personal security while traveling abroad is provided in the Department of State pamphlet, "A Safe Trip Abroad," which is available from the Superintendent of Documents, U.S. Government Printing Office, Washington, D.C. 20402. Also available from the same address is the Department of State publication, "Tips for travelers to Central and South America."

DRUG PENALTIES: U.S. citizens are subject to the laws of the country in which they are traveling. Penalties in Brazil for possession, use and trafficking in illegal drugs are strict, and convicted offenders can expect lengthy jail sentences and fines.

AVIATION OVERSIGHT: In November 1992, the U.S. Federal Aviation Administration assessed Brazil's civil aviation authority as in compliance with international aviation safety oversight standards for Brazil's carriers operating to and from the U.S. The same level of safety oversight would typically be applied to operations to other destinations. For further information, travelers may contact the Department of Transportation at 1-800- 322-7873.

REGISTRATION/ EMBASSY LOATIONS: U.S. citizens may register with the consular section of the U.S. Embassy or consulates and may also obtain updated information on travel and security within Brazil.

The U.S. Embassy is located in Brasilia at Avenida das Nacoes, Lote 3, tel. (55-61) 321-7272. There are consulates in Rio de Janeiro at Avenida Presidente Wilson 147, tel. (55-21) 292-7117; in Sao Paulo at Rua Padre Joao Manoel 933, tel. (55-11) 881-6511; in Porto Alegre at Rua Coronel Genuino 421 (9th flr.), tel. (55-51) 226-4288; and at Recife at Rua Goncalves Maia 163, tel. (55-81) 221-1412.

There are also consular agencies in Belem at Travessa Padre Eutiquio 1309, tel. (55-91) 223-0800; in Manaus at Rua Recife 1010, Adrianopolis, tel. (55- 92) 234-4546; in Salvador da Bahia at Avenida Antonio Carlos Magalhaes, S/N Edificio Cidadella Center, Suite 410, Candeal, tel. (55-71) 358-9166; and in Fortaleza at the Instituto Brasil-Estados Unidos (IBEU), Rua Nogueira Acioly 891, Aldeota, tel. (55-85) 252-1539.

CHAPTER NINE

REPUBLICA DE CHILE

SALT STARS ICE EARTH & FIRE

*"The sea flowers all year round. Its rose is white. Its petals
are salt stars. ...everything flowers"*
-Pablo Neruda

Neruda wrote those lines at **Chascona**, (meaning: "Woman with the Tousled
Hair"), it was the place in time and space that he loved more than any other. Its
name was derived from a lovers rebellious hair. We thought it might be a good
way to open our section on Chile, the long thin land whose spirit has again been
born anew. Chile's troubled past is not a secret; a 1982 popular film, *Missing*,
which starred Jack Lemon and Sissy Spacek depicted the violent coup that
overthrew the socialist government of Salvador Allende. For the next sixteen
years of dictatorial rule under Agusto Pinochet, Chile's lack of freedom became
an international *cause célèbre*. Finally, in March of 1990, Chile returned to
democracy. With each passing year Chile improves, which in itself is wonderful, but what is better is that it's improvement has grown and continuously
grows in a way both extemporaneous and exponential. It is not just as good as
it once was, it is better. Everything flowers.

It is difficult for us to imagine a better destination-country for a creative expatriate. Chile is really on a roll. A country that didn't even seem like a contender
has become the champion of South America. Not only that, if one ignores the
air pollution of Santiago, it's a terrific place environmentally. It's got it all; ski
resorts, lakes, mountains, rivers, great beaches, great wine, good schools &
Universities, (the literacy rate at 96%, is one the world's highest), good telecommunications, open access to the web, an understanding of what makes business work, plenty of culture, ranchlands, forests and enough snow-capped volcanos to keep a vulcanist-skier eternally happy. Chile has such dynamic environmental diversity that it may well be a geographical cross-section of the world.
Chile has such successful commerce that it is rivaling heavyweight countries
that once scorned it as a mining camp at the ends of the earth. Chile is nobody's
fool. We like her.

Chile is open for business. Both the consumer and the industrial markets are open and eager for imported products; so someone who wants to import into Chile should investigate this potentially lucrative opportunity. Using Chile as our base for importing goods from out of the United States and into Chile and goods out of Chile back to established contacts inside the United States offers tremendous possibilities. With such a fast growing per capita GDP, Chile should be high on the list of viable countries of choice. Todays smart expat should be looking for any upward moving market such as Chile's. A country with more and more of its consumers arriving at the position of being able to afford more consumer luxuries with each passing day. Who would be better suited to understanding the concept of luxury, and providing the access to the commodities of luxury than an American expat? Chile is filled with many thousands of people who for the first time are able to look beyond the rudimentary necessities of survival towards luxury items. Chile may represent a sellers paradise for the creative expat. Additionally, with its unrestricted access to the World Wide Web Chile is an excellent location for anyone who wants to be involved in Internet commerce. Knowledge about computer hardware or software would also be a very important asset in Chile. Additionally; it seems obvious to us, that in the field of computer-technology, some of the best and easiest money to be made is away from the crowd. Rather than lamenting a multitude of missed opportunities, we could be spending our time creating some exciting new opportunities. Few people inside of a vibrant nation use the old cliché which states that there's more room at the bottom than there is at the top. The excitement of opportunity inside of an upwards moving economy is like a breath of fresh air. Old bromides and clichés apply best to those who enjoy being forever stuck inside of a stagnant nation part way to the middle of their dreams.

Two factors we might mention is that the existing Chilean business community has developed close trading ties with Taiwan, Japan, Australia, New Zealand, as well as several other Asian nations. Also, Saudi Arabia has entered into the Chilean market through the action of helping Chile pay off some external debt that Chile was buried under. What Chile gave to the Saudi's in exchange was ownership-interest in a number of Chilean companies mostly engaged in fishing, forestry, and fruit packing. It seems to us that the Saudi's obviously aim is to insure agricultural proficiency in the coming millennium. It also gives us a very secure feeling about Chiles future knowing that the Saudi's are playing a long range Chilean trump card. How an expat can make a play on these factors is entirely up to the degree of thought we put into the field of interrelated issues. Strategy is the science and art of employing forethought, as opposed to the artlessness of simply stumbling along blindly.

As we have mentioned elsewhere, the majority of Web Sites in the world are either totally or partially in English. Sometimes the English is comical, but it is used anyway, because English has become the language of information and commerce. Two other languages will be important in the coming millennium; Chinese and Spanish. Expats moving to Chile will need to learn Spanish, but it is doubtful we will be speaking it like a native for many years. We should be able to learn to speak it well enough to function within a year of immersion; for there is nothing like immersion as a means of instruction. Depending on our facility with English we should always be slightly better at working in English then someone who grew up immersed in Spanish. Our psycho-automatic command of English, coupled with some capacity in another language is an asset, especially on the Internet. If the Internet is a labyrinth, English is its cipher. We should note that we have not seen much Chinese on the Web. Even the Home Page of the Tsinghua University of Beijing is mostly in English. Admittedly, we do see some pages in Japanese, but we know, and we're sure the Japanese know, that someone in the Czech City of Prague, or in Rio de Janerio, Brazil, is going to be a thousand times more likely to read English then Japanese. Conji, as lovely as it is to look at, is simply too cumbersome a written text to use internationally, in that it requires one image for each concept it wishes to express. (which is why the Koreans abandoned it.) If the Japanese want to interact globally, they, like everyone else, will more than likely have to use English on the Internet. We suspect that few if any Japanese companies are still foolish enough to use a Japanese advertising agency to sell inside the United States. For the Japanese have realized, as should we, that isn't just the language that is different; its the nuance, which is a subtlety that may at times be next to impossible for speakers of another language-culture to grasp. What we are saying, poorly perhaps, is that speaking and writing English is an asset to an expat. It has become the international language. Every other language we learn, Spanish, Japanese, Chinese, French, Italian; will all act to increase our global capacities, but English as the global language is here to stay, even with computerized translators available. Computers understand the definition, but never the meaning. Meaning is a human capacity. We believe that ultimately there will only be two languages on the Internet; English and French.

Copper continues to be the major Chilean export, accounting for about 43% of the export total. Agricultural products follow, with 30% of the export market; and what we mean by agriculture, is timber/pulp products, fish products, nuts, wine, fruit, as well as frozen foods. Even though the full list of export products totals more than 1500 items, (and the list is growing), the majority of the remaining 27% is comprised of gold, other minerals, women's apparel, some biotechnological products, and industrial machinery. It is obvious that mining remains the largest industry in Chile. In addition to owning approximately 20% of the worlds copper reserves, Chile also has significant deposits of molybdenum, rhenium, sodium nitrate, lithium, and coal. The forestry and related wood pulp and paper manufacturing is fairly large. Chile has 1.1 million hectares of radiata pine forests. Commercial fishing and fish processing is an industry that is expanding 10% per year and it is the fastest growing export segment of the past decade, accounting for 13% of Chilean exports.

HOT SECTORS

The hot sectors for expats to consider are:

✓ **TELECOMMUNICATIONS, TELEPHONY, & COMPUTER-TECHNOL-OGY** There is so much opportunity in this sector in Chile that it goes to the front to the class. If we know what we're doing in any of these fields we should be booking our travel reservations.

✓ **FOOD PROCESSING, packaging**, (enjoying an 8 to 10 percent annual growth) We'd take a look at items like sorbé, (with all the excellent fruit in Chile, this might be a natural), jams, jellies, and so forth. Anything that would capitalize on Chiles great agricultural bonanza combined with some noveau-American culinary innovation would probably create a winning product for both domestic and export market.

✓ **The AGRI-BUSINESS** is growing at 32% a year. We suspect that most of the agri-business is of the 'tried and true' variety. With Asia buying so much from Chile, some innovations directed at that market would be worth looking into.

✓ **SHIPBUILDING** requires heavy capitalization, but boat building is within reach.

✓ **WOODWORKING** equipment and wood products.

✓ Additional vacancies exist in **medical and scientific instruments and equipment, safety and security equipment**, (this market is quadrupling yearly).

✓ **ENVIRONMENTAL PRODUCTS** Sad to say, that pristine, unpolluted Chile has a Capital with some of the worst air pollution in the world. Santiago's air pollution is a disaster. Chile wants the problem solved, which spells bonanza for anyone with the wherewithal to design and/or sell pollution control products.

The government of Chile would like to address the following problems: they would like to build new and better roads, refurbish the ports, improve and expand the rail system, (access to the southern section of Chile is poor, and the south is partially isolated from the rest of the country), improve existing water pumping and purification systems and build new ones where they are needed, build new and improve existing secondary and primary schools, improve health care, develop worker training programs, build new and improve existing sewage drainage and sanitizing facilities, build low income housing, build shopping malls. What all this says to the alert reader, is that everything the average American knows about, understands, and takes for granted is needed in Chile. It is simple to say we could go back in time and create what we now take for granted, however the innovation didn't occur to us or we would have done so. As expats, we can go back in time by emigrating to another country and in that way take advantage of the knowledge that we ourselves already do possess but too often ignore and take for granted.

STUPID STORY TIME

We could name anything and it would be of value in Chile.
EXAMPLE: Air-conditioning and refrigeration equipment, the knowledge of how to repair it, the knowledge of how to install it. Let us explore this avenue just as an example of possible directions. (I'd appreciate it if the reader will indulge my rather simplistic example, I'm a simplistic kind of guy.)

[1] It would be quite simple for any American to take a few community college courses in air-conditioning and refrigeration repair, an opportunity we take for granted.

[2] Many manufacturers in the United States would jump at the chance to have a sales representative in a foreign country. By contracting an agreement with two or three good manufacturers, to export their products to Chile, here is what we could accomplish just with these two simple steps:

● Sell air-conditioners and refrigeration in Chile.
● Install air-conditioners and refrigeration in Chile.
● Teach air-conditioner and refrigeration repair in Chile.
● Repair air-conditioners and refrigeration in Chile.
● Learn to manufacture air-conditioners and refrigeration in Chile.
● Develop a relationship with a large manufacturer in the United States which allows us to manufacture their air-conditioner and refrigeration product in Chile. It is even conceivable to us that we could purchase used equipment in the United States, (where it does exist), refurbish it, and ship it to our own company in Chile for resale (where it is scarce). If we did this, we'd want to make sure we guaranteed our product. We could hire any number of refrigeration and air-conditioner repairman, (who earn nearly nothing in the United States) and have them work for us. Or, hire one or two good teachers to train our Chilean employees. But why go on with this walking fantasy, we believe that the point is made. We also believe that this simplistic approach could be used universally. The steps are: Look at a country. Analyze what it needs. Calculate the number of different approaches possible to meet those needs. Calculate what it would take to set our plan in motion.

We are not implying that it is simple, we are implying that **tremendous opportunity exists**.

Chile has not yet developed a full network of **Free Trade Zones (FTZ's)**, and only two have thus far been developed. Chile is also holding back on joining **MERCOSUR**, (see sections on Argentina, Uruguay, and Brazil). Chiles reasoning is based on several factors; but the ultimate reasoning is that it may not be to Chiles best interest to belong to Mercosur ever though Brazil and Argentina are Chiles third and fourth largest trading partners. Chile is doing pretty well trading with the Asian market and Chiles Pacific seaboard location lends itself well to that end. Correspondingly, both Argentina and Brazil are much larger than Chile and Chile could conceivably end up not getting the best end of any sort of economic commitments such as Mercosur entails. We predict greater and greater cooperation between South American countries in the coming decades. Working together the nations of South America will make a formidable economic force. note: It is interesting that the combined human population of Mercosur nations would be around 200 million in a land area 25% larger than the United States [pop: 260 million] and 20% larger than China [pop:1.2 billion]

MONEY

CURRENCY: Peso ($1.00 = 410.70 Chilean Peso as of this writing.
EXCHANGE RATES: As at December 31, 1995 the observed rate closed at Ch$407,95=US$1, compared to Ch$404,09 one year earlier, that is, a 0.9% devaluation. The observed rate is the actual average between buying and selling for the previous day and is the rate used in the so called Formal Exchange Market. The values on the Informal Exchange Market were very similar. The fact that inflation was 8.2 percent and devaluation 0.9 percent, has meant a continued increase in the strength of the peso compared to the US dollar
FOREIGN EXCHANGE POLICIES: Most of the foreign exchange policies remained unchanged during 1995. However, in July 1995 the Central Bank eliminated the requirement to bring export proceeds back into the country. They may now be kept indefinitely outside Chile. Before that change, all export proceeds had to be brought back into the country within 270 days of shipment.
INFLATION: Inflation for 1995 was 8.2%, in line with the Government's target of 8 percent. Inflation is expected to be around 6.5 percent in 1996.

ECONOMY

ECONOMY: Chile is the most prosperous country in South America. The currency (Peso) is even appreciating against the dollar. The GDP has grown annually since 1984, (and in the 90's it has grown by anywhere from at least 5.8% to 10% annually) The government has run a surplus since 1990 and has simultaneously increased its expenditures proportionately on health, education and housing. Inflation is under control which makes the soaring GDP more significant. Unemployment is below 5% and perhaps best of all per capita income is going up. Chile has even run a trade surplus with Japan, something which most nations appear incapable of achieving, including the US. Poverty is gradually becoming a thing of the past thanks to some very innovative programs which are continuously aimed at reducing it even further. Chile remains the world's largest producer of copper. But times have changed. By looking at its Internet Web Sites we quickly become aware we are looking at a country cognizant of the future and not some sort of backwater mining outpost on the moon. Chile also remains heavily dependent on agriculture for its export revenue, which is a pretty good situation for Chile in our opinion, because its entirely possible that agriculture (and water) may become a form of money at some point in the next millennium.*

*Agriculture: accounts for about 7% of GDP (including fishing and forestry); major exporter of fruit, fish, and timber products; major crops - wheat, corn, grapes, beans, sugar beets, potatoes, deciduous fruit; livestock products - beef, poultry, wool; self-sufficient in most foods; 1991 fish catch of 6.6 million metric tons.

FACTS AT A GLANCE

GDP: $96 billion (1993 est.)

GDP PER CAPITA: We have seen widely disparate figures, ranging from: a.] $2,500 (1991 Cambridge) b.] $ 7,000 (CIA 1993 est) c.] $8,410 (Freedom House 1996 PPP). We would guess that the GDP is somewhere in between these figures in the $5,000 to $6,000 range. The most current figure: $5,120 is one that we've seen in recent news releases on **CHIP On-Line News Service** from Santiago. CHIP's Web Page:URL: http://www.chip.cl/

COUNTRY REPORTS Economy Overview: Chile has a prosperous, essentially free market economy, with the degree of government intervention varying according to the philosophy of the different regimes. Under the center-left government of President AYLWIN, which took power in March 1990, spending on social welfare rose steadily. At the same time business investment, exports, and consumer spending also grew substantially. The new president, FREI, who took office in March 1994, has emphasized social

spending even more. Growth in 1991-94 has averaged 6.5% annually, with an estimated one million Chileans having moved out of poverty in the last four years. Copper remains vital to the health of the economy; Chile is the world's largest producer and exporter of copper. Success in meeting the government's goal of sustained annual growth of 5% depends on world copper prices, the level of confidence of foreign investors and creditors, and the government's own ability to maintain a conservative fiscal stance.

National product: GDP - purchasing power parity - $97.7 billion (1994 est.)

National product real growth rate: 4.3% (1994 est.)

National product per capita: $7,010 (1994 est.)

Inflation rate (consumer prices): 8.7% (1994 est.)

Relative costs:

- Cheap meal: US$5
- Restaurant meal: US$15
- Cheap room: US$10
- Hotel room: $US25

Unemployment rate: 6% (1994 est.)

💻 TELECOMMUNICATIONS & THE WORLD WIDE WEB

"Traditionally, a researcher in Chile works with papers published last year, written three years ago and discussed five years ago. Now he or she can take part in the discussion, or at least "listen" to it."

WWW: As already mentioned, there seems to be a proliferation of very good Web Sites in Chile. In all of South America, only Brazil has more Internet-connected networks then Chile. As of May 1995 there were a total of 102 known Internet connected networks; we would guess that number has increased significantly since then. There are at least nine known Access Providers in Chile. As is usually the case in other growing and developing Internet Access locations around the world, most of the early servers (and developers), were the Universities. As in many countries, one very good site to locate is Chile's Internet Sun Site, which is at: http://sunsite.dcc.uchile.cl/ This page gives access to some very good information sites, including most of the major newspapers and magazines, the cultural sites; such as Museums, Libraries, Art Galleries, the Services, Industry, Web Site Providers, Weather, Business and Commerce Indices, Science, Government & Law information sites, Universities, Tourism, and a large number of local Search Sites available for current information. The word in Spanish for search is Buscar, and directions for entering a page are Volver, meaning to go to, and Vuelve to return to. We estimate that about 30% of the Sites and Pages are in English. And even those in Spanish are laid out logically enough that even the most rudimentary understanding of the language might suffice. The Interconnectivity is so good and the Sites so interesting, that one could easily spend a week just surfing the Republic of Chile. According to the U.S. Department of Commerce office in Santiago, Chile is one of the top three users of the Internet in Latin America. Within the first six months of 1994, usage of this service jumped 170 percent, the highest growth rate in Latin America. They have about a hundred servers in Chile.

INTERESTING SITES

The Chilean Internet Connection
URL: http://sunsite.dcc.uchile.cl/chile/cl/inet93/paper.html
An interesting and scholarly discussion of the Internet in Chile.
Except: "The Internet growth in recent years is impressive, and a large part of the planet is now interconnected [3]. This global network presents outstanding opportunities for under-developed countries, which have now access to a wealth of online information, including live discussions on research and application topics [10]. The main problem that countries like Chile face is the distance separating them from the technology, and in particular, from the decision-making process. Traditionally, a researcher in Chile works with papers published last year, written three years ago and discussed five years ago. Now he or she can take part in the discussion, or at least "listen" to it."

U.S. Embassy - Santiago, Chile
Use this home page to find out more information on American Foreign Policy, issues of concern for Americans living in Chile, and visa information, as well as for connections to other World Wide Web sites that might be of interest. **URL:** http://www.rdc.cl/usemb/

U.S. Embassy Address Avenida Andrés Bello 280 Santiago, Chile   Phone: [56] (2) 232-2600
Embassy Fax: [56] (2) 330-3710   Commercial Section Fax: [56] (2) 330-3172
Consular Section Fax: [56] (2) 330-3005   Economic/Political Section Fax: [56] (2) 330-3191

The CHIP News, a daily English-language summary of Chile's most important national, business and mining news, featuring a state-of-the art search engine to help you research Chile's news from 1990 to the present. **URL:** http://www.chip.cl/
Steve Anderson, Publisher
Tel: (562) 777-5376
Fax: (562) 735-2267
email: anderson@chip.mic.cl
PO BOX 53331, Correo Central, Santiago, Chile.
NOTE: There are several Spanish language newspapers of note inside Chile. Those with Internet access can bring them up at: URL: http://www.business1.com/cacc/english/chilinks.htm

UT-LANIC Resources in Chile
URL: http://lanic.utexas.edu/la/chile/
WWW Servers Science and Technology Travel & Tourism News & Periodicals Network and Information Services Government Education Business & Economy Arts & Humanities Academic Research Resources

CHILE SCHOOLS
List of schools in Chile: Regular Universities
Plus: Learn Spanish & French in Chile
Country Information for Chile WorldWide Classroom
Box 1166 - Milwaukee, WI 53201-1166, USA
Phone: (414) 224-3476 - FAX: (414) 224-3466
email: study@worldwide.edu

Chile Business Directory
Chilnet S.A.
Av. Ricardo Lyon 1789 Providencia,
Santiago, Chile.
Telefono 56-2-2516440
fax   56-2-2514187
email: info@chilnet.cl
URL: http://www.chilnet.cl/

Internet en Chile
URL: http://sunsite.dcc.uchile.cl/chile/cl/index.html

Chilean-American Chamber of Commerce
San Francisco, California U.S.A.
URL: http://www.business1.com/cacc/english/welcome.htm
See video and audio clips of a recent Chamber-sponsored event using the latest in Internet technology -- U.S. - Chilean Relations: Expanding Trade Opportunities in the Americas: Live broadcast and text of speech by the U.S. Ambassador to Chile, Gabriel Guerra-Mondragón in San Francisco, California.
Contact the Chamber at:
Chilean-American Chamber of Commerce
870 Market St., Suite 1058
San Francisco, California 94102 USA
tel. 415-391-7174 fax 415-982-2384
A newly established chamber formed in recognition of the expanding business opportunites that exist between the United States and Chile.

A Latin World - Latin America on the Net
URL: http://www.latinworld.com/
A directory of Internet resources on Latin America and the Caribbean.

Internet Resources for Latin America
URL: http://lib.nmsu.edu/subject/bord/laguia/lag1.html

Embassy of Chile
1732 Massachusetts Avenue, NW, Washington D.C. 20036;
telephone (202) 785-1746; fax (202) 887-5579.
URL: http://minnie.iafrica.com/~chile/english/chile.htm

Communications in Chile (statistics)
Telephone system: 768,000 telephones; modern telephone system based on extensive microwave radio relay facilities intercity: extensive microwave radio relay links and 3 domestic satellite stations international: 2 INTELSAT (Atlantic Ocean) earth stations Radio: broadcast stations:
AM 159, FM 0, shortwave 11 Television: broadcast stations: 131

FREEDOM HOUSE RATING FOR CHILE

FREEDOM HOUSE RATING:
Political Rights: ② Civil Rights: ②
Democratic institutions are better established in Chile than in any other country in South America. The press media has been almost fully restored to full levels of freedom. Freedom House notes improvements in accountability. If what we've seen on the Internet is any indication, freedom of expression is alive and well in Chile. It is nice to able to speak of a country so much improved as Chile.
We hope it continues.

US STATE DEPARTMENT COUNSULAR TRAVEL SHEET

COUNTY DESCRIPTION: Chile has a stable government and a strong economy. Civil disorder is rare. Facilities for tourism vary according to price and area.

ENTRY REQUIREMENTS: A passport is required. U.S. citizens do not need a visa for a three-month stay. However, those considering scientific, technical or mountaineering activities in areas classified as frontier areas are required to obtain authorization from the Chilean government. Requests for authorization must be presented to Chilean authorities at least 90 days prior to the beginning of the expedition. The portions of Antarctica claimed by Chile are exempt from these pre-approval requirements. For current information concerning entry and customs requirements for Chile, travelers can contact the Chilean Embassy at 1732 Massachusetts Avenue N.W., Washington, D.C. 20036; tel: (202) 785-1746 or the nearest consulate in Los Angeles, Miami, Philadelphia, New York, Houston, or Chicago.

MEDICAL FACILITIES: Medical care is good but may not meet U.S. standards. Doctors and hospitals often expect immediate cash payment for health services. U.S. medical insurance is not always valid outside the United States. Supplemental medical insurance, which includes specific overseas coverage, is highly recommended. In-country medical evacuation from outlying areas to Santiago costs $2000 (U.S.) or more. Cost for international evacuations begin at about $10,000 (U.S.). For travelers to the Antarctic, additional insurance to cover the cost of air evacuation specifically from that remote region is strongly recommended. In the event of illness, injury or even death, the cost of evacuation from the Antarctic region to Santiago can exceed $10,000 (U.S.). This is in addition to the evacuation costs indicated above. For additional health information travelers can contact the Centers for Disease Control's international travelers' hotline at (404) 332-4559.

CRIME INFORMATION: In Santiago and other large cities, thieves thrive on rush hour crowding on the street and aboard public transportation. Persons wearing expensive looking jewelry or carrying luggage or cameras are particular targets. Walking in the downtown area after dark, or on weekends in the late afternoon, even in the well-traveled areas, is considered risky.

DRUG PENALITIES: U.S. citizens are subject to the laws of the country in which they are traveling. Penalties in Chile for possession and trafficking in illegal drugs are strict, and convicted offenders can expect lengthy jail sentences and fines.

ADOPTIONS: The Consular Section of the U.S. Embassy can provide updated information on Chilean adoption procedures and on immigrant visa matters related to adoptions. Consular officers are not authorized to act as agents on behalf of Americans seeking to adopt Chilean children. Additional information is available by writing the Office of Citizens Consular Services, CA/OCS/CCS, Room 4817, Department of State, Washington, D.C. 20520, or by telephoning (202) 647-3712.

EMBASSY LOCATION / REGISTRATION: Americans who register with the Consular Section of the U.S. Embassy at 2800 Andres Bello, Vitacura, Santiago; telephone (562) 232-2600, can obtain updated information on travel and security within Chile.

FACTS AT A GLANCE (STATISTICS ON CHILE)

ECONOMIC STATISTICS

LOCAL NAME: Conventional long form: Republica de Chile
TIME ZONE: GMT-4
AREA: 292,958 sq mi (not including territory in Antartica) [slightly larger than France]
STATUS: Republic
DATE OF INDEPENDENCE: 1818
CAPITAL: Santiago (pop: 4,400,000 est.)

PEOPLE STATISTICS

POPULATION: 14,251,000 (est. #1) Population: 14,161,216 (July 1995 est.WFB)
Age Structure:
0-14 years: 29% (female 2,014,877; male 2,099,450)
15-64 years: 64% (female 4,574,947; male 4,529,251)
65 years and over: 7% (female 549,385; male 393,306) (July 1995 est.)
Population growth rate: 1.49% (1995 est.)
Birth rate: 20.29 births/1,000 population (1995 est.)
Death rate: 5.42 deaths/1,000 population (1995 est.)
Net migration rate: 0 migrant(s)/1,000 population (1995 est.)
Infant mortality rate: 14.3 deaths/1,000 live births (1995 est.)
Life expectancy at birth:
total population: 74.88 years
male: 71.89 years
female: 78.01 years (1995 est.)
Totality fertility rate: 2.49 children born/woman (1995 est.)
LANGUAGES: Spanish (official)
ETHIC GROUPS: European and European-Indian: (95%) Indian: (3%)
RELIGIONS: Catholic: (89%) Protestant: (10%) there is a small Jewish and Muslim minority.

There is an uneven distribution between urban and rural sectors of the population. Eighty-four percent of Chile's population is in the urban areas. Chileans have a strong cultural background. About two-thirds of Chileans are mestizos (mixed Indian and European descent). A small amount of Chilean ancestry comes from Germans, Swiss, Italians, British, French, and Yugoslavs who settled in Chile during the 19th and 20th centuries. Some Araucanian Indians still reside in the forests south of the Bío Bío River. While most of these people still retain their native languages, the official language of Chile is Spanish and eighty percent of the population practices the Roman Catholic faith.

TALL & SLENDER

In summary Chile has become one of the strongest economies in the entire world. The explanation that we have heard for this occurrence is rather interesting.

The U.S. Government withdrew it's Foreign Aid from Chile because of the excesses of General Pinochet. (This is verifiable fact.) The lack of U.S. handouts left the country of Chile no other course of action other than to excel. The lack of burdensome debt furthered their ascent. We think the lesson is for the citizens of the U.S. who have been footing the tremendous foreign aid bill being run up by government employees in Washington.

Chile as we've pointed out has more than just the best economy in South America. Being 2,666 miles long, (and only 250 miles wide at its widest point,) Chile is blessed with a number of different geographical conditions and climates. It has the purest desert in the world in that no rainfall has ever been reported there. The land mass of Chile rises rapidly from sea level to 20,000 feet. In its snow capped mountains it has that truly magnificent region known as the Lake Region that is as beautiful as any place on earth. Chile also has rich agricultural lands and a region of fjords and glaciers which has been described as other-worldly. The fjord and glacier area is in the south and is of monolithic proportions. Walls of water stream down huge rockfaces into immense river valleys that eventually flow out unto rich green grasslands and forests. Chile's mountain slopes in the Andes have five-star ski resorts. There are beaches on the Pacific Ocean, rivers everywhere, volcanos, the highest lake in the world, areas filled with enormous crops of wine-grapes and high, isolated peaks where the llama and the vicuña still roam.

Chile also lays claim to the offshore territories of Easter Island (2,300 miles west), Juan Fernánde (425 miles west) and half of the southern island of Tierra del Fuego (which it shares with Argentina). The variety of it's habitat supports distinctive flora and fauna, which are eco-protected by an extensive system of national parks -- one of the country's major drawing card for the estimated 1,000,000 tourists per year . In the parks, are animals such as the endangered vicuña (a wild relative of the alpaca), the Patagonian guanaco (a wild relative of the Andean llama), flamingos, pelicans, penguins, otters and sea lions Chilean plant life includes stands of araucaria (the monkey-puzzle tree), cypress and rare alerce trees (similar to the giant redwoods of California.)

Trying to describe Chile's meteroric economic ascent from zero to the top is a pleasure. Being able to see that a respect for human rights and civil rights have improved is also a pleasure. The fact that even the poor are being regarded is astounding. Trying to describe Chile's geography and climate is like trying to describe the geography between New York City and Los Angeles, or for a more accurate analogy; the geography and climate between the Ocotillo Lodge in Palm Springs and an Eskimo Village near Prudhoe Bay, Alaska. No matter how we look at her, Chile is really something.

CHAPTER TEN

URUGUAY

"...Their heroic disposition to differentiate themselves, their persistence in being themselves, their searching and early-rising soul. If on many occasions, they not only search but find, it will be mean to envy them for it. The sun, in the mornings, passes by San Felipe of Montevideo before it comes here."

-JORGE LUIS BORGES

Uruguay is a fertile land, given mostly to rolling plains with low hills, about 78% of the land being meadows and pastures. Forests and woodland make up about 4% and 8% is used as crop land, although we suspect that Uruguay's crop production potential could be enormous, as the land is highly fertile, coupled with an almost profound water availability. Water, within its many lakes and rivers, is one of Uruguay's distinguishing geographical characteristics. We have seen a statistic which states that Uruguay has 125,057 sq km of jurisdictional waters, which is a number almost proportionately equal to its total land area. Bordered by the **River Uruguay** to the east and the **River Plate** to the south, Uruguay is also dotted with many lakes. Along the coast there are great marshes filled with endless variety of waterfowl. We remember reading a fine article about these great marshlands some years ago written by **Vance Bourjaily** in *GEO Magazine*;* and we have never been able to think of Uruguay without recalling Bourjaily's wonderful descriptions of this majestic land. Uruguay's rugged four hundred mile coast is filled with rustic fishing villages, where solace is the way of life, and, to quote Uruguayan journalist **Oscar Bonilla**, "...the harsh and wild land is inhabited by gauchos as rooted in the sea as the fishermen are rooted in the land." Uruguay's climate is warm and temperate; with freezing temperatures almost unheard of. Uruguay has a very low population growth rate, excellent real estate prices and even though it is very urban in a statistical sense there is much that is wild about it, in the most wonderful sense of the word wild.

The population growth rate is 1.1%, which is the lowest in the whole of Latin America and comparable to that of the world's most highly-developed countries. This fact is attributable to the high cultural and educational level of the population, ** reflected in a greater sense of family responsibility. The very low birth rate (17.3 per thousand inhabitants) and the very low death rate (10.0 per thousand, with a life expectancy at birth of 72.4 years -data 1992-) account for another singular feature of Uruguayan demography: 16.5% of the population are over 60, 27% are under 17.5, and 66.1% are between 15 and 60. It's a very balanced culture reminiscent of much that used to be agreeable once upon a time in the United States.

---

* GEO February 1985 VOL 7 /2   The reader who is lucky enough to find a vintage collection of the old English-language editions of GEO will consider themselves fortunate.

** As a result of long standing tradition, both men and women continue on to college for degrees in the Republic of Uruguay and they have one of the highest literacy rates in the world: 95.8%

ESCAPE FROM AMERICA

POPULATION IN URUGUAY

URUGUAY'S POPULATION: 3,222,716 (July 1995 est.)

AGE STRUCTURE:
- 0-14 years: 25%   (female 392,262; male 409,580)
- 15-64 years: 63% (female 1,026,314; male 995,492)
- 65 years and over: 12% (female 233,377; male 165,691) (July 1995 est.)

POPULATION GROWTH RATE: 0.74% (1995 est.)

BIRTH RATE: Birth rate: 17.57 births/1,000 population (1995 est.)

DEATH RATE: 9.27 deaths/1,000 population (1995 est.)

NET MIGRATION RATE: -0.93 migrant(s)/1,000 population (1995 est.)

INFANT MORTALITY RATE: 16.3 deaths/1,000 live births (1995 est.)

LIFE EXPECTANCY AT BIRTH: total population: 74.46 years
male: 71.24 years   female: 77.83 years (1995 est.)

TOTAL FERTILITY RATE: 2.41 children born/woman (1995 est.)

LANGUAGES: Spanish, Brazilero [Portuguese & Spanish mixed.]

ETHNIC GROUPS: European 88% [mainly Spanish & Italian] Mestizo 8% [Brazilian] Black/Mulatto 4%

RELIGIONS: Catholic 66% [less than half the adult population attends church with any degree of regularity.] Protestant 2% Jewish 2% Nonprofessing: 30% [The number of people who might follow one or the other of the Brazilian Afro-Spiritualistic practices, such as Macumba, Candomblé, or Umbanda, is not reported in any of the reference text, but we suspect there may be instances of such along the Uruguay-Brazilian border.

POPULATION FACTS

The population of Uruguay is 3,222,716 [July 1995 est.] this equals a density of 17.8 inhabitants per square kilometre.* Even though in absolute figures the population of Uruguay is one of the smallest in South America, owing to the country's small size the population density is double that of South American countries as a whole, since the entire territory of Uruguay is habitable under what can only be called excellent conditions.

A special feature of Uruguay is that in contrast to the rest of South America there is no native population. Settled by Spanish colonizers, it received large waves of European immigrants, mainly Spanish and Italian in the late 19th century and in the early part of the 20th century. Uruguay is a markedly urban country. 87.3% of its population are town dwellers and only 12.7% live in rural areas despite the fact that the economy depends mainly on agriculture and livestock farming. It is the most urbanized country in the world. Montevideo accounts for 44.5% of the total population of Uruguay. This is an exceptionally high proportion that is equalled by no other capital city in the world.

* Ipanema, in Brazil had 23,000 people per square kilometre when we were there.

The population growth rate is between 0.74% and 1.1% depending on whose statistics we are to believe. In either case it is still the lowest in the whole of Latin America and comparable to that of the world's most highly-developed countries. The fact is attributable to the high cultural level of the population, reflected in a greater sense of family responsibility.

THE ECONOMY OF URUGUAY

The government of Uruguay has learned the lessons of statism the hardest way. Once one of the richest countries in the world, Uruguay initiated the first welfare state in the western hemisphere, with a system that included free education, free medicine, and overall benefits that were equal to the level of salary. This giveaway program was financed by the rich cattle market of the early 1900's. When the bottom fell out of the cattle market, Uruguay found itself unable to continue its 'free lunch' program, so it began printing money in order to keep itself afloat. (Hello, America!) The statist mentality of the government encouraged the growth of unions, which became coercive monopolies willing to go on strike at any sign of a decrease in any of the established 'free lunch' programs. Continuously rising rates of inflation forced the government to institute wage-price controls, import-export allocations, and (yes,) foreign exchange controls, in an attempt to keep its sinking ship afloat. Capital fled the country. (Hello, America!) factories closed down, and many workers went on welfare. The government reacted by raising tax rates, broadening the welfare benefits, increasing the rate of currency debasement and expanding the size of its own bureaucracy. (Hello, America!) The revolution that followed led to the establishment of a military government that ruled Uruguay under a state (more or less) of martial law.

In the twelve years from 1973 to 1985, one in every fifty Uruguayans was arrested at some point for presumed subversive activities against the government. (as the cartoon character Pogo once said, "...we have seen the enemy and he is us.") One in every 500 was sentenced to six or more years in prison. Almost 15% of the population fled the country; somewhere in the numerical vicinity of 400,000 people became expatriated from the land they loved. When the country of Uruguay finally hit the bottom, they had one distinct thing going for themselves and that was that there was nowhere further to fall. What kind of people could have been so foolish?

The people of Uruguay have one of the highest literacy rates in the world. They are the world's *most* urban country; not the second, or third most urban country, they are number one. They produce more Medical Doctors than any other country in Latin America. They are bright, proud, intelligent and honest. It would be difficult to find a better people anywhere in the world. That is the kind of people who allowed statism to destroy their country. (Hello, America, are you listening?)

It has taken Uruguay almost a full decade to recover and they are not totally recovered yet. However, they do recognize to some degree that statism was the cause of their fall. They were once one of the richest if not *the* richest country in the world. They were called the Switzerland of South America. Where are they at today? Let's take a look.

A NEW URUGUAY

Uruguay's new goals are to create conditions which encourage sustainable economic growth. They are actively seeking investment and people who know how to create prosperity. To accomplish this they have initiated the following policies:

✔ The elimination of all exchange controls, both domestic and foreign.
✔ Privatization of the public sector and modernization of those sectors remaining under government control.
✔ The intention of attaining and then maintaining stability and consistency in economic policies.
✔ Reduction and control of the rate of inflation and the policies which cause it.
✔ A willingness to understand and to set in motion other sound policies which attract foreign investments in order to increase their industry and export market.

The progress already achieved has been somewhat remarkable considering that Uruguay only began to turn away from statism in 1985. The **GDP** grew from 0.9% in 1990 to 2.9% in 1991 and reached 7.4% in 1992. As a result of its policies Uruguay has come to be seen as a banking center by much of South America, with *unrestricted* capital inflow and outflow, free determination of interest rates paid by banks, (independent of any determination on the part of the Central Bank,) tax exemption for non-resident financial assets; and the establishment of a system of bank confidentiality decrees. These are very, very healthy signs. Uruguay, of course is not totally out of the woods. The principals of property rights and freedom from government control are somewhat difficult principals for governments to understand and maintain. Governments have a difficult time limiting their own activities, much as we. The government of Uruguay, like governments everywhere, must stay its heavy hand. Generally, we feel very good about Uruguay's capacity to do so, and generally, we also feel very good about Uruguay's economic outlook. We place Uruguay on our list of most highly recommended country-destinations for expats. Additionally, we view its investment markets as currently undervalued, (as of this writing 4th quarter 1996,) and would suggest further investigation in both regards.

ECONOMIC OVERVIEW FROM THE 1995 WORLD FACT BOOK:

Uruguay's economy is a small one with favorable climate, good soils, and substantial hydropower potential. Economic development has been restrained in recent years by excessive government regulation of economic detail and 40% to 130% inflation. Although the **GDP** growth rate slowed in 1993 to 1.7%, following a healthy expansion to 7.5% in 1992, it rebounded in 1994 to an estimated 4%, spurred mostly by increasing agricultural and other exports and a surprise reversal of the downward trend in industrial production. In a major step toward regional economic cooperation, Uruguay confirmed its commitment to the Southern Cone Common Market (**MERCOSUR**) customs union by implementing MERCOSUR's common external tariff on most tradable's on 1 January 1995. Inflation in 1994 declined for the third consecutive year, yet, at 44%, it remains the highest in the region; analysts predict that the expanding fiscal deficit and wage indexation will force the inflation rate back toward the 50% mark in 1995.

URUGUAY'S ECONOMIC STATISTICS

NATIONAL PRODUCT: GDP - $23 billion [1994 est.]   PPP: US$19 billion [1993 estimate]
NATIONAL PRODUCT REAL GROWTH RATE: 4% [1994 est.]
NATIONAL PRODUCT PER CAPITA: $7,200 [1994 est.] We have seen per capita estimates that range from US$4,174 to US$6,000
INFLATION RATE: (consumer prices): 44% (1994 est.)
UNEMPLOYMENT RATE: 9% (1994 est.)
BUDGET: revenues: $2.9 billion expenditures: $3 billion, including capital expenditures of $388 million (1991 est.)
EXPORTS: $1.78 billion (f.o.b., 1994 est.) commodities: wool and textile manufactures, beef and other animal products, leather, rice partners: Brazil, Argentina, US, China, Italy
IMPORTS: Imports: $2.461 billion (c.i.f., 1994 est.) commodities: machinery and equipment, vehicles, chemicals, minerals, plastics partners: Brazil, Argentina, US, Nigeria
EXTERNAL DEBT: $4.2 billion (1993)
INDUSTRIAL PRODUCTION: growth rate 3.9% (1992); accounts for 28% of GDP
ELECTRICITY: capacity: 2,070,000 kW   production: 9 billion kWh consumption per capita: 1,575 kWh (1993)
INDUSTRIES: meat processing, wool and hides, sugar, textiles, footwear, leather apparel, tires, cement, petroleum refining, wine
TOURISM: 1.3 million visitors annually
AGRICULTURE: accounts for 12% of GDP; large areas devoted to livestock grazing; wheat, rice, corn, sorghum; fishing; self-sufficient in most basic foodstuffs
ECONOMIC AID: recipient: US commitments, including Ex-Im (FY70-88), $105 million; Western (non-US) countries, ODA and OOF bilateral commitments (1970-89), $420 million; Communist countries (1970-89), $69 million

TIME & PLACE

LOCAL NAME: Uruguay; República Oriental del Uruguay
TIME ZONE: GMT/UTC minus three hours
AREA: Total area: 176,220 sq km (60,018 sq mi)
             Land area: 173,620 sq km
             [Slightly smaller than Washington State, slightly larger than Missouri.]
COAST LINE: 660 km (approximately 410 miles)
STATUS: Republic
DATE OF INDEPENDENCE: 1828

CAPITAL: Montevideo
Supposedly a linguistic corruption of:*Monte vi eu!* [I saw a hill!]

CURRENCY [PAPER MONEY] PAST & FUTURE

CURRENCY: 1 Uruguayan peso ($Ur) = 100 centesimos
EXCHANGE RATES: Uruguayan pesos ($Ur) per US$1 - 5.6 (January 1995), 4.4710 (January 1994), 3.9484 (1993), 3.0270 (1992), 2.0188 (1991), 1.1710 (1990)

Note: on 1 March 1993 the former New Peso (N$Ur) was replaced as Uruguay's unit of currency by the Peso which is equal to 1,000 of the New Pesos   The rate of inflation remains high, although we believe that this is not a tremendously crucial matter for the prudent expat, as long as there is a continued absence of exchange controls. As always, we suggest keeping ones money in a stable currency (and not in the Uruguayan Peso,) and then exchanging into the local currency only in amounts sufficient to meet monthly expenditures.

Just to determine Peso Performance in recent years, we checked to see what the Peso was on this evening over that past three years. Here are the results: November 1995: 6.43 or 15.5¢, November 1994: 5.09 or 19.6¢, November 1993: 4.35 or 23¢. Today, it's: 8.18 or 12.2¢. We cannot stress enough how important it is for the reader to read the section on Tax Havens and the section on Offshore Real Estate carefully before disembarking on their life as an expatriate. In just three years the Peso of Uruguay has fallen by approximately 50%.

INFLATION RATE: [consumer prices]: 44% [1994 est.]
EXCHANGE RATE AS OF NOVEMBER 1996: [$Ur] per US$ - 8.18 [or a value of: 12.2¢.]

RELATIVE COSTS:
● cheap meal: US$2-3
● restaurant meal: US$8-15
● cheap room: US$5-10
● hotel room: US$15-20

SOAP BOX & STUPID STORY TIME

In terms of overall analysis of the economic opportunities and potential of the market, a good degree of what applies to **Argentina**, also applies to Uruguay; but definitely not across the board. Argentina and Uruguay are two separate countries, and the Uruguayans feel quite strongly about this, (which is what the opening quotation from Borges implies.) We have seen comparisons between the relationship Canada has towards the United States applied to Uruguay's relationship to Argentina. While we are not sure how precise this is, it may work loosely by way of analogy. We believe that Uruguay's greatest asset is it's location between two of South Americas heaviest players, **Brazil** and **Argentina**. This locational aspect may indeed be the trump card to play for the perceptive investor-expat. Brazil is the largest producer of the so-called third world, and it's overall potential is absolutely staggering. To give its potential some sort of perspective let's liken it to Australia, a country which is not considered a third world country by any stretch of the imagination. Australia has a Gross Domestic Product of US$340 million and a human population of 18 million. Brazil has a Gross Domestic Product of US$785 billion and human population of 158 million. Brazil's economy is 2000 times greater than Australia's and Brazil has at least two cities whose overall population just within themselves exceeds the entire population of Australia. There is no word to use for Brazil's size and potential other than staggering. (Anyone who has had several *caipirinha,* Brazil's deservedly popular national drink, will surely agree with our assessment.)

Argentina is also a heavy favorite by any analysis. These two countries, Brazil and Argentina, with a combined population of almost 200 million, each filled with fertile land and abundant resources, are poised to dominate the 21st century. And sitting between them like a toll booth on a bridge is Uruguay. We are reminded of a futuristic story we read some years ago by the science fiction writer, Ray Bradbury, about someone who had opened a hamburger stand on some remote, mostly uninhabited planet. When asked why he was there when there wasn't anyone to sell hamburgers to, he replied, "...well, I figure it's only a matter of time. It's a good location, there's plenty of parking, and I've got the best hamburger on the planet."

THE INTERNET IN URUGUAY

We have been more than a little impressed with the WebSites we've seen coming out of Uruguay. We must remember that Uruguay has a population of only 3.25 million people. Many cities around the world far exceed 3.25 million inhabitants but we've seen few cities anywhere with WebSites as fine as those from Uruguay. The reader must see the quality of the Site for the Newspaper *EL PAIS* which is a Motevideo daily paper. We aren't sure if it could be called 'third generation' WebSite, because we aren't too sure about the subtle technological distinctions but it in any event it manages to impress us quite a bit. See the WebSite for the Newspaper *EL PAIS* at:
URL: http://www.web2mil.com/EL_PAIS/

There is a multitude of Web Services and information listed at the Site called: **Servidores WWW de URUGUAY** They have a huge WebPage that lists everything imaginable. Radio, Television, Sports, Cultural information, Politics, Uruguayan Personal Web Pages, Education, Health, Directories [including classified ads for apartments, real estate, cars and so forth,] Computers, the Internet, Banks, Organization & Publications, Export Information, Import Information, Search Engines for Uruguay & the world, and more. [mostly in Spanish]
URL: http://www.multi.com.uy/presenta/america/Uruguay/servers.htm#Diarios

URUGUAY, THE WEB SITE is the name of a Site at URL: http://www.adinet.com/
We found some excellent Sites on smaller towns in Uruguay including some nice photos of some of the countryside.

Cronicas Economicas On-Line is the name of a Site at
URL: http://lsa.lsa.com.uy/cronicas/
The Site is totally on the economy of Uruguay and totally in Spanish. Uruguay doesn't have English options on too many of it's WebSites as do some of it's larger neighbors.

One Site that *does* have optional English is the Dirección Nacional de Comunicaciones which is the page for the **Department of Communications in Uruguay.**
URL:http://dnc.comintur.com.uy/$dnc-1a.htm

It is possible to hear Uruguayan **Radio** [X FM 100.3 (Edición Internet)]
URL: http://multi.com.uy/Xfm/Index.htm
Montevideo Uruguay - 18 de Julio 1220 Piso 4 . Tel (05982) 925979 Fax 925992
Was it just ten years ago we had to use a Short Wave to listen to Samba, Tango and other Latin American music? We remember listening to the music on Short Wave radio as the signal would fade in and out and wondering how we could go about improving the audio. Today we can hear live radio from anywhere in the world and have video along with.

Another newspaper with a fine WebPage is the Newspaper *El Global Observador de Uruguay*. The site has a number of Tangos which can be played, [as does *EL PAIS*] it is the best kind of music to go with the Uruguayan news; they can be found at
URL: http://www.zfm.com/observador/

A very important site for those of us deciding on moving to Uruguay or to Argentina is the site for: **THE CHAMBER OF COMMERCE of Uruguay & the United States of America.** The Site *does* have English options and the people at the C of C do speak English. Those without a computer can address inquiries to the Chamber's Manager, Mr. Carlos Boubet, at the following address:

Cámara de Comercio Uruguay - Estados Unidos
Bartolomé Mitre 1337 Of. 108 Montevideo 11000, <u>URUGUAY</u>
Phone: (598)2 959048 Fax: (598)2 959059 e-mail: amchamuru@zfm.com

The Uruguay & US Chamber have their WebPage at
URL: http://www.zfm.com/amchamuru/
The Chamber WebPage and the Chamber itself can help us find useful information about Services that the Chamber offers. They provide information on the Financial and Legal Regulations of Uruguay, Foreign Investment regulations and also on the aspects of how Uruguay is focused within Mercosur and what opportunities that will provide for investors and expatriates.

Publications that are provided by The Chamber of Commerce:
The following publications are available from the chamber. For more information about their publications you can contact them by email at: amchamuru@zfm.com. or by fax, phone or post.
- *Membership Directory*
- *Doing Business in Uruguay*
- *Investor's Guide*
- *Uruguay Investment System*

TELEVISION WEBSITE: There is an Internet access to Uruguayan Television station from Montevideo. Channel 10 has a very nice WebSite, all in Spanish. If we plan on moving to Latin America and we have a PC then the first thing we should purchase is a software program that translates. The software translators that we've seen in action tend to give decent but rigid approximations of the human language, but they suffice. The WebSite at the URL listed below provides enough daily information to keep in total contact with Uruguay. What a pleasure the Internet is at times! It is easy to be informed of many things not available from the NorthAmerican news media.
CANAL 10 - Montevideo - Uruguay Edición INTERNET
URL: http://www.multi.com.uy/canal10/

COMMUNICATIONS RELATED STATISTICS
Telephone system: 337,000 telephones; telephone density 10/100 persons; some modern facilities
Local: most modern facilities concentrated in Montevideo intercity: new nationwide microwave network
International: 2 INTELSAT (Atlantic Ocean) earth stations
Radio: broadcast stations: AM 99, FM 0, shortwave 9
Television: broadcast stations: 26
Electricity: 220V, 50 Hz

FREEDOM HOUSE RATINGS FOR URUGUAY

Freedom House granted Uruguay a score of 2 in each of the rights ratings; a ② for political rights, and a ② for civil rights. They point out that constitutional guarantees regarding free expression, freedom of religion, the right to organize political parties, labor unions and civic organizations are generally respected in Uruguay. The judiciary is relatively independent and is headed by a Supreme Court appointed by the congress. The system includes courts of appeal, regional courts, and justices of the peace. The press is privately owned and broadcasting is both commercial and public.

In 1995, the new President of Uruguay, Julio Sanguinetti pushed through an austerity package that cut back on the overburdened social security system. The action led to immediate labor stoppages by the over-abundant labor unions. Despite the obvious social and political improvements Uruguay has undergone since 1985, it still remains the most statist and union-dominated nation in South America. We would not consider it a worthy candidate for the expat if Uruguay did not have so much going for it that is positive. We believe what prevents Uruguay from being a total basketcase, is its low population density. Uruguay has a very low birth rate, somewhere on the order of one half of one percent increase per year, (compare this figure with Mexico's almost three (3%) percent, which is five times as high.) While Uruguay is just slightly larger than Missouri, one of America's less-populated states, Uruguay with a population of only 3,186,000 people has not even 60% of Missouri's population of 5,200,000.

LIVING IN URUGUAY AS AN EXPAT

Because Uruguay is so sparsely settled, most people tend to live either along the ocean coast, or along the River Plate. In the Spanish idiom, River Plate is *Rio de la Plata,* which means: River of Silver or Silver River. (Actually the River Plate is coffee colored due to the immense amount of sediments from the many rivers that enter it.) Directly across the River Plate from Buenos Aires, lies the city of **Colonia Del Sacramento**. (or **Colonia Suiza**) About 85 west of Montevideo, this city is filled with 300 year old houses built of stone; houses whose walls are over two feet thick. Built in the Portuguese style, (with wrought-iron balconies and ceramic tiles;) many of these houses have woodwork on their doors & shutters whose craftsmanship is a century or more old. The quiet streets are made of cobblestone and the houses themselves for the most part are for sale. Yes, for sale. There's no factories, no commerce, no manufacturing. It's just a sleepy and wonderful city on the Rio de la Plata. One hour away by hydrofoil is the "Paris of South America", Buenos Aires, with its night life, its culture, its opera, its bookstores, its coffee houses and its many fine restaurants. The pace of Colonia itself is very, very slow. Many Portenos, (Buenos Aires city dwellers,) have weekend or summer houses in Colonia, but it is definitely not overbought, nor do we expect a sudden surge of buyers. Things move slowly in Uruguay, and probably will for some time to come. Most young Uruguayans have traditionally gone to Argentina in search of work, a fact that the end of the Nation-State may soon change. Along with the tremendous improvement inside Uruguay over the last several years, the advent of MERCOSUR and the wonderful ambience of Uruguay itself; it is a more than excellent destination for the more rugged type of expatriate. Those individualists who can think independently should give careful consideration to this wonderful country. Uruguay is also an excellent destination for retirees. If Uruguay is looked at, Colonia is definitely a spot worth looking into.

The City of **Tacuarembó** in the department (State) of Tacuarembó is also a very agreeable town. The air is permeated with the sweet smell of sycamore from it's sycamore-lined streets and the lovely sycamore shaded plazas. Founding in 1832, the town is filled with statues and monuments commemorating military figures, writers, clergy members and educators. In late March, they have a three-day gaucho festival that features exhibitions, riding skills, music and other activities. But if you prefer a really peaceful seaside town, visit **Aguas Dulces** in the department of Rocha. It's a quaint, unprepossessing fishing village with modest facilities, great seafood and a local speciality, the messy to eat but flavorful fruit of the butía palm.

Montevideo is the Capital of Uruguay and it's largest city. Poetically described as the city 'we dreamed of in our past and wish to escape to from our present.' *"...city, whose name sounds like a verse, streets with patio light."* Borges said of it. In Montevideo modernization hasn't yet arrived. Montevedio has broad stately boulevards that criss-cross narrow streets dotted with tree-shaded parks and plazas. The air smells of eucalyptus, of pine and of sea salt. The lay out is simple. On one side of the city is the estuary of the Plata, on the other side of the city is the Atlantic Ocean. The breezes are warm. The ambience mellow. On the eastern edge of town are the great beaches and the casinos. Today they are mostly deserted by the modern world, Montevedio plays like a memory. Everyone that's hip has gone to **Punta del Este**.

Briget Bardot discovered Punta del Este, at least that's what we're told. It would have been wonderful to watch with the bemused eyes of the Uruguayan fishermen who were already living there as Briget came ashore with her crew, in a long boat perhaps, having braved the Atlantic Ocean in ship that looked like the Pinto or the Santa Maria. We can see her drawing her sunglasses from their sheath and claiming the city in the name of all the jet setters of the world.

Punta is a resort known mostly to Europeans and Argentinians, though international it is, with some Americans having discovered its many wonders. Punta is considered one of South America's most glamorous and exclusive destinations. The place is awash with yacht and fishing clubs, golf courses, casinos and beautiful holiday homes. There are excellent beaches for swimming and serious sunbathing. Offshore are two islands, Isla Gorriti, which also has superb beaches as well as the ruins of an 18th-century fortress that is worth seeing. The other island, Isla de Lobos, is a nature reserve that is the home to a fairly large sea-lion colony.

North of Punta, the coast seems deserted, it's solitude is dotted with tiny fishing villages. If we would find a reason to go there and look, we would assume that we've gone back in time to a more tranquil era. Yet, amidst these tranquil time encased fishing villages is the enigma that is Punta del Estes. Punta itself. And Punta is a jet-setters jewel. Even the taxis are Mercedes Benz. We can expect to find very few real estate bargains here, although this might be the spot to go if we are capable of opening a restaurant with something special to offer, or if we have a product or service that has that necessary fascination. Nothing quite glitters like the fascinating brilliance of enjoyment. We can of course check out Punta on the Internet at Punta's WebSite **URL:** http://www.adinet.com/terre/urumald.html

Inland, Uruguay's interior is lovely and sparsely populated, with very little tourism, few towns and much open country. We can still buy a farm house here on 10 acres for $20,000. If we do, we'd better have a way to make a living. Wages everywhere in Uruguay would do little to excite an expat. This is country to which we must bring our own expertise. It is a lovely and lonely land.

EVERYTHING YOU NEED TO KNOW ABOUT URUGUAY
We thought we would mention this especially large and impressive Web Site on Uruguay with numerous links, many in English.
URL: http://www.reu.edu.uy/varela/wwwsp1095.html

FACTS ABOUT LIVING & RETIRING IN URUGUAY

The **United Nations Program for Human Development** has categorized Uruguay as the country with the highest standard of living in all of Latin America and the thirty-second highest in the world. Below is some useful information about Uruguay that will help us to understand why:

Visa Requirements for U.S. Citizens: None
We can stay up to 3 months without a visa, if we want to stay longer than 3 months we may ask for a visa after we are in the country.

Real-Estate: Non-Citizens are subject to the same rules, laws and privilege as citizens when buying real estate.

Business: A foreign investor is treated the same as a domestic investor under Uruguayan law, without needing special authorization to set up a business in the country, to make deposits or perform other banking transactions in any currency, to access loans and receive promotional benefits. There is even total freedom to transfer capital or profits abroad, as well as to enter into contracts expressing the obligations in any currency. Additionally, there are no controls on foreign exchange transactions.

Taxes: There is no difference between non-citizens and citizens for tax purposes. There is no personal income or inheritance tax. The basic tax system is as follows: A) **State Taxes**: 1) Value-added tax, the value-added tax is not imposed on business income but rather is a method of taxing the domestic consumption of the population. The tax is calculated on net amount invoiced for sales and services. The basic tax rate in Uruguay is 23%. 2) Capital tax - The capital tax is assessed at the rate of 2% on the net worth employed in business at year-end and is not therefore directly related to business profits. However significant restrictions on deductible liabilities are imposed. A Capital tax is collected on the wealth of individuals at a progressive rate (0.7% to 3.5%) 3) Tax on real estate transfers - both parties to the transfer contract of real estate are subject to this tax at a rate of 4% each on the property tax value (generally below market value).
B) **Local Taxes:** 1) residence tax - paid by the owner of a property - about $ 25 a month.
2) **automobile tax** - paid by the owner of the car - 4% of the market value of the car yearly.
3) **local property tax** - paid once a year by the owner of the property - about 1% of market value.

Another advantage of Uruguay are it's people. Uruguayans have a high percentage of educated people. They are mostly of European origin (the indigenous population was all but extinguished by 1830.) There are no racial or religious problems. The literacy rate is 95.8%. Life expectancy at birth is 72.41 years. In a world where crime rates are always increasing, Uruguay has a static or decreasing crime rate.

COST OF LIVING [Standard prices in U.S. dollars]

Basic Foods
- Milk - $0.60 (1 lt.)
- Flour - $0.50 (1 kg.)
- Eggs - $1.25 (1 dozen)
- Oil - $2 (1 lt.)
- Potatoes - $1 (1 kg.)
- Meat - $2.5 (1 kg.)
- Coke - $1.25 (1 lt.)
- Beer - $2 (1 lt.)
- Wine - $5 (1 lt.)
- Rice - $0.50 (1 kg.)
- Mineral Water - $0.5 (1 lt)

Garments
- Men's Suit - $300
- Men's Shirt - $35
- Pants - $50
- Coat - $200
- Leather Shoes - $80
- Brand Name Jeans - $60

Food and Drink
- Tea or coffee - $ 1
- Chocolate - $2
- Small Sandwiches - $ 3
- Hot dog - $ 0.75

Misc.
- Private schools - $ 200 per month.
- Gas - $ 2 (1 lt.) about $ 6 per gallon.
- Electricity - $ 20 per person, per month (approx.).
- Telephone - $ 80 plus international calls, per month.

Real Estate Cost A Simple house or condominium in an average area costs approximately $ 45.000. In addition there is a real state agent commission of 2%, a Notary Public fee of 3%, and a registration tax of 1%.

Medical Cost There are many medical plans in Uruguay, each with its own Hospital. The monthly fee is, on average, $ 60 per person.

Health Requirements For Pets: The standard documents required to export a pet from the U.S. is sufficient. A consular visa is not needed, and there is no quarantine period.

Television Standard System - PAL-N. There are four public access channels in Montevideo, five in Punta del Este and cable is installed in the country's main cities. Current Voltage - 220 Volts. Power outages are preprogrammed. If you suffer a power outage for more than 24 hours caused by problems at the Electric Company (state owned) you receive one month of electrical usage free of charge.

RETIRE IN PUNTA DEL ESTES

For those who want to retire the mayorship of Maldonado is promoting Punta del Estes and the nearby area as a retirement haven. The Mayorship points out that there are no reports of violent crimes against senior citizens in the last 5 years (such as rape, robbery, etc.); nor have there been any reports of crimes related to drugs in the area. All rates of crimes against people are very low and with one exception, that occurred in 1992, have not had fatal consequences. Crimes against property (robberies) also have a low rate. The robberies that do occur are mainly focused on summer houses which are empty during the winter. The Cost of Living in Punta del Este varies substantially. This is due to fact that housing prices are higher in the peak season (Summer - January thru March). The cost of living at the middle-class level in the summer is approximately $1,500 a month total. It is statistically demonstrated that the cost of living in Punta del Este is about 50% higher than living in the rest of the country. Local Services Water and electric power service are more than sufficient, although minor inconveniences may arise during the peak season with water services. The Mayorship is currently working out these problems in order to assure the service and to ultimately eliminate inconveniences.

Mayorship services include: trash pickup, street sweeping, public lights, etc. Local taxes in Maldonado are 100% higher than in other places in the country. If you would like more information about living in Punta del Este, you should contact the "Intendencia Municipal de Maldonado". Their address is:
INTENDENCIA MUNICIPAL DE MALDONADO
Montevideo 745 Maldonado, Uruguay Ph: 011 598 42 23906 Fax:011 598 42 29132

GOVERNMENT DEGREES REGARDING EXPATS [VERBATIM]

Decree 333/972 Allows residence applicants to bring into the country all types of home appliances, furniture and a car for personal use. The resident must pay for transportation, insurance and port use (2.5% of CIF value) and 60% over the car invoice as tax. These general decree apply to everyone who wants to emigrate into Uruguay. Uruguayan citizens have some limits of time and special documentation to present in order to return to Uruguay.

Decree 416/964 Allows applicants for residency to bring into the county all the tools and equipment needed for their jobs or business enterprises (except cars or trucks).

PASSPORT FOR INVESTORS [VERBATIM]

Decree 289/990 **PASSPORT FOR INVESTORS** A national passport can be obtained after some years of legal residence if you acquire Uruguayan citizenship, or immediately if you make an investment in Uruguay that will come to maturity in no less than ten years. There are many different options: a) an investment project (subject to government approval if it represents a risky project). A warrant deposit of the 30% of the project of at least $ 40.000 must be made before asking for the approval. b) Buy **"TITULOS DE FORESTACION"**, a special kind of public debt dedicated to the promotion of the reforestation of the country; the minimum amount to buy is $70,000. The forestry bonds earn 6.5% interest, payable annually; the entire principal is repayable at the end of ten years. A Passport can also be obtained for your spouse and minor children by making an additional deposit of $ 10,000 for each of them. c) Deposit in the New York branch of the Bank of the Uruguayan Republic for at least $100,000, or buying public debt for that amount and deposit it in the said bank. In order to receive your passport you have to present all the basic documents and travel to Uruguay. You do not have to renew the investment after the initial ten years and if you die before the ten years are up, the investment forms part of your estate. You do not have to reside in Uruguay either before, or after, the passport is issued.

l Basic Documents and Other Requirements To Apply For Residence in Uruguay
1.Police Record - with no arrest, certified by the Uruguayan Consulate.
2.Financial Statement - to prove that you can financially support your family group.
3.Documents That Allow The Applicant And His Family To Return To His Original Country - in case the application is rejected, the person must return to his country of origin. For American citizens the U.S. passport is enough.
4.Health Examination - once in Uruguay, doctors will examine the candidate in order to certify that he or she is healthy.
5.Documents Of Marital Status - legalization in the Uruguayan Consulate of birth certificate, license of marriage and decree of divorce from vital records will be required for your own convenience in order to establish your marital status in Uruguay.
6.List Of Personal Property Moved To Uruguay - In case you decide to move your home appliances and furniture to Uruguay, you have to legalize a list of them in the nearest Uruguayan Consulate.
7.Car Documents - If you want to take a car for personal use (not truck or business vehicle you must legalize its title (it must be in the name of the person who immigrates into Uruguay) and invoice (to fix its value at customs and other services). This Information Last updated: 1/27/96.

THE EMBASSY OF URUGUAY IN THE UNITED STATES

The Embassy of Uruguay is located at:
1918 F Street, N.W.
Washington, D.C. 20006
Telephone: (202) 331-1313
FAX: (202) 331-8142 email: uruguay@embassy.org
They have a WebPage at URL: http://www.embassy.org/uruguay/

CONSULATES OF URUGUAY IN THE UNITED STATES

Uruguay has Consulates in the U.S. in the following locations:

New York
747 3rd Avenue, 21st Floor, New York, NY 10017
Phone: (212) 753-8581
Fax: (212) 753-1603

California
429 Santa Monica Blvd. #400, Santa Monica, CA 90401
Phone: (310) 394-5777
Fax: (310) 394-5140

Florida
1077 Ponce de Leon Blvd., Coral Gables, Florida 33134
Phone: (305) 443-9764
Fax: (305) 443-7802

Washington, D.C.
1918 F Street, NW Washington, D.C. 20006
Phone: (202) 331-4219
Fax: (202) 331-8142

New Orleans
Honorary Consulate
540 World Trade Center
2nd Canal Street, New Orleans, Louisiana 70130
Phone: (504) 525-8354
Fax: (504) 524-8925

San Francisco
Honorary Consulate
564 Market Street, Suite 221, San Francisco, CA 94104
Phone: (415) 986-5222
Fax: (415) 989-4502

STATE DEPARTMENT TRAVEL WARNING INFORMATION

COUNTRY DESCRIPTION: Uruguay is a medium-income nation with a developing economy. The quality of facilities for tourism varies according to price and area.

ENTRY REQUIREMENTS: A passport is required. U.S. citizens do not need a visa for a three-month stay. For current information concerning entry and customs requirements for Uruguay, travelers can contact the Uruguayan Embassy at 1918 F Street N.W., Washington, D.C. 20006, tel: (202) 331 1313 or the nearest consulate in Los Angeles, Miami, Chicago, New Orleans, or New York.

MEDICAL FACILITIES: Facilities for medical care are limited. Doctors and hospitals often expect immediate cash payment for health services. U.S. medical insurance is not always valid outside the United States. The Medicare/Medicaid program does not provide payment of medical services outside the United

States. In some cases, medical insurance with specific overseas and medical evacuation coverage has proved to be useful. For additional health information, travelers can contact the Centers for Disease Control's international travelers' hotline at (404) 332-4559.

CRIME INFORMATION: Street crime, including pickpocketing, is on the increase. Persons carrying items of value in open display have been victimized by teenage muggers in the downtown area of Montevideo and near the old city and port. While criminals often have weapons at their disposal, to date foreigners have remained relatively free from assault.

The loss or theft of a U.S. passport abroad should be reported immediately to the local police and the nearest U.S. embassy or consulate. Useful information on guarding valuables and protecting personal security while traveling abroad is provided in the Department of State pamphlet, "A Safe Trip Abroad". It is available from the Superintendent of Documents, U.S. Government Printing Office, Washington, D.C. 20402. Also available from the same address is the Department of State's publication, "Tips for Travelers to Central and South America."

CIVIL AVIATION OVERSIGHT: In September 1993, the U.S. Federal Aviation Administration assessed Uruguay's civil aviation authority as not in compliance with international aviation safety oversight standards for Uruguay's carriers operating to and from the U.S. Typically, the same level of safety oversight is applied to operations to other destinations. For further information, travelers may contact the Department of Transportation at 1-800-322-7873.

EMBASSY LOCATION/REGISTRATION: Americans who register with the Consular Section of the U.S. Embassy in Montevideo at Lauro Muller 1776, telephone: (598-2) 23-60-61, may obtain updated information on travel and security within Uruguay.

CHAPTER ELEVEN

ARGENTINA

"The air is thick with the medicinal smell of the eucalyptus trees, that ancient balm which, beyond time and ambiguities of language, brings back vanished country houses."
-- Jorge Luis Borges

We have heard a very interesting anecdote concerning Argentina, and it is one which we have little reason to disbelieve. Argentina is said to be so complete and so balanced a country, that if every other country in the world were to suddenly disappear, Argentina would have no trouble going on just with what it contains within itself. It's top soil is said to be 10 feet deep, it has almost every known mineral in the world, every possible geographical and climatic condition imaginable and enough water and sunshine to grow anything. Argentina's climate covers the full range; subtropical, temperate, arid, semiarid, and cold. This extreme range of climatic conditions exist within three totally separate climatic zones each covering approximately one-third of the country.

Over half of continental Argentina consist of grasslands and about a quarter of Argentina is classified as forested. It is assumed that Argentina could raise any crop it chose. It is already one of the worlds major crop producers in addition to the cattle and sheep production for which it is justifiably famous. Its mineral resources include oil and natural gas, manganese, lead, zinc, iron, copper, tin, and uranium.

It is bounded on the east by the Andes upon which lies its border with Chile. The Andes rise to a height of 22,834 feet at Aconcagua, the highest elevation in the Americas. In and along the Andes are many breathtakingly beautiful lakes and lake resorts, the skiing in these resorts is just as good, or better than any place on earth. The local population of these mountainous lake region was settled by Italian-Swiss and the area has about it a very Italian-Swiss cultural ambience in architecture, food and life-style.

The Republic of Argentina is one of our personal favorites. We expect that Argentina along with Chile, Uruguay and Brazil are going to be the nations to beat in the coming century. These four nations plus Paraguay are in fact banding together economically into a unified front called **MERCOSUR**. We find it very significant that the combined human population of the Mercosur nations would be around 200 million in a land area 25% larger than the United States [pop: 260 million] and 20% larger than China [pop:1.2 billion]. What is interesting is that the average American doesn't seem to be aware of what it is happening in this area of the world, either culturally, economically or recreationally. Those who remain uninformed are cheating themselves out of one of the world's more interesting destinations.

COMMENTS ON THE ECONOMY

Argentina was the most promising nation in the world at the turn of the century, and possibly one of the least promising ones a mere decade ago. Today it is coming back into its own. Argentina, Chile, and Brazil are poised to dominate the world economy in the next century. While Argentina has usually been noted for its commodity agricultural products and exports, Argentina's reawakening industrial sector is beginning to produce and export a broader range of coemptive, higher-value-added industrial products. Although labor costs are generally more expensive in Argentina than they are in many competing countries these costs are still lower than in fully developed economies, and Argentine workers are also better trained than most of its competitors. After half a century of statism and populist policies geared towards protectionism, Argentina has opened up its markets. Argentina has recognized that the global economy has much more to offer than a closed statist controlled economy, having experienced the effects of statistic practices to such a degree that Argentina could easily be the nation held up to serve as the model demonstrating the ill effects a top-heavy government has when it acts to intervene into the free affairs of its people. Accordingly, it has dismantled many of its trade barriers and has opened up its economy to foreign participation and investment, and through its Convertibility Law, which removed foreign exchange controls, has revised its financial structure to put its domestic and international dealings on an open and solid footing. Argentina is completing the privitization of its far reaching state sector industries, opening them to outside interests, and returning them to the free market and to profitability. Argentina is also looking outward, as evidenced by its adoption of the General Agreement on Tariffs and Trade (GATT) and its participation in **MERCOSUR**, the Southern Cone common market arrangement with Brazil, Paraguay, and Uruguay. Chile has recently implied that it may join Mercosur.

Mercosur, which stands for Mercado Común del Sur, or Southern Common Market. This alliance has the objective of establishing the free circulation of goods services and factors of production, achieving unified customs coordination fiscal and exchanges pollices and setting a common external tariff and trade policy. They are also creating a unified free trade zone.

Argentina is a more than intriguing market from a number of perspectives. For buyers, Argentina is becoming one of the world's stronger markets for its incredible variety of traditional raw materials and commodity resource products, as well recently created nontraditional intermediate processed products. Its industrial sector as we've said, is moving swiftly away from statism pushing Argentina into the spotlight as one of the world's more competitive producers. As part of this effort, Argentina is also beginning to actively import a wider variety of goods. This factor would allow the expat to operate as an intermediary between products still being produced in the United States and desperately required in Argentina.

Annual growth rates in five Argentine industrial sectors are expected to meet or exceed 10 percent by the year 2000. What's needed?

1) Telecommunications equipment markets, in 1991-92 were already totaling US$145 million. These markets were expected to experience an annual growth rate in excess of 27 percent and did. Privatization of the nations telephone system is just a prelude to a massive refurbishing effort, which will entail a significant ongoing demand for state-of-the-art switching gear and components, transmission stations and lines, satellite equipment, and related receivers, and transmitters. Demand for cordless and cellular phones and related electronic consumer goods systems is accelerating. If we knew and understood any aspect of this market we would be on our way to Buenos Aires in the morning.

Another set of statistics we've seen claims that the Telecommunications Equipment market is projected to continue to grow at 10 percent in 95-96, reaching $1.6 billion. They state that 1995, U.S. exports to Argentina are expected to have totaled $450 million, accounting for 18 percent of imports. As basic telephone services become more available throughout the country, demand for specific telecommunications equipment is expected to continue to increase. Recent developments in this market have been driven by the privatization of the Argentine telecommunications sector. The continuing effects of privatization, liberal trade policies, firms' desire for state-of-the-art telecommunications equipment, and an expanding local market will provide increasing opportunities for U.S. companies and individuals.

2) Oil and gas field equipment markets are expected to increase by 13 percent a year. This would entail a need for, drilling rigs, support gear, transport facilities, refining capacity, and distribution equipment and materials.

3) Electronic components market estimates range from 11% to 13%. Entails all electronic appliances, electronic security systems, etc.

4) Computer and peripheral markets totaling US$105 million will experience 10 percent annual growth. We've already heard reports of one American couple from the USA going to Buenos Aires, Michael and Luchi Schmitz. Michael, now 31 and Luchi 32, opened a computer distribution firm in Buenos Aires. Sales exceeded US$1 million in 1993, which was their second year in business.

Argentina is also initiating a full-scale program called Project Maria, which entails total computerization of all areas of Argentina's customs service nationwide, which will establish a mechanism to expedite exporting and importing products in a matter of hours, provide daily information on foreign trade to improve control over unfair trading practices, and reduce the number of illegal acts by providing better valuation and control of imports. Anyone who has been berating themselves for having missed so many opportunities in the computer field over the last decade or so, now has those same opportunities available in four of five major countries in South America.

5) Food processing and packaging equipment markets of US$92 million are expected to grow by 10 percent a year.

OTHER ITEMS & MARKETS.

Other high demand markets include:
- Medical and scientific equipment
- Building materials and off-road construction vehicles
- Designer clothing and textiles
- Power tools
- Laboratory equipment
- Mechanical security systems
- Industrial chemicals
- Pharmaceuticals
- Private aircraft and aircraft parts
- Office equipment and supplies (especially fax machines & copiers)
- Synthetic resins, rubber, and plastic materials
- Civil engineering and other construction services.

If we already knew something about providing any one of these goods or services we would pursue the following course of action. We would visit Argentina and spend some time there. We would use our expertise to determine how long it would take us to set up the facilities to manufacture these goods and services in Argentina. We would begin by importing these goods and or services to generate capital for the establishment of our own Argentine company to provide those same goods and services. We will eventually be able to provide these same goods and services within Argentina at a lower cost then we could by importing them, we will part of growing countries industry at a competitive level, which is an enviable position. A very enviable position.

The items currently being produced in Argentina are so numerous, that it would be impossible to list them all. Here is a brief sample: Apples, apple juice, apricots, asparagus, barley, berries, beef, biscuits, butter, candies, canned fruit and vegetables, cereals and subproducts, cheese, cherries, chicken, chocolates, common bulk wines, cookies, corn, corn oil, corned beef, cotton, cottonseed oil, crackers, cucumbers, dairy desserts, jam, eggs, fine wines, fruit juices, garlic, glucose, grapefruit, grapefruit juice concentrate, grapes, grape juice, grapeseed oil, hams hamburger and ground meat, heat-processed meats, ice cream, jams, jellies, lemons, lemon juice, liquid eggs, mandarins, marmalade, mate, melons milk,nuts, oats, oilseeds, olive oil, olives, onions, oranges, orange juice and concentrate, organic meats and other foods.

THE ARGENTINE ECONOMY WORLD FACT BOOK OVERVIEW

Argentina, rich in natural resources, benefits also from a highly literate population, an export-oriented agricultural sector, and a diversified industrial base. Nevertheless, following decades of mismanagement and statist policies, the economy in the late 1980s was plagued with huge external debts and recurring bouts of hyperinflation. Elected in 1989, in the depths of recession, President Menem has implemented a comprehensive economic restructuring program that shows signs of putting Argentina on a path of stable, sustainable growth. Argentina's currency has traded at par with the US dollar since April 1991, and inflation has fallen to its lowest level in 20 years. Argentines have responded to the relative price stability by repatriating flight capital and investing in domestic industry. The economy registered an impressive 6% advance in 1994, fueled largely by inflows of foreign capital and strong domestic consumption spending. The government's major short term objective is encouraging exports, e.g., by reducing domestic costs of production. At the start of 1995, the government had to deal with the spillover from international financial movements associated with the devaluation of the Mexican peso. In addition, unemployment had become a serious issue for the government. Despite average annual 7% growth in 1991-94, unemployment surprisingly has doubled - due mostly to layoffs in government bureaus and in privatized industrial firms and utilities and, to a lesser degree, to illegal immigration. Much remains to be done in the 1990s in dismantling the old statist barriers to growth, extending the recent economic gains, and bringing down the rate of unemployment. Unemployment rate: 12% (1994 est.)

GROSS STATISTICS

GDP: US$185 billion (1993 est) per capita: $5,500 (1993 est) We have seen updated figures for 1994 and 1995, these figures are as follows: GDP: US$255.7 billion end of the year 1993 GDP: US$279.4 billion end of the year 1994

NATIONAL PRODUCT: GDP - PPP: $270.8 billion (1994 est.)

NATIONAL PRODUCT REAL GROWTH RATE: 6% (1994 est.)

NATIONAL PRODUCT PER CAPITA: $7,990 (1994 est.)

INFLATION RATE (consumer prices): 3.9% (1994 est.)

RELATIVE COSTS: cheap meal: US$4-6 Restaurant meal: US$10-20 cheap room: US$20-25 Hotel room: US$30-40

CURRENCY: 1 nuevo peso argentino = 100 centavos

EXCHANGE RATES: pesos per US$1 - 0.99870 (December 1994), 0.99901 (1994), 0.99895 (1993), 0.99064 (1992), 0.95355 (1991), 0.48759 (1990)

EXCHANGE RATE AS OF THIS WRITING: 1.00 US Dollar = 0.9997 Argentine Peso (1.00 Argentine Peso = 1.00010 US Dollar)

ESCAPE FROM AMERICA
PRIVATIZATION AND EMPLOYEE OWNERSHIP IN ARGENTINA

A percentage of the Argentine economy was nationalized in the past, including trains, planes, phones, utilities, and other basic services. The figure given for the nationalization of the private sector was 7% of the total. Today, the government's goal is to sell back (privatize) most of the nationalized companies.

A shared ownership program is currently being made available in Argentina. The Argentine program involves reserving 10% of the shares in companies being privatized for purchase by employees. The program is called "Programa de Propiedad Participada" (Shared Ownership Program), or PPP. Workers must buy shares at market price; however, special "privatization bonuses" that can pay up to 50% of the stock price are available for this purpose. The remaining 50% is paid directly by the employees, mostly through payroll deductions and/or dividend payments on the stock (dividends can pay off only a small amount of the loans, however). The number of shares that each employee can purchase is determined by the employee's years of employment, salary, and other factors.

Worker-shareholders have the right to vote a representative on the company's board of directors. Upon retirement, death or employment termination, employee shares are sold back to the company through a special "Fondo de Garantia y Recompra" (guarantee and repurchase fund). The share price at departure is either the purchase price or, if higher, the last stock price as approved by the shareholders meeting for that year. The first large state-owned company to set up a PPP was the Argentine National Gas Company.

We admit that we don't know a great deal about this program. Information regarding the PPP program was derived from the WebSite of The National Center for Employee ownership (NCEO) phone 510/272-9461; email: nceo@nceo.org; URL: WWW http://www.nceo.org/

CURRENTLY MANUFACTURED ARGENTINE INDUSTRIES: food processing, motor vehicles, consumer durables, textiles, chemicals and petrochemicals, printing, metallurgy, steel

AGRICULTURE (Including fishing): accounts for over 8% of GDP and produces abundant food for both domestic consumption and exports. As noted on the previous page Argentina's agriculture is diverse and places Argentina on the list of the world's top five exporters of grain and beef. Principal crops: are wheat, corn, sorghum, soybeans, and sugar beets.

💻 TELECOMMUNICATIONS & THE WWW

Argentina has Chile and Brazil as close neighbors which fact tends to give Argentina some pretty stiff competition for WebSite quality, quantity and artistic creativity. However we're going to go on record by saying that Argentina certainly leads the pack in content and efficacy.

We do a lot of web-surfing. Probably more surfing than the average person. We personally spend about five hours a day on the Internet looking at the WebSites and Network Infrastructure of many different nations around the world. That fact gives us some sort of subjective view of what different nations have going Web wise. Speaking of the Mercosur nations and including Chile in the equation, we would have to evaluate them as follows: Brazil has the artistic edge. Chile the technical. Argentina has the edge in dependable data. Surprisingly, Uruguay also has good quality WebSites, which is amazing considering the fact that Uruguay has only 3 million people. Paraguay still has a way to go.

ELECTRICITY: capacity: 17,330,000 kW production: 54.8 billion kWh consumption per capita: 1,610 kWh (1993)

COMMUNICATIONS:
Telephone system: 2,650,000 telephones; 12,000 public telephones; 78 telephones/1,000 persons; extensive modern system but many families do not have telephones; microwave widely used; however, during rainstorms, the telephone system frequently grounds out, even in Buenos Aires.
intercity: microwave radio relay and domestic satellite network with 40 earth stations
international: 2 INTELSAT (Atlantic Ocean) earth stations
Radio: broadcast stations: AM 171, FM 0, shortwave 13
Televison: broadcast stations: 231

🖥WWW WEBSITES & RESOURCES FOR ARGENTINA:

● This WebSite here was voted the best Argentine Personal Homepage on the Web! note: We have to admit that it is pretty good and highly informative.
URL: http://www.middlebury.edu/~leparc/htm/argent2.htm

● **ARGENTINE REFERENCE DESK** / A LARGE REFERENCE PAGE ON ARGENTINA
URL: http://lanic.utexas.edu:80/la/argentina/

● **The World Wide Web Virtual Library Latin American Studies**
URL: http://lanic.utexas.edu:80/las.html

● TRAVEL FILE

URL: http://www.travelfile.com/go
Also try: http://www.travelfile.com/$mapimage/tvl/maps/dmr_tbar.imagemap?342,7
Travel File is a series of searchable directories containing over 100,000 files of information on travel suppliers, tourism offices, attractions, and events for destinations worldwide. TravelFile has been available to professional travel agents through their airline reservation systems since 1989 and is now available to us regular folks to make our traveling easier. TravelFile provides a direct link between travel suppliers and travel planners through their global on-line network. You can make reservations and send messages to many of the travel suppliers listed in the TravelFile directories.

INTERNET ACCESS PROVIDERS IN ARGENTINA

We aren't quite sure if they list all of them, but here's a WebSite that lists **Access Providers** in Argentina: **URL:** http://www.best.be/iap/

● ARNET

Ministerio de Relaciones Exteriores y Culto - Reconquista 1088 1er. Piso - Informatica
(1003) Buenos Aires, ARGENTINA
Phone : +541 313 8082 Fax : +541 814 4824 email : noc-arnet@atina.ar

● GES de Argentina S.A.

Phone : 011-541-814-0592
URL: WWW : http://www.ges.com

● ImpSat

Alferez Pareja 256
1107 Buenos Aires
Services : Dial Up and leased interNet Services
POPs : 28.8 Kbps
Contact : Sofia Pescarmona Phone : (54-1) 318 8333 Fax : (54-1) 318 8444
email : spescarmona@impsat.com.ar email : atombesi@impsat1.com.ar
URL: WWW : http://www.impsat.com.ar
Note : ISP present in Argentina, Colombia, Mexico, Venezuela and Ecuador. It is the second ISP in Argentina.

● Proyecto Wamani -CCI

Centro de Comunicacion de Informacion - Talcahuano 325 - 3F
1013 Buenos Aires - Argentina
Contact : Carlos E. Alvarez (tecnica de operaciones)
Phone : 54 (1) 382-6842 / 793-1502 email : carlos@wamani.org.ar

● Red Cientifica y Tecnologica Nacional RECyT

Av. Cordoba 831 3er. Piso
Republica de Argentina
Contact : Estela Barone (Coordinador RECyT) Phone : (54-1)312-8917
Fax : (54-1)312-414201-054
email : ebarone@secyt.gov.ar

● **REDUBA (ex RAN)**

Servicio de Informacion-Centro de Comunicacion Cientifica (UBA)-Universidad de Buenos Aires
Pab. I, Cdad. Universitaria-Intendente Guiraldes s/n
Contact : Julian Dunayevich Phone : (54 1) 783 0729 (voz y fax) Fax : 54 (01) 311-0516
email : postmaster@ccc.uba.edu.ar

● **RETINA** Asociacion Ciencia Hoy Corrientes 2835 - Cuerpo A - 5o A
1193 - Buenos Aires
Phone : 54 - 1 - 961 - 1824 Fax : 54 - 1 - 962 - 1330
email : rtperez@arcriba.edu.ar

● **SatLink S.A.**

Sarmiento 944 - Piso 7
(1041) Buenos Aires
Phone : +54-1-474-4512 email : info@satlink.com
URL: WWW : http://www.satlink.com
Note: SatLink is the major Internet Service Provider in Argentina. Services available are analog & digital leased lines, dialup access up to V.34 and has POPs (Point of Prescence) in major cities in Argentina. Other services are UUCP and E-mail to international fax gateway.

● **SiON**

Av. Gaona 4455, Ciudadela (1702) - Buenos Aires, Argentina.
Services : E-Mail, Newsgroups (All), FTP, Gopher, Archie, etc...
Phone : (+54-1) 656-9195 (Rotary lines) Fax : (+54-1) 653-0413 EMail : Info@SiON.COM.ar
Last Update : 10/06/96

● **SISCOTEL, S.A.**

Rivadavia 822, Piso 1- Buenos Aires
Phone : (54-1) 331-6249 Fax : (54-1) 342-5437

● **Stardel S.A.**

25 de Mayo 637 2 piso
1002 Buenos Aires Argentina
Services : full internet
Phone : 54-1-318-6000 Fax : 54-1-313-4327 email : info@startel.com.ar
URL: WWW : http://www.startel.com.ar
Note: Startel is a commercial internet provider from Argentina and also is the operator for the national IP backbone.

● **Universidad Nacional de la Plata**

Director General Cientifico y Tecnico. CESPI
50 Y 115, 3er piso - (1900)La Plata
Contact : F. Javier Diaz Phone : (54-21)35102/43179/43552 Fax : (54-21)257240
email : jdiaz@unlp.edu.ar

FOR NEWSPAPERS IN ARGENTINA: AGENCY INTERIOR BUENOS AIRES (AIBA)

Street 48 [nº] 641- 1900 The Silver- Argentina

Tel./ Fax (54 21) 230823/ 24- BBS: (54 21) 259368

Fax-on-Demand data base: (54 21) 240288

URL: [http]:// [www.satlink.com]/ [aiba] email: [aiba]@ [satlink.com]

AIBA is an independent news agency in Buenos Aires that contains the contact numbers & addresses of 40 different journalistic resources. They publish a periodical called *Advances.*

📖 **The U.S. House of Representatives**

Internet Law Library

Argentina **URL:** http://law.house.gov:80/118.htm

WEB SERVER ARGENTINA:

URL: http://www.cts.com/browse/intervox/index.html

InterVox Argentina

Tel (54-1) 788-5395 Fax: (54-1) 788-0436

email: informes@intervox.com.ar

CLARIN NEWSPAPER URL: http://www.clarin.com/

Argentine companies related with foreign trade: **Net Group S.A.**

URL: http://www.externa.com.ar/ExIng/COM/compa.htm

Net Group S.A. Pueyrredon 860 12th Floor (1032) Buenos Aires, Argentina

Tel. (541) 963-9191; Fax: 54-1-964-0801

email: info@externa.com.ar

Asociación World Wide Web Argentina

URL: http://www.ibmpcug.co.uk/%7Eawwwa/index.html

Ⓞ**Telefónica de Argentina Home Page**

Argentina Phone Directory (White, Yellow and Blue Pages)

URL: http://www.telefonica.com.ar/GUIAS/Paginas.htm

A LIST OF ALL OF THE SCHOOLS IN ARGENTINA IS LISTED AT:

WorldWide Classroom

URL: http://www.worldwide.edu/ci/argentina/fargentina.html

Box 1166 - Milwaukee, WI 53201-1166, USA

Phone: (414) 224-3476 - FAX: (414) 224-3466

E-Mail: study@worldwide.edu

NOTE: Student Visas are issued to students that are going to study for a period of 360 days or less. Documents to be presented are the same as other Visa applications (listed in this section) with the inclusion of a parental authorization form that can be obtained at the Argentine Consular Office

FINAL COMMENTS ON THE ECONOMY OF ARGENTINA

Statistics, as we are fond of saying, are quite slippery fellows. Nonetheless, we would like to give some closing comments regarding Argentinas economic situation. From 1991 through 1994 Argentina's economy grew almost 55 percent in current dollar terms, second only to China's growth during that same period. Per Capita growth was also impressive. The GDP per capita for 1994 was US$8,159 up from 1993 by anywhere from 60 percent to 67 percent, depending on which set of figures we are to accept. Measuring Argentina's growth is difficult because in the past the Peso was so subject to bouts of heavy inflation and devaluation. As the economy comes out from under the burden of government domination these figures should be clearer and clearer to read with each passing year. Hopefully, Argentina will separate its Federal Reserve from government control, making it a separate office totally free of any governmental restraints. This will make not only the figures and the facts clearer to read, it will put Argentina in front of the pack, and insure its position as a world leader. By any standard, despite the absence of unwavering facts and figures, economic growth in Argentina has become an undeniable fact of reality. In current dollar terms, its growth has been second only to Chinas during the same period.

It is obvious that we like Argentina. Decidedly so. We like its people, its culture, and its rugged natural environment. We believe that the future of hope is in Argentina and not in China. We believe strongly in Mercosur, and the combination of South American countries of which it is comprised. Having abandoned statism, heavy with talent, abundant with resources, let us see what they can do working in unison.

FREEDOM HOUSE

CURRENT FREEDOMS: Freedom House granted Argentina a score of:

Political Rights: ② **Civil Liberties:** ③

This score, reflects an unfortunate downward trend caused by the current president, Carlos Menem. Because it is impossible to know the inner working of every political intrigue, we cannot comment at this time on this unhappy note. We suspect that it is the usual wrangling's of politicos trying to have their way; however we cannot see behind closed doors and cannot yet understand every aspect of every political maneuver. What we suspect, is that the privitization of the state-owned sectors is causing unhappiness with those who have been getting a free lunch. This is exactly the sort of issue we hope to update in our fax-on-demand service, which we will explain in detail in another section. (Our hope is to be able to constantly update readers as to political changes, economic opportunities, real estate opportunities as they come available due to shifting markets, currency opportunities and so forth. We hope to be able to be on site to be able to evaluate these things for our readers in a way that expresses the philosophy of our book.)

What we will say regarding the Argentine situation is that we believe that President Menem has overstepped his bounds in the view of Freedom House, and we won't argue with that evaluation. We do note that freedom of the press is still strong in Argentina, and what has occurred can be related to President Menems attempt to free the economy and deal with the pressures of doing so. The economy has continued to grow, economic freedom is continually on the increase, and the Gross Domestic Product per capita has increased by a very large margin, which speaks well for the personal life and fortunes of the individual citizens of Argentina. They have just reelected President Menem for a second term, by a fairly wide margin. The consensus is that Menem is liked and appreciated by the Argentines. Again, we do not disagree with the conclusions of Freedom House, their analysis is across the board, and that is the only way they could possibly give a fair and accurate analysis. For instance, President Menem granted a pardon to the convicted military personnel involved in the 'dirty war' and halted further prosecutions of the military. Freedom House would rightly see this as an intervention into the Judicial System; and did. However, President Menem used the opportunity to reduce the military budget by half, while privatizing defense industries and abolishing universal conscription, which move, places the armed forces under effective civilian rule for the first time in decades. We must view these events in context, even if Freedom House, in order to be of value, cannot. This doesn't mean that we have turned our back on the issues of morality. We cannot. By the same token, we cannot turn our back on reality. The top-heavy power of the military needed to be brought into balance, and placed at the disposal of the will of the people of Argentina. The moral thing to do would be to pen them up and make them eat grass like domesticated cattle; but we know in our heart of heart's that tigers don't eat grass; so why pretend that they might? Menem acted pragmatically, we are not asked to like it, or to assume that Judicial procedures were properly followed. In view of actual events such as these, Freedom House will give us the facts, unbiased, impartial, and across the board. We, in turn, are left to interpret them.

SOAP BOX TIME

With luck, evolution may carry us away from government oppression, and perhaps someday injustice may become less frequent in human affairs. With really good luck we may be free of governments altogether; it's not impossible. More then once I have been accused of romanticism for these statements and the naivete my optimism implies. Okay, I am sophomoric, half-baked, and half smart ...it is undeniably true. Who would deny that I am a fool? I'd like to believe that the mothers of the Plaza de Mayo may learn to sleep once again without burning hearts. Because I believe that the idiocy that took their children never should have happened. More. I believe that without governments it never would have happened. But I am not so dumb as to believe that the lion will ever lay down with the lamb. We will never be free of the responsibility of making judgements and forming interpretations from the judgements that we make. Perhaps it is recognition and fear of that responsibly that causes incapable fools to create and continuously maintain bad governments. Somehow they intuitively grasp what the psychological and spiritual requirements of independent judgment actually entail and they fear the responsibility. It is obvious, or it should be, that in order to learn to make judgements we must prepare our own selves to be judged.

GETTING IN & STAYING IN

EMBASSY OF ARGENTINA
1600 New Hampshire Ave., N.W., Washington, DC 20009
Tel: 202-939-6400 - Fax: 202-332-3171
email to: mjr@atina.ar or aln@atina.ar
The Argentine Embassy has a website at: http://www.ar/cwash/homepage/

PERMANENT VISAS (IMMIGRATION VISAS)

A form must be filled out at the Consular Office to be sent to the National Direction of Migration in Argentina for review and further instructions. (fee)
Permanent resident visas-for spouses, sons/daughters and parents of Argentine citizens
The following documents must be presented to the Consular Office:
Valid passport 2 photographs (1.5 x 1.5, color, light background, 3/4 right profile, head and shoulders).
Health certificate- (HIV and AIDS test must be included). Check with the Consular Office for forms. **
Good conduct certificates for everyone over 16 years old, from the areas where you lived in the past five years. **
Birth and marriage certificates. ** (must be the long form proving relationship) - .
** Documents must be legalized by the Consular Office of the State where document was issued.

LEGALIZATION OF DOCUMENTS: All documents to be presented in Argentina, must be legalized by the Argentine Consular Section or a Consulate (please check jurisdictions). Documents that must be legalized are: Power of Attorney, Company Certifications, Affidavits, Birth, Marriage, Death and Divorce Certificates, Diplomas and School Transcripts and Phytosanitary Certificates. If the document to be presented is a public one, you must get an apostille. To do so you must check with the Secretary of State of the state where the document was issued. Apostilles are only valid on public documents which are sent directly to Argentina. Only an original document can be legalized (no photocopies, faxed copies or erasures will be accepted). Signature must be in original form; also print name and title under the signature. Signatures must first be registered at the Consular Section or Consulate. Call the Consulate in your jurisdiction for further instructions and fees. Translations of any type of document to be presented in Argentina, must be done within the jurisdiction where the document will be presented (in Argentina). To avoid unnecessary delays, check with the Consulate before mailing documents for legalization to make sure you have followed the proper procedures.

Photocopies of documents can be legalized only if presented to the Consulate with the original document.

Check for fees. If you are traveling with your pet (dogs and cats only) a certificate of rabies vaccination and a health certificate signed by the veterinarian and a notary public registered at the consulate or the USPHIS, and two pictures of the animal (only for ID purposes) must be sent to the Consular Office ten days prior to departure, so that the animal will not stay in quarantine upon your arrival. (Check for fees)

CUSTOM REQUIREMENTS

To enter a vehicle and personal belongings into Argentina, all foreign citizens moving to Argentina will need to show Custom authorities the proper visa and certificate. A custom fee will be assessed as to the Blue Book value of the car. Check with the consular office as to how to obtain a certificate of residency. (fee) Travelers entering Argentina as tourists will be assessed a customs fee for articles they are introducing into the country as gifts over a limit of u$ 300.00 All electronic articles will have a duty of approximately 50% of its value. If you are entering Argentina with your automobile, you must send the vehicle title in your name and the sales receipt to the Consular office for a visto.(fee) Only those over the age of 21 years are allowed to enter an automobile. Tourist Visa

TEMPORARY RESIDENT VISAS

Issued to those that need to stay in Argentina for a period longer than six months. The following documents   must be presented to the corresponding Consular Office:
Valid passport
Letter from the sponsor and a letter from the organization in Argentina where you will be working or studying. (a contract or an acceptance school certificate legalized by the Ministry of Education.)
One photograph
Fees (must check with Consular Office)
Good Conduct Certificate for those over 16 years of age, from their local Police Department and the areas where person resided in the past five years. **
Good Health Certificate (HIV and AIDS test must be included). Check with the Consulate Office for medical form.**
Birth certificate and marriage certificate if applicable. **
 ** Documents must first be legalized by the Consulate that has jurisdiction over such document. Example: if a birth certificate from California is going to be presented in Washington, DC, it must first be legalized by the Argentine Consulate in Los Angeles.

STUDENT VISAS

They are issued to students that are going to study for a period of 360 days or less. Documents to be presented are the same as above with the inclusion of a parental authorization form, that can be obtained at the Consular Office. (fee).

CONSULATES

ARGENTINE CONSULATES IN THE UNITED STATES
URL: http://members.aol.com/sealandtou/consul.htm

CONSULATE GENERAL OF ARGENTINA IN ATLANTA, GA:

229 Peachtree Street, Suite 1401
Altanta, GA 30303
Ph: (404) 880-0805   Fax: (404) 880-0806
Territorial Jurisdiction: Alabama, Georgia, Kentucky, Mississippi, South Carolina and Tennessee.

CONSULATE GENERAL OF ARGENTINA IN CHICAGO, IL:
205 North Michigan Ave., Suite 4208
Chicago, IL 60601
Ph: (312) 819-2610   Fax (312) 819-2612
Territorial Jurisdiction: Illinois, Indiana, Iowa, Kansas, Michigan, Minnesota, Missouri, Nebraska, North Dakota, Ohio, South Dakota, Wisconsin.

CONSULATE GENERAL OF ARGENTINA IN HOUSTON, TX:
1990 Post Oak Blvd., Suite 770
Houston, TX 77056
Ph: (713) 871-8935   Fax: (713) 871-0639
Territorial Jurisdiction: Arkansas, Colorado, Louisiana, New Mexico, Oklahoma and Texas.

CONSULATE GENERAL OF ARGENTINA IN LOS ANGELES, CA:
5055 Wilshire Blvd., Suite 210 & 208
Los Angeles, CA 90036
Ph: (213) 954-9155   Fax: (213) 937-3841
Territorial Jurisdiction: Alaska, Arizona, California, Idaho, Montana, Nevada, Oregon, Utah, Washington,   Wyoming, Hawaii, Pacific Islands and Carolina Islands.

CONSULATE GENERAL OF ARGENTINA IN MIAMI, FL:
800 Brickell Ave., PH 1
Miami, Fl 33131
Ph: (305) 373-7794 Fax: (305) 371-7108
Territorial Jurisdiction: Florida, Puerto Rico, Bahamas and US Virgin Islands.

CONSULATE GENERAL OF ARGENTINA IN NEW YORK, NY:
12 West 56th St.
New York, NY 10019
Ph: (212) 603-0400   Fax: (212) 541-7746
Territorial Jurisdiction: Connecticut, Maine, Massachusetts, New Jersey, New Hampshire, New York, Rhode Island, and Vermont.

ON THE GROUND IN ARGENTINA

Argentina is possibly the best expat destination in the world. It has almost every-thing. With the addition of a stable government it *will* have everything. Anyone who could bored in Argentina should stay in Seattle buy a television and live in a board-ing house.

BUENOS AIRES

To the city's poet laureate, Jorge Luis Borges, Buenos Aires was as eternal as air and water. To many Argentines, their capital city is synonymous with the country itself, and indeed 40% of the population lives in the city's massive, sprawling suburbs. Buenos Aires is situated on the banks of the Río de la Plata in the Federal Capital district, and not, as one would expect, in Buenos Aires province. A city transported from its European parent, its compact and regular centre is reminiscent of Paris, but its tree-lined avenues and frequent plazas have a beguiling, faded elegance. The city throngs with bankers on the make and sophisticated dressers mingling with the gaunt beggars and unemployed from the surrounding shanty-town suburbs. Downtown, the Plaza de Mayo is the traditional focus of activity, while nearby Avenida 9 de Julio is popularly known as the world's widest thoroughfare and is truly a pedestrian's night-mare. Avenida Santa Fe is the most fashionable shopping area.

Buenos Aires' attractions include the Catedral Metropolitana, which contains the tomb of José de San Martín, a hero of Argentina's struggle for independence; the Teatro Colón, a world-class facility for opera, ballet and classical music; a cluster of worthwhile and popular museums, including the Museo Nacional de Bellas Artes, Museo del Cine and Museo Histórico Nacional, which presents a panorama of the Argentine experience; the colourful Italian suburb of La Boca, which features brightly painted wooden houses lining the Riachuelo waterway; and the Cementerio de la Recoleta, the place to go to witness the national passion for death.

Buenos Aires is an expensive city but regardless whether you're after a cheap or a top-end hotel, it is possible to stay right in the centre of things. Congreso is a good place to look for inexpensive lodgings, while mid-range hotels are concentrated on Avenida de Mayo. Food bargains can be had in the suburbs of La Boca and San Telmo. Downtown, Lavalle and Avenida Corrientes are the places to go for pizza, coffee with the city's intellectuals or one of those ubiquitous meaty dishes.

MAR DEL PLATA

If summer means the beach to the inhabitants of Greater Buenos Aires, Mar del Plata is most often the beach they are thinking of. Situated on the northern Atlantic coast, 400 km from the capital, beaches in this area sprawl for eight km, with sophisticated mansions (reflecting the area's upper-class origins) mingling with the new middle-class resorts. Sea lions keep an eye on the fishing activities around the wharves, and a replica of the grotto of Lourdes is a kitsch paradise.

CORDOBA

Argentina's second city, Córdoba, long rivalled Buenos Aires for political, economic and cultural supremacy; indeed, while Buenos Aires languished through neglect, Cordoba was the country's architectural treasure house. Today, a fine collection of colonial buildings is concentrated in its compact centre. They include the old market, the Iglesia Catedral (featuring a Romanesque dome) and the Jesuit Iglesia de la Compañía. The Museo Históricao Provincial Marqués de Sobremonte is one of the most important historical museums in the country.

THE PAMPAS

The unrelentingly flat Pampas is Argentina's agricultural heartland and the home of that symbol of romantic nationalism, the gaucho. Comprising the provinces of Buenos Aires, La Pampa and major parts of Santa Fe and Córdoba, its varied environments include forested hills, extensive grasslands and flamingo-coated salt lakes. The Parque National Liahué Calel is a popular detour, with wildlife including some puma and many guanaco, rhea, native hares and a variety of wild chinchilla called a vizcacha. The cities of La Plata, Luján (whose basilica to La Virgen de Luján receives four million pilgrims a year), Rosario and Santa Fe are worth seeing for their many museums, churches and faded colonial buildings.Iguazú Falls

Situated in the Parque Nacional Iguazú near Puerto Iguazú, these spectacular falls lie just east of the confluence of the Iguazu and Paraná rivers. At least 5000 cubic metres of water per second plunge the 70 metres into the abyss below. If they look familiar, it's because they were the supporting actors in the film The Mission; appropriately, the area has historic ruins of Jesuit missions which also draw many visitors. San Ignacio Miní, built in a style of architecture known as 'Guaraní baroque', is especially popular. Above the falls, the waters are suitable for canoeing, kayaking and other water sports. The surrounding park is home to 55,000 hectares of pristine subtropical rainforest, with abundant wildlife and plant species.

GETTING THERE & AWAY

Argentina has excellent worldwide air connections, with Aeropuerto Internacional Ezeiza, outside Buenos Aires, the main international airport. A departure tax of US$13 is payable on international flights; the tax is US$5 on flights to Uruguay.

Argentina Airport Information:
Capital: Buenos Aires Airport Information
Name of airport: Ministro Pistarini (Ezeiza) Airport
Distance to city: 51 km
Airport tax: USD 13
Transportation between airport and city: Bus fare: ~USD 14 frequency: every 30 min (05:00 - 23:00) Taxi fare: ~USD 49
A multitude of land and river crossing points connect Argentina with neighbouring Uruguay, Brazil, Paraguay, Bolivia and Chile. Travel from Chile usually involves a hike through the Andes, while over land travel to Bolivia can go through the border

towns of La Quiaca, Tarija, Pocitos/Yacuiba. Paraguay can be reached by bus and/or river launch, and the most common crossing to Brazil is via Foz do Iguaçu or Uruguaiana. Uruguay is linked to Argentina by road bridges, and ferries sail between Buenos Aires and Colonia in Uruguay.

GETTING AROUND

Three Argentine airlines attempt to make this big country appear smaller: Aerolíneas Argentinas handles domestic as well as international routes, Austral covers domestic routes only, and Líneas Aéreas del Estado serves mostly Patagonian destinations. Discount deals and passes are advisable as fares are expensive. Argentine domestic flights carry a departure tax of around US$2.50.

Long-distance buses are fast and comfortable; some even provide on-board meal services. However, fares are expensive and fluctuate wildly according to inflation.

The country's extensive rail network is unfortunately under threat.

US STATE DEPARTMENT TRAVEL WARNING INFORMATION

COUNTRY DISCRIPTION: Argentina is a medium income nation with a developing economy. The quality of facilities for tourism varies according to price and area.

ENTRY REQUIREMENTS: A passport is required. U.S. citizens do not need a visa for a tourist stay. For current information concerning entry and customs requirements for Argentina, travelers can contact the Argentine Embassy at 1600 New Hampshire Avenue N.W., Washington, D.C., tel: (202) 939- 6400, or the nearest consulate in Los Angeles, Miami, New Orleans, Chicago, New York, Houston, or San Juan.

MEDICAL FACILITIES: Medical care is good but varies in quality outside major cities. Doctors and hospitals often expect immediate cash payment for health services. U.S. medical insurance is not always valid outside the United States. The Medicare/Medicaid program does not provide payment of medical services outside the United States. In some cases, medical insurance with specific overseas and medical evacuation coverage has proved to be useful. For additional health information, travelers can contact the Centers for Disease Control's international travelers hotline at (404) 332- 4559.

CRIME INFORMATION: There are no specific threats directed against American visitors or tourists at the present time. Street crime is a problem in the metropolitan Buenos Aires area. Most crime affecting tourists or business travelers in Argentina is of the non-violent type: pickpockets, purse snatching, hotel burglaries and fraudulent dealings.
However, it is recommended that caution be exercised when traveling about the city. Street robberies (muggings), while not common, are not unheard of in Buenos Aires. For additional crime information, travelers can contact the Consular Section of the U.S. Embassy either before or upon arrival.

ADOPTIONS: Argentine adoptions often involve complications and delays. In general, the adoption of Argentine orphans is possible but discouraged by the Council of Minors due to a waiting list of qualified Argentine couples wishing to adopt children. Updated information on Argentine adoption proceedings and U.S. immigrant visarequirements is available from the Consular Section of the U.S. Embassy. Additional information is available byrequirements is available from the Consular Section of the U.S. Embassy.

Additional information is available by writing the Office of Citizens Consular Services, CA/OCS/CCS, Room 4817, Department of State, Washington, D.C. 20520, or by telephoning (202) 647-3712.

DUAL NATIONALITY: U.S. citizens also considered to be citizens of Argentina who remain in Argentina more than sixty days, are required to leave the country on their Argentine passports. They might also be subject to compulsory military service while in Argentina. Those who may be affected can inquire at an Argentine embassy or consulate to determine their status. In some instances, dual nationality may hamper U.S. government efforts to provide protection abroad.

DRUG PENALITIES: U.S. citizens are subject to the laws of the country in which they are traveling. Penalties in Argentina for possession, use and trafficking in illegal drugs are strict, and convicted offenders can expect lengthy jail sentences and fines.

AVIATION OVERSIGHT: In October 1992, the U.S. Federal Aviation Administration assessed Argentina's civil aviation authority as in compliance with international aviation safety oversight standards for Argentine carriers operating to and from the U.S. The same level of safety oversight would typically be applied to operations to other destinations. For further information, travelers may contact the Department of Transportation at 1-800-322-7873.

EMBASSY OF THE UNITED STATES IN ARGENTINA: LOCATION/ REGISTRATION: Americans are encouraged to register with the Consular Section of the U.S. Embassy in Buenos Aires at 4300 Colombia, 1425, telephone: (54-1) 777-4533.

EMBASSY OF ARGENTINA IN THE UNITED STATES
1600 New Hampshire Ave., N.W., Washington, DC 20009
Tel: 202-939-6400 - Fax: 202-332-3171
email to: mjr@atina.ar or aln@atina.ar
The Argentine Embassy has a website at: http://www.ar/cwash/homepage/

RESOURCES FOR ARGENTINA

Argentina Airport Information:
Capital: Buenos Aires Airport Information
Name of airport: Ministro Pistarini (Ezeiza) Airport
Distance to city: 51 km
Airport tax: USD 13
Transportation between airport and city: Bus fare: ~USD 14 frequency: every 30 min (05:00 - 23:00) Taxi fare: ~USD 49

AGENCY INTERIOR BUENOS AIRES (AIBA)
Street 48 [n°] 641- 1900 The Silver- Argentina
Tel./ Fax (54 21) 230823/ 24- BBS: (54 21) 259368
Fax-on-Demand data base: (54 21) 240288
URL: [http]:// [www.satlink.com]/ [aiba] email: [aiba]@ [satlink.com]
AIBA is an independent news agency in Buenos Aires that contains the contact numbers & addresses of 40 different journalistic resources. They publish a periodical called *Advances*.

ADVENTUROUS TRAVEL BOOKSTORE
SOUTH AMERICA BOOK, TAPE, VIDEO & MAP RESOURCES:
Call: (800) 282-3963/(802) 860-6776 Fax: (800) 677-1821/(802) 860-6667
URL: http://www.gorp.com/atb/samer.htm
PO Box 1468
Williston, VT 05495
email: books@atbook.com

Argentine companies related with foreign trade: Net Group S.A.
URL: http://www.externa.com.ar/ExIng/COM/compa.htm
Net Group S.A. Pueyrredon 860 12th Floor (1032) Buenos Aires, Argentina
Tel. (541) 963-9191; Fax: 54-1-964-0801
email: info@externa.com.ar

For more information on travelling to Argentina, contact the Argentine National Tourist Office. The heardquarters is located in Buenos Aires.
National Tourist Office
Santa Fe 883
Buenos Aires, Argentina
Ph: [54](1) 312-2232/-6560

A LIST OF ALL OF THE SCHOOLS IN ARGENTINA IS LISTED AT:

WorldWide Classroom URL: http://www.worldwide.edu/ci/argentina/fargentina.html

Box 1166 - Milwaukee, WI 53201-1166, USA

Phone: (414) 224-3476 - FAX: (414) 224-3466

E-Mail: study@worldwide.edu

NOTE: Student Visas are issued to students that are going to study for a period of 360 days or less. Documents to be presented are the same as other Visa applications (listed in this section) with the inclusion of a parental authorization form that can be obtained at the Argentine Consular Office.

THE LARGEST ARGENTINE LAW FIRMS (Listed without endorsement.)

● Abeledo Gottheil Abogados, Avienida Madero 1020, 5th Floor, Buenos Aires, 1106, Argentina, Tel: (54) 1-3154721, Fax: (54)1-3127526, Contact: Julio Gottheil

● Allende & Brea, Maipu 1300, Buenos Aires, 1006, Argentina, Tel: (54) 1-3139191, Fax: (54) 1-3125288, Contact: Teodosio Cesar Brea

● Basilico Fernandez-Madero & Duggan, Marcelo T de Alvear 684, Piso 2, Buenos Aires, 1395,

● Argentina, Tel: (54) 1-3133030, Fax: (54) 1-3113903, Contact: Carlos A. Basilico

● Cardenas Cassagne & Asociados, Avienida Corrientes 545, 7th Floor, Buenos Aires, 1043, Argentina, Tel: (54) 3266690, Fax: (54) 1-111577, Contact: Juan Carlos Casssagne

● Estudio Beccar Varela, Cerrito 740, Buenos Aires, 1309, Argentina, Tel: (54) 1-3725100, Fax: (54)1-3726619, Contact: Marcelo P Saravi

● Estudio Bruzzon & Asociados, Av. Corrientes 222, 4th Floor, Buenos Aires, 1356, Argentina, Tel: (54)1-3154123/4134, Fax: (54) 1-1-3154218/8739, Contact: Juan Carlos Bruzzon

● Hope, Duggan & Silva, Av Leandro N Alem 1110, 3 piso, Buenos Aires, 1001, Argentina, Tel: (54)1-3151314, Fax: (54) 1-3150606, Contact: Adrian F.J. Hope

● LePera & Lessa, Avinida Leandro N Alem 1110, Piso 6, Buenos Aires, 1001, Argentina, Tel: (54)1-3119163, Fax: (54) 1-3119165, Contact: Sergio A.C. Le Pera

● Maciel, Norman & Asociados, Tte. Gral. J D Peron 328, 3rd Floor, Buenos Aires, 1038, Argentina, Tel: (54) 1-3429190, Fax: (54) 1-3343735, Contact: Rogelio N. Maciel

● Marval O'Farrell & Mairal,Carlos Pellegrini 887, 3rd Floor, Buenos Aires, 1338, Argentina, Tel: (54)1-348-0600, Fax: (54) 1-3224122, Contact: Alfredo Miguel O'Farrell, Esq.

● Marval O'Farrel & Mairal is one of the oldest law firms (founded in 1923) in Buenos Aires, as well as the largest one, as it presently has over 80 attorneys. The firm is in the general practice of law and is the Argentina member of Lex Mundi, a global association of 133 independent law firms.

● Negri Teijeino & Incera, Avenida Corrientes 330, 4th Floor, Buenos Aires, 1378, Argentina, Tel: (54) 1-328-1273, Fax: (54) 1-3285628, Contact: Mafalda Curutchet

● Quattrini, Laprida & Asociados, Av Del Libertador 602-4 Piso, Buenos Aires, 1001, Argentina, Tel: (54) 1-8141190, Fax: (54) 1-8141091, Contact: Sergio Quattrin

FACTS AT A GLANCE (CURRENT STATISTICS)

TIME & PLACE

LOCAL NAME: Argentina
TIME ZONE: GMT-3 (UTC minus three hours; Buenos Aires observes day-light-saving time.)
AREA: total area: 2,766,890 sq km (1,073,115 sq mi ±)
       land area: 2,736,690 sq km
Argentina claims a total surface area of 3,761,274 sq km (1,452,228 sq mi) of which three fourths; just under 2.8 million sq km (1.1 million sq mi) - - is located on the South American continent (the rest consists of a sector of Antarctic and three groups of islands in the South Atlantic.) Based on area, continental Argentina is the eighth largest country in the world.
COAST LINE: 4,989 km (3,093 mi)
STATUS: Republic
DATE OF INDEPENDENCE: 9 July 1816
CAPITAL: Buenos Aires (means 'good air') population: approximately 10 million '*porteno's*' live in Buenos Aires which amounts to one third of the total population of Argentina.

SORTED STATISTICS:

Total Budget: revenues: $48.46 billion expenditures: $46.5 billion, including capital expenditures of $3.5 billion (1994 est.)
Exports: $15.7 billion (f.o.b., 1994 est.) commodities: meat, wheat, corn, oilseed, manufactures
Export Trading partners: US 12%, Brazil, Italy, Japan, Netherlands
Imports: $21.4 billion (c.i.f., 1994 est.)
Commodities: machinery and equipment, chemicals, metals, fuels and lubricants, agricultural products
Import Trading partners: US 22%, Brazil, Germany, Bolivia, Japan, Italy, Netherlands
External debt: $73 billion (April 1994)

ESCAPE FROM AMERICA

PEOPLE

LANGUAGES: Spanish, Italian, Guarani (an Indian dialect), Brazilero (Portuguese & Spanish mixed, spoken along the Brazilian border.)
ETHNIC GROUPS AND DIVISIONS: European 85% (mostly Italian and Spanish, large groupings of Welch and British.) Mestizo 15%
RELIGIONS: Catholic 90%, Protestant 2%,
OFF THE RECORD: Argentine Roman Catholicism, the official state religion, is riddled with popular beliefs which diverge from official doctrine. Spiritualism and veneration of the dead are deep-seated, with pilgrimages to the resting places of relations and of the famous dead a common sight. Spanish is the official language, but some immigrant communities retain their language as a badge of identity. Italian is widely understood, reflecting the influence of the country's single largest immigrant group, and BBC English is the preserve of the Anglo community. There are 17 native languages, including Quechua, Mapuche, Guaraní, Tobas and Matacos.
POPULATION OF ARGENTINA: 33,912,994 (July 1994 est)
Population growth rate: 1.12% (1994 est.)
POPULATION OF ARGENTINA: 34,292,742 (July 1995 est.)
Population growth rate: 1.11% (1995 est.)
Age structure:
0-14 years: 28% (female 4,706,793; male 4,903,589)
15-64 years: 62% (female 10,680,074; male 10,689,728)
65 years and over: 10% (female 1,922,552; male 1,390,006) (July 1995 est.)
Birth rate: 19.51 births/1,000 population (1995 est.)
Death rate: 8.62 deaths/1,000 population (1995 est.)
Net migration rate: 0.19 migrant(s)/1,000 population (1995 est.)
Infant mortality rate: 28.8 deaths/1,000 live births (1995 est.)
Life expectancy at birth: total population: 71.51 years
male: 68.22 years
female: 74.97 years (1995 est.)
Total fertility rate: 2.65 children born/woman (1995 est.)
Literacy: age 15 and over can read and write (1990 est.) :total population: 95%
male: 96%
female: 95%

CHAPTER TWELVE

COSTA RICA

O QUE RICA!

BEAUTIFUL COSTA RICA

Everyone (just about everyone,) speaks wonders about Cost Rica. Over 20,000 Americans live there, the highest number of expatriates for any Latin American country, which may indicate something about its livability if plurality indicates livability. Its climate, natural beauty, politics, as well as its economy are all spoken highly of. The United Nations places Costa Rica among the top 20 nations in the world in terms of health care. The general level of care in Costa Rican hospitals is said to be equal to or superior to that of the United States. The cost of living is low by American standards. Americans are allowed to own real estate and to operate a business there. And, the telephones work.

There is no shortage of books on Costa Rica providing information on everything from the ecology to the means of reestablishing our life there. In fact it is one of the few countries of the world that has books providing expatriate information specifically written about it. John Howell's **Choose Costa Rica**[1] is the classic and granddaddy of them all, but there is also **The Golden Door to Retirement and Living in Costa Rica,**[2] by Christopher Howard. These and other publications are listed at the end of the chapter as well as in the appendix. We are not as blindly excited about Costa Rica as many of it's numerous promoters claim to be. We'll tell you why.

ESCAPE FROM AMERICA

CONVENTIONAL NAME: Conventional long form: Republica de Costa Rica
TIME ZONES: GMT-6 Area: 19,694 sq mi (slightly smaller than West Virginia)
STATUS: Republic
DATE OF INDEPENDENCE: 1821
POPULATION: 3,343,154 (1994 est.) 3,130,000 (source: World Bank)
CAPITAL: San José (Population: 893,000 est)
LANGUAGES: Spanish (official) English is widely spoken.
ETHNIC GROUPS: European (87%), mestizo (7%), black/mulatto (3%) Approximately 70,000 blacks live in the Limón Province on the Caribbean Coast mostly Creole English-speaking descendents of Jamaican immigrants. The Limón Province is also the home to the Bribri and Cabécar Indians. Amerindian (1%) Religions: Roman Catholic (85%), the remaining 15% is made up of Protestant, Methodist, Baptist, Episcopalian, Jewish, and Bahai.
PHYSICAL FEATURES: Second smallest republic in Central America. Formed by a series of volcanic ridges: highest peak, Chirrpó Grande (12,529 feet). Tropical. Costal plains on both coasts are separated by rugged mountains.
CLIMATE: Perfect.
CURRENCY: Colón = (185.00 colones = US$1.00 July 1996)
ECONOMY: Capitalist-statist The economy is still based on agriculture: (coffee, bananas, sugar, cattle.) There is significant mining: (silver, bauxite, and there is currently exploration for petroleum underway.) Costa Rica has several free trade zones.
GDP: US$19.3 billion (1993 est.)
GDP Per Capita: $5,480 (1995 est.)
FOREIGN DEPT: $3.2 billion (1991) American Foreign Aid: $1.5 billion
FREEDOM HOUSE RATING: **Political Rights:** 1 **Civil Liberties:** 2
WWW: Costa Rica is online! There is a proliferation of Web Pages and of Web Presence Providers, but as of this writing, there is not open-competition for Internet Service Providers. (see the Costa Rica section on TELECOMMUNICATIONS & THE WWW)

CLIMATE

Costa Rica seems to offer something for everyone. It has three sperate climate zones. The area surrounding the capital, San José is called the central valley. It has temperate to cool weather. The mountain slopes surrounding the central valley and some of the small towns surrounding San José are blessed with perfect temperatures. San José boasts a daily high temperature that is usually in the 70's — and seldom goes into the 80's. Low temperatures are always in the 60's.

CULTURAL DIVERSITY

Because Costa Rica has two coast lines, one on the Atlantic and one on the Pacific, it also boasts two different tropical zones; the Atlantic being the tropical-wet zone, and the Pacific being the tropical-dry zone. The temperatures at sea level tend to fluctuate between the high 80's and low 90's in the summer. There is more humidly at sea level than there is in the central valley.

Costa Rica offers everything from pine forests to a fairly sophisticated urban scene. It has jungles, rivers, hot springs, good colleges, good schools, friendly people, rich farm lands, nightlife, entertainment, sports, diving, river rafting, casinos, fishing, low prices, good food, fresh fruits and vegetables, good coffee, movies, television, television-cable access, Internet Access, opera, dance, a good symphony orchestra, art galleries, libraries, bicycling, birdwatching, latin dancing, golf, running, surfing, horseback-riding, camping, bridge clubs, roller skating, mountaineering, eco-excursions, alpine lakes, great beaches, a Caribbean Culture on the Atlantic coast with its own native arts, museums, zoos, business opportunities, beautiful real estate, and quite probably an opportunity to live our life with a greater degree of interest and latitude then exists in the United States.

It is impossible to get bored in Cost Rica. It is a country of adventure that allows the physical freedom that is sadly missing in America today. But is more than that: its also a country that has decent schools and colleges with tuitions that are much lower than most American Universities. Foreigners can enroll in these schools and in some cases receive a degree recognized in the United States. With one of the highest literacy rates in the world and one of the best health care systems in the world, Costa Rica is far from being just another banana republic.

Costa Rica is the second-largest exporter in the Caribbean Basin It has a proliferation of Free Trade Zones (**FTZ's**), with foreign investors claiming the larger share of manufactured products, and Costa Rica having a thriving agricultural export market. There are approximately 130 foreign companies operating in the FTZ's, employing about 11,000 workers. All the FTZ's offer:

- 100 percent exemption from import duties and export taxes.
- Foreign exchange facilities independent of the Central Bank
- 100 percent exemption from municipal and capital taxes for ten years.
- 100 percent exemption from Costa Rican income taxes for twelve years, plus a 50 percent exemption for an additional six years.

Additionally, Costa Rica has enacted four other incentives to attract foreign investment

- Tax exemption on the import of capital goods and raw materials.
- Negotiable tax credits based on access to locally generated foreign currency.
- A guarantee of profit and capital repatriation.

Costa Rica has a number of governmental as well as privately owned facilities for promoting and encouraging investment into Costa Rica. For information regarding the Free Trade Zones contact:

Corporacion de la Zona Franca P.O. Box 96 Montes de Oca San José, Costa Rica
Phone: 506·222·5855 Fax: 506·233·5090

ESCAPE FROM AMERICA

There is an office called the **Center for Export and Investment Promotion (CENPRO)**, which assists prospective investors with information and the completion of forms required to set up a facility. (We have heard that their efforts to streamline investment regulatory procedures have been helpful and effective.) CENPRO helps exporters secure the necessary export approvals and obtain marketing information:

Center for Export and Investment Promotion CENPRO Ministry of Foreign Trade P.O. Box 5418-1000 San José, Costa Rica Phone: 506·221·7166 FAX: 506·223·5722

There is an office in the United States that promotes Costa Rican exports called the **Costa Rica Investment Promotion Offices (CINDE)**, they can be contacted at:

CINDE 992 High Ridge Road Stamford, CT 06905 Phone: 203·968·1448 FAX: 203·968·2591

Costa Rica has developed a reputation as being an attractive country for foreign investors in many areas, including exporting and in the utilization of the Free Trade Zone facilities. Costa Rica is known for its highly educated work force and for its record of having less racial, religious, or crime-related problems than many other so-called third world nations. Additionally, there has been a recent DOLLARIZATION of the economy proposed. Already almost every restaurant and store in Costa Rica accepts the U.S. dollar. There is currently much debate and speculation regarding pressures to abandon the national currency, the colón and to make the dollar the national currency. This would have the effect of preventing the Costa Rican Central Bank from manipulating the economy by printing worthless money. We believe that the overall effect would be a positive move for Costa Rica. While we are not exactly bullish on the dollar, the choice between the dollar and the colón is a choice between Americas rate of inflation and Costa Ricas. Costa Rica had a rate of inflation of 43% in 1995, which is many times worst than Americas rate of inflation vis a vis the dollar. Many Costa Rican politicos will undoubtedly fight this move; however the fact that some Costa Rican politicos thought it up is encouraging. Further demonstration that the Costa Ricans can be a very smart people.

TELECOMMUNICATIONS & THE WWW

Costa Rica has a reputation as having good telecommunications. This may be true from a functional perspective; the telephones work, which is always a surprise in any event. However, there are some stumbling blocks on the road to globalism. Two government subsidized monopolies, **Costa Rican Electricity Institute (ICE)**, and **Radiográfica Costarricense S.A. (RACSA)** have control over the industry. ICE has a state monopoly on telephone service and electrical generation. Congressional Opposition Deputy Hernán Fournier, a one time ICE executive director, has recently introduced a bill into the Costa Rican Congress designed to preserve this state monopoly. However, the government is currently preparing legislation that would open both sectors to competition, requiring ICE to compete with private companies for contracts on future projects. It is said, although we cannot confirm this, that Mr. Fournier is trying to booster ICE's position prior to ICE putting its company on the selling block.

Until such time as there is legislation to open these industries to market competition there exists the typical problem of competitive Internet Service Providers not being allowed to offer local internet access. Although both ICE and RACSA have governmental approval to provide Internet Access Services, RACSA is currently the only entity that is handling internet access. RACSA offers a $30.00 a month SLIP (serial line Internet protocol-connectivity) dialup connection at speeds of up to 28.8kbps. The $30.00 pays for 30 hours with additional hours paid at a rate of $1.00 per hour. Faster speeds and ISDN are not yet on the block. Included in the RACSA package is an Internet email address, but no installation or support. There are private companies that provide support, and there are Web Page Providers and from our observations, there certainly seems to be a high degree of competent support inside Costa Rica.

We have given some thought to the issue of government-subsidized monopolies controlling the Internet Access Providers market. While we do not pretend to have the hard technological knowledge required to develop computer related products; we have often pondered the interesting potential of someone with such knowledge developing Long Distance Internet Access Providers Services using Computer-Telephony technology. We have wondered how possible it might be to use some sort of High Performance Communication Processor-sibling related to that used in Callback in order to develop such a system. We are aware that Digital Signal Processor chips have amazing capacities to take digital information and turn it back into any number of analog components from voice to image; and vice versa; but we don't understand why this cannot take place at a distance. i.e. We assume, perhaps because of our naiveté, that there may be some really inexpensive way via Callback to be logged unto a distant Internet Service Provider, rather than a costly local provider.

We have had numerous discussions with competent people in the field who assure us that satellite access is going to be a fact quite soon; and we have also been told that the price of placing ones own satellite in orbit is now down in the $250,000 range; well within the range of a small company. We suspect that these companies will sell access to anyone with the proper equipment to log on, or perhaps even supply the equipment for customers to log on. It probably doesn't need to be pointed out that there has been tremendous advancements made in television dish receivers in just a few short years. The new satellite T.V. home antenna is of a very convenient size, and the reception remains excellent. More important, the technology that made such an antenna possible is evolving. It will be fairly difficult for any government to stop anyone from accessing a satellite in this manner, and if the Service Provider providing the satellite is outside of their jurisdiction they won't be able to do much about it. All the money that such government subsidized entities spend trying to monopolize the market would produce more and better returns if it was spent developing or utilizing better technology. However, in the meantime we suspect that with the current technology existing today, it might be possible for some enterprising individual to become very rich by figuring out a way to provide Long-Distance Internet Access Service to monopoly-locked individuals and corporations. Callback is just a phone call away, and if 'our' computer has a way to call 'your' computer, well maybe Long-Distant Internet Access Service is economically viable. (Did we hear someone say, LDIAS?)

LOOKING AT COSTA RICA ON THE INTERNET

Costa Rica has a number of Web Pages. Most of the Web Pages we've seen from Costa Rica, as might be suspected, are related to tourism. There are several information pages; here is a partial list of some of those we feel are of value:

The Tico Times Online
URL: http://magi.com/crica/ttimes.html
The Tico Times is an English-language newspaper based in San José. Unlike many foreign based English-language newspapers that we've seen, The Tico Times is not afraid to handle thorny issues. The copies we have seen have addressed issues and problems that are not necessary favorable to Costa Rica. i.e. The Tico Times is not a house-organ for the government of Costa Rica, nor do they appear to be controlled by the tourist industry. They seem to print the facts. However we have only seen several issues, and admittedly our impression results from a cursory glance. Nonetheless, we are favorably impressed. Their online service is well worth looking at; with daily updates on the Costa Rican scene. If you don't have a computer, you can subscribe: from the USA by writing Dept. 717 P.O. Box 025216, Miami, Florida 33102. In Costa Rica: Apartado 4362 in San José. Their fax number in Costa Rica is: 506·233·6378 We would like to note with some emphasis the fact that the Tico Times is openly vocal about issues seems to demonstrate that freedom of the press is alive and well in Costa Rica. [3]

There is another English-language news service based in San José, which has news from all over Central America. This service is strictly an On-line news service, and it is probably a good idea. The service, **Central American News (CAN)**, can be accessed at
URL: http://www.magi.com/circa/news/news.html Their email address is: iiclayton@magi.com

One interesting Web page we've seen is called **Goldnet Costa Rica** which is on the **Cafe Internet**. It offers an Online version of the Costa Rica Yellow Pages, which we think is a fine idea. They also list a number of services and information sources about Costa Rica in addition to a gateway to other Costa Rican Links. We found them at:
URL: http://www.goldnet.co.cr/

REAL ESTATE IN COSTA RICA

In our opinion, Real Estate Prices in Costa Rica have reached the level of the 'greater fool phenomena,' that is economically related to chain letters and games of chance. There were great bargains in Costa Rica in the 1970's, there were great bargains in the 1980's, and we'd be willing to bet that there are probably still great bargains even today; but we believe that portions of the market are extremely overbought. The fact is, that we personally would currently be looking to short our investments into Costa Rican real estate. This is of course only a personal opinion, and we could certainly be wrong about this situation; we've been wrong plenty of times in the past. On the other hand we've also been right a number of times, so we'll pass along our opinion and let readers make their own decisions.

Over the years, Central America has been greatly influenced by the USA; perhaps far greater than any other region in Latin America; if not the world. Over the last 150 years, the United States has basically owned Central America; and we don't care to get into the politics of this, we are merely stating what we have come to view as the facts of reality, the reader is asked to indulge our opinion, and then draw their own conclusions.

Costa Rica has recieved far and above, the largest portion of US foreign aid of any nation in the region. In fact, on a per capita basis, it has been receiving almost twice the amount of aid when compared to most of its neighbors. [4] Why?

We took the time to compare the per capita US foreign aid for each country from Belize to Panama, and we found that aid generally increases as we approach the Panama Canal. It is no secret that the US Government has always believed very strongly that the Panama Canal was quite crucial to its national defense; perhaps even to the point of obsession. We believe that it is this historic obsession that is responsible for the amount of US foreign aid to Costa Rica as well as the continuous encouragement given to the American public by certain departments of the US Government to invest in and retire in beautiful Costa Rica. The defense department has simply viewed Costa Rica as a buffer that protects its defensive interests; a stalwart domino that will not fall because it is well-supported.

However the Panama Canal is now technically obsolete. Today's ships have grown to the point where they are now too long to go through the canal. Additionally, with today's advanced marine-engines it is quite easy (and economical) to round the horn in a few days with ships that are built to super size. It might additionally be noted, that the real Naval power of our time is the submarine and no longer the destroyers, cruisers, and other Naval ships that once depended on the Canal for strategic defense; plus, it is more or less common knowledge, that the Canal could be knocked out with one missile sent from a lot further away than Central America. (Most school children know this.) Further, even the US Government is having trouble trying to maintain the illusion that there is some sort of an enemy somewhere whose existence requires the astronomical expenditures required for conventional warfare and especially for traditional methods of defense. [5]

What does the Canal's almost-defunct status portent for Costa Rica? Will the boys in Washington pull the plug on the giveaway programs to beautiful Costa Rica? One thing we have learned down through the years, is that there are very few altruists in Washington D.C. If they are stealing from Peter to pay Paul, we can be sure that there is some reason involved beyond a general concern for Paul. When they no longer need Paul he'll be dumped into the trashcan along with other defunct friends. Let us call this Conjecture number One in our Critique of Costa Rica's Over-priced and Cherished Homesites. (COCROACH, if you like acronyms.) The conjecture is this: 'whatever the degree to which the US Government has encouraged and subsidized investment into Costa Rica may represent to a corresponding degree the manner in which Costa Rican Real Estate values may be falsely inflated.' Dominoes fall both ways.

Our second concern is one we've voiced elsewhere in this book; and that concern resides in the wide degree of disparity between the average wage of the average Costa Rican (GDP Per Capita,) and the common gringo-directed advertised sale price of Costa Rican Real Estate.

We have seen figures for the Per Capita GDP, that range widely; from a 1992 figure of $2,096 to a 1995 figure of $5,480 At the very same time, we are seeing resident properties as of this writing, advertised in the $200,000 to $700,000 price range. Let's see, if we earn $5000 per year total and we spend every nickel of our earnings just on Real Estate, we can purchase a $700,000 house in only 140 years (This quick payoff can only happen so long as no interest is charged. The charging of 9% interest on $700,000 is $63,000 per year in itself without amortization. If however we reduce our principal by using the total of our yearly income as a downpayment, our first years earnings of $5000 brings the principal balance down to a more manageable figure of just $695,000 which at 9% interest gives us a first year interest deficit of only $62,550 without amortization. To accomplish this entire feat, will require that our average Costa Rican does not eat or otherwise splurge any money on anything but house payments for 140 years.) We have only one thing to say about houses costing $700,000 in Costa Rica: Bullshit! If you will forgive the colloquial. This observation represents conjecture number two in our critique. Conjecture: Home prices are determined by comparative analysis. As there are no slums in Costa Rica and home ownership is high among Costa Ricans, the prices of a suitable home based on Per Capita purchasing power, is likely to be in the $20,000 price range.6 For the sake of analysis, let us assume that a house in Costa Rica has sold for $700,000. (Many have.) How was such a price reached? What created the price? Building costs? Land costs? Labor costs? Taxes? We are curious. We suspect that in order to get to a figure of $700,000 for a house in Costa Rica, one of two things has to be true: 1) The property and the house are really, really, something and it compares favorably to a $3 million house in, say Portland, Oregon, or: 2) Some smart gringo found a dumb gringo buy an overpriced property.

There are additional factors that drive the prices of real estate artificially high in America such as the number of mindless governmental requirements; and these factors simply don't exist in Costa Rica. In the United States, the fees, requirements for licenses, building codes, building restrictions and bureaucratic roadblocks add 30% to the cost of construction. Thirty percent. Thirty percent of ones hard earned capital, that simply goes straight down the drain in the United States. Zoning contributes additional problems. In America zoning has more or less destroyed the quality of traditional American life, what it adds to construction costs is difficult to determine, but the figure is astronomical. Costa Rica has had zoning laws since 1974, but they have never been enforced; although that may soon change. Additionally, labor costs in the United States add another 25% to 30% to the cost of construction. The average electrician and plumber on a construction site in the United States make at least $35 an hour; even a laborer makes $14 per hour, six times what the average Costa Rican makes. Overall construction costs in the United States are between $100 to $200 per square foot.

We believe that a very, very conservative estimate of the costs for home construction in Costa Rica places them at least 50% lower than in America and we are being extremely generous with this estimate. If we are correct and we certainly believe that we are and if raw land prices in Costa Rica are traditionally 90% lower, and if the property taxes are 90% lower, and if capital gains can all but be totally avoided;7 than the $700,000 houses being sold in Costa Rica are equivalent in comparison to $2-$4 million dollar houses being sold in the US in their amenities, size and attribute. If you live in Costa Rica and you did buy a house for $700,000 and it does not compare favorable to a house that in the United States would sell for $2-$4 million dollars, we think that now is a good time to sell. (If you can.) This represents conjecture number three in our analysis and it is based on the supposition that: 'the price of a house has be determined by; a.] its replacement value, b.] its utility value, c.] comparative analysis, or d.] some measurable fact of reality.'

We don't necessarily believe that the situation in Costa Rica has reached the proportions of the 'Tulip Bulb bubble' of 17th century Holland, because there are still bargains in Costa Rica. How to evaluate fair market value is the question. One method might be replacement value. We believe that it is possible to build a 'modern' 1500-2000 sq ft, two bedroom house in Costa Rica for, at the very most, $75,000 including property costs, so that might be a good figure to start from. The best method of determining current market value, is to go to Costa Rica and spend some time there. (away from other gringos, and gringo house sellers!) We wouldn't be surprised to find nice bungalows starting in the $30,000 price range. If prices are significantly higher, or if we talk to a real estate agent (fresh from Malibu, California) who looks at us incredulously, as if we are idiots to expect to find a $30,000 house, then so be it. These are same people who will laugh at us when we are stupid enough to think that the $14 price on a wine-list in some quaint Beverly Hills restaurant is for a bottle and not for one single glass of wine; they are very clever individuals.

If norm prices are in the over $100,000 price range for a 'moderate' house, our current recommendation is to hang back and wait for the prices to collapse. Everyone will tell you this cannot happen; however there is nothing abnormal about price changes. Costa Rica has gone broke four times; something most noveau real estate agents in Costa Rica don't even have a clue to. Their mentality is a short-range mentality with no comprehension of historic or economic reality. 'Never burned, so never shy, and never asked the question why.' sums up the philosophical depths of most noveau real estate agents. Their view of history stretches back to their last dinner party.

ANOTHER VIEW

There is of course a contrary view to what we've just said. There are mitigating factors that are pushing the price of Costa Rica's real estate upwards, not least of which is the inordinate number of expatriates moving to Costa Rica. Costa Rica itself has initiated a process which is attracting a large number of expatriates from around the world through the sale of citizenship by way of passive investment. An investment of $50,000 or more into specifically approved sectors of the market will qualify an investor for residency, citizenship and a Costa Rican passport. Many investors into these schemes are people from areas of the world that are on the brink of potential disequilibrium, such as Hong Kong. The most popular of these schemes involves the purchase of real estate by way of so-called 'reforestation' projects; which are purchased in many cases by investors who never set foot into Costa Rica. Investors of the sort who would purchase $50,000 worth of real estate sight unseen and never care if their investment yielded a nickel are bound to have some rather odd repercussions on the cost of land, no? 8

It is also quite true that Costa Rica has a large number of very legitimate expatriates who go to Costa Rica for good reason. Costa Rica may have the most perfect climate in the world. There is no question that it does have a strong economy compared to many nations. Its many Free Trade Zones are attractive incentive to manufactures wishing to escape the crippling bureaucracy and regulations that have rendered manufacturing in the United States impossible. Good labor is plentiful and cheap. The government has developed an impressive record of being democratic, peaceful, and pro-business. People go to Costa Rica. More Americans live in Costa Rica than any other country in Latin America; which is pretty impressive when we consider its size. Additionally, many Europeans have been visiting and emigrating to Costa Rica. Considering these various contributing factors, it would take little imagination for us to assume that Costa Rica with a population of around 3,400,000 in a land area comparable in size to the state of West Virginia, (population: 1,800,000;) could conceivably be experiencing a legitimate real estate boom. The question we must then ask is; at what point in the boom cycle do we find ourselves?

Those who tell us, with a mouthful of smiling good cheer, that 'the rest of the world has finally discovered Costa Rica,' must not have been conscious twenty-five years ago when going to Costa Rica to buy real estate was a smart idea. Those like myself, who tell everyone that the cycle may be far past the point of being overbought, are common doom-sayers. It is difficult to know wherein lies wisdom.

FREE WISDOM

According to investment consultant Harry Browne, the best rule of thumb in a potentially overbought real estate market is for us to insure that our total real estate holdings not exceed 20% of our total investment portfolio. Which for many of us would just about be the price of our own home. If we have to pay more than 20% of our total holdings just for our home, then we should probably back off and keep our powder dry. By doing so, we could conceivably miss out on some opportunities; perhaps even some once-in-a-lifetime opportunities, so I must add a personal note to this discussion. Most of the money I've made in life has come from real estate. While I have never considered myself a genius at it, I have never lost money at it. I have always bought extremely low, and managed to make a good profit. Investment decisions such as those we are discussing would be very difficult if there were nowhere else in the world where real estate bargains existed. However when we can buy Caribbean ocean front houses in Venezuela for $30,000, or a 1000 acre dairy farm in Mozambique for $10,000 total, then the extreme suffering we might endure by opting to error on the side of caution could be mediated by investing elsewhere, away from the maddening crowd. One note I must also add, and I hate to say anything so simplistic, but I really must admit that I have a gut feeling that a bunch of people are being fleeced for their life savings in Costa Rican Real Estate. If I'm wrong, I guess I'll have to settle for a couple of thousand acre estancia some place else.

MAS MAS OR MAS MENOS?

The information already available in books,[1] videos, and tapes for those considering emigrating to Costa Rica easily exceeds that of any other country in the world.[2] There is little we could add to the overwhelming abundance of what is already available, (at least in terms of the positive, good cheer, pro-Costa Rica aspects about choosing the place.) The schools are good. Damn good. Their system of preventive medicine exceeds the level of preventive medicine which is available in the United States. To our knowledge, the United States leads the world in Medicine, hands down. If history will remember the United States for any form of greatness, we believe it will be for it's amazing contribution to the field of Medicine. So, for a tiny country like Costa Rica to have such a fine level of preventive medicine openly available to its people, is a great compliment to Costa Rica and to it's Universities. In many cases, a Degree from a Costa Rican University can be recognized within the United States. The culture as a whole, is interesting and tends towards lucidity. Their fine arts are adequate and ambitious. The people friendly. The climate superb.

We can give the name of a dozen books that becry the greatness of Costa Rica, so we will only advise readers as to the few caveats of which we are aware and move on.

WARNINGS CAVEATS AND MORDIDAS We've already mentioned our concern with the coming change of ownership in the Panama Canal, and the decreasing value of the Canal as may be perceived in the eyes of our great heroes and manipulators of America's defense policies. What this portends for Costa Rica is uncertain, however, if we ourselves chose to move to Costa Rica it would be something we would keep foremost in our mind. It would be an issue we would monitor and consider closely as we made our investments. Those noveau real estate agents with the gushing good cheer and the short-range mentalities could conceivably wake up one day and discover that they were simply pawns in a game of complex political manipulations which they themselves knew nothing about. Knew nothing about, not so much because they could not find the facts, but because they refused to look.

ADIOS PENSIONADO

The retirement of the **Pensionado** program, is a very sore spot with us. Costa Rica reneged on its promise to those retirees who came to Costa Rica based on the Pensionado program. In our opinion, this broken promise constitutes an act of utter barbarity against the elderly, the very people least capable of doing anything about it. Perhaps the economic pie has gotten a bit grander and sweeter for other incoming investments. Why should Costa Rica continue to give promised benefits to the elderly, when **Marriot** is willing to come in and build a 246 room $40 million hotel? Tourism is booming! And just look at real estate!

We'd like to make our position on this issue very clear: anyone who would renege on their promise to the elderly has lost a great deal of stature in our eyes. It is for this reason more than any other we are negative on Costa Rica. If they will lie and cheat the elderly, they will lie and cheat anyone. How long until they renege on the next policy? Is it to be assumed that someone who lies to the elderly would treat us any better? The lemmings investing into Costa Rica should take heed: Any government that changes policies towards the elderly is not to be trusted.

Corruption is alive and well in Costa Rica, all rhetoric to the contrary. There have been numerous substantiated charges of human rights violations against the police, and Costa Rica's prisons are a disaster, with well documented cases of secret jails and human torture. As we are writing these lines two gruesome cases involving Costa Rican rights violations are currently headline news in Germany, but seemingly not being covered at all in the US press, both case involve tourists who were visiting Costa Rica. In one case Hennes Their, a German tourist disappeared while on vacation in Costa Rica. After weeks of absence stretched into months with no word from Hennes, his brother Hermann decided to go to Costa Rica and look for him. Tragically, Hermann discovered that his brother had been shot in the head and killed by a Costa Rican. Hennes embalmed body was at the Latin American University of Science and Technology awaiting dissection by medical students. Though Hennes had a Passport among his possessions, nobody, neither his family nor the German Embassy was notified of his death. Why wasn't anyone notified? The Costa Rican Director of Criminal Investigations (OIJ), Gerardo Láscares told the press that in Costa Rica informing an embassy or family members of a death "isn't the law ...it's a courtesy." [11]

210

This case followed on the heels of a previous case involving the kidnapping of another German tourist, Nicola Fleuchaus and her Swiss tour guide. The couple was kidnapped from a Costa Rican 'nature lodge' in the northern part of Costa Rica. They were finally released after a ransom of $194,000 was paid. They spent a total of 71 days in captivity. In yet another case two Americans were taken into the jungle where they were beaten and robbed. Their injuries were so extensive that they required hospitalization. Upon release from the hospital, none of the Costa Rican 'nature tours' which they had paid for and been scheduled to take would give them a refund despite the fact that they hadn't been able to take the tours. They were so upset with the treatment they recieved from everyone in Costa Rica, that they started up a Web Page to bring their treatment in Costa Rica to the attention of the world. You can visit their Web Page at: http://www.primenet.com/ bbethel/costarica.htm

One final tale about visitor treatment in beautiful Costa Rica. Jim Rogers who teaches at Columbia University as well as co-hosting a popular television program on CNBC, is a world famous investment analyst who specializes in analyzing foreign countries for potential investment. He and the very lovely Tabitha Esterbrooks were traveling through Costa Rica on motorcycles; having traveled around the entire world on them. They traveled through over 14 countries just in Latin American and of all the countries in Latin America, Costa Rica is the only one where they were stopped by a corrupt policeman trying to get a 'Mordita.' Additionally, the policeman who stopped them decided to preform a more creative and much more lucrative 'Mordita Coleando'[12] on them. It seems that Rogers and Esterbrook were taken to Police Headquarters where after a rather involved donnybrook they began to realize that the police were trying to 'plant' drugs on their motorcycles; hence turning the simple Mordita into the much more lucrative imprisonment-and-ransom-for-release Mordita Coleando, a situation which would have cost them their motorcycles, their freedom, and ultimately a huge ransom for their release. Only by keeping cool heads and using their wits were they able to avoid going to a Costa Rican jail. The situation was stressful to say the least; Rogers didn't have a particularly high opinion of Costa Rica to begin with, having pointed out, among other things, that it has 'an extremely high debt per capita, a huge fiscal deficit and high inflation.'

To be fair to Costa Rica, everything we have just mentioned could and often does happen in New York City in a single day. But why single out New York? One of the least populated counties on the West Coast of the United States is Pacific County on the Washington State coast which has Highway 101 running directly through it. Pacific County has a reputation for issuing very costly tourist traffic tickets for meaningless infractions, (in addition it has a reputation for activities that are a bit more serious involving police brutality and outright theft of real property through its court system.) The corruption said to be occurring in Pacific County is becoming openly talked about, but thus far no one has done anything about it, possibly because it is so isolated. It is all but impossible for a tourist to get through Pacific County without getting a ticket and if you put up a fuss, worst things can happen to you.[13] The fact that the mordita money may possibly go into the Pacific County coffers rather than into the officers pocket is an irrelevant issue; armed robbery is armed robbery. There no difference between a corrupt police force and judicial system in the United States and one in Costa Rica. We despise injustice.

It should also be pointed out that Costa Rica continues to have freedom of the press.[3] As long as there is freedom of the press there is hope. There are many wonderful people in Costa Rica; and we have no wish to disparage them or their beautiful country. In our view it has simply become the current vogue land-of-scams. We don't like scams.

If we really want to buy Costa Rican Real Estate, an excellent way to start is to understand Real Estate Law in Costa Rica and the best way of understanding Costa Rican Real Estate Law is by reading the book, **Purchasing Real Estate in Costa Rica**, by Alvaro Carballo Pinto. Mr. Carballo is a Costa Rican lawyer specializing in real estate law. Additionally he has taught Commercial and Real Estate Law, and has served as the Costa Rican Vice-Consul in the United States in Miami. He has studied law both in Costa Rica and in the United States, and he has degrees in both countries. His background is quite extensive both in the private and public sector of Costa Rica. He is well qualified to write about Costa Rican real estate. In fact, he may be the most qualified person in the world. The book is available from Carballo Abogados P.O. Box 6997-1000 San José, Costa Rica FAX: 506·223·9151 TEL: 506·233·0348 The book is advertised for $10; contact Mr. Carballo for shipping charges. If trouble is experienced in contacting Mr. Carballo, check with our fax-on-demand system for possible information updates.

REFERENCES, NOTES, CAVEATS & AVATARS

NOTE: The first two references below refer to books which are written entirely about emigrating to and living in Costa Rica. These books contain from 150 to 250 pages devoted entirely to the subject of Costa Rica; we cannot hope to cover in a dozen pages what these books contain. The reader who is serious about Costa Rica should read these two books.

1) *Choose Costa Rica* by John Howells Gateway Books, San Rafael, California [252 pg] 1992 Howells has written a lot of books on Latin America. He is a happy traveler and his positive enthusiasm is very contagious. He has come under criticism from others for not discussing enough of the negatives; and while this might be true to a degree, what he does discuss is better discussed then any of his counterpart discuss it. We like him. For those who have made up their mind to go to Costa Rica his book is must reading. Five stars.

2) *The Golden Door to Retirement and Living in Costa Rica* by Christopher Howard. Costa Rica Books, Thousand Oaks, California [149 pg] 1994 Filled with useful information, including current telephone numbers and addresses. If you are moving to Costa Rica, this book and Howells book would supply you with a good deal of what it takes to get you started.

3) Among the various technique used by some governments to silence any form of opposition reporting in the press is to a.] create a paper shortage to a disobedient newspaper, b.] impose very high taxes on imported newsprint, and c.] deny them advertising revenues. This type of auxiliary pressure is less conspicuous than out and out censorship; and it doesn't ruffle as many feathers. Costa Rica does have inordinately restrictive libel laws which can place some undue pressure on freedom of the press, but thus far Costa Rica's record of media freedom is exemplary. That is to say: Much to the credit of Costa Rica and its people, Freedom of the press is alive and well in Costa Rica.

4) Belize, the Central American Country furthest away from the Panama Canal receives only $104 million compared with $1.4 billion for Costa Rica, which is a pretty profound disparity. If this disparity is the result of per capita causes, then why does Nicaragua with a population 25% greater than Costa Rica only receive $620 million? Guatemala with a population almost four times larger than the population of Costa Rica also receives less foreign aid.

5) In 1989, immediately following the fall of the Berlin wall the United States invaded Panama killing thousands of civilians. No one seems to know or care how many civilians were killed in order to perform what amounts to a 'drug bust.' Are we really supposed to be so stupid as to assume that the invasion of Panama had anything to do with Noreiga's drug business? His affairs in drug trafficking were common knowledge as far back as 1972, yet Noreiga remained on the CIA payroll until 1986. The invasion of Panama took place in 1989, the Panama Canal was due to be turned over to Panama on January 1, 1990. What a coincidence. That the United States could invade another country, kill thousands of civilians and do it all on national television without too much protest from anyone tells us a great deal about the power and morality of the United States government and the ability of the media-conditioned human mind to only see what it has been instructed to see when viewing the media.

6) We <u>have</u> seen homes priced in the $20,000 range for moderate houses. The term 'suitable' is an esthetic term and so remains an abstraction.

7) It is our understanding that property in Costa Rica can be purchased by way of a Costa Rican corporation and through such a modality, most if not all of the capital gains taxes can be avoided. Talk to a good attorney and study the ramifications of this technique thoroughly before trying it. [see our section on Tax-Havens, Offshore Corporations, and Offshore Banks for further input regarding this and other methods of protecting ones assets.]

8) The reforestation projects are methods of gaining a second passport for those to whom $50,000 is not a great deal of money. How well these same methods work as investment vehicles is another question. We know of one company that will answer questions regarding these investments; however we have never dealt with this company, nor can we vouch for the investments themselves. Gerald Shaffer is the **Cana Teca** Senior Account Manager, and he can be reached at Cana Teca International S.A. 2nd Floor, 827 West Pender Street, Vancouver British Columbia, <u>CANADA</u> V6C 3G8 tel: 604·681·8423 fax: 604·689·5284 <u>gshaffer@canateca.com</u> They have a Web Page at http://vanbc.wimsey.com

10) The **Pensionado** programs were a type of residency statues that allowed a number of perks for retirees. The best of the perks involved duty free importation of household goods and duty free importation of their family car. These very important statues have been revoked. As if this wasn't bad enough, the Costa Rican government is now considering increasing the amount of taxation on retirees. We see the issue in these terms: those retirees who went to Costa Rica based on the Pensionado program probably bought heavily into Costa Rica, both emotionally and financially. Now they can no longer bring in items that they may want for their personal life without paying a high duty. This sounds rather trite, but to those on fixed incomes such matters are not trite. It is easy enough to say that they could sell their homes and move on to cheaper places. The elderly don't make such changes with the same degree of simplicity as someone younger. For the elderly such things can be extremely stressful. Costa Rica now has for itself a fat American chicken that it can pluck because the chicken is more or less immobile. How courageous.

11) We took the time to read *Oro*, by Cizia Zykë. While it must be admitted that the author of *Oro* is less than admirable in much of his behavior, his book does provide yet another view of Costa Rica. Zykë's stated ambition in his very own words is: "...to amuse myself, to seek pleasure, and to live as intensely as possible." Much of the way that Zykë goes about accomplishing these complex desires is by knocking other people around and by being a thug. Zykë does offer us a view of Costa Rica that is entirely unique, a view that many of us may otherwise not even have known existed. Though we read *Oro* a number of years ago, the moment we read Láscares thoughtless statement to the press regarding law and *'courtesy'* in Costa Rica we were reminded of Zykë's candid description of Costa Rican police behavior.

12) We suspect that everyone now knows the definition of the word, *'mordida,'* or 'little bite,' which is a term used in much of Latin America for a 'bribe.' The compound term, *'mordida coleando'* is the worst kind of situation when a bite turns into a combination armed robbery and kidnapping.

13) The last time we were in Pacific County a group of concerned citizens were placing leaflets on tourist car windows warning drivers to use caution. There were also leaflets implying that one of the Pacific County Court Judges was a cocaine user and a dealer. We cannot comment on this because we don't know any of the details, but it seems that a great many people in Pacific County are saying the same thing and they seem frightened. Our last visit to Pacific County was our last visit.

US STATE DEPARTMENT CONSULAR TRAVEL INFORMATION

COUNTRY DESCRIPTION: Costa Rica is a developing country. Tourist facilities, particularly in the capital, are generally adequate.

ENTRY REQUIREMENTS: A valid passport is required to enter Costa Rica. At the discretion of Costa Rican authorities, travelers are sometimes admitted with a photo I.D. for tourist stays up to 90 days. Additional information on entry requirements may be obtained from the Consular Section of the Embassy of Costa Rica at 2114 S Street, N.W., Washington, D.C. 20008, tel.: (202) 328-6628, or the nearest consulate in Los Angeles, San Francisco, San Diego, Denver, Miami, Honolulu, Atlanta, Chicago, New Orleans, Las Vegas, New York, Houston or St. Paul (Minnesota).

MEDICAL FACILITIES: Medical care in the capital city of San Jose is adequate. However, in areas outside of San Jose, medical care is more limited. Doctors and hospitals often expect immediate cash payment for health services. U.S. medical insurance is not always valid outside the United States. Supplemental medical insurance with specific overseas coverage, including provision for medical evacuation, has proven useful in many emergencies. For additional health information, travelers may contact the Centers for Disease Control and Prevention's international travelers' hotline at (404) 332-4559.

CRIME INFROMATION: Crime is on the upswing, with tourists as well as the local populace frequent victims. Pickpocketings, muggings, house and car break-ins and thefts are common, and becoming increasingly violent in nature. Car-jackings are also on the rise and, recently, several motorists were confronted at gunpoint while stopped at traffic lights. Two U.S. citizens have been killed during robbery attempts over the past two years. In January 1996, a foreign tourist and guide were kidnapped from their hotel in the northern border region. Incidents of crime commonly occur in downtown San Jose, at beaches, at the airport, and at national parks and other tourist attractions. There have been several assaults on tourist buses as well. Travelers who keep valuables out of sight, do not wear jewelry, and travel in groups during daylight hours lessen their risk. Local law enforcement agencies have limited capabilities. Money exchangers on the street will pass off counterfeit U.S. dollars and local currency. Credit card fraud is growing. Vehicles should not be left unattended, nor any items left inside.

Some trails in national parks have been closed because of low numbers of visitors and reported robberies of hikers in the area. Tourists may wish to check with forest rangers for current park conditions.

INVESTMENT ISSUES: Costa Rica has a long history of investment and real estate scams and frauds perpetrated against U.S. citizens and international visitors. In addition, some U.S. citizen landowners have had longstanding expropriation disputes with the government of Costa Rica, and others have had their property invaded by squatters, whom they have been unable to evict. Pavones, on the south Pacific coast, and Sarapiqui, in northeast Costa Rica, are the areas most affected by squatter/landowner disputes. Persons contemplating buying land may find it useful to seek competent legal advice concerning their rights as landowners, to inspect the property, and to assess local conditions prior to purchase.

AVIATION OVERSIGHT: In October 1991, the U.S. Federal Aviation Administration assessed Costa Rica's civil aviation authority as in compliance with international aviation safety oversight standards for Costa Rica's carriers operating to and from the U.S. The same level of safety oversight would typically be applied to operations to other destinations. For further information, travelers may contact the Department of Transportation at 1-800-322-7873.

REGISTRATION/ EMBASSY LOCATION: U.S. citizens may register with the Consular Section of the U.S. Embassy in San Jose and may also obtain updated information on travel and security within Costa Rica. The U.S. Embassy in Costa Rica is located in Pavas, San Jose, Tel. (506) 220-3050. The Embassy is open Monday through Friday, and closed on Costa Rican and American holidays. For emergencies arising outside normal business hours, call (506) 220-3127 and ask for the duty officer.

CHAPTER THIRTEEN

VENEZUELA

"Matilda... matilda... matilda, ...she take my money and run Venezuela."
- Calipso song from the 1950's

Venezuela has the distinction of being the oldest unbroken democracy in Latin America. It has been called 'the Switzerland of the South' due to its mostly stable, peaceful politics. It has also been called 'the Saudi Arabia of the South' due to its immense oil wealth. While these 'handles' are easy enough to sling around and just about every place is called the 'Switzerland of this or that,' Venezuela does have a history of freedom. Simon Bolivar, the liberator of most of Latin America, (a sort of hispanic Thomas Jefferson,) was born there. Venezuela was the first colony to win independence from Spain. That is not to say that Venezuela doesn't have it's share of problems, it certainly does. Venezuela's major problem is corruption. But amidst the muck of the problems are some real estate gemstones.

Venezuela has a very large number of unspoiled regions, including designated natural parks and wildlife reserves. What is significant is that it has more tropical coastline than any other country in the Caribbean, yet at the same time has peaks with snow just a short drive away from the coast.

It is possible to eat papayas at our beach house for breakfast and build a snowman before we eat our dinner at our mountain cabin. The drive will be pleasant because we will be paying the lowest Gasoline prices in the world; less than 40 cents a gallon. (Venezuela has the largest proven oil reserves in the Western hemisphere.) We can also mine for precious and semi-precious stones and/or pan for gold, Venezuela is rich in minerals. Prices on consumer goods are close to fabulous. A main course meal in a restaurant costs $2 to $3. Excellent locally-produced rum is priced at $1 to $2 a bottle. Low taxes or no taxes on some imports, including cars. (Unlike most other Latin-American countries where cars are taxed as luxury imports even for expats.) Communications are modern: the Internet is up and running. Telecommunications are good, with a fairly high concentration of PC's and with what is perhaps the highest number of cellular phones per capita in the entire Latin and Caribbean basin.

There are wide, modern highways. There is high-tech architecture. There is a daily English-language newspaper and several other English-language publications which are produced locally for the expat community. Top quality vacation homes can be rented at decent prices when compared to the rest of the Caribbean. We can buy our own tropical beach hideaway, with prices starting at just $25,000 to $30,000 and ranch land in the interior along the Orinoco River is going for under $100 an acre. If we had to make a choice between Costa Rica and Venezuela, we'd pick Venezuela in a heartbeat... it's way more than twice the ground for way less than half the price. If that's not enough, the people are good looking, the weather is fine and there's plenty of economic opportunity.

If we view Venezuela as a Caribbean nation it has some of the advantages of being a large land based nation. Whereas on an island everything has to be shipped in at inflated import-prices Venezuela has most of lives necessities at hand. Venezuela has its own agriculture/food industry and food prices are significantly lower than most countries, let alone Caribbean islands. It is cheaper living in Venezuela than in most other places in the world. If we have a limited budget and want to be expats, we can't afford to stay away from Venezuela, or at least check it out. There is a lot to do in Venezuela. The country is modern, yet has a real abundance of wilderness and wild-life sports, activities and attractions. Additionally, for those who might miss them there are more McDonald's Blockbuster's and KFC's in Venezuela than anywhere else in the region. South Caribbean in nature, with merengue rhythms and warm tropical summer nights Venezuela is perched between two worlds. Serious business can be done during the day in modern cities in close proximity to where happy faces dance all night and the rum is flowing. Venezuela might be said to be one of the greatest secrets of the Caribbean. In some people's opinion it is superior to the Caribbean. Perhaps we should forget about overpriced, overcrowded Caribbean islands. In Venezuela we can still discover the true creole. Plus there are numerous Venezuelan islands off the coast that are not yet spoiled by tourism, if it is islands that are our true desire. Venezuela remains a place where rum and salsa blend together in the old fashion and romantic way of a Bogard and Bacall movie. Venezuela is a country with an incredible coastline and some magnificent real estate bargains. Expats should place Venezuela on their list.

CAPITAL: **Caracas** is located 3,000 feet above sea level in a high riff valley. It has a **metropolitan population** of 3,000,000 and is one of South America's more developed and cosmopolitan cities. It is Venezuela's center for foreign commerce and it is the center of the nations prosperous petroleum industry. The city's climate is mild, characterized by a dry summer from May to October and a rainy winter. Diego de Losada founded Caracas in 1567 and named it Santiago de Leon de Caracas. The forests and Avila mountain have remained virtually untouched over the centuries, protecting the city that has gradually expanded along the valley. Ten years after its foundation, Caracas was already an important administrative, military and religious center sought out by pirates due to its great commercial possibilities and proximity to the port of La Guaira.

ECONOMY

Venezuela is currently suffering the effects of an economic downturn that was triggered early last year [1995-1996] by the near collapse of its commercial banking system. The usual methods to resolve this crisis have thus far been ignored. If Venezuela could sperate it's Central Bank from government intervention such as has been done recently in New Zealand and some time ago in West Germany then the situation could be rectified. There is some recognition inside of Venezuela of the need for open markets, competition, privatization of inefficient government owned companies as well as for installing a sound juridical system. The question of the moment seems to be how to achieve those conditions without destabilizing the country's financial sector and/or its institutional set-up. The answers are easy, though it is most probable in that the will may be lacking. The Venezuela bureaucracy remains horrendously cumbersome. Additionally, there is the ongoing problem of corruption at every level and every sector; government, military and business. What does this mean for the expat? Our judgement is to move now and buy now before the situation stabilizes. Anyone can buy in a stable market. ...and they probably will. Keep in mind that regardless of periodic downturns caused by inept politicos, Venezuela is not going to run out of oil.

What we have seen of **real estate** prices in Venezuela is as good as anything we have seen on the planet. With good Caribbean beach front houses going for $25,000 in Venezuela and good arable land going for under $100 per acre, now is definitely the time to buy. Let's keep in mind that this is the Caribbean that we are talking about when we talk beach front and land on the Oniroco River when we talk about rancheros. There is an international expat community in Venezuela left over from the oil rush of the 1970's. Many who came then liked what they saw and stayed. It is both a cosmopolitan and a tropical setting.

When you travel to Venezuela for a reason that has anything to do with business, you must travel with a business visa. This visa is valid for one year, and you can renew it in Caracas. Please check the Embassy's home page at http://venezuela.mit.edu/embassy for further information and the consular offices nearest to you. The requirements for Venezuelan citizenship can be obtained through the immigration office in Caracas. These types of transactions can be done only in Venezuela, at that office. Real estate can be purchased by a foreigner There are no exchange controls at this point in time. Local currency is stable at around Bs470 per $1. **Margarita** is the largest free trade zone in Venezuela.

CIA WORLD FACT BOOK 1995 ECONOMIC OVERVIEW: Despite efforts to broaden the base of the economy, petroleum continues to play a dominant role. In 1994, as GDP declined 3.3%, the oil sector - which accounts for 24% of the total - enjoyed a 6% expansion, provided 45% of the budget revenues, and generated 70% of the export earnings. President Caldera, who assumed office in February 1994, has used an interventionist, reactive approach to managing the economy, instituting price and foreign exchange controls in mid-year to slow inflation and stop the loss of foreign exchange reserves. The government claims it will remove these controls once inflationary pressures abate, but the $8 billion bailout of the banking sector in 1994 has made it difficult for the government to make good on its promise. Economic controls, coupled with political uncertainty driven by recurrent coup rumors, continue to deter foreign and domestic investment; private forecasters see the recession persisting for a third year in 1995.

FREEDOM HOUSE RATING:

Freedom House gave Venezuela
Civil Liberties ③ **Political Rights.**③

Admittedly, this rating isn't overly-inspiring for the timid expat, nor for the expat with a family to worry about. The reasons for the low ratings are due to problems which have their roots in economics. The roots of the economic problems seem to reside in the murky mud of corruption. Nothing seems to increase social unrest so swiftly as a rumbling stomach and too many people in Venezuela have rumbling stomachs when in fact they shouldn't have. Freedom House shows a per head gross domestic product of $8,520, much higher than our own estimates. If indeed the GDP per capita was that high we believed we would be seeing less social unrest. What we believe is happening is that too few at the top have too much while too many at the bottom have too little. This in itself is not a crime. But the modality of keeping what's at the top up there seems to be a consistent policy of corruption. For some reason those at the bottom who don't have too awfully much and can't find any possibilities of earning too awfully much are upset. Social unrest is causing the military to feel itchy. The ongoing unrest has also caused the Caldera administration to act by way of suspending a number of civil liberties, which in turn has caused increases in the unrest. The fact that President Calderas own family has been accused of corruption is not helping the situation.

Voter abstention reached 60% in 1995 and voting is mandatory. Human rights organizations inside and outside of Venezuela report widespread arbitrary detentions and torture of suspects, as well as dozens of extrajudicial killings by military security forces and the notorious corrupt police. Indigenous communities trying to defend their legal land rights have been subject to abuses by goldminers and corrupt rural police. Since the 1992 coup attempts, weakened civilian governments have had less authority over the military and the police, and rights abuses overall are committed with a larger degree of impunity than is acceptable. In 1995 rights activists remained targets of intimidation.

The press is privately owned. There are nearly a dozen daily newspapers. Radio and television are mostly private, supervised by an association of broadcasters under the government communications ministry. The practice of journalism is restricted by a licensing law and threatened by government control of foreign exchange required to purchase newsprint and other supplies. Since 1994 the media in general have faced a pattern of intimidation. Government and military officials, including the president, frequently attack the media verbally and the Congress passed a series of restrictive laws involving the right of reply and journalistic conduct.

TELECOMMUNICATIONS & THE WWW

COMMUNICATIONS

Telephone system: 1,440,000 telephones; modern and expanding local: NA intercity: 3 domestic satellite earth stations international: 3 submarine coaxial cables; 1 INTELSAT (Atlantic Ocean) earth station

Radio: broadcast stations: AM 181, FM 0, shortwave 26 Television broadcast stations: 59

INTERNET SERVICE-PROVIDER WEB SITES WE'VE LOOKED AT

Eldish
Area/Country Codes:+58
Automated email: info@eldish.lat.net
Human email: sysop@eldish.lat.net
Phone: (+58) (2) 564-9889   Caracas
(+58) (2) 562-4246   Caracas
(+58) (51) 54-7446   Barquisimeto
(+58) (86) 23-5550   Puerto Ordaz
(+58) (41) 59-5949   Valencia
Fax: (+58) (2) 561-1741 Caracas
(+58) (41) 59-4912   Valencia
(+58) (86) 23-5652   Puerto Ordaz
(+58) (51) 54-7446   Barquisimeto
URL: http://eldish.lat.net/
note: Eldish has a very sophisticated main page

Internet Communicaciones, c.a.
Area/Country Codes: +58
Local Area Codes: 02
Automated email: admin@ccs.internet.ve
Human email: admin@ccs.internet.ve
Phone: +58-2-9599550
Fax: +58-2-9594550
URL: http://www.internet.ve/

Servicios Omnes De Venezuela, S.A.
Area/Country Codes: +58
Local Area Codes: 02
Human email: omnes@sa.omnes.net
Phone: (+58) (02) 9765323   Helpdesk
(+58) (02) 9765233   Master
Fax:(+58) (02) 9750892
URL: http://www.sa.omnes.net/

The Web Pages & Sites we've seen from Venezuela have been extremely sophisticated. Why this is, we aren't sure. Venezuela doesn't look like a country with problems when we look at it over the internet. We'd like to believe that the internet gives us a sort of cross-section of a nation, but after viewing the images of Venezuela portrayed on the Web we are forced to admit that there may be a greater disparity between actual reality and the illusion of reality seen over the Internet than we first imagined. It should have been obvious to us that if the average income is below $8,000 per year then not exactly everyone has the money to be surfing the Web or putting up a Web Site. Maybe just trying to eat enough to stay alive is more important. In some nations there is a fairly large base of middle class people, despite the lower overall income. The proliferation of Internet users in Brazil is a good example. There are students and housewives surfing the Web in Brazil. In many so-called third world countries such activity may not be the case across a sufficiently wide enough spectrum to draw meaningful conclusions about that society as a whole. If the upper-class segment of a society is sufficiently rich enough to never have to worry about going hungry and they are sufficiently ignorant enough not to be concerned about prevailing injustice and corruption then we aren't going to know too much about that society by looking at their Web Sites if only the rich can afford to have Web Sites. We certainly aren't saying this about Venezuela, because we don't know if that is the case. They may just be an extremely resilient people.

Our assessment of Venezuela remains unchanged. We would not hesitate to purchase real estate in Venezuela for ourselves. Our reasons are surprisingly straightforward. Adjacent to Venezuela is the nation of Columbia. The price of real estate in Columbia is many times higher than that of Venezuela, yet both Columbia and Venezuela are geographically similar. Additionally, Columbia has a GDP of only $172.4 billion compared to Venezuela's $178.3 billion, so we can see that Venezuela is doing pretty well with less people than Columbia. The per capita income in Venezuela is said to be $8,670 which compares favorably to Columbia's $4,850. All things considered Venezuela is alright and real estate prices are a bargain. Venezuela has no major problems with the exception of its having an idiot for a president. Idiots come and go, the land remains. An American just went to Venezuela and purchased a 10,000 acre estancia complete with buildings. The land is rolling hills and quite lovely. He paid $100,000 total price. That's a pretty hard price to beat. Venezuela, despite it's ongoing problem of political corruption is not in chaos. It is for the most part a pretty peaceful place.

Doug Casey has something interesting to say regarding timing in purchasing foreign real estate. Doug say's that the best time to go and invest in any country is when they've run it totally into the ground. As Doug put's it, 'until the wheels have fallen off.' When things can't get any worst, is the time to buy. All things considered, while the wheels may be off the cart in Venezuela, the situation is not actually too terribly bad. Venezuela's peaceful history probably tells us that it could and should begin to move upwards from it's current problems. Doug recommends the place himself. Doug has traveled to 110 countries and lived in seven. Eight, if you count the United States.

Escuela Bella Vista . .is an American school located in the city of Maracaibo, in western Venezuela. Founded in 1948, it was run by a consortium of international oil companies prior to the nationalization of oil resources by the Venezuelan government in 1978. It was *The* School to many Americans and Europeans whose parents lived and worked there, and still proudly serves that function today.

P. O. Box 290
Maracaibo, Venezuela
Phone: 011-58-61-911674 or 911696
FAX: 011-58-61-919417
or S.A. Escuela Bella Vista
Buzoom C-MAR-P1815 P.O. Box 02-8537
Miami, FL , 33102-8537 USA

TRADE INFORMATION
CUCIVA

CUCIVA is a non-profit, private entity, whose members are mainly Florida based Venezuelan and American businesses and individuals linked to the trading activity with Venezuela.

1101 Brickell Avenue Suite G2 Miami, Florida 33131-3104
Phone: (305) 530 3526 / (305) 530 8958 Fax: (305) 530 3527

Some of CUCIVA's goals are: To promote trade between United States and Venezuela by making information available to exporters and importers of both countries. Organize trade missions to and from Venezuela. Promote Business seminars and workshops. They publish a newsletter.

They have a Home Page at **URL:** http://www.netpoint.net/virtual/cuciva.html

LOCALIZED INFORMATION ABOUT VENEZUELA

There's a **Sensitive Map** at **URL:** http://venezuela.mit.edu/sensitive.html

There is information about each of the States of Venezuela, including population, surface area, mortality, economics, tourism, science, maps, current media, schools, parks, universities, attractions, cities and much more ...available from the Sensitive Map. Lots of Links.

Venezuela's Web Server
URL: http://venezuela.mit.edu/
This page collects information about Venezuela. and links to places in Venezuela.

NEWSPAPERS

The Newspaper **El National** has a Home Page at:
URL: http://www.el-nacional.com/

The Newspaper El Observador has a Home Page at:
URL: http://200.30.8.5/observador/default01.htm

News about Venezuela in English on the Internet (We are impressed; fairly extensive.)
URL: http://www.vzla.com/weekly/

CURRENCY: 1 bolivar (Bs) = 100 centimos

EXCHANGE RATES: bolivares (Bs) per US$1 - 169.570 (January 1995), 148.503 (1994), 90.826 (1993), 68.38 (1992), 56.82 (1991), 46.90 (1990)

EXCHANGE RATE 10/08/96: US$1 - 473.30 [each bolivar is worth .002¢ It would take five bolivars to make one penny.] It is crucial to keep all currency-assets out of Venezula and/or in a different currency.

WHAT TO TRADE INTO VENEZUELA: The following products look good at this time:● Food processing and packaging equipment ● machine tools ● transport equipment ● telecommunications equipment ● computers, peripherals and software ● medical and diagnostic and treatment equipment ● chemical processing machinery ● safety and security products.

TRADE WEB SITE: There is a Total Search Directory for Venezuela Export Web Site on the Internet. This is an excellent tool for anyone thinking of trading into or out of Venezuela.
URL: http://www.ddex.com.ve/

EXPORTING REGULATIONS: The best place to get additional information about exporting regulations and protocol as well as about procedures for selling to the government of Venezuela is:

Latin American/ Caribbean Business Developing Office
U.S. Department of Commerce
14th Street and Constitution Avenue NW
Washington DC 20230
tel: 202.377.0703

MORE BUSINESS CONTACTS:

The Venezuelan-American Chamber of Commerce of Florida
1101 Brickell Avenue Suite 1102-A Miami, Florida 33131-3104
Phone: (305) 530 3526 / (305) 530 8958 Fax: (305) 530 3527

CARACAS Camara de Industriales de Caracas
Venezuelan Chamber of Commerce
piso 2 y 3, Esq. Puente
Anauco, P 2,100,000, tel (02) 5714202, 5714224, fax: 5712009

Links to Venezuela
Links to Venezuela is a WebSite that provides numerous links to Veneauela.
URL: http://www.mse.berkeley.edu/Groups/cooper/JoseFolder/Venezuela.html

There is also **CONAPRI.** CONAPRI assists private investors to invest in Venezuela. Providing information on: investment opportunities, legal framework, areas/sectors of activities and possible business partners. Besides this, CONAPRI promotes investments in competitive sectors such as agribusiness, mining, tourism, finance and telecommunications. Publications: CONAPRI offers up-to-date political and economic information on Venezuela to people and organizations anywhere in the world showing an interest in Venezuela.

They also have a publication called: **Venezuela Now Faxnews**, which is a fairly informative one page report that summarizes what's news in Venezuela related to private investment, economics, finance and politics. Venezuela Now Faxnews also includes two statistical pages per month, one page of financial indicators and the other of macroeconomic indicators. These stats pages are included alternatively every two weeks together with the news summary page. Additionally, once a month they include a special news analysis page investigating an important issue in greater detail.
note: CONAPRI is a private company. Their inclusion here is not an endorsement.
For more information call: Tamara Guerrero
Phone 011 582 2376142 / Fax 011 582 2376028 /
Internet: email at conapri@dino.conicit.ve / Compuserve: 73000,2147
URL: http://lanic.utexas.edu/la/venezuela/conapri/venezuela_now.html

Mailers/Shippers APO
The **POBA Group** does remail, courier, and cargo. Serving Miami and Latin America, with special emphasis on the Venezuelan market. The group is comprised of P.O. Box Air International C.A., POBA Cargo Inc., and POBA Aduana. Their company was established more than 10 years ago with the intention of providing safe, confidential, and rapid deliver for Venezuelans. It is possible to both send and receive international correspondence and packages via POBA. They presently have more than 7,000 active clients served by offices in Caracas, Miami, Maiquetia and Valencia. They also have their own customs broker, POBA Aduana, to serve customers' needs.
P.O. Box Air International C.A.
Torre Las Mercedes, Mezz. Sur Avda. La Estancia, Chuao
Caracas, Venezuela
Tel:(02) 993-0250, 993-7525
Fax: 923469

POBA Cargo Inc
10421 N.W. 28th St. #D-105
Miami, Fl. 33172
Tel: (305) 477-8334
Fax: (305) 477-8916

POBA Asuana C.A.
Galpon Triple A, Planta Baja
Local 4 Zona Aeropuerto Maiquetia
Tel: (031) 23319 Fax: (031) 23128
Also: in Valencia, Venezuela Tel: (041) 240059 Fax: (041) 224331

225

EMBASSY OF VENEZUELA, WASHINGTON DC

Location: 1099 30th St., N.W., Washington D.C. 20007.
Office hours: 9:00am - 1:00pm and 2:00pm - 5:00pm Monday to Friday. Consular Section: 9:00am - 1:00pm Monday to Friday.
Phone: 202 342 2214 Fax: 202 342 6820 Home Page: http://venezuela.mit.edu/embassy
E-Mail: embavene@dgsys.com
Personnel Directory: Ambassador's Office: Pedro Luis Echeverría, Ambassador (202) 342 6804/05
Petroleum, Economic and Commercial Affairs Unit: (202) 342-6807 342-6822
Consular Section: (202) 342-6842 Visas and waivers 342-6843 Legalizations 342-6841
Embassy Library: (202) 342-6852 342-6853
Periodical published by the Embassy: Venequela Up to Date A quarterly publication concerning present topics of political, social and economic nature, to which we can subscribe. Free of charge by calling (202) 342 6849.

When you travel to Venezuela for a reason that has anything to do with business, you must travel with a business visa. This visa is valid for one year, and you can renew it in Caracas. Please check the Embassy's home page at http://venezuela.mit.edu/embassy for further information and the consular offices nearest to you. The requirements for Venezuelan citizenship can be obtained through the immigration office in Caracas. These types of transactions can be done only in Venezuela, at that office. Real estate can be purchased by a foreigner There are no exchange controls at this point in time. Local currency is stable at around Bs470 per $1. **Margarita** is the largest free trade zone in Venezuela.

Venezuela is Beautiful URL: http://venezuela.mit.edu/tourism/brochure
Loaded with pictures, this 60-page on-line brochure explores the coral beaches, rain forests, and mountain peaks of Venezuela. The guide is organized by locale and, though it doesn't contain specific expat info, it is well worthwhile for inspiration. There are some transportation tips.

For all of Latin-America there is the Institute of Latin American Studies at the University of Texas with a page called **LANIC** or **UT-LANIC**. With joint projects and hosted databases for all of Latin America. A mass of linked information. Arts & Culture, Business & Economics, Education, General Information, Government, Libraries, Network & Information Services, News & Electronic Forums, Travel & Tourism, WWW Servers, and more. It can't get more complete than this.
URL: http://lanic.utexas.edu/

An example of some of the very interesting things we can find on the Internet is the formative page of the State of **Zulia**, in the Republic of Venezuela, that is published by the local government and the State University of Zulia. The pages are in English and Spanish at: URL: http://www.luz.ve/Zulia/Maracaibo/zulia.htm

Newspapers & Magazines all over Latin America
URL: http://latinoweb.com/favision/newspapers.html

FACTS AT AT GLANCE (ADDITIONAL STATISTICS ON VENEZUELA)

PEOPLE

POPULATION: 20,185,000 [1992 est]   21,004,773 (July 1995 est.)

AGE STRUCTURE:

l 0-14 years: 35% (female 3,650,705; male 3,795,032)

l 15-64 years: 60% (female 6,350,466; male 6,313,887)

l 65 years and over: 5% (female 486,020; male 408,663) (July 1995 est.)

POPULATION GROWTH RATE: 2.1% (1995 est.)

BIRTH RATE: 25.11 births/1,000 population (1995 est.)

DEATH RATE: 4.57 deaths/1,000 population (1995 est.)

NET MIGRATION RATE: 0.46 migrant(s)/1,000 population (1995 est.)

INFANT MORTALITY RATE: 26.5 deaths/1,000 live births (1995 est.)

LIFE EXPECTANCY AT BIRTH:

total population: 73.31 years

male: 70.48 years

female: 76.29 years (1995 est.)

TOTAL FERTILITY RATE: 2.97 children born/woman (1995 est.)

LANGUAGE: Spanish is the official language. Italian is spoken fluently. Indian dialects are spoken and we have seen statistics that claim that native dialects are spoken by about 200,000 Amerindians in the remote interior. More than 30 Amerindian languages still survive, predominantly belonging to the Arawak, Cariban and Chibcha ethnolinguistic categories.

ETHNIC GROUPS: Mestizo [69%], European [20%], African origin [9%], Indian [2%]

RELIGIONS: nominally Roman Catholic 96%, Protestant 2% Roman Catholicism is by far the dominant religion in Venezuela, and has been adopted by most indigenous people - only those living in isolated regions still practise their ancient tribal beliefs. The Protestant church has a significant presence, and recently has been gaining some ground, attracting adherents from the Catholic Church. An unusual and obscure pantheistic sect, known as the Cult of María Lionza, exists in the north-west and combines pre-Hispanic indigenous creeds, African voodoo and Christian religious practices. The country's largest, most exuberant festival is Carnaval, which takes place on the Monday and Tuesday preceding Ash Wednesday. Characterized by music, dancing, parades and masquerades, the flavor of the event varies from region to region. The town of Carúpano is famous throughout the country for its elaborately staged Carnaval. Given the strong Roman Catholic character of Venezuela, most other national celebrations are tied to the Christian calendar. Apart from Easter, Christmas and Corpus Christi, which are celebrated enthusiastically, there are many saints' days spread over the calendar year.

SOME ECONOMIC STATS

NOTE: Some of the following figures differ from the figures supplied by the CIA World Fact Book and some of them are the figures supplied by CIA researchers. That is because we usual use several sperate sources for our analysis. If we supply more than one set of figures for something [as we do with the GDP] its because we suspect that the true figures may exist somewhere in between. Statistics are slippery.

GDP: US$59 billion

GDP ranking in the world: 38th

GDP PER CAPITA: US$2,900

ANNUAL GROWTH RATE: -1%

INFLATION: 66%

TOURISM: 550,000 visitors in 1991

MAJOR TRADING PARTNERS: USA, Germany, Japan

RELATIVE COSTS: ● Cheap meal: around $2-3 ● Restaurant meal: US$8-10 ● Cheap room: US$6 ● Mid range hotel room: US$20/35 single/double

NATIONAL PRODUCT: GDP - purchasing power parity - $178.3 billion (1994 est.)

NATIONAL PRODUCT REAL GROWTH RATE: -3.3% (1994 est.)

NATIONAL PRODUCT PER CAPITA: $8,670 (1994 est.) note: This figure is pure hyperbole. The figure for GDP per head is somewhere around $2,500 [if we don't happen to be an Indian.] If we're an Indian, we don't count.

INFLATION RATE: (consumer prices): 71% (1994 est.)

UNEMPLOYMENT RATE: 9% (1994 est.) note: Again we have a case of hyperbole. If this is an example of CIA humor it isn't funny; if it isn't humor, its laughable. We cannot venture a guess as to what the unemployment figures are. Probably double this figure.

BUDGET: revenues: $10.3 billion expenditures: $14.6 billion, including capital expenditures of $103 million (1994 est.) Exports: $15.2 billion (f.o.b., 1994 est.) commodities: petroleum 72%, bauxite and aluminum, steel, chemicals, agricultural products, basic manufactures partners: US and Puerto Rico 55%, Japan, Netherlands, Italy Imports: $7.6 billion (f.o.b., 1994 est.) commodities: raw materials, machinery and equipment, transport equipment, construction materials partners: US 40%, Germany, Japan, Netherlands, Canada External debt: $40.1 billion (1994) Industrial production: growth rate -1.4% (1993 est.); accounts for 41% of GDP

ELECTRICITY: capacity: 18,740,000 kW production: 72 billion kWh Electricity: 110V, 60 Hz

INDUSTRIES: petroleum, iron-ore mining, construction materials, food processing, textiles, steel, aluminum, motor vehicle assembly

AGRICULTURE: accounts for 6% of GDP; products - corn, sorghum, sugarcane, rice, bananas, vegetables, coffee, beef, pork, milk, eggs, fish; not self-sufficient in food other than meat

ILLICIT DRUGS: illicit producer of cannabis, opium, and coca leaf for the international drug trade on a small scale; however, large quantities of cocaine and heroin transit the country from Colombia; important money-laundering hub

ECONOMIC AID: recipient: US commitments, including Ex-Im (FY70-86), $488 million; Communist countries (1970-89), $10 million

PHYSICAL FEATURES:

Area: total area: 912,050 sq km, land area: 882,050 sq km; comparative area: slightly more than twice the size of California. Land boundaries: total 4,993 km, Brazil 2,200 km, Colombia 2,050 km, Guyana 743 km Coastline: 2,800 km Maritime claims: contiguous zone: 15 nm continental shelf: 200-m depth or to the depth of exploitation exclusive economic zone: 200 nm territorial sea: 12 nm International disputes: claims all of Guyana west of the Essequibo River; maritime boundary dispute with Colombia in the Gulf of Venezuela Climate: tropical; hot, humid; more moderate in highlands

Terrain: Andes Mountains and Maracaibo Lowlands in northwest; central plains (llanos); Guiana Highlands in southeast

Natural resources: petroleum, natural gas, iron ore, gold, bauxite, other minerals, hydropower, diamonds

Land use: Arable land: 3% permanent crops: 1% meadows and pastures: 20% forest and woodland: 39% oter: 37% irrigated land: 2,640 sq km (1989 est.)

Environment: current issues: sewage pollution of Lago de Valencia; oil and urban pollution of Lago de Maracaibo; deforestation;soil degradation; urban and industrial pollution, especially along the Caribbean coast natural hazards: subject to floods, rockslides, mudslides; periodic droughts international agreements: party to - Biodiversity, Climate Change, Endangered Species, Marine LifeConservation, Nuclear Test Ban, Ozone Layer Protection, Ship Pollution, Wetlands, Whaling; signed, but notratified - Hazardous Wastes, Marine Dumping Venezuela is on major sea and air routes linking North and South America Venezuela is situated on the northern coast of South America, north of Brazil and between Colombia and Guyana. The south east is dominated by the Guayana Highlands, and a further 30% of the country is taken up by the vast grassland plain of the central Llanos, which is drained by South Americas third largest river, the Río Orinoco. The continent's largest inland lake, Lake Maracaibo, lies in the north-east, surrounded by marshy, fertile lowlands. South of the lake, rise the northern end of the Andes, known here as the Cordillera de Los Andes, which climb to 5,007 metres at Pico Bolívar. Boggy highland meadows in the Andes, known as páramos, are home to some of Venezuela's most amazing plant species. Equally diverse flora can be found on the tepuis (huge flat-topped mountains) in the south-east of the country, particularly Roraima.Flora of the páramos, the Andes (10K) Flora of the tepuis (10K)

LOCAL NAME: Repúblic de Venezuela Digraph: VE (The name means "Little Venice".) When Columbus arrived he saw the houses the indians had built on stilts in the lagoons and was reminded of Venice.

TIME ZONE: GMT-4

AREA: 352,051 sq mi [slightly more than twice the size of the state of California]

STATUS: Republic

DATE OF INDEPENDENCE: 5 July 1811 [from Spain]

CLIMATE:

The country's climate is predominantly tropical, with a warm temperate zone extending along the coast. Temperatures rarely vary more than a few degrees (Caracas 18.3 - 20.6 degrees Celsius, Maracaibo 27.2 - 29.4 degrees Celsius); consequently Venezuela's climatic zones are defined by rainfall rather than by differences in temperature. The northern coastal lowlands are relatively arid, but rainfall increases over the Llanos and the Guayana Highlands, with average yearly readings reaching 1,500 mm in both regions. The dry season (called the verano) extends from December to April, and the wet season (invierno) covers the remainder of the year. The Amazon region has no distinct dry season, and annual rainfall exceeds 2000 mm, distributed evenly throughout the year. The dry season is more pleasant for travelling, particularly if you plan on hiking.

Venezuela is a country of striking natural beauty and dramatic contrasts: the snowcapped peaks of the Andes in the west, and steamy Amazonian jungles in the south; the hauntingly beautiful Gran Sabana plateau, with its strange flat-topped mountains, in the east, and 3,000 km of white-sand beaches fringed with coconut palms line the Caribbean coast. South America's largest lake, Lake Maracaibo, and third-longest river, the Orinoco, are also here, and the country boasts the world's highest waterfall, Angel Falls. It is also home to a wide variety of exotic plants and animals, including the jaguar, ocelot, tapir, armadillo, anteater, and the longest snake in the world, the anaconda.

CHAPTER FOURTEEN

DOMINICAN REPUBLIC

ONE OF A KIND

The **Dominican Republic** (or D.R. as it is known) is definitely one of a kind. It is on a very large island that it shares with **Haiti**. The island of **Hispaniola** [hIS-Pan-yó-laa] which is a mountainous island, having the highest and the lowest points in the Caribbean on its shores. The capital of the DR is **Santo Domingo**, located next to the largest port on the island. About 50% of the people live in rural and agricultural centers; many are small landowners. The Dominican Republic is an agriculturally rich island. The country has five universities, including the Autonomous University of Santo Domingo (UASD) dating from 1538, which makes it the oldest university in the Americas. Santo Domingo also has the oldest street in the Western World, and in the Colonial Zone many buildings which are some of the oldest, if not the oldest European buildings in the new world. Founded on August the 4th in 1496, Santo Domingo is indeed one of a kind. The DR is an especially lovely island. In the mountains are valleys that are as nice as anything we could hope to see. Europeans (especially the Germans and the Italians,) have more or less kept the DR their Caribbean secret and it is only recently that Americans have seriously began to visit there. There are miles of unspoiled beaches and overall it is a very peaceful spot to be.

In business and commerce the DR continues to be one of a kind. In 1992, inflation dropped from triple digits to zero, while real economic growth went from zero up to 3% at the same time. Despite these very positive indicators the nation suffers from an abysmally low per capita GDP. Some statistical sources show the per capita income to be as low as $1,000 per year. We have seen figures of $3,000; however knowing what we know, our inclination is to believe that the lower figure is closer to reality. Additionally, we have seen reported unemployment statistics approaching 30 percent. There are 27 **Free Trade Zones (FTZ's)** in the Dominican Republic, which must be some kind of a record for its size. Tourism plays a close second to the FTZ source created revenue, followed by agriculture. The FTZ's are a mixture of public and private sector managed facilities and they offer numerous incentives that are worth investigating. The DR FTZ program is said to be one of the best in the world and the most successful. Nearly all foreign investment over the last few years has been concentrated in the FTZ's and in tourism. The DR may also hold some sort of record in it's large number of American Expatriates per capita; the estimated number being claimed is 80,500 American Expats. [A figure which we find questionable.]

Real Estate prices in the Dominican Republic are better than most of it's Caribbean neighbors. While prices are not as good as Venezuela's or Dominica's, there are still some great bargains to be found in the Dominican Republic if we pay attention.

FREEDOM HOUSE RATINGS:

FREEDOM HOUSE RATINGS: Political Rights: ④ Civil Liberties: ③
Freedom House states that the citizens of the Dominican Republic cannot change their government through democratic elections because of widespread fraud and corruption. The current President Balaguer controls all of the police, the armed forces and the bureaucracy preventing legitimate and fair elections. Constitutional guarantees regarding free expression, freedom of religion and the right to organize political parties and civic groups are general respected, however. Yet, despite this, the courts offer little recourse to those without money or influence. Newspapers are independent and diverse, but subject to governmental pressures. With so many borderline bad things to say about the Dominican Republic perhaps the reader wonders why it is a recommended country.

The Dominican Republic is one of those nations where there is a great disparity between what happens to an expatriate trying to improve the situation by bringing in jobs and innovation as compared to what happens to an impoverished citizen. With this said, many will wonder if I have all my wits about me in continuing to recommend the Dominican Republic. We believe that the only way to make the situation better in the Dominican Republic, or anywhere else for that matter, is to bring legitimate jobs and innovations that create better working standards for the nation. The situation in the Dominican Republic is much improved from what it once was. Add to this, that there are innumerable Free Trade Zones and a heavy influx of both European and American Expatriates and we have a fairly positive situation despite the continuing presence of election fraud. We fully expect that the political situation is going to greatly improve over the next decade. Real Estate in the Dominican Republic is both attractive and reasonably priced, especially in some of the more remote areas. By investing now, before the political situation is completely stabilized, the expat stands to purchase at a significant savings. This is one of those situations we will run into around the world. Wherein lies morality? I certainly consider myself moral, but I recognize there are better ways to create change than at the point of a gun or at a public protest. Whatever negatives we might say about the Dominican Republic, the Dominican Republic does accentuate free market enterprise. And where there is the means to sway the market, there is ultimately, also the means to sway morality. With that said, we must repeat that we are cognizant of the problems and at times almost abysmal conditions faced by the many citizens inside of the Dominican Republic. We believe their situation can best be remedied by supplying them with solid good-paying jobs, and by filling the country with well-educated expatriates who can exert positive influence where it counts the most; in the economy of the nation. The government of the Dominican Republic knows where its bread is buttered. Add to that, that a new group of younger political aspirants is slowly entering the scene and gradually pushing out the last remanent of Trujullo legacy.

TELECOMMUNICATIONS & THE WWW

WWW, TELEPHONY & TELECOMMUNICATIONS: There are at least two Service Providers that we know of to the Dominican Republic and we suspect that there may be more. How fully the Service Providers cover the island we cannot say in absolute detail; Mr. Francisco Vinoly of **GBM Corporation** is one of the Service Providers to the Dominican Republic. He informed us that not all of the Dominican Republic has Internet Access at this time. They are moving slowly into the interior with service at the time of this writing. [4th quarter 1996] We will continue to monitor progress of Service into the interior and we will try to have this information in our Fax-On-Demand system by the time you are reading this. The available statistics & data claim that there are currently some 190,000 telephones and a relatively efficient domestic system based on island-wide microwave radio relay network. Whether or not this means that Internet Access is ultimately going to be available island-wide we cannot yet state in fact, but we suspect that such is the case. There are 120 radio stations and 18 domestic television stations, plus the other thousands of stations worldwide that we can pickup with a satellite dish. We do know that electrical service in the DR is subject to sporadic power outages and that this is an ongoing problem. In terms of access to high tech equipment, the DR is definitely a bring your own baseball kind of game. But that also means we'd be the first kid on the block.

For Service Providers contact: **GBM Corporation** at http: //www.gbm.net/ email them at: webmaster@gbm.net and telephone them in Miami at: 305·539·3450 or 305·539·3477

Embassy of the Dominican Republic
Chancery: 1715-22nd St., NW Washington, DC 20008
Tel: (202) 332-6280 Fax: (202) 265-8057
URL: http://gurukul.ucc.american.edu/uiwww/fg6414a/embassy/embassy.htm

Dominican Republic: This page offers an updated list of links of several sites concerning the Dominican Republic. The information is divided in : general information, general pages, homepages, pictures, travel, accommodation & sports, Internet, studies and education, human rights & unrest and cultural & food.
URL: http://huizen.dds.nl/~henkm/dominic.htm

Tropical Weather Resources:
Numerous Caribbean-related weather sites:
URL: http://www.webcom.com/earleltd/common/weather/wthr.html
This page is continually updated. Includes tracking info and satellite shots of Tropical Storms and Hurricanes. Excellent information on this past year's and the current Hurricane season including charts of all the storms and satellite pictures.

There is a WebSite on the Dominican Republic put together by **Dolores Vicioso** called **D.R. ONE** It's **URL** is http://www.drl.com It is a great WebSite that is well put together.

As we stated on the opening page in business and commerce sectors the DR continues to be one of a kind. In 1992, inflation dropped from triple digits to zero, while real economic growth went from zero up to 3% at the same time. Despite these very positive indicators the nation suffers from an abysmally low per capita GDP. Some statistical sources show the per capita income to be as low as $1,000 per year. We have seen figures of $3,000; however knowing what we know, our inclination is to believe that the lower figure is closer to reality.* Additionally, we have seen reported unemployment statistics approaching 30 percent. There are 27 **Free Trade Zones (FTZ's)** in the Dominican Republic, which must be some kind of a record for its size. Tourism plays a close second to the FTZ source created revenue, followed by agriculture. The FTZ's are a mixture of public and private sector managed facilities and they offer numerous incentives that are worth investigating. The DR FTZ program is said to be one of the best in the world and the most successful. Nearly all foreign investment over the last few years has been concentrated in the FTZ's and in tourism. Information regarding the **Dominican Republic Free Trade Zone programs** is available at: **Dominican Republic Investment Promotion Council**, P.O. Box 25438 Washington D.C. 20007 Telephone: 703·247·8445 Fax: 703·247·8569 Also try; **Dominican Association of Industrial Free Zones** Telephone: 809·566·0437 Fax: 809·566·0570

The American Chamber of Commerce in the Dominican Republic is at Telephone: 809·544·2222 and can be Faxed at: 809·544·0502

There is the Association of Industries of the Dominican Republic at telephone: 809·535·9111, and they can be faxed at: 809·533·7520

National Hotel & Restaurant Association Would probably the ones to contact regarding the possibilities in the Tourist Industry. 809·687·4676 Fax: 809·687·4727

It is probably instructive to look at the **1995 World Fact Book Overview of the Dominican Republic Economy** According to them: "The Dominican economy showed some signs of slippage in 1994, although its overall performance in recent years has been relatively strong. After posting an increase of nearly 8% in 1992, GDP growth fell to 3% in 1993 and 1994 as mining output decreased and erosion of real wages caused private consumption to decline. A pre-election boost in government spending in early 1994 led to the first government deficit in four years and bumped inflation up to 14% for the year. Continued dynamism in construction and the services sector, especially tourism, should keep the economy growing in 1995. Tourism, agriculture, and manufacturing for export remain key sectors of the economy. Domestic industry is based on the processing of agricultural products, oil refining, and chemicals."

* We believe that the method of determining the per capita GDP seldom reveals anything much like the very thing it is meant to define, which is supposed to be the average income of people living in a country. It is also necessary to consider the purchasing power of the income earned. *If the value of the paper money is absolutely determined by government fiat with exchange controls in place,* then earning five hundred Zapolotés which have a government value of U.S. One Hundred Dollars, doesn't mean too much if the 'street value' of the Zapoloté is something like: Two Thousand Zapolotés for U.S. Fifty Dollars. Economics is a slippery science, especially in the hands of government employees who tend to be slippery people.

The Central Bank of the Dominican Republic Telephone: 809·221·9111 Fax: 809·686·7488 We have heard that outside of the Free Trade Zones the Central Bank has a tight grip on all foreign exchange transactions, both incoming and outgoing. i.e. All individuals or businesses generating foreign exchange are required to exchange it with the Central Bank through commercial banks. Imports can be purchased only with dollars furnished by the Central Bank. How this effects the people in the tourist business we cannot say at this point. We can think of innumerable methods of having our bank offshore, however this method might not work in every circumstance when doing business within a country. Those who operate outside of the Free Trade Zones and whose business generate large amounts of revenue will have to deal with the Central Bank. We will welcome any information passed on to us about how different expats deal with this issue and certainly relay such information in our fax-on-demand system. The corporate tax base outside of the Free Trade Zone is 46%, the highest in the Caribbean Basin; while those corporations operating inside of the Free Trade Zones enjoy a 100 percent exemption from all taxes for fifteen years.* Duty free imports of machinery and equipment, spare parts, construction material, and other items needed to construct and operate a facility. Duty free import of raw materials, supplies, and other goods destined for reexport, exclusion from foreign currency holding and exchange restrictions, and exemption from financial reporting requirements, except those dealing with local expenses. Wages inside the Free Trade Zones is running about US$0.56 per hour, including fringes. Labor supply is plentiful, although skills are at the lower end of the spectrum. Management talent is very scarce and expatriate managers are necessary. Foreign companies can freely repatriate profits and capital and can totally own 100 per cent of their own free trade zone based businesses. Outside the free trade zones the loudest complaint from foreign investors is concerning the poorly managed customs operations and corrupt customs officials. This hampers the movement of goods and services in and out of the country.

AGRICULTURE

A very dynamic sector is the **agribusiness**. The problem in this sector thus far has been concerning government restrictions about expatriate/foreign ownership of agricultural land. (Does this effect those who become DR citizens? We doubt it, but do not know the facts.) Ownership of more than 50% of the land must be in DR hands. Numerous conflicts have been reported over contractual rights and land tenure. The government has done little to correct this situation. However a joint US-DR group has been set up to help agricultural investors. Further information can be obtained by contacting either of the following: ✓ Oscar Benitez, Executive Director, **Joint Agricultural Consultative Committee** Apartado Postal 38809 Santo Domingo, Dominican Republic. Telephone: 809·567·7207 Fax: 809·541·4564 ✓ Lawrence Eisenberg, **Commercial Officer U.S. Embassy**, Santo Domingo APO Miami, Florida 34041-3470 Telephone: 809·541·2171 Fax: 809·688·4838

*It is interesting to note what Consulate-General Jim Howell of New Zealand has to say about Free Trade Zones. Among other things he states, "If you have a Free Trade Zone and it's tax-free, then in our view it is government subsidized. Somebody has to pay for it." See our interview with Mr. Howell in the New Zealand section for greater detail.

It should be noted that government price controls keep agriculture exports from being competitive in international markets, severely restricting the development of this sector. The DR exports more to the United States than any other independent country in the Caribbean basin, exceeding $2 billion annually. Just slightly less than of half this amount comes from companies in the free trade zones. The balance is derived mostly from those firms outside of the FTZ's exporting sugar, sugar by-products, ferronickle, gold, silver, coffee, cocoa, and the mineral bauxite.

The best market for American products exported to the DR is in the areas where hotel development and foreign owned villas and condominiums are being built. Additionally there are several very upper class neighborhoods around Santo Domingo an other larger cities with a sufficiently large population of affluent DR citizens who are susceptible to American products. Many expats are making a great deal of money in the **real estate** market. The real estate market seems uneven to us. We have noted a great deal of disparity between prices in undeveloped sections of the DR and those sections where expats have built villas. We suspect that our faithful caveat is to be closely observed in this matter. Don't buy any real estate until you have lived in the DR for at least a year. The difference in price between what a knowledgeable person pays versus some dude 'fresh-off-the-boat,' may be somewhere on the order of a 80 to 90 percent difference in price.

GETTING IN & DOING BUSINESS

Getting in and doing business inside the Dominican Republic is rather simple. We will quote directly from correspondence we recieved from an acquaintance in the Dominican Republic based on some questions we asked:

"Yes, there are tariffs (import taxes) assessed for bringing a vehicle into the DR. Rates vary considerably and usually will not be quoted until the vehicle is actually here on the dock, but it seems to vary from 20 to 30 percent of vehicle value depending on age, motor size, etc. A vehicle is one of the expensive items here; either to import or to buy here."

"Yes, you can live here year round without citizenship by holding a residency permit. (has no effect on U.S. citizenship) which a DR lawyer can obtain for you in 1 to 2 weeks at a cost of approx. U.S.$1800 to $2000. This allows you to operate a business legally. Many people here live full time and operate a business without residency but you are technically illegal. I do know of many doing so. A permit or license to operate a business is very simple to obtain and in most cases only requires a visit to the City Hall by yourself or lawyer and a small fee. They do not even inspect the premises. Liquor does not require special permits here to be sold."

"If you wish a corporation under which to operate or to own your business it cost approx. U.S.$1200 to $1400 and you own the corporation even though it is a Dominican Corp. and operates with those benefits. I would not be surprised if you find out that the DR is about the easiest country to enter and operate in. Naturally there are disadvantages here such as frequent power outages or poor maintenance of some of the roads etc., but something has to suffer."

We spoke with a second expat-resident of the DR, and asked similar questions, here is the response they gave us:

"Moving to the Dominican Republic is much easier than moving to Costa Rica. My husband is quite familiar with all the procedures as we were pioneers in moving first to Costa Rica and then later to the Dominican Republic. Most people who move here to live year round to do business purchase a Dominican Corporation and then obtain their residency. The cost of a residency is now U.S.$1,500 per person. Within a 3 month period of obtaining this residency you are able to bring in your automobile providing it is at least one year old, there is a charge for this (tips etc.) but we do work with people who do this for a living and it is not that difficult. Opening a business is still uncomplicated here. You must be accepted by the health department and business bureau and have an operating permit which is usually under $100. No one needs a liquor license so that is not a problem."

Another person we spoke with told us that most people coming to the Dominican Republic simply dispense with the residency requirements (along with most other legal requirements,) and that enforcement is very lax. This may certainly be true, we have seen much of this sort of thing elsewhere in the world; however we suggest as we always do that it is best to spend a year or so in a place and learn the rules before making any sort of commitments or dangerous moves. Writing this book requires that we advise readers to error on the side of caution, so of course we are going to suggest that the rules be followed to avoid surprises further down the trail. This said, we will comment that we have heard from more than one expat that the Domincan Republic is very lax about enforcing expatriate requirements and that living there is a very relaxing laidback sort of experience as a result.

All in all, we see the Dominican Republic with rather clear eyes. It is a lovely place with many real estate bargains. It has a good climate, because it is easy to live at different elevations where we can pick and choose our climate. It is a very large island. The people are extremely friendly and there is no great crime or pollution problems outside of the capital city of Santo Domingo. (See the US State Department Consular Travel Information Sheet in this chapter.) There are any number of excellent economic opportunities in the DR. The country is the number one trading partner of the US in the Caribbean, and is a major player in the world market even if we don't compare it to other Caribbean nations. It is doing many things right in an economic sense. It is smart enough to keep its hands off of business and business ventures and while it does little to prevent business from flourishing it seems also to know how to promote it. It is very welcoming to expats from any nation and has a sizeable expat community. There is much open land and excellent agricultural potential. It is strategically located between the US and Latin American Markets; and it sells a great deal of its products to the European market. Many, if not most of its tourists are from Europe. Tourism is booming, because of its vast unspoiled open beaches and its reasonable prices vis a vis other Caribbean destinations.

The disadvantages are obvious and that is why the Dominican Republic still remains somewhat of a bargain. It has the wrong language if we don't speak Spanish, and even for us that do speak a bit of it, the Spanish of the DR is an almost 'pure' Spanish which differs from most other Latin American Spanish. This language-problem is not insurmountable; but it has stopped or slowed down enough other expats to a degree that keeps the Dominican Republic a bargain. Additionally, it must be kept in mind that the Dominican Republic government has been less than forthright in its past attempts to hold fraud-free elections. However, we are happy to report that the situation seems to have taken a very recent turn for the better. As we pen these lines a new president is being sworn into office in the Dominican Republic. In fact, this turn of events is so recent that we are having to revise this section even as we write it.

The new president, Dr. Leonel Fernández was born in a small house in the San Carlos area of Santo Domingo, the son of a former Army mayor Jose Antonio Fernández and Yolanda Reyna. At age 9 Fernádez moved to New York City with his parents and attended school in the United States for several years. He is thus very fluent in English and even taught high school English and French while attending law school. He is a member of the DR party called the Partido de la Liberación Dominicana (PRD), which for the first time occupies the presidency. We believe that this is a major step towards a new era in DR politics. Fernádez, 42, replaces Joaquin Balaguer, 90, the last of the politicians to serve under dictator Rafael Trujillo. Some of the themes touched upon in the new president's election speech pledges were the DR's participation in the emerging global economy in the aftermath of the Cold War, the need to update the nation's knowledge and use of modern technology in the areas of production and communication.

Fernádez is also working towards the privatization of state-controlled industries a total reform of the judicial system and the passing of a General Electricity Law which may prevent the recurrent power outages,. He also pledged to fight against poverty and promised the development of public education and adequate housing. There we have it, what we have longed and hoped for, has perhaps been given to the Dominican Republic. While we are aware that political talk is cheap, we will state, that we believe that now is probably the best time in history to go to and invest in the Dominican Republic. To be sure, we have not seen Fernádez preform and it is possible he might be a disappointment, but we doubt this will be so. The reasons, for us, are obvious. The man is a past high school teacher and as totally different in orientation from his predecessor as day is from night. (He is not an ex-general.) From what we have seen he is already addressing issues that Balaguer couldn't even recognize. There will still be problems, as remanent of the old guard are forced to give way (and influence) to a younger, perhaps more moral generation of politicians. We, who are notably apolitical and anti-government, are willing to give the new President a vote of confidence. We have very high hopes for the Dominican Republic and for it's people based on this fortuitous outcome.

Leonel Fernández, don't let your people down.

REAL ESTATE IN THE DOMINICAN REPUBLIC

As we mentioned, real estate in the DR is a bargain for the selective buyer. The July 23, 1992 issue of **Island Property Report** has a front page feature on the Dominican Republic entitled, *'Dominican Republic, Still a Bargain for the Cautious Homebuyer.'* The **Island Property Report** is available from telephone: 813·495·1604, Fax: 813·495·1738 or by writing them at 4061 Bonita Beach Road Suite 201, Bonita Springs, Florida 33923 Back issues are available. They also write about Costa Rica, Belize and Central America as well as writing about the Caribbean.

SOME TIPS ABOUT BUYING & RENTING REAL ESTATE

Some Spanish terms we might see regarding real estate are: *Inmobiliaria* and/or *Bienes raices.* These are the most common terms for real estate. Immobiliaria refers more to a business that buys and sells real estate. A *solar* or *parcela* is a tract of land, and a mortgage is a *hipoteca.* Watch out for the words *alquiler* and *alquilar*: the first is a noun, referring to renting or letting, while the second is a verb. In a Purchase Agreement, watch out for the words:*promesa de venta,* which refers to the specific date upon which an agreement must be finalized to avoid loss of deposit. Of course it is better to use a good attorney; try checking with the American Chamber of Commerce in Santo Domingo for recommendations.

The American Chamber of Commerce in the Dominican Republic is at Telephone: 809·544·2222 and can be Faxed at: 809·544·0502

LAWYERS IN THE DOMINICAN REPUBLIC The American Chamber of Commerce of the Dominican Republic gave us the following names of lawyers in the Dominican Republic:

✓ **Ricardo Pellerabi Pellerano & Herrera** Fax: 809·541·5200

✓ **Luis Heredia Bonetti Russin, Vecchi & Heredia Bonetti** Fax: 809·535·6649

Finding suitable housing in Santo Domingo is usually done through the newspaper just as it is in the United States. There is one English Language newspaper of good repute: *The Santo Domingo News*, telephone: 809·535·7173 Fax: 809·535·0788. They are highly recommended as a newspaper; however we are not totally sure they are the best place to find a reasonably priced rental or sale property. We would compare the Spanish speaking newspaper advertisements with the English speaking newspaper advertisements to determine if there are any disparities between the prices when compared. The Santo Domingo News is a fine paper. They can be viewed online at the wonderful Web Site of **Dolores Vicioso** called **D.R. ONE** Its **URL** is http://www.drl.com It is nothing less than a gold mine of quality information about the Dominican Republic. Ms. Vicioso is doing an excellent job, every country should have someone so talented. There are real estate companies which post available properties on her Web Site. Again, it is best to live in a country at least a year before buying any real estate.

239

In seeking a rental or bargain property we might also run an advertisement in the local paper stating what it is we are looking for. The cost for an advertisement would be about $5 to $10, and Spanish would be almost a necessity for this method, or someone who can answer your calls in Spanish, such as a hotel clerk or hired helper. In the paper, those advertisements placed by agents are obviously going to be appreciably higher in price then those placed by the average DR citizen. Driving around and asking questions is something that we have to do no matter where we live in the world. It can be a slow but enjoyable process. If we don't want to meet the people then we might be better off staying at home in the US rather than going abroad. We usually find that the average person is worth meeting in most foreign countries.

In the Dominican Republic it is required that we ask about the electrical situation in any place we rent or buy. The requirements are the existence of an auxiliary generator or *planta,* or preferably, an 'inversor' which is a power back-up system. It is further required that we determine thoroughly the extent of the back-up systems capacity: i.e. does it provide full power, including air conditioners and elevators?

It is technically legal for foreigners to purchase DR real estate only after receiving what is called a 'presidential approval.' However we have been told (repeatedly) that the rules are so broad and loosely enforced that it is usually possible to purchase a property without any requirements or difficulties. We must stress that this is exactly the type of situation for gringos to beware of. Having lived in Latin America, and indeed, having Latin American relatives in my immediate family; I have come to know that legalities can, and often do change suddenly and without notice. Nowhere can rules change so rapidly as they do in Latin America then in that moment when something becomes extremely valuable and all of the paperwork is suddenly discovered to be improperly filed. It is always sad to discover that the property which you purchased ten years ago for $10,000 (and is now worth $400,000) actually belongs to the Mayor's cousin ...unless of course you are the Mayor's cousin. (But cheer up, you will be released from jail and deported as soon as you pay the ten years back rent.) Perhaps the reader believe's I am talking about the Dominican Republic, or Mexico, or Brazil, or Costa Rica. They are right. Dot your eyes, cross your heart, and cover your assets; and if you don't trust your attorney then get a second or even a third opinion. (...if it's Mexico, you might also check to see how much real estate is owned by your attorneys cousin.) In my immediate family that would be my second-cousin Fendizio who now owns most of Cabo San Lucas.

Our understanding, which we arrived at third hand, is that no approval is required in the Dominican Republic for a single first time purchase of real estate, providing that the property is less than 22,000 square feet in size. That is approximately a half acre in size. (one acre is 43,560 square feet) There are numerous other things we've heard third hand; regarding length of time in the DR, marriage to a citizen exemptions and so forth. We recommend that the reader use prudence in purchasing real estate by understanding the law as well as possible. See an attorney. We understand that presidential approval for the purchase of real estate by foreigners is liberally granted in the DR, so jumping through the hoops shouldn't be too much of an ordeal for what it may be worth in ultimate peace of mind.

It is possible to determine who has Legal Title to a piece of property prior to signing any papers in the DR just as it is in the United States. Property can be appraised by a DR appraisal firm for a reasonable fee. Try: ✓ **Instituto de Tasadore Domincanos**, Inc. telephone: 809·686·4433 Another firm that does appraisals is:✓ **Edmundo Garcia Iglesias** telephone: 809·687·0508. Mr. Iglesias speaks English. [I like that.]

Using a real estate agent may be easier, but it will cost a lot for the ease. It should also be noted that several of the gringo backed villas and condominium projects have never reached completion. They were ill-planned, under-funded, or simple rip-offs. Buying from a gringo is not a means of avoiding getting ripped-off. On the contrary; we personally feel that we would be much more comfortable buying a home or farm from a Dominican family than from a real estate agent. Of course we would consult with a DR attorney to understand the fine print in any event, but we don't believe that much is accomplished by dealing with a real estate agent beyond ease of transaction. If ease of transaction triples the price or buys us a gringo villa in a gringo village, then we didn't accomplish too much beyond making it easy to spend our money. It's the same old story. Americans go to the DR and buy a villa on a lot near the beach for $250,000 from another American. The transaction is simple. The brochures divine. All the photographs look like Cinemascope. (today that's called wide angle ...and the angles are wide.) What we could have bought by taking some time and learning the ropes is perhaps 25 acres of land and a beautiful house for half the money. If you think that villas on subdivided lots near the beach for $250,000 are great things, then buy a few acres of land on the beach for $40,000 and develop your own.

The U.S. government provides some services for individuals interested in doing business in the DR. A central office that provides the names of other offices is **Dominican Republic Desk Officer, Caribbean Basin Division**, Room 3025, US Department of Commerce, Washington D.C. 20230 telephone: 202·377·2527; Fax: 202·377·2218

Also try: **Dominican Republic Investment Promotion Council**, P.O. Box 25438, Washington D.C. 20007, telephone: 809·532·2381; Fax: 809·533·7029

There is a book entitled: *Living In Santo Domingo*, that is published by the **Santo Domingo News**. We have not read the book; but advertisements for it state that it is a compilation of answers to more than 1,000 of the most asked questions by foreigners moving to the capital of the Dominican Republic. The advertisement claims that the book not only tells how to find goods and services in Santo Domingo but gives advice on the unwritten rules of Dominican society and culture. The newspaper itself is available by mail. For the book, information about other publications and newspaper rates, contact: The **Santo Domingo News**, CPS 1215 P.O. Box 149020 Coral Gables, Florida 33114 Fax: 809·535·0788

The Dominican Republic: A National History, by Frank Moya Pons, is also available from the Santo Domingo News. The book is a history book as the title indicates, published in 1995 with maps and a bibliography updated to cover events up to the year 1991.

ESCAPE FROM AMERICA

Two rather gloomy books; *Dominican Republic: Beyond the Lighthouse* by James Ferguson 1992 Latin American Bureau, London; and *The Dominican Republic: A Caribbean Crucible*, by Howard J. Wiarda and Michael J. Kryzanek 1992 Westview Press, are both worth reading for anyone serious about the Dominican Republic. These books concentrate on the many broken promises and political fraudulence perpetuated upon the Dominican people.

The *Hippocrene Insiders Guide to the Dominican Republic* is a good travel book that is wider in scope than the average travel book. By Jack Tucker and Ursula Eberhard, Hippocrene Books, New York 1993.

Harry S. Pariser, the world traveling travel-writer has an adventure guide to the D.R., called: *The Adventure Guide to the Dominican Republic*, from Hunter Publications, New Jersey 1995.

There is also a nice little guide called the *Practical Travel A to Z: Dominican Republic*, from Hayit Publishing, London 1992

Commerce and Trade in the Dominican Republic
The Dominican Republic 1995
1995, 36 pages
Published by Publicaciones en Inglés
P. O. Box 106-2
Santo Domingo, Dominican Republic
Tel. (809) 535-7131 Fax (809) 535-0788

FACTS AT A GLANCE ON THE D.R. ECONOMY

CURRENCY: 1 Dominican Peso = (official foreign exchange rate: 14.28 RD Peso = US$1.00 That makes each Peso worth .07¢ as of this printing, 4th quarter 1996.) Note: A parallel market exists in the RD Peso.
ECONOMY: Recently moved from agricultural based economy to tourist based
GDP: US$10.8 billion (1994)
GDP PER CAPITA: US$1,532
GDP GROWTH RATE: 4.3%
NATURAL RESOURCES: Nickel, gold, silver, beaches
AGRICULTURAL PRODUCTS: Sugar cane, coffee, cocoa, tobacco, beef, fruits and vegetables
TYPES OF PRODUCTS: Sugar and petroleum refining, rum and beer, textiles, pharmaceutical, cement, light manufacturing, food processing, metallurgy
PRINCIPAL GOODS EXPORTED: Ferronickel, gold, silver, coffee, cocoa, tobacco, meats, fruits and vegetables (US$1.9 billion)
PRINCIPAL IMPORTS: Foodstuffs, petroleum, industrial raw materials, capital goods (US$2.2 billion)

**PRINCIPAL STEPS FOR INSTALLING A FREE ZONE COMPANY IN THE DO-
MINICAN REPUBLIC** (Supplied by the Chamber of Commerce in Santo Domingo)
[Verbatim]

1. Identification of the legal vehicle for the operation of the free zone in the Dominican Republic.

Despite the fact that Law 8-90 foresees granting the status of free zone to individuals
as well as corporation, the investors usually prefer to utilize a corporation for this. To
that effect, a company is formed pursuant to the laws of the Dominican Republic
(this is not obligatory and the company may be constituted pursuant to the laws of a
jurisdiction other than that of the Dominican Republic), which can be made up entirely of foreign shareholders.

2. Negotiation and obtaining the industrial bay where the free zone operation will be
located.

Once the legal vehicle to be used has been identified, negotiations must be undertaken for obtaining the leasing or, in exception cases, the purchase of the industrial
bay in which the free zone plant will be established.

The investor selects an industrial bay in the park of his preference as a function of
transportation facilities, available labor, etc. offered in the different industrial parks
of the country, whether belonging to the State or private parties. In the former case,
negotiations are taken up with the Industrial Promotion Corporation ("Corporaci—n
de Fomento Industrial").

3. Obtaining the benefits granted by Law 8-90.

In order to become established as an export free zone and qualify for the benefits of
Law 8-90, the company must obtain an installation permit that will be issued by the
National Council of Export Free Zones. The company must present the following:

a) Completed installation permit form (available in the office of the Council)
b) Lease contract and/or a letter of intent from the park in which the company will be
installed.
c) Definitive or preliminary formative documents for the company, indicating a list
of shareholders, nationality and contributions.
d) Certified check for the publication of the installation of the company in a newspaper of national circulation, on two (2) consecutive days, to the order of the publisher.
e) Sample of the product to be manufactured.
f) Letter of solvency, or some document that identifies the investor.

PRINCIPAL STEPS FOR INSTALLING A FREE ZONE COMPANY IN THE DOMINICAN REPUBLIC CONTINUED:

4. Obtaining the Export License.

Once a Resolution to Permit Installation has obtained from the National Council of Free Zones, the company must obtain an Exporter License, which is the document that verifies the capacity of the company in question to export. Said document can be obtained in the Dominican Center for the Promotion of Exports ("Centro Dominicano de Promoci—n de Exportaciones - CEDOPEX"). The Exporter License Application form ("Solicitud de Licencia de Exportador - SLE") must be presented.

At the time of filing the form for applying for the exporter license, the amount of RD$750.00 must be paid to CEDOPEX to cover the cost of handling and processing the information.

PROCEDURE FOR ACQUIRING NATURALIZATION AND RESIDENCY IN THE DOMINICAN REPUBLIC (Supplied by the Chamber of Commerce in Santo Domingo) [Verbatim]

Naturalization as a Dominican citizen is governed by Law No. 1683 of April 21, 1948, as amended.

A. Naturalization Prerequisites: In order to qualify for naturalization, one of the following conditions must be met:
1. An authorization from the Chief Executive to establish domicile in the country and to maintain said domicile for a period not less than six months;
2. Continuous residency for at least two years in the Dominican Republic;
3. Continuous residency for at least six months in the Dominican Republic and having either founded or currently be operating a business in the Dominican Republic or owning real estate in the Dominican Republic;
4. Continuous residency for at least six months in the Dominican Republic and being married to a Dominican at the time the application for naturalization is submitted;
5. An authorization from the Chief Executive to establish domicile in the country, and within 3 months after obtaining the authorization, owning a piece of land under cultivation at least 30 hectares in size;
6. Continuous residency in the country for six months and having performed technical or special services for the Armed Forces.

PROCEDURE FOR ACQUIRING NATURALIZATION AND RESIDENCY IN THE DOMINICAN REPUBLIC CONTINUED:

Absence from the country due to a trip abroad for a period of less than one year and made with the intention of returning to the Dominican Republic will not be considered as breaking the continuity of residency in the country.

The spouse of an applicant for naturalization need not fulfill the residency requirements for naturalization if the applications are made jointly and the spouse is in the country at the time the applications are submitted. A married woman residing in the country can also be naturalized after her husband, but she must have his consent for her naturalization if such consent is required by the laws of her native country.

Children over eighteen year of age may obtain Dominican citizenship after one year of residency, if the application is made jointly with the mother's.

Unmarried children under eighteen years of age, if legitimate or recognized by the father, receive Dominican citizenship automatically upon the naturalization of the father. In this case, the child has the right to renounce his or her Dominican naturalization within a year of obtaining majority (18 years of age).

B. Residency Visas: In each of the cases above mentioned (except as indicated), a residency requirement must be fulfilled. The procedure for obtaining residency in the Dominican Republic is established in Law 95, as amended, dated April 14, 1939.

First of all, in order to enter the country, a visa must be obtained. Visas are classified as Diplomatic, Official, Courtesy, Business NS (limited), Business NM (broader), Dependent, Tourism, Residency and Student.

The visa to be applied for depends on the applicant's initial purpose for coming to the Dominican Republic. Dependent visas are issued based on family relations and are valid for a period equal to that of the visa given to the head of the family. A person entering the country with one visa, a business or tourist visa, for example, may later apply for a residency visa.

Applications for business and tourists visas can be made at any Dominican Consulate. The documentation to be submitted for tourist and business visas are Visa Application Form 509 and a letter from a Dominican citizen attesting to the identity of the applicant and the applicant's behavior in the Dominican Republic. In the case of a business visa, the applicant also must submit a letter stating his or her business purpose in the Dominican Republic (for multiple entry). Form 509, which must indicate the date of birth and passport number.

PROCEDURE FOR ACQUIRING NATURALIZATION AND RESIDENCY
IN THE DOMINICAN REPUBLIC CONTINUED:

For residency visas, the following documents must be submitted at the Dominican Consulate nearest the place of actual residence:

1. Three 2" x 2" frontal photos of the applicant's face.
2. A certification of good behavior issued by the Police Department of the applicant's place of residence.
3. An employment agreement or, if a real estate investment has been made, a copy of a land purchase agreement, or any other documentation proving the applicant's financial solvency in the Dominican Republic.
4. A guarantee letter from a Dominican citizen or legal resident of the Dominican Republic.
5. If a real estate investment has been made, a copy of the Presidential authorization.
6. The results of medical examination acknowledged before a Notary Public and certified by the Dominican Consul.
7. Birth Certificate.
8. Results of Physical Examination.

Visas must be picked up at the Dominican Consulate within 60 days after the date of authorization. Consular taxes must be paid on business, dependent, tourism, residency and student visas. Visas granted to any person can be revoked at will by the Ministry of Foreign Affairs, without prior notification.

C. Provisional Residency Card: Once the residency visa has been granted, the applicant must arrive in the country within 60 days to submit an application to the Immigration Department for a provisional residency card. This card takes about two months to obtain. It is valid for one year and can be renewed annually. If an expired card is not renewed for five years, the applicant loses his or her residency.

The requirements for applying for a provisional residency card are:
1. Application Form C-1 Ref. in Triplicate.
2. 2 copies of the Residency Visa.
3. A copy of the applicant's Birth Certificate, translated into Spanish.
4. 5 frontal photos of the applicant's face.
5. 3 profile photos of the applicant's face.
6. A copy of the land purchase agreement and a Certificate of Title or certification by the registrar of titles, if applicable.
7. A notarized letter from a Dominican citizen or a legal resident in the country, guaranteeing before the Dominican Government the financial support of the applicant during his or her stay in the country, including repatriation costs.
8. The results of a physical examination, including a blood examination (V.D.R.L./ H.I.V.) and a chest x-ray, conducted by a doctor who is a citizen of the Dominican Republic.
9. Immigration taxes (which may be changed without prior notification, but currently are RD$245.78).
10. Work Contract (if any).

PROCEDURE FOR ACQUIRING NATURALIZATION AND RESIDENCY IN THE DOMINICAN REPUBLIC CONTINUED:

D. Naturalization Application: After six months of legal residency in the country, a person can apply for naturalization, which takes about 4 months to obtain. The naturalization is granted by a Presidential decree and is processed through the Ministry of Interior and Police.

The following documents must be submitted with the application for naturalization:
1. A certificate of non-delinquency, issued by the State Prosecutor.
2. A Birth Certificate duly legalized by the Dominican Consul located in the applicant's birth place or place of last residence and translated into Spanish. If a Birth Certificate is not available, a statement of public knowledge ("Acto de Notoriedad") can be submitted. This statement must be made before a Justice of the Peace by three persons of legal age, who attest to the applicant's identity, nationality, date and place of birth, and parents' names.
3. Photocopy of an up-to-date residency card.
4. Two certifications from the Immigration Department, stating that (1) the person is a resident of the country, and (2) his or her file contains the guarantee letter required for the residency.
5. An additional guarantee letter signed before a Notary Public by a person assuming responsibility for the moral and economic welfare of the applicant.
6. An Internal Revenue naturalization duties.
7. An Inernal Revenue Stamps for publications in the Official Gazette.
8. Five 2" x 2" frontal photos of the applicant's face.
9. If the person has made an investment in real estate or operates a business, a copy of the Certificate of Title or a certification from the Registrar of Titles.

E. Physical Presence in the Dominican Republic: The applicant for naturalization must be physically present in the Dominican Republic to do the following:
1. Make a real estate investment or establish a business.
2. Apply for residency and wait for the Provisional Residency Card to be issued.
3. Obtain a Personal Identification Card (C☐dula).
4. Apply for naturalization.
5.Take the oath of naturalization.

F. Timing: The time required to complete the naturalization process varies between one and one and a half years.

G. Liabilities of Domnican Citizenship: A naturalization citizen must maintain his or her residency in the Dominican Republic. For a new citizen, residency must be continual during the first year after naturalization. After the first year, residency will be considered as not maintained if the naturalized citizen does not maintain his residence as stated and thus his residency is subject to revocation. In practice, the power or revocation is seldom exercised.

NOTE: All residents are subject to Dominican income taxes and their estates (except for real estate located outside the Dominican Republic) are subject to Dominican inheritance taxes.

Embassy of the Dominican Republic
Chancery: 1715-22nd St., NW Washington, DC 20008
Tel: (202) 332-6280 Fax: (202) 265-8057
National Holiday: Independence Day, February 27
HOME PAGE
URL: http://gurukul.ucc.american.edu/uiwww/fg6414a/embassy/embassy.htm

COUNSULAR INFORMATION SHEET

COUNTRY DESCRIPTION: The Dominican Republic has a developing economy. Tourist facilities vary, depending on price and area.

ENTRY REQUIREMENTS: A passport or proof of U.S. citizenship and a tourist card or visa are required. For further information concerning entry requirements, travelers may contact the Embassy of the Dominican Republic at 1715 22nd St. N.W., Washington, D.C. 20008, tel: (202) 332-6280, or the nearest consulate in Los Angeles, Miami, Chicago, New Orleans, Boston, New York, Philadelphia, or San Juan.

MEDICAL FACILITIES: Medical care is limited. Doctors and hospitals often expect immediate cash payment for health services. U.S. medical insurance is not always valid outside the U.S. Supplemental medical insurance with specific overseas coverage, including medical evacuation, has proved to be useful. For additional health information, travelers can contact the Centers for Disease Control and Prevention's international travelers' hotline at (404) 332-4559. Internet: http://www.cdc.gov/.

CRIME INFORMATION: Petty street crime involving U.S. tourists occurs infrequently. Valuables left unattended in parked automobiles, on beaches, and in other public places are subject to theft. Burglaries of private residences have increased. Resort areas on the north coast, for example Puerto Plata, Sosua and Cabarete, have experienced an increase in violent crime. Some incidents have involved foreign residents and tourists, including U.S. citizens. The larger, better-known resort complexes, which rely on private security services, have generally not been affected.

The loss or theft of a U.S. passport overseas should be reported to the local police and the nearest U.S. embassy or consulate. A lost or stolen U.S. birth certificate and/or driver's license generally cannot be replaced outside the United States. U.S. Citizens may refer to the Department of State's pamphlet, "A Safe Trip Abroad," which provides useful information on guarding valuables and protecting personal security while traveling abroad. Both this pamphlet and "Tips for Travelers to the Caribbean" are available from the Superintendent of Documents, U.S. Government Printing Office, Washington D.C. 20402.

CURRENCY REGUALTIONS: It is legal to exchange currency only at banks and exchange booths in hotels. The exchange rate is set by the Central Bank, based on prevailing market conditions. No more than $5000.00 U.S., may be taken out of the Dominican Republic at the time of departure. U.S. tourists have been arrested for even minor illegal currency transactions.

DRUG PENALTIES: U.S. citizens are subject to the laws of the country in which they are traveling. Criminal penalties for possession, use, and dealing in illegal drugs are strict, and convicted offenders can expect lengthy jail sentences and fines.

AVIATION OVERSIGHT: In January 1993, the U.S. Federal Aviation Administration assessed the Dominican Republic as not providing oversight in compliance with international aviation safety standards for Dominican carrier operations. As a result, Dominican carriers arrange to have their flights conducted by an air carrier from a country meeting international safety standards in order to provide commercial passenger service to the U.S. For further information, travelers may contact the Department of Transportation at 1-(800) 322-7873.

EMBASSY LOCATION/ REGISTRATION U.S. citizens may register with the consular section of the U.S. Embassy in the Dominican Republic. The Embassy is located at the corner of Calle Cesar Nicolas Penson and Calle Leopoldo Navarro in Santo Domingo; telephone (809) 541-2171. The Consular Section is a half mile away at the corner of Calle Cesar Nicolas Penson and Maximo Gomez; telephone (809) 221-5036. There is a consular agency in Puerto Plata at Calle Beller 51, 2nd Floor, Office 6; telephone (809) 586-4204; office hours Monday through Friday, 8:30-12:00 p.m., and Thursday, 2:00-4:00 P.M. U.S. citizens who register at the U.S. Embassy may obtain updated information on travel and security in the Dominican Republic.

ADDITIONAL EMBASSY INFORMATION

Mailing address: Unit 5500, Santo Domingo; APO AA 34041
Telephone: [1] (809) 541-2171, 8100
FAX: [1] (809) 686-7437

DOMINICAN REPUBLIC FACTS AT A GLANCE

TIME & PLACE
LOCAL NAME: Republica Dominicana
TIME ZONE: GMT-4
AREA: 18,699 square miles
DATE OF INDEPENDENCE: February 27, 1844
CAPITAL: Santo Domingo (pop. 2.4 million)
PHYSICAL FEATURES: mountainous, valleys, costal plains
CLIMATE: Maritime tropical; the mountainous terrain allows a wide range of climatic variation

NOTE: We were surprised to discover that the Dominican Republic has about 1,000 miles of railroad, we haven't heard any tourist information regarding these rail lines, so possibly they are used strictly for freight. We admit to be curious and fascinated with this obscure fact. It is something we eventually plan on looking into, just for fun.
RAILROADS: total: 1,655 km (in numerous segments; includes 4 different gauges from 0.558-m narrow gauge to 1.435-m standard gauge)
PEOPLE
POPULATION: 7.1 million growth rate 2.4% annually
Age structure:
 0-14 years: 35% (female 1,288,210; male 1,336,162)
15-64 years: 61% (female 2,246,791; male 2,312,555)
65 years and over: 4% (female 178,388; male 149,157) (July 1995 est.)
Population growth rate: 1.17% (1995 est.)
Birth rate: 23.92 births/1,000 population (1995 est.)
Death rate: 6.15 deaths/1,000 population (1995 est.)
Net migration rate: -6.04 migrant(s)/1,000 population (1995 est.)
Infant mortality rate: 49.5 deaths/1,000 live births (1995 est.)
Life expectancy at birth:
total population: 68.73 years
male: 66.57 years
female: 70.99 years (1995 est.)
Total fertility rate: 2.72 children born/woman (1995 est.)
LANGUAGE: Spanish (official) English is widely spoken in resort areas.
ETHNIC GROUPS: Spanish Caucasian 16%, Black 11%, Mixed 73%
RELIGIONS: Roman Catholic (90%)
EDUCATION: Years compulsory — 8 years
Adult literacy rate — 74%
Primary school enrollment — 90%
HEALTH: Infant mortality rate - - 56 per 1,000
Life expectancy — 65 years men, 69 years women
ESTIMATED NUMBER OF AMERICAN EXPATRIATES: 80,500 (If this number is correct it is the largest number of American expatriates outside of Canada.)

PART III

ASIA-PACIFIC

"ALL LANGUAGE IS A SET OF SYMBOLS WHOSE USE AMONG ITS SPEAKERS ASSUMES A SHARED PAST." **-JORGE LUIS BORGES**

We'll go out on a limb and make a prediction: We believe that the Philippines is going to constitute one of the best manufacturing sites in the opening years of the 21st century. In terms of investment, it has further to climb than the rest of Asia thereby allowing the greatest upturn potential. If we are correct and if we get on for the ride at the beginning either as manufacturers or investors, we stand to do better than most even if we start with less. We have no doubt that the ride will be bumpy.

People who talk about New York City describe the 'energy' there. We suspect that what they mean by 'energy,' is confusion. People talk about the enormous potential of Asia. We suspect that what they are talking about is the areas population. There are an enormous number of people in Asia and if the word *'people'* equates to the word *'consumer,'* then there are indeed a lot of potential consumers in Asia. What that has to do with true human potential we cannot say. We often get the feeling when we hear others talking about 'consumers' that they are describing some sort of subspecies that has developed an uncontrollable attachment to bargains. A sort of *Genus Consumo* that wanders the sidewalks of the world in search of commodities.

Perhaps.

If humans are 'consumers' and not thinking-beings, then sheer numbers of them indicates sheer consumption potential. China is said to have one-point-three billion souls poised on the brink of consumption. The shoemakers of the world are working themselves into a fervor with these numbers. One-point-three billion Chinamen each giving one shoemaker one dollar means a one-point-three billion dollar yield. What a deal!

Anyway, that's the level of conceptual thinking that is getting everyone very excited here in the latter parts of the twentieth century. Let's look at it.

We are being told that each person in China is earning $38 a week This is unlikely. What is more probable is that a percentage of male Chinese (under the age of sixty) may earn $38 a week. Unless they are being reeducated.

With that $38 they may buy anything they have access to: Big Mac's, Video Players, Pentium Chips, the new Lexus...

251

We are also told that 'things' have improved in China and that the *trickle down* forces of the 'new world order economics' is alive and healthy. We're not sure what 'things' have improved in China. What we do know is that the Chinese government has increased is military expenditures by over 50% since the end of the cold war, so we know for a fact that there has been a dramatic increase in spendable revenue.

The fact is, that worldwide government military spending is now running $600 billion dollars a year, which is one million dollars a minute. Some markets are better than others.

Last year China spent ten times as much on military expenditures than it did on education. Who are they planning on killing? The zebra? Martians? Perhaps their own people?

The truth is brutal and it is sad. China, along with Burma and Vietnam have slaves. The terms used to describe a human slave in the modern world requires the use of doublespeak. In China slaves are not called slaves. The reason? Because they are not simply being forced to labor against their will without compensation. No. In China although they are not paid money for their forced labor, they are being *'reeducated'* by the state free of charge. This doublespeak distinction allows de facto slavery. If it's called education it couldn't be slavery, right? We are all being reeducated a bit these days.

Cheer up. Investors are lining up to utilize the 'manufacturing sites' where the 'education camps are.

Countries, corporations, and individuals are falling all over themselves to be the first to use nations such as China, Burma and Viet Nam as locations for their manufacturing. The list of investors reads like an international Who's Who.*

SOAP BOX TIME

"With no standard nothing has merit and man is capable of using every sublimity to degrade himself." So said the philosopher Jose Ortega y Gasset more than a half century ago. We hope those readers who go out into the world recognize that humanity needs standards. As expatriates we become powerful and capable of being influential. We best serve ourselves by making a world our children can live in.

We have been told that observations such as these are inappropriate and have no place in a book such as this. We will try to watch ourselves.

* **Listing of Investors in Burma**   Companies doing business in Burma. Some of the companies listed *knowingly* use slave labor, or products purchased from slave labor camps. Some data on this list may be outdated, incorrect or incomplete. For the most complete and authoritative list, contact the Investor Responsibility Research Center, 1350 Connecticut Ave, NW, #700, Washington DC 20036-1701. Phone 202-833-0700 fax 202-833-3555 email irrc@aol.com. URL:http://sunsite.unc.edu/freeburma/

EXPATRIATES IN ASIA

The most frequent destination of expatriates to this region of the world has usually been Australia and New Zealand. The reason for this is no great mystery. Australia and New Zealand are English-speaking immigrant nations with multi-racial populations.* These attributes are not quite as important as they were just a few short years ago. Today, countries without diverse ethnic populations are much more accepting of foreign views and foreign presence. It is still very romantic to live in Bangkok, but we would not be surprised to see a twenty year old American Coed shoot by us navigating Bangkok streets on a motorbike. We no longer need a pith helmet and a safari guide to make the trip. ...and yes, when we get there we can dial up the Internet from one of Bangkok's several different Internet Service Providers. We are instantly in touch with the world. We see you on our screen, we hear your voice... you can show us text, photos, graphs, art, or turn us on to a music video. You may be in Bangkok and we may be in Rio, it may be raining for us and shining bright for you, but we are as in touch as if you lived across the street from us. For this reason, Sydney today (and especially tomorrow,) is not that much greater than Surarbaya today as an expat destination. (In relative terms of course.)

Civilized countries and civilized people will find difficulty maintaining traditional barriers to friendship** for the very same reasons that fiends will soon have a more difficult time hiding their crimes. Global communication allows an almost speed of light cross-border transfer of information that is difficult for governments to jam with traditional jamming methods. They can continue to force children to build roads in Burma with impunity only until the Burmese have Internet Access, then no longer. We are more welcome where our face is the face of a friend. We are welcome now in Bangkok. With hope we may be welcome soon in Burma. As an expat destination in the Asia-Pacific, Australia is no longer our only option.

PERMANENT residence in Australia and New Zealand have now become rather expensive. There are ways to qualify for entrance into these countries without purchasing residency, but for many of us qualifying for permanent residence without shelling out cash is going to be a bit difficult to achieve. For instance, because of my age, qualification for permanent residence to New Zealand is out of the question. Those without a college degree might also face difficulties. The qualification requirements to enter these countries is not unreasonable, but it is stiff. Understandably so. Residency can be purchased. The price is high, but if escaping from intolerable conditions is our goal, then price is probably a secondary matter. Many people have recently moved from Hong Kong to other nations in an attempt to escape the unknown and unknowable conditions that will occur when China takes control of the island. It's sort of like turning Tel Aviv over to Saddam Hussien, no?

* At least to a degree that is greater than most Asian nations. We have heard one American expat who lives in Australia remark about the more or less racial 'samenesss' of the people in Australia when compared with the richer racial mixture of some of the places where he once lived in America.
** It should be pointed out that when we talk to each other by way of the internet we are not using the 'filter' of government to 'interpret' our friendship. This will and already is allowing international friendship. Government employees will find it more and more difficult to trick human beings into killing each other for government gain.

The **Philippine Islands** remains a personal favorite of ours. A fact we admit to openly. If we were to drop everything we are doing today and become Asia-Pacific expats tomorrow we would pick the Philippines in a heartbeat. There are numerous reasons for this. English is openly spoken in the Philippines. Set-up costs are immensely lower than they would be in either Australia or New Zealand. The Phillipine people have developed some very nice Free Trade Zones. The Phillipine work force is very highly educated and most education is in English. They are excellent workers and hospitable people with a rich and interesting culture. They have long-standing ties to the American people and to America, but they are extremely independent. i.e. They don't bow and scape to the American government, but the ties are close enough, that the Philippines have been considered for American Statehood. (Which we suppose isn't any more absurd a proposal than considering Hawaii for statehood might have once been.)* There is a tremendous range of locations within the more than 7,000 islands that make up the Phillipine archipelago. Many islands are white-sand palm covered gems that have the look and ambience of a tropical paradise. Additionally, with their ultra-modern deep water shipping ports the Phillipine Islands are equipped to take full advantage of the fact of their location. (Of being centrally located with excellent access to the entire Asia-Pacific region.) Telecommunications in the Philippines has just recently made a quantum leap in capability and technology. We discuss all of these positive attributes and much more in the upcoming section on the Philippines. We also discuss some of the problems and some of the negatives that have kept the Philippines in their position as Asia's odd man out.

The unfaltering stability of **New Zealand** stands in sharp contrast to the mismanagement problems that have plagued the Philippines. New Zealand has become the country to beat in many ways. Its rapid economic recovery and accelerating economy are impressive by any standard. It has adopted some of the most brilliant economic policies in the world. As a comparative example of New Zealand's meteoric assent, let us compare it to the accomplishments of another country; Chile. Chile is another of our personal favorites and it is justifiably famous for its stellar economy. The Gross Domestic Product of Chile is $96 billion with a population of 14 million. New Zealand has a Gross Domestic Product of $46 billion with a population of only 3.5 million. Pretty impressive. Chile is often seen as having the most transformed economy in the world. Wait until you read our section on New Zealand. New Zealand is in a class of its own.

Perhaps we have the reader wondering. In one paragraph we say we'd go to the Philippines in a heartbeat and in almost the very next paragraph we state that New Zealand is the country to beat. The explanation is rather straightforward. It could take us as much as $250,000 to qualify for admittance to New Zealand, even if we have all the of the necessary attributes required for admittance, and those skills that NZ immigration holds as being in demand. Of course, admittance to New Zealand

---

* We are sure that no one today is seriously considering the idea of Philippine statehood. It is doubtful, after Marcos, (who most Filipinos viewed as an American-puppet,) that the people of the Philippines would view such a proposal with anything other than disdain.

would put us inside one of the safest, most stable nations in the world. If we had that kind of money, the required attributes and skills and we had a family with children we'd start making applications to New Zealand in the morning. Especially if stability and social order were important to us.

Half of that sum of money could easily set us up in a prosperous business in the Philippines without having to jump through any qualification hoops. The stability might come and go in the Philippines. We might be subject to chaotic conditions from time to time... but we'd seldom get bored. There are some of us who would go to the Philippines regardless of our qualifications, just because we like the ambience. There are some of us who wouldn't go to the Philippines on a bet. New Zealand has one of the lowest crime rates in the world. It is a wonderful place to raise a family. The Philippines has crime, but we're willing to bet that anyone who brings their family there will find excellent conditions and an openness unequaled.

Where we go is as personal a choice to us as the choice we make in choosing the one we choose to love.

Asia Business Network
URL: http://infomanage.com/asia/abn/contactsdata.html
ABN is a web service that allows a networker to place their name and products on site. Through ABN businesses can advertise their businesses, products, or service. The list is amateur though extensive.

A better page **Asiannet Search Engine** can be found at URL: http://www.asiannet.com/

Asian Links is for people who have decided to invest in Asia and are interested in science and technology.
The purpose of this site is to provide a launching pad for searching Asian science and technology www sites. . Much information, nicely rendered.
URL: http://www.atip.or.jp/asialink.html

There is a series of business books we find excellent. From **World Trade Press**
1505 Fifth Street
San Rafael, California 94901
phone toll free 800.833.8586 or 415.454.9934 fax 415.453.7980
In Asia they include: Japan, China, Korea, Taiwan, Singapore, and Hong Kong.
They call their books, "The portable encyclopedia for doing business."
We recommend them. See Resources for more details.

"I would like [the west] to see us not as a country rather far away whose sufferings do not matter, but as fellow human beings in need of human rights and who could do so much for the world, if we were allowed."

- Daw Aung San Suu Kyi

While in July 1995 the Slorc* released Aung San Suu Kyi, Nobel Peace Price Laureate and leader of the opposition National League for Democracy (NLD), it has continued on a campaign of random arrests, extrajudicial executions, rape, forced labor and military service and other human rights abuses. They have terrorized their people and pilfered the economic infrastructure that could otherwise prosper in Burma. The human rights situation in Burma [Myanmar] is truly deplorable.

* As the reader may or may not already know, Burma is governed by a military junta, known as the State Law and Order Restoration Council (SLORC), that took power in September 1988 after President Ne Win stepped down.

CHAPTER SIXTEEN

NEW ZEALAND
THE LAND THAT SAID I CAN... AND DID!

Applications [for admittance] increased by 25 percent between the years 1994 and 1995.
-New Zealand Immigration Service

"Always bet against central banks and with the real world."
--Jim Rogers

We know of very few people who have anything bad to say about New Zealand. Oh, they engendered Washington's anger a few years back, with their very courageous stand regarding nuclear policy. But for a time anyone who opposed lunacy was in a heroic minority. What was it Amos Oz said? ...something to the effect that "...after we have tried every form of violence perhaps we shall try reason."

New Zealand has been using reason for a long while now.

Mostly.

They had an economic policy for awhile that resembled the 'incredible bread machine.' (Only New Zealand tried it with sheep.)

Others in the world have tried it, those well-meaning social systems. In fact some nations have never been able to fully abandon such systems and the system eventually kills them by killing quality production and human incentive. (Australia's powerful trade unions for instance, are crippling Australian evolution.) New Zealand had the courage. Even Australians we've talked to are gaining hope that New Zealand will be an example to the boys in Canberra. But that's a different story. One story at a time.

This is a story about New Zealand.

Once upon there was a magic land that had so many sheep they didn't know what to do... there were 3 million human beings surrounded by 100 million sheep. Let us observe how despite the fact they found themselves baad-ly outnumbered, they refused to have the wool pulled over their eyes.

ESCAPE FROM AMERICA

TIME ZONE: GMT-12
AREA: 103,756 sq mi
STATUS: Independent member of the Commonwealth.
DATE OF INDEPENDENCE: 1947
POPULATION: 3,542,000 (1995 est) population growth rate: 1.4%
CAPITAL: Wellington (population: 325,000) While Wellington is the capital of New Zealand, Auckland (pop:841,700) is the real metropolitan center of New Zealand. Auckland has so many islanders from the Pacific Islands, that it now has the largest concentration of Polynesians in the world. This tends to give Auckland a rather cosmopolitan atmosphere. Wellington, at the south end of North Island is a major travel crossroads between the two islands. It is a pleasant lively harbor city sur- rounded by steep hills. (...from what we understand Wellington gets frequent gale force winds.)
LANGUAGES: English and Maori
ETHNIC GROUPS: European (mainly British, Australian, and Dutch) [87%], Maori [9%]
RELIGIONS: Christian (59%): (Anglican 25%, Presbyterian 18%, Roman Catho- lic 16%)
PHYSICAL FEATURES: New Zealand is actually two islands, called North and South Island, the combination of which is comparable in size to either Great Britain or Japan. Great Britain has a population of approximately 50 million, and Japan a population of approximately 124 million; compared with New Zealands 3.5 million. This low population factor may be New Zealands greatest asset an as an expat desti- nation.

Most of the urban action is on the North Island and that is where the majority of the population lives. There are also some sizable outlying islands. The North Island, contains the two major cities, Auckland, and the Capital of NZ, Wellington. The climate on the North Island tends to be tropical in the extreme North and more temperate as one goes south; with the extreme south of South Island being alpine. NZ generally has pleasant weather year round with the only freezing temperatures occasionally occurring in the far south of South Island. There is no pollution in NZ.

CURRENCY: The New Zealand Dollar has recently appreciated strongly and as of this writing stands at 0.697 US$ per NZ dollar. (every NZ dollar is worth US$1.43) This appreciation has resulted from a recent economic growth of 6.4% which pushed the NZ dollar up 14% last year vis a vis the dollar. This has caused a slight slow down in exports, because they are now more expensive for outlanders to buy, but it has made imports much cheaper for NZ and lowered the burden of external debt. Unemployment is down and interest rates have fallen from 20% to 10% making funds more available for commerce.

This is to say that the **NEW ZEALAND ECONOMY:** is definitely on the move. This hasn't always been the case. In the 1970's the Russians were buying wool from New Zealand at high volume, and at the same time, the prosperity in the Middle East allowed the Arabs to indulge themselves in their taste for lamb. This caused a coun- try of 3 million human beings to surround themselves with 100 million sheep. When the Russians stepped away from the table the price of wool plummeted and when the

258

Arabs folded up their tents and rode away on their camels, the price of mutton fell like a rock. That's bad. The government of NZ at the time was socialist, and in their infinite wisdom they decided to support the price of wool. That's really bad. In essence, the NZ govenment was borrowing money to buy sheep in order to finance its farmers lifestyle. So, the farmers raised more sheep and produced more wool. (...not too complicated is it?) The problem was; there was no real buyers and when the situation got as bad as it could get, the people of NZ threw out the socialist government and 'hired' a conservative government. The first thing the Tories did, was to sperate the Central Bank from governmental control*. They instructed the Central Bank to stay at arms length from politics and to 'get the rate of inflation under 2% and to keep the rate of inflation under 2%.) There you have it. That is how they managed to produce a currency that has just appreciated by 14% against the dollar and has created widespread prosperity in NZ.

GDP: $46.2 billion (1991 est) We suspect this figure is low.
GDP PER CAPITA: $14,000 (This figure was derived from the same data source as above and was based on the 1991 estimate when the rate of economic growth was 0.04%) We have seen a recent figure of $15,700 for Per Capita GDP, but we cannot substantiate it.
FREEDOM HOUSE RATINGS: Political Rights: 1 Civil Liberties: 1
TELECOMMUNICATIONS & THE WWW: We are more than a little impressed with the proliferation of Web Sites and Service Providers available in NZ. There is no shortage of information available on every aspect of NZ life. There are 2.11 million telephones in NZ, which comes out to: 46.04 lines per 100 inhabitants, 24.4 business lines per 100 employees, and 2.64 Facsimile Machines per 100 mainlines. Additionally, there are 2.72 cellular phones per 100 inhabitants. (Compare to 4.33 cellular phones per 100 inhabitants in the USA.) There is open competition for public service telecommunications. There are 356 Internet-Connected Networks (ICN) in NZ. (Compare to 165 Internet-Connected Networks in Brazil with a population of 160 million.) No restrictions exist with regards to constructing public services network infrastructure. If Brazil had the discipline to follow a program like NZ, Brazil could break loose from the chains that bind her and become the world power she was meant to be. New Zealand, (as we are fond of saying,) ...is on line, and open for business! In terms of Per Capita ICN proliferation, NZ may just have the world record; which is quite an accomplishment. From this fact we can extrapolate, not unreasonably, that NZ is on it's way to being a heavyweight contender with a minuscule population. We predict, if NZ can correct its problem with unions, curb its welfare-statist mentalities and slightly lower its rate of taxation, that it will soon have one the highest Per Capita GDP's in the world. What could happen if they would dedicate themselves to Information Technology (IT) is anyone's guess. Perhaps a world leader with a population under 5 million?

* Much like separating the sheep from the goats, no?

YESTERDAY'S ISLANDS

Kei muri i te awe kapara he tangata ke,
mara te ao, he ma.

New Zealand's beauty precedes her. Anything we might add would be superfluous. We will therefore get right to the heart of the matter and discuss commerce and immigration.

For the expat, New Zealand can be approached and considered from several perspectives. It is a credibly good entrance to the Australian market. Manufacturing cost are considerably less than those of Australia, and NZ and Australia have a free trade agreement. This would allow us to manufacture our product in NZ and ship it to Australia without tariff. Keep in mind that NZ is also a trading partner with Chile. Those readers more enamored with NZ than Chile, but shorn to ignore Chile's exponential economic growth can use NZ as their homebase to trade into Chile from NZ, or conversely, to trade into NZ from Chile. New Zealand's Corporate Tax Rate of 33 percent is more than twice that of Chile's and the foreign branch rate in NZ is 38 percent, while Chile's remains at 15% like its domestic Corporate Rate. (The foreign branch rate is what we would pay in taxes, if we had a company, such as a food-processing company or whatever, that was owned and based in another country other than NZ, but had a branch which operated in NZ.) New Zealand's tax rates need to be lowered across the board. However we believe that most expats will be balancing the high tax rates with the quality of environment and other factors, which may balance everything out when the scales of judgement are hung in the right perspective. Agriculture accounts for 70 percent of NZ export. At world market prices, NZ food producers would have little difficulty competing. Some of the lowest-cost meat and dairy farming in the world is in NZ. Yet, there is an unfortunate de facto boycott which has left NZ farmers out in the cold, despite their low production cost in agriculture. The de facto boycott results from the enormous agricultural subsidies given farmers in the USA and European Community countries. To further protect their farmers, the US and ECC place very restrictive import quotas which they impose against competitively priced foreign agricultural products. This forces Americans and EC Community consumers to pay a much higher price for their own homegrown products than they would for [unpolluted] New Zealand imports. The subsidies used to pay the farmers comes from our tax dollar, the higher price for food for our family comes from what money we have left after the taxes are paid. (Welcome to the real world.) Rather than lamenting all this, recognize that there is opportunity somewhere in the equation.

On the other hand, because NZ is such a small market to import into, most multinationals have not bothered with it. This also sounds like opportunity to me. We must keep in perspective that NZ has a total population that is less than the City of Chicago or Central Los Angeles; [not counting suburbs.] This leaves the door open to smaller firms willing to service smaller markets. While no big multinational finds a population of 3.5 million overly attractive, we have but imagine what a City like Los

Angles is capable of buying and we have a pretty good idea what might sell in NZ. New Zealanders are a very sophisticated people with sophisticated tastes and with their increased spendable income burning a hole in their pockets, we can be fairly sure that not all of their modern consumer needs are being fully being met by importers. Look towards personal care items, speciality clothing, (swimware, etc.,) security systems, computer hardware, plus anything having to do with tourism. On the industrial side; food processing machinery, office equipment, and possibly hotel & restaurant supply equipment as the tourism industry continues to heat up.

Establishing a position in the NZ tourists industry is a good idea. We believe that NZ, like Argentina and Belize, and going to become very hot ticket destinations for the tourist industry. We believe that the number of people whose taste is becoming too sophisticated for the 'Disney-World meets Beverly-Hills' type of resort has reached the critical level. Many tourists, especially younger people, seem to have had their fill of the colored floodlights shining on the eratz palmtrees type of resort. Not to mention being tired of Europe, which is one hell of an interesting museum, but expensive, filled with rude people, and not very physically invigorating. More and more people are looking for *Environment* with a capital 'E,' and fewer and fewer people seem to be returning to the Honolulu-meets-Beverly Hills type of vacation. People today want to experience life, not sit in a smoke filled version of their own downtown Mariott. NZ sure as heck fills the bill as one of the world's foremost Environments with the capital 'E.' In fact, the US government has more or less boycotted New Zealand and placed it in a category along with Cuba and other tyrant-nations, as a result of New Zealand's heroic environmental positions. Well, he who laughs last, laughs best, and we believe that NZ may be the one who will be doing the laughing. (Why was no Nobel Peace Prize suggested or given for New Zealand's heroic stand against nuclear arms? They stood alone, it cost them *'friends'* and it cost them money. If that doesn't earn NZ a Peace Prize then Sweden might consider changing the name of the award.)

EMIGRATING TO NEW ZEALAND

Actually emigrating to New Zealand is relatively easy. After years of restrictive policy, NZ has more or less opened its doors to immigration. Anyone is welcome to apply and the rules for acceptance are clearly spelled out. **The standards are high,** as they should be in a restricted geographical island nation the size of New Zealand. New Zealand has no shortage of resources; natural gas, iron ore, coal, timber, gold, limestone and a very excellent supply of hydropower. As we have said before, we believe that agriculture is going to be the gold of the next century and NZ is an agricultural horn of plenty. The only thing that NZ has a finite amount of is space. It could certainly support twice or even three times the population it currently has, but at what price to its quality of life we cannot say. Therefore, NZ must be a picky and selective host.

There are several types of application for entrance into NZ: to visit, to study, to live and so forth. **Applications increased by 25 percent between the years 1994 and 1995.** The anticipated annual total number of applications is now around 318,000 according to the New Zealand Immigration Service and around 1.5 million people a year now contact the Service by telephone, in person and by mail. This has thrown the Service into the constant role of decision-making. Most New Zealand Applicants receive a decision regarding their residence application within six months of applying. In Canada the wait for residency decisions is around a year, in Australia about a year and a half, and in the United States the wait can take up to three years; so the six month wait in NZ is quite reasonable.

Under the current system, anyone who wants to immigrate to NZ needs to apply for residency. The gaining of residency allows us to live, study and work indefinitely in NZ. In addition to the usual requirements regarding good health and good character, NZ has a lengthy statue regarding general skills. General skills includes specific demonstrable skills as well as certain college degrees. The skills and degrees are judged on a basis that awards a certain number of points per attribute. For example; 10 points is awarded for the equivalent of a NZ 'base degree' (bachelor degree) or trade, or for a three year diploma/certificate. An additional trade or professional qualification is worth 11 points, and a Masters degree or better is worth 12 points. A minimum of 25 points is required for acceptance as a New Zealand residence.

An existing job offer is worth 5 points. Work experience is worth one point. Age is awarded points on the following scale:

- 20-25 years: 8 points
- 25-29 years: 10 points
- 30-34 years: 8 points
- 35-39 years: 6 points
- 40-44 years: 4 points
- 45-49 years: 2 points
- 50-55 years: 0 points

NOTE: We believe that there is a seperate retirement category for those over the age of 55.

Settlement factors: If after all debts are paid we have $100,000 to purchase a house, business or to deposit in a NZ bank we earn one point. Two points for $200,000.

Let's take a look at all this. If we are 26 years of age, with a Masters Degree and a job offer waiting in NZ, we have the necessary points to qualify. This is admittedly rough, but not unfair. We cannot expect to NZ to ask for less; they are looking for a certain grade of immigrant. If you are looking at all this and feeling discouraged, don't despair; I just got a zero because of my age.

There are other avenues into NZ. There is the **Business Investor Category**, which requires a NZ$750,000 investment into New Zealand.* Additionally, there are numerous skills which are given the equivalency of a college education. (Based on the number of years at the job, we can gain up to 10 points for work experience.) Additionally, we can get a work permit under certain conditions and possibly even gain a sponsor in some cases to aid in gaining residency. In order to know if we qualify, the best route is to contact **New Zealand Immigration Service** in New Zealand. There are seven offices; so there is one in most of the major cities of New Zealand. There is a private company which gives professional immigration advice and assistance for a fee. **Malcolm Pacific Ltd.** has offices in New Zealand, Taiwan, Hong Kong, and London. They also have agents in Cape Town, Johannesburg, Moscow, Seoul, Dacca, Sao Paulo and Antwerp. Their email address is: intl@malcompacific.co.nz

PURCHASING REAL ESTATE IN NEW ZEALAND

From what we've seen real estate prices in New Zealand are on average comparable with U.S. prices. Please note that we really have not looked too closely at NZ real estate and it may be that there are some real property bargains. (There usually are.) From what we have gathered we would say that despite price similarities with U.S. prices, that in NZ we might be getting some great ocean and mountain views for our money. (We can compare square footage with a tape measure, but ambience requires a different yardstick.) The rules regarding purchase of real estate in New Zealand by *Overseas Persons* has been relaxed (to use NZ-speak) as of December 1995. The effects of these changes are:

● Any purchase of land by overseas persons, with an area greater than 5 hectacres will require the consent of the Overseas Investment Commission.
● Consent by the OIC is similarly required where land greater than 4,000 square metres adjoins the foreshore or a lake or forms part of an offshore island.
● Consent by the OIC is also required if the purchase price is greater than $NZ10 million.

The above rulings would not effect us once we became NZ citizens.

* Ten points are scored for $3,000,000

ESCAPE FROM AMERICA

NEW ZEALAND SPEAKS ABOUT EXPATS We had the good fortune and privilege to speak with **New Zealand's Consulate-General**, Jim Howell and **New Zealand's Director of their North American Investment Promotion Unit,** Mr. Kelly Beeman, about immigrating to New Zealand. They shed a great deal of light on the subject of immigration as well as New Zealand's investment potential.

Q What is New Zealand's position regarding the establishment of a **Free Trade Zones**?

A A Free Trade Zone implies a level of government support and protection. New Zealand's policy is that the whole country is a Free Trade Zone. We are close to a zero tariff country now and the government is committed to arriving at a zero tariff within a few years. If you have a Free Trade Zone and it's tax-free, then in our view it is government subsidized. Somebody has to pay for it.

Q What is the corporate tax rate?

A Same as the individual tax rate; 33 percent and within our program of total tax reduction that rate is scheduled to be reduced.

Q We appreciate New Zealand's need to maintain a highly selective standard on the issue of immigration. While New Zealand is about the same size as Japan or Great Britain, New Zealand nonetheless is not enormously large and obviously must consider long-range consequences in its immigration policy. That said, talk to us a bit about your policy.

A We are admittedly selective. Our selectivity is not founded on race, religion or such matters, but on issues that as you state consider the impact of immigration on New Zealand as a whole. We targeted twenty-eight thousand for immigration last year; whereas in actual fact the number of immigrants last year was exactly double that; somewhere between fifty-six and fifty-eight thousand. We are learning as we go along; we are not merely looking for those who are rich and can invest a fortune into New Zealand so much as we are looking for capable individuals who want to better themselves and who can fit into New Zealand.

Q If you could talk to Americans right this moment, what would you say to them? Who would you be inviting and what would you be advising them?

A Obviously, those who want to invest their time, money and energy into a viable future and have the capacity to do so. It would be difficult to deny that Americans as a whole fit in easier than just about anyone else who comes to New Zealand. They have less trouble fitting into the community. Most New Zealander's have an easy time relating to Americans even though you tend to drive on the wrong side of the road. If you were to ask me, how would the New Zealand government react to the book you are writing, Mr. Gallo; our reaction would have to be: why not? If you want a go at a country that is low on crime and long on quality of life, New Zealand is the place to be.

Q What about in terms of investment, trade and so forth; we were under the impression that computer software might be something attractive to New Zealanders.

A Well, I think that you might be in trouble there. I think a lot of software development is being done in New Zealand. You look at all the companies and see who it is developing the software; you'll find New Zealand high on the list. My son develops software for American companies. We think that the tourism area is a good place to be looking to invest. American tourists and tourists in general are looking for a lifestyle type of tourism; and it doesn't take a lot of money to go a long way towards developing this sort of thing. Communications, transportation and so forth, are also worth looking into.

Q Where is New Zealand selling its agriculture?

A All over the world. Since we've eliminated farm subsides, New Zealand has become one of the most competitive nations in the agricultural sector. Our major trading partners are, Australia, the United States, Japan, Korea, China, and most of the Pacific Rim, however the European Community is a close second. Our agriculture is as famous for its quality as it is for its competitive price.

Q What else is worth looking at?

A Forestry. Paper. Food processing. Hunts just did a major investment into New Zealand so that it can take advantage of our agriculture and position relative to Pacific Rim buyers of processed foods.

Q What about retirees?

A Our best recommendation is to come and enjoy New Zealand six months out of the year and then enjoy some other place for the rest of the year.

Q You have no specific program encouraging retirees?

A No. But the fact that our summer is your winter, and the opposite, means that American retirees could enjoy endless summers by spending six months of the year.

Q Is there any chance that New Zealand could become the first Libertarian Country in the world? One totally free of government.

A No. While Roger Douglas the Minister of Finance, in his book *Unfinished Business*, does recommend that New Zealand go to a system free of all income taxation and his proposals could indeed be considered radical; his theory and ours does not lead to a government-free state. We're a small player in a pretty big game, and you need a captain of the team, you need a coach. We believe in someone to steer the ship.

265

Q We have heard it said, that in Spain they believe that those who jump the highest are those who begin with their feet most firmly planted on the ground. We would like to take this opportunity to tell you that from our perspective it appears that New Zealand is prepared to make a quantum leap in every way. You are to be congratulated for an excellent job very well done. Thank you very much for taking the time and sharing your ideas with us.

A Well, thank you for the compliment. Come visit New Zealand and see for yourself what we're all about.

RESOURCES FOR NEW ZEALAND

New Zealand Immigration Services
Auckland V&P Branch
Level 4 College Plaza
Corner Gudgeon & Hargreaves Streets
Private Bag
Wellesley Street
Auckland, New Zealand
Telephone: 09 377 6855
Facsimile: 09 366 4466
See the **NZ Immigration Service** Web Site at: http://www.immigration.govt.nz

As stated; there are several offices in NZ. Please check our fax-on-demand services for additional information.

New Zealand Immigration Service

West Coast
New Zealand Consulate-General Suite 1150, 12400 Wilshire Boulevard, Los Angeles, CA 90025 Telephone: 310·207·1605 Facsiimle: 310·207·3605 Contact: Ms. Dianna Clockley Consulate-General: Mr. Jim Howell

East Coast
New Zealand Embassy 37 Observatory Circle NW Washington DC 20008 Telephone: 202·328·4848 Facsimle: 202·667·5227

NOTE: There are New Zealand Consulates throughout the United States. Call either of the two sites listed above for the number of the consulate nearest to you, or check our fax-on-demand service for updated New Zealand information.

INVESTMENT INFORMATION

New Zealand has an investment office that provides information and answers specific questions regarding investments in New Zealand. The investment officer is Mr. Kelly Beeman and he can be contacted at either of the above consulates. Mr. Beeman is a storehouse of knowledge about New Zealand investments. He is himself an expat and currently has dual American-New Zealand citizenship. He can be contacted for information regarding investment questions and issues relating to New Zealand. Note that his field is investments, but those considering investing into New Zealand may also be able to seek his advice on issues regarding adjustment to life in New Zealand.

BOOKS, GUIDES, NEWSPAPERS & WEBSITES

There are a plethora of travel books on New Zealand. **Insight Guides** has one of it's magnificent books dedicated specifically to New Zealand. If you know the Insight Guides series, you'll want the book, and if you don't know the series, New Zealand is a good place to start. We have a our own collection of the Insight Guides, and we always find them enjoyable. They are nothing short of wonderful.

Insight Guides /New Zealand Houghton Mifflin Company 222 Berkely Street Boston, Massachusetts 02116

On the Internet, **Globe Corner Bookstore** handles the entire series of **Insight Guides**. Find them at their URL: http://www.globecorner.com They also have other travel series, as well as maps and a book of the month series on travel. They can be reached by telephone: 800·358·6013 by fax: 617·227·2771 and by email at: info@gcb.com

It should be noted, that **Insight Guides** are not travel guides in the specific sense of the definition. What they are is much wider in scope than a travel guide. They give us a total introduction to a country; a brief history, a profile of the people and the culture plus a description of the places that make up the country. They are filled with photographs, maps and timely tips on visiting the country. If one had nothing more than an Insight Guide about a particular country one would have at the very least a cross-section of that country and at most, the very best guide we have encountered.

For a more meat & potatoes style of guide, try: **Lonely Planet**.

Lonely Planet / Travel Survival Kit for New Zealand Lonely Planet Publications PO Box 2001A Berkeley, California 94702

There is a Travel Guides Web Site at: http://www.omnimap.com/catalog/guides that handles Lonely Planet Guides. This Web Site also has Flodor's Guides, Michelin Guides, APA Insight Guides. Check our fax-on-demand for updates and see **RESOURCES** for recommended book sources.

There's a complete **New Zealand Commerce** WebSite at: http://icair.iac.org.nz/nz/commerce/index.html

ESCAPE FROM AMERICA

There's a total **New Zealand WebPage** at: http://www.nz.com The site includes access to a number of other informative sites, including a virtual tour of New Zealand, commerce and real estate pages.

The **Wilson White Group** are a 'professionals' recruitment agency. They can assist us if we have the proper credentials to gain professional employment. Telephone them at: +64 9 307-3869 Fax them at: +64 9 379-7910 or direct mail them at: PO Box 976, Auckland, New Zealand. email them at: admin@wilsonwhite.co.nz Visit their WebSite at:http://www.infonetx.co.nz/wilson_white/

Another agency which assists with employment is: **Positive Business Relations** Phone or fax:
Joy Paxton at: +64 9 529-2487. PO Box 28 559 Remuera, Auckland, New Zealand

NOTE: The above two agencies also assist in immigration. But unless it is fairly obvious that we qualify they probably wouldn't be able to help us much. They can't work magic. They are agencies that help with job searches, real estate searches and placement. They can assist the qualified.

A company which we have heard can help with immigration needs is **Malcolm Pacific** PO Box 6219 Welleslely Street Auckland, New Zealand. tel: 64.9.309.4187 fax: 64.9.366.4730 email
intl@malcolmpacific.co.nz

The **New Zealand Herald** will airmail copies of any edition of their newspaper to anywhere in the world: telephone: +64 9 303-0265 or direct mail them at: PO Box 32, Auckland, New Zealand.

STATE DEPARTMENT TRAVEL INFORMATION

COUNTRY DESCRIPTION: New Zealand is a highly developed stable parliamentary democracy which recognizes the British monarch as sovereign. It has a modern economy and tourist facilities are widely available.

ENTRY REQUIREMENTS: A passport is required. A visa is not required for tourist/business stays of up to three months, and visitors must have onward/return tickets and a visa for the next destination. Proof of sufficient funds may also be required with prearranged accommodations. Specific information is available through the Embassy of New Zealand, 37 Observatory Circle, N.W., Washington, D.C. 20008 - telephone: (202) 328 4800 or the Consulate General of New Zealand in Los Angeles - telephone: (213) 477-8241.

MEDICAL FACILITIES: Good medical care is widely available. Doctors and hospitals may expect immediate cash payment for health services. U.S. medical insurance is not always valid outside the United States. Supplemental overseas medical insurance, including coverage for medical evacuation, has proven useful. The Medicare/Medicaid Program does not provide payment of medical services outside the United States. The international travelers hotline at the Centers for Disease Control (404) 332-4559 has additional useful health information.

INFORMATION ON CRIME: Crime in New Zealand is comparatively low but has increased in recent years. Foreign visitors, including those from the U.S., are seldom victims of crime. The most prevalent incident is occasional theft or attempted theft. The loss or theft abroad of a U.S. passport should be reported immediately to the local police, and the nearest U.S. Embassy or Consulate. Useful information on guarding valuables and protecting personal security while traveling abroad is provided in the Department of State pamphlet, "A Safe Trip Abroad." It is available from the Superintendent of Documents, U.S. Government Printing Office, Washington, D.C. 20402.

DRUG PENALTIES: Travelers are subject to the laws and legal practices of the country in which they travel. Penalties for possession, use, or trafficking in illegal drugs are strict, and convicted offenders can expect jail sentences and fines.

REGISTRATION: Americans who register at the U.S. Embassy or Consulate can obtain updated information on travel and security within the country.

EMBASSY & CONSULATE LOCATIONS: The U.S. Embassy in New Zealand is located at 29 Fitzherbert Terrace, Thorndon, Wellington - telephone: (64 4) 472-2068. The U.S. Consulate General in Auckland is located on the 4th floor, Yorkshire General Building, Corner of Shortland and O'Connell Streets, - telephone: (64) (9) 303-2724. TheU.S. Consular Agent in Christchurch may be reached c/o Price Waterhouse Center, 119 Armagh Street, tel. (64-3) 379-0040.

CHAPTER SEVENTEEN
AUSTRALIA

TIME & PLACE
TIME ZONE: GMT+8 (In Western Australia) GMT+10 (In New South Wales, Queensland, Tasmania, Victoria, and the Capital) GMT+9.5 (In South Australia and the Northern Territory)
AREA: 7,686,850 sqkm (2,969,228 sq mi) Slightly smaller in size than the continental US.

POPULATION TOTAL: 18,322,231 (July 1995 est.) Population: 18,077,419 (July 1994 est.) Population growth rate: 1.38% (1994 est.)
Birth rate: 14.29 births/1,000 population (1994 est.) Death rate: 7.38 deaths/1,000 population (1994 est.)
Net migration rate: 6.91 migrant(s)/1,000 population (1994 est.) Infant mortality rate: 7.3 deaths/1,000 live births (1994 est.)
Life expectancy at birth: Total population: 77.57 years Male: 74.45 years Female: 80.84 years Total fertility rate: 1.83 children born/woman (1994 est.)
Ethic divisions: Caucasian 95% Asian 4% Aboriginal and other 1%

CAPITAL: Canberra (pop: 311,000 approx.) The City of Canberra shares with Brasília and Belmopah the distinction of being an artificially created capital city. We were told that the decision regarding Canberra's location was based on finding a sheep ranch that was an inconvenient distance from anywhere else. Australians can be both wry and dry. More often than not it is totally impossible to determine which part they are being. They themselves have described Canberra as the ruin of a perfectly good sheep station. We are advised not to agree. Australians can be amusingly self-deprecating. However, they are quickly miffed and totally unamused with any type of slight regarding their fine country. Canberra is the home of the Phillsbury BakeOff.

LANGUAGES: Australian ('Bait-Rice' translates as 'Boat-Race.')

RELIGIONS: Anglican (30%), Roman Catholic (25%)

GEOPHYSICAL FEATURES OF AN ANCIENT LANDSCAPE: The first descriptions of Australia to reach the civilized world occurred right after they won the America's Cup in Yachting. The descriptions were met with disbelief. Here were a people that were unlike anything seen on any other continent. Not only were they capable of winning the America's Cup, they were also adept at rubbing salt in Americas wounds. Boisterous, cocky and iconoclastic, they also had the audacity to be competent. In fact, considering their degree of boisterousness these blokes were a little too competent. ...besides that, they talked funny. Where was the magnanimity? The propriety? The civilized humility? Weren't they half British?

271

It was not until one was actually brought to the British Museum of Anthropology that their existence was scientifically accepted. Even still there are many disbelievers and those who consider their existence an elaborate hoax. How can nature ever have produced a race of humans that lived upside down? ...and while doing so, being capable of stealing the America's Cup.

Other unusual creatures live in this unusual land. It is common knowledge that Australia is considered a land apart. But why should we tell the reader what the reader already knows. To fill pages describing Australia would in a sense be like filling pages describing America. There are very few Americans are not fully familar with Australia. It is probable that we know more about Australia than we do about Canada. We cannot turn on the television without seeing a special on Australia. It is a popular land with much that is good about it. But it is certainly not America despite the similarities.

CURRENCY: Australian Dollar. One Australian Dollar = US$ .78

ECONOMY: Australia is currently having some economic troubles. The national debt is at an all time high. The yearly obligations on the foreign debt are A$26 billion and the overall debt is at A$166 billon (at the time of this writing.) This represents a seven fold debt increase in less than a decade. About 42% of Australia's investment capital goes into paying the foreign debt. With the

GROSS DOMESTIC PRODUCT: at $374.6 billion, this gives Australia a debt to income ratio that is far from attractive. As a means of comparison we will refer back to the nation of Chile as we did earlier. Chile's total foreign debt is $1 9 billion with a GDP of $96 billion. This means that Chile has a total debt that is equal to 20% of one years gross income. Australia has a total debt of $US130 billion with a GDP of US$374.6 billion. That gives Australia income. Australia has a total debt of $US130 billion with a GDP of US$374.6 billion. That gives Australia a total debt that is equal to 35% of one years gross income.

We have seen several conflicting explanations for Australia's economic problems. As it is with each nation we talk about, we gather what information we can and we make whatever recommendations that we do make based either on what we know personally, or on what we are able to learn from insiders living there. As always, our predictions come with a caveat. Fortunately we know an American expat who has lived in Australia since 1964 who because of his background has every reason to know the probable causes and possible solutions of the economic problems currently facing Australia. As we've mentioned repeatedly, no one can really know the future. This is especially true in todays world where so much is changing so rapidly. None the less, we think the reader will be very interested in what this expat has to say.

INTERVIEW WITH AN AMERICAN EXPAT IN AUSTRALIA

Q You moved to Australia in 1964. That makes you a fairly early-on expatriate, at least by our standards. The big push to immigrate away from the United States started in 1968 following the Democratic Convention in Chicago. (At which time inquires to the Australian consulates in the United States jumped from a trickle to 8,000 in one month.) We know that you had a college education and were successfully employed inside the United States doing laboratory research. What made you decide to leave America and to start living in a new country?

A First of all, 1 don't see your time-frame distinction. People have been migrating since they could walk upright. If its a compliment, I'll accept it, but there have always been migrations. Secondly, 1 didn't leave for any political reasons; nor was it necessarily dissatisfaction. I was living in California prior to my migration and while I was vaguely dissatisfied with the increasing population and auto traffic, my actual motivation wasn't to escape anything negative. I was young and adventuresome. The surf in Australia was fantastic and I was a consummate surfer. At the time I was surfing a lot in Huntington Beach, and the waves were getting crowded, so I thought I'd go where the surfing was better. The Australian Government offered me some excellent incentives. I was what was called an Assisted Migrate; they paid part of my fares and gave me £500 to come to Australia. That would equate to about $10,000 by today's standards. That was the Crown that did that. Things have changed a bit. I had a job waiting for me in Australia and it looked like a pretty good deal to me at age 27. In Los Angeles I had a decent job working in a Laboratory, but I had a few things from my youth that kept following me about. Childish things I'd done as a teen were preventing me from making the kind of career advancement I wanted to make. Today the same sort of thing wouldn't be looked at twice. But as I say, it wasn't the negatives pushing me, as much as it was the sense of adventure pulling me. I wanted adventure and I wanted freedom. Australia was the new frontier.

Q After living in Australia a few years you opened your own company. That must have been around 1966. Are the opportunities the same for a young expatriate going to Australia today as they were in 1966?

A I opened my own company in 1970. I'd been in Australia six years, 1 was settling down. I had married an Australian girl and I felt pretty much at home by that time. Something I must point out, is that it takes years to get to know a culture; five to ten years in my opinion. You can't adapt in three weeks. It's the same opportunity today, or probably similar. The key in my opinion is that the newcomer take the time to establish themselves and understand the culture.

Q Your business required that you know a great deal about economic conditions. About how economic conditions effect markets inside Australia and about what factors encourage economic growth. In past conversations you have mentioned 1975 and then 1980 as being pivotal years for Australia. It is our impression that you believe that Australia's economic problems began then and not recently. What were the events and conditions that precipitated the economic down-turn and in your opinon have those conditions been alleviated?

ESCAPE FROM AMERICA

A The years were actually 1974 and 1981. Australia has had one socialist administration after the other. These administrations, and the country itself have been held ransom by the Trade Unions. They have all but destroyed the economy. The government controlled sector employs 30% of the work force. They give themselves constant pay raises by keeping the socialist in power and their productive performance overall isn't vaguely commensurable to what we could be getting from the private sector for less money. There is a now a new, less socialistic administration in power and they are trying to straighten out some of the mess. Some things are starting to improve slightly and the economy is stating to turn around slowly, but to answer your question, no, the conditions have not been alleviated. In order to pay the bill they were running up the socialist administrations borrowed heavily or floated bonds. Now they are paying the piper. Bob Hawke [a past Prime Minister of Australia,] was a former Trade Union representative before becoming the Prime Minister. In my opinion he almost brought the country to ruin.

Q New Zealand managed to turn itself around after years of socialistic programs. Their economy is coming on strong. Will Australia follow suit?

A New Zealand is amazing! I would not have believed it. In answer to your question, the current Australian government won't do it. But if New Zealand can do it, then Australia can do it. We are the more or less same kind of people. If New Zealand succeeds it will be helpful to Australia, if only by example.

Q You went to Australia when you were 27 years old. If you were 27 today and starting out, would you be choosing Australia.

A I would say to any guy that age: Christ, yes! I can't think of a better place

Q What would you tell a young couple headed for Australia today? What sectors look interesting? Where are the caveats?

A Communications. Information technology. Computers and software. The caveats remain the same, take the time to become established and to get to know the culture.

Q We realize that it is outside your area of expertise, but would you comment on Australia's situation with water. We know that the United States is facing an eminent crisis due to rapidity decreasing water tables. This coupled with large agricultural demands for water may spell grave problems for America in the coming Millennium. It is no secret that portions of Australia are water-deficient, but what is the real situation overall? With less than 20 million people in an area the size of the continental United States, it wouldn't seem to us that Australia has any short-term water worries. Have you heard anything you could pass along to us?

274

A There is plenty of water in the north. The far north is tropical. There is a wet season and a dry season. The wet season means exactly that. It rains continuously. One of the problems is harnessing the available water. Lake Argyle and the Ord River scheme is an attempt at doing this. [note: Lake Argyle and the Ord River are in the extreme north-west, in the Western Australia Territory.] More could be done for Agriculture. Your assessment is essential correct. The low population of Australia prevents any sort of water crisis. As is, we have plenty of water, with the exception being in certain agricultural regions, where the problem could alleviated by harnessing the water we have.

Q If there's no water problems with a population of 20 million, would there be a problem with a population of a hundred million?

A Fifty million is enough.

Q And more than that?

A It's anybody's guess. Fifty million is probably the limit, beyond which troubles could begin.

As we pointed out, the above interview was conducted with an expat who has lived in Australia for many years. What we did not point out is that this American-expat made a considerable fortune in Australia. We also happen to know that he and his wife worked tremendously hard, so we are not implying that Australia is a place where it is simple to strike it rich. It is not. There is *usually* a greater degree of possibilities in a smaller expanding economy than there is in a large slow moving economy. Whether or not this is still true in Australia is a matter of conjecture. That is to say, we cannot determine how we would fare economically in today's Australia compared with today's Chile or today's New Zealand. There is of course much more that makes Australia an attractive place to live than it's capacity to make us wealthy.

Australia is long on quality of life. Additionally, we suspect that it is much easier for Americans as a whole to 'fit- in,' in places like Australia and New Zealand than it might be in other places. We also suspect that if we were raising a family, we'd be much better off in Australia they we would be in today's America. (At least in those ways that are truly important to parents.) We recognize of course that such declarations may be viewed as subjective and conjectural, but we don't think that the matter is purely so. Too many people and too much circumstantial evidence seems to indicate that such opinions about the high quality of Australian life is corroborated by facts. There are some, including the World Bank who have begun measuring a nation's Standard of Living by measuring factors other than economic. Even while we concur we remain slightly unsure how accurate such indicators can be because it seems to us that such factors as 'quality of life' are quite possibly subjective. In any event, some us believe that such subjective factors are possibly more important than economic factors. For most of us however, such issues as 'quality of life' are so highly interrelated and dependent upon the economic conditions of a nation we would have a difficult time trying to guess as to where one leaves off and the other begins.

WORLD FACT BOOK OVERVIEW OF AUSTRALIAN ECONOMY

Australia has a prosperous Western-style capitalist economy, with a per capita GDP comparable to levels in industrialized West European countries. Rich in natural resources, Australia is a major exporter of agricultural products, minerals, metals, and fossil fuels. Primary products account for more than 60% of the value of total exports, so that, as in 1983-84, a downturn in world commodity prices can have a big impact on the economy. The government is pushing for increased exports of manufactured goods, but competition in international markets continues to be severe. Australia has suffered from the low growth and high unemployment characterizing the OECD countries in the early 1990s. In 1992-93 the economy recovered slowly from the prolonged recession of 1990-91, a major restraining factor being weak world demand for Australia's exports. Unemployment has hovered around 10% and probably will remain at that level in 1994 as productivity gains rather than more jobs account for growth.

National Product: GDP - purchasing power equivalent - $339.7 billion (1993) National product real growth rate: 4% (1993)

National product per capita: $19,100 (1993) Inflation rate: (consumer prices): 1.1% (1993)

RELATIVE COSTS

● Cheap meal: US$3
● Restaurant meal: US$7
● Hostel accommodation: US$8
● Cheap room: US$20

Unemployment rate: 10% (December 1993)

Budget: Revenues: $71.9 billion Expenditures: $83.1 billion

Exports: $44.1 billion (1992) commodities: coal, gold, meat, wool, alumina, wheat, machinery and transport equipment

Export trading partners: Japan 25%, US 11%, South Korea 6%, NZ 5.7%, UK, Taiwan, Singapore, Hong Kong (1992)

Imports: $43.6 billion (1992) commodities: machinery and transport equipment, computers and office machines, crude oil and petroleum products

Import trading partners: US 23% Japan 18% UK 6% Germany 5.7% NZ 4% (1992)

External debt: $141.1 billion (1993)

OTHER SOURCE ECONOMIC INDICATORS

GDP: US$340 billion
GDP ranking in the world: 13th
GDP per head: US$19,007
Annual growth: 3.3%
Inflation:5.1 %

TELECOMMUNICATIONS & THE WWW

Good international and domestic service is provided to Australia's 8,700,000 telephones. There are 134 television broadcast stations. We spent some time looking at some of Australia's Internet Service Providers Net Pages and we were favorably impressed. There is no question that Australia has full Internet connections. There are over 2,000 Internet Connected Networks in Australia. (Mary Cronin's *Global Advantage on the Internet* published early 1996 claimed that there was 207,426 Internet-Connected Host Computers in Australia. A figure that is probably increasing daily.) We cannot say what current Internet Access conditions are in the Australian outback, but with the advent so much new technology being created so rapidly we wouldn't be surprised to see full Internet Access globally by satellite within five years. We know we have said this before, but we will repeat it anyway. Soon you will be able to sit on the deck of your yacht and talk with anyone anywhere using full video telecommunications. If we don't have a yacht, we can opt for a sheep ranch in the outback. From there, when it is 100 degrees in whatever shade we can find, we can spend our free time with full video telecommunications talking with someone sitting on the deck of their yacht. (...while listening to the bleating of sheep in the background.)

☎ TELECOMMUNICATIONS:
good international and domestic service;
✓8.7 million telephones;
✓broadcast stations - 258 AM, 67 FM, 134 TV;
✓submarine cables to New Zealand, Papua New Guinea, and Indonesia;
✓domestic satellite service;
✓satellite stations - 4 Indian Ocean INTELSAT, 6 Pacific Ocean INTELSAT earth stations
ELECTRICITY: 220-240V

Australian WWW servers
✏URL: http://www.csu.edu.au/links/ozweb.html
We thought it would be nice to list the servers in Australia. Sorry. If you need servers, go to this website yourself. They are listed: Alphabetically by Site (Complete Listing,) by Topic and they are listed by State. The number of servers on the list goes quite high, perhaps over a hundred, and the details of their services just in themselves would take an entire chapter. Check out this site for details. If you are going to Australia, this site will tell you who, what, where and why as to service providers and access information.

① **Telstra White Pages** URL: http://www.whitepages.com.au/ The Australian Alphabetical Phone Books
①**Telstra Yellow Pages** URL: http://www.yellowpages.com.au/ The Australian Business Phone Books (by business category) 2 MILLION LISTINGS
1996 Australian Broadcasting Corporation
URL: http://www.abc.net.au/

Newsgroups
URL: http://coombs.anu.edu.au/CoombswebPages/Newsreader/aus. html

📖 **National Library of Australia**
NLA Collections, Govt Info, Electronic Journals, Govt Policy documents. Indexed.
URL: http://www.nla.gov.au/

🖳 RESOURCES ON THE INTERNET

Sydney 2000 Olympic Games
URL: http://www.sydney.olym pic.org/i ndex. htm
Everything you wanted to know about the games. Including details of the sports, environmental and security considerations and more.

Tasmania At A Glance
Statistics about Tasmania. Includes Agriculture, Building, Education, Finance, Foreign Trade, Labour force, Manufacturing, Mining, Population, Price Indexes, Retail Trade, Road Traffic Accidents, Tasmania Compared with Australia, Tourism, Transport, Vital Statistics, Wages
URL: http://www.statistics.gov.au/d33101 07/1 ha. htm

♟ Tax on Australia
URL: http://www. csu.ed u.au/faculty/commerce/account/tax/tax. htm
Information about Tax in Australia and links to related sites

The Australian Enterprise Review
URL: http://www.icic.com.au/aer/index.html
The Australian Enterprise Review is the largest and most ambitious publication ever produced to showcase Australian goods and services being exported to the Asia-Pacific region.

Australian Visa Application
URL: http://www.anzac. com/ausVvisa. htm
If you're travailing to Australia as a tourist, then you can download a copy of the visa application form from here. Simply print the page then fill it out and mail the application and your passport to the appropriate visa office as listed for your geographic location.

Tandanya - National Aboriginal Cultural Institute
Aboriginal Art and Culture
URL: http://203.8.94.2/Tandanya.html

Education - Australia The World-Wide Web Virtual Library: Education - Australia
URL: http://www.csu.edu.au/education/aust.html
The Australian entries in the WWW Virtual Library: Education.

AUSTRALIAN STOCK EXCHANGE WEBPAGE
URL: http://www.asx.com.au/

Travelling Australia - on the Internet
URL: http://v~wv.travelaus.com.au/
Travelling Australia provides a comprehensive listing of tourist attractions and travel facilities within Australia. You may search for Tourist and Travel Facilities within Australia or by State, Region, City/Town. Their Australian travel database is divided into categories and sub-categories to enable you to quickly find what you want.

LONELY PLANETS: DESTINATION AUSTRALASIA
URL: http://www. Ionelyplanet.com.au/desVaust/aus. htm Yet another of Lonely Planets' fantastically wonderful WebSites. Lonely Planets are becoming the travel book writers to beat thanks to their innovative WebSites. Check them out.

SUNSITE Information About Australia
URL: http://sunsite.an u.ed u.au/aus. html
Yet another Sunsite and another of their usual fine jobs at presenting informative sites from Universities worldwide.

✈Chisholm Travel, Inc.✈
URL: http://www.cl.ais.net/chisholm/
BUSINESS HOURS: Monday through Friday, 8:30 AM - 6:00 PM CST
Telephone 312-263-7900 1-800-631-2824 (Outside Illinois) Fax 312-759-9234
Pacific Rim BARGAIN Travel
Chisholm Travel sells discounted air fares with the following airlines:
- ●✈United Airlines
- ●✈Korean Air
- ●✈Air New Zealand
- ●✈Cathay Pacific
- ●✈Thai Airways
- ●✈Japan Airlines
- ●✈Malaysian
- ●✈Garuda Indonesia

✈**Qantas Airways Ltd** ✈ Qantas Airways Limited is headquartered in Sydney, Australia and has offices worldwide. You can contact Qantas at their address: 841 Apollo Street, Suite 400, El Segundo, CA 90245 or Phone: their Reservations and Customer Service representatives at (800)227-4500. **AUSTRALIAN WEBSITE URL:** http://www.anzac.com/qantas/qantas.htm
THE QANTAS AMERICAN WEBSITE IS AT URL: http://198.68.191.76/

📖 **Australian Directories** LIST OF UNIVERSITIES IN AUSTRALIA
URL: http://staff.connect.com.au/mrp/phone.html

📖 **THE AUSTRALIAN FINANCIAL SERVICES DIRECTORY**
URL: http://www.afsd.com.au/

AUSTRALIAN BUREAU OF STATISTICS
Level 5 St Andrews House Sydney Square
Sydney 2000 GPO Box 796
Sydney 2001 Phone (02) 9268 4611 Fax (02) 9268 4668
URL: http://www.statistics.gov.au/d3110120/213a.htm
For general statistical and data enquiries, E-mail to
Client Services%ABS@notes.worldcom.com
(please note the ABS operates on a fee-for-service basis)

GUIDE TO AUSTRALIA
URL: http://www.csu.edu.au/education/australia.html
Editors... David Green and Wendy Moir
This GUIDE TO AUSTRALIA WebSite project aims to compile links to all available
on-line information resources about Australia for distribution via the World Wide
Web. Their aim is that ultimately it will grow into an on-line, hypertext encyclopaedia.

THE AUSTRALIA INDEX VIRTUAL LIBRARY
URL: http://sin.csu.edu.au/australia/library.html
URL: http://sin.csu.ed u.au/australia/all. html
Further Information Small at: ozindex@sin.csu.edu.au

The Department of Foreign Affairs and Trade, Australia
Maintains an online service forthe Australian Department of Foreign Affairs and Trade.
The Department is responsible for the Australian Government's international relations, trade and development assistance programs through their headquarters in
Canberra and Embassies, High Commissions and Consulates around the world. Their
site inicudes:
Facts at a glance - States and territories - People - Cultural expression - A sporting
lifestyle - Olympic host - The island continent - European settlement - Unique flora
and fauna - Care forthe environment- Tourist destination - Government - International relations - Economy - Reforms for productivity - Labour and industrial rela-
tions- Trade - Resources and energy- Manufacturing industry- Rural industry - Services industry - Transport and communications - Media - Science and technology-
Defence - Social security -Education - Health - Housing.
All this from DFAT online at: **URL:** http://www.dfat.gov.au/

AUSTRALASIAN IMMIGRATION SERVICES
298 Palmer Street, Darlinghurst, Sydney, NSW 2010 Australia
Telephone 61 (02) 9360 5699, Facsimile 61 (02) 9360 5677, International Fax 61 2
360 5677 Registered Migration Agent No: 73510, ACN 074 511 318
URL: http://www.magna.com.au~gerwyn/dgsaisj6.html

MIGRATING TO AUSTRALIA

Most migrants go to Australia as:

Family migrants - we must have a relative in Australia who will sponsor us.
Skill migrants - we must have skills or outstanding abilities that will benefit Australia
Refugee, humanitarian and special assistance migrants-
Interdependent migrants -

POINTS SCORE

In order to gain entrance into Australia we need to qualify for admission based on one of the above categories. As most readers will be entering under the skill category we will discuss the point system that is used to determine our qualification for acceptance in that category. We need 115 points to be considered for acceptance into Australia.
Fluency in English: 20 points
Trade certificate/degree/diploma (acceptable),with at least three years post-qualification work: 80 points.
Post-secondary school qualifications: 25 points
12 years or primary and secondary schooling: 20 points
10 years of primary and secondary schooling: 10 points
Less than 10 years schooling: 0 points
18 to 29 years of age: 30 points
30 to 34 years of age: 25 points
40 to 44 years of age: 10 points
45 to 49 years of age: 5 points
Less than 18 or more than 50 years of age: 0 point

It should be pointed out that some of these factors are on a sliding scale, and that one does not always earn full points for a particular attribute. It is safe to say that if we are 27 years old, speak English and we have a medical degree that we qualify, but that doesn't imply that if we are 37 years old and a sheet metal worker with seventeen years experience that we will not qualify. As in all things of a bureaucratic nature the rules may not be infinitely elastic, but they are something approaching that.

In the Business Skills class there are five sub-classes: 1] Business owner, 2] senior executive, 3] State/ Territory sponsored business owner,4] State/Territory sponsored senior executive, and 5] investment linked. It is our intention to have details concerning these sub-classes in our Fax-On-Demand system as well as other details regarding Australian Migration. This sort of detail can run into countless pages. Attempting to Include exhaustive details for each country would obviously require a book hundred times this size. We will try to make our Fax-On-Demand system as accommodative as possible.

HOW TO APPLY

The place to apply is at a Australia Diplomatic Mission. In the United States:
New York: 212.408.8400 fax: 212.408.8485
Washington DC: tel: 202.297.3000 fax: 202.797.3100
Houston: tel: 713.629.9131 fax: 713.622.6924
San Francisco: tel: 415.362.6160 fax: 415.956.9729
Los Angeles: tel: 310.229.4840 fax: 310.227.5620
Honolulu: tel: 808.524.5050 fax: 808.531.5142

Ask for an appointment with the migration officer. If it appears that we meet the requirements for migration under one of the Business Skills classifications, the officer will: 1] provide information on migration to Australia, as well as specific forms for the Business Skills class. We may also be provided with general information on business conditions in Australia, and a directory of organizations and contacts to help us find out more about business and living conditions in Australia. 2] The officer will assist us with visa arrangements for an exploratory visit. 3] Provide details of Australia State and Territory Government business development agencies to which we must provide notification and which can provide us with further assistance. 4] Provide details on how to contact agencies offering Designated Investments in Australia. There may be a small fee for these forms.

Additionally, in order to apply, the following forms must be submitted: 1] an application for migration to Australia form number: 47. 2] business skills supplementary information form 928. 3] business skills State 1 Territory notification form number 927. 4] business skills declaration form number 926. Business skills migrants receive visas which give them the right to travel into and out of Australia as they wish. These visas are valid for four years. At the end of that period the migrant can apply for a further multiple re-entry visa if they meet certain residence requirements, or can demonstrate that they have engaged in a business of benefit to Australia.

About 1.5 million people worldwide enquire every year about immigration into Australia. Of that number, about 500,000 actually apply. Somewhere in the vicinity of 150,000 applicants are accepted. Of the total accepted the largest percentage usually already have family in Australia [75,000 or 50%.j The second largest percentile will be those whose skills are in demand [60,000 or 40%.] The remainder are refugees and special admittance cases. Over thirty-five percent of the population of Australia was born outside of Australia, or their parents were. What is clear, is that despite the difficulty of gaining admittance to Australia; the issue of acceptance is not based on race, religion, sex, or ethnic origin. The acceptance is unbiased and fair. Australia, per capita, is the largest [refugee] resettling receiving country in the world. Since the second world war they have accepted over a half million refugees; that number represents 2.5% of the population. Many of these have been Asian refugees. Australia is a multiracial open society.

FREEDOM HOUSE RATING

FREEDOM HOUSE RATING: Political Rights: ☐   **Civil Liberties:** ☐

As might be suspected Australia's only civil liberties issues have to do with its indigenous population of Aborigines. Approximately a quarter million in number they have an incarceration rate twenty-nine times higher than that of whites. Additionally, because they often do not have a fixed address or cannot afford to pay fines they have been denied bail, even for minor offenses.

Native land has also been an issue. In June of 1992 the High Court formally overturned the concept of *terra nullius* (no man's land), which from a legal standpoint had considered Australia to have been vacant when the British settlers arrived. The Mabo Decision (after claimant Eddie Mabo) formally recognized that Aborigine groups inhabited the land prior to the British arrival, and that native titles to land would still be valid in government-owned areas provided the indigenous people had maintained a 'close and continuing" connection to the land. The probability is that these new rulings will be argued and debated for many years. Indigenous peoples worldwide face the same problem. As a species we seem to have a tendency to flow much as a unified river flows. Cultural pockets get eroded away and eaten up by the force of the river. We might not like the cold impersonal force of this cultural evolution, it might not seem fair to us and it may cost us much of our cultural heritage; but there doesn't seem an effective way to sandbag against it.

Australia has a fairly low crime rate and is probably one of the worlds preeminent safe-havens. It's low population per land mass will probably insure that it remains socially safe for many years to come. Its legal and judicial system are far above average by world standards, and what civil liberties problems do exist do not exist unobserved. Australia is a free and open society subject to the rule of its people and scrutinized by an unrestricted press and television news media. Australia is not perfect, but it will never cease in trying to be so.

Something that we find extremely interesting is that Australia has no Bill of Rights written into any of its Commonwealth or State Constitutions. However, Australia has one of the best human rights records in the world. Perhaps the innate national characteristics of tolerance and a 'fair-go' are of more importance than the letter of the law. There are several relevant Web-links regarding Parliamentary Protection of Rights in Australia. Some interesting materials may be found at:
ACT Government Discussion Paper on a Bill of Rights
URL: http://www.vicnet.net.au/~victorp/vphuman.htm#3

ESCAPE FROM AMERICA

For immigration assistance, there are services. One such is:

AUSTRALASIAN IMMIGRATION SERVICES

298 Palmer Street, Darlinghurst, Sydney, NSW 2010 Australia

Telephone 61 (02) 9360 5699, Facsimile 61 (02) 9360 5677, International Fax 61 2 360 5677 Registered Migration Agent No: 73510, ACN 074 511 318

Much as in the United States, Australia has private services and attorney that help with migration. Australasian Immigration Services is an experienced professional Registered Migration Agency firm specializing in Australian immigration. *They state* "they are committed to ensuring that every person interested in migrating is given the best possible chance to succeed." *They claim:* "that their services involve quick and effective forward planning for all business, skilled, family, spouse and student visa applications, expert advice on all areas of the migration process, firm control of a visa application and efficient dealing with all the Australian government officials who make crucial decisions on the visa."

That: "their experience, detailed knowledge and understanding of Australian Migration Law, Policy, Procedures, Regulations and directives, allows them to perform the highest quality representation available to potential migrants or temporary residents." They have a WebSite:

URL: http://www.magna.com.au/~gerwyn/dgsaisj6.html

Download an **Australian Visa Application**

URL: http://www.anzac.com/aus/visa.htm

If you're travelling to Australia as a tourist, then you can download a copy of the visa application form from here. Simply print the page then fill it out and mail the application and your passport to the appropriate visa office as listed for your geographic location.

Note that some travel agencies and tour wholesalers can now issue visas for you themselves as part of their total tour planning services. Endeavour Travel would be pleased to do this for you. You need a current passport to visit Australia. In addition, everyone except holders of Australian and New Zealand passports requires a visa to enter Australia. You must have received a visa before you travel to Australia. You can either apply in person for a visa at the closest Australian Consulate or by mail. If applying in person, you will normally be granted a short-stay visa while you wait. If you are sending your application by mail, you should allow 21 days, although this can be expedited if you need rush handling. There is no fee for a standard short stay visa. If you are seeking to stay for more than three months, or if you wish a visa good for multiple visits anytime in a four year period, then a fee (currently US$21/C$28) would apply.

As a visitor, you are not normally allowed to stay more than six months in any given year in Australia. Additionally, you can not work or study. If you are interested in a working stay, a visa to allow for further education in Australia, or if you wish to move to Australia as a permanent resident, then you should contact your closest Australian Consulate, Embassy, or High Commission.

You can obtain visa application forms by contacting your closest Consulate office. In addition, many travel agencies and airlines flying to Australia stock the forms also. If seeking an expedited visa, you may wish to send your application by courier and to arrange for its couriered return.

SOME OF THE BENEFITS OF AUSTRALIAN LIFE

Let's make it plain from the get-go that Australia is very much a statist nation. If Statism is your bag, then Australia is the country to migrate to. That is not to say that Australia is lacking in opportunity or excitement. But we want to make it plain that when we discuss the 'benefits' of Australia, that they are the type of benefits that might appeal more to a statist mentality than to a libertarian. None the less, Australia is a great place despite its socialistic leanings.

We are more or less obligated to illustrate some of the advantages enjoyed by people who live in Australia from a statist perspective; it is not our view of 'beneficial benefits', but we will remain neutral, (or at least semi-neutral) and report the facts as they exist from and for a statist mentality. Australia is the country which in 1995 was assessed as the richest country in the world by the World Bank. The assessment was based on factors such as wealth of resources, standard of living and well being of the population, rather than traditional methods such as GDP. Whether or not we choose to agree with the methods used in making such a judgement, there is little doubt about the high quality of living which exists in Australia. Here are some of the benefits enjoyed in Australia:

● Stable government: Australia has a democratic system in which every adult Australian citizen can vote and speak according to their beliefs. They have avoided the widespread political violence of Europe and Latin America, as well as the street crime of the United States. Additionally, they have established an independent legal system monitoring the actions of private citizens and all those in power according to fairly consistent rules of fairness and accountability.

●Inflation is fairly low: 3% (with less than 2% claimed for consumer goods)

● Australia is a progressive society in technological terms and one of the world leaders in IT and Computer services industries. They have the second highest use of PC's in the world, the growth of Internet use is approximately 5-10% per month. This fact reflects the significance of computers both in the general and business communities. Opportunities for employment and business growth are plentiful.

● Good pay for workers: In May, 1 996, the average earnings in Australia for full time workers was AUD$ 37190 per annum (US$ 29380). A skilled professional with some experience can expect to earn much more than the average wage.

● For better of for worst, Australian working conditions are protected (or dominated) by trade and professional unions as well as the independent Industrial Court of Australia. Common conditions for an office worker are a 37.5 hour week, 4 weeks paid holidays per year, a superannuation scheme where the employer pays 6% of your wages into a fund to be collected by you at retirement, 10 paid public holidays per year, 5 to 10 paid sick days per year as well as legally enforced workplace safety.

● Medicare: After the initial waiting period, permanent residents have access to free or greatly discounted medicine or health care. For example, the Australian government-run health insurance scheme Medicare pays 85% of scheduled fees for out of hospital services. If a family or individual pays more than A$270.10 in a single year, then they will get back 100% of all claims over that figure for the rest of the year. How we might interpret this depends on the degree of confidence we have in statism and socialized medicine. In Australia, with a few exceptions, a public patient in a public hospital pays nothing. Insurance under Medicare only costs a worker 1.7% of their salary. What these benefits do to increase taxation and what the taxation does to an individual's incentive or to the economy long range is another issue.

● Pharmaceutical Benefits Scheme. The commonwealth government subsidies certain medicines, meaning a working Australian will pay no more than A$20 for these medicines. The Australian government pays the rest. (Again, there is no such thing as a free lunch. Someone, somewhere has to earn the money it takes to make up the shortfall between actual cost and subsidized price. The subsidy comes from somewhere.)

● Free education: Australia has a high quality primary and secondary education system that is free of cost to the student, although school books and uniforms must be bought. Education is compulsory for children, and children who are unable to speak English, or who speak English poorly, are brought up to Australian standards by government run English education classes. The Australians not only mean well, for the most part they do well. (My anti-statist sentiments aside.)

● Family Payment: Families with children (even those earning more than the average national wage) can be eligible to receive Family payment which is A$22.70 every two weeks. (YIKES!) Move over Uruguay.

● Parenting Allowance: A spouse who stays home to look after the children can receive parenting allowance of A$64 per fortnight (that's every two weeks in the American vernacular) while their spouse works. Only the income of the spouse at home is looked at in deciding eligibility for this benefit. It is paid in addition to any money brought home by the working spouse. (Let's go to Australia and get pregnant!)

●Job search Allowance: After a qualifying period of residence, a permanent resident who is looking for work is able to receive AUD$285 every two weeks, job and skill enhancement programs, subsidized transport, rent assistance and further medical and other benefits. (In The Netherlands if we are artists, the government has to buy our art if no one else will. The idea is to support artists who have not been recognized, hence increasing the cultural ambience of the Netherlands. Let's go to Holland and be artists!)

● Telephone Interpreter Service: This is an extremely successful free service to migrants or to anyone whose first language is other than English. For the cost of a local call, a person can telephone into the service which has skilled translators available in more than 100 different languages. This is a very valuable help to all new arrivals organizing their new life here. (I admit that I actually like this idea, but I'd also like to see Jazz and Bossa Nova subsidized, so maybe my ideas of what constitutes a good government handout wouldn't fill a constituency.)

● Multicultural Australia: Once, Australians were almost all English speaking people of British background and the institutions of the country were the same. That is all in the past. Today one out of every four Australians was born overseas. Correspondingly, one out of every six do not speak English in the home. The institutions and attitudes of the country have altered, hopefully with each culturally disparate part enriching the whole.

● Australian law gives court enforced guarantees that people cannot be discriminated against on the basis of race, colour, sex or ethnic background. This applies in employment, housing, access to government services, membership of clubs and numerous other areas, including it being illegal to make racial insults. Both the Equal Opportunity Commission and the Racial Discrimination Board exist to enforce this. Fortunately, Australians are fairly easy going by nature and their successful multicultural society has nowhere near the amount of racial trouble seen in the United States and Europe.

● Protection of rights: It is a fundamental part of the Australian attitude that causes them to respect the rights of others. They recognize that humans would like to have personal rights which are protected both from infringement from other citizens and by the government and its officers. Most of the white settlers who came to Australia in the early days chose to leave behind the cultural and religious intolerance in Europe as well as their prevailing unaccountable and oppressive political systems. A firm resolve that the purpose of government is to serve and not to oppress the people has been at the basis of the Australian social system. Almost every government body has an internal complaints section and an external independent tribunal or court to ensure that all decisions by government officials are in accordance with the law and with the principles of justice and fairness and efficiency that the law protects. Something that we've already mentioned and that we find extremely interesting is that Australia has no written Bill of Rights. Not in its Commonwealth nor in it's State Constitutions. However, it is more or less common knowledge that Australia has one of the best human rights records and attitudes in the world. Perhaps the innate national characteristics of tolerance and a 'fair-go' are of more importance than any written Constitution. The human spirit and the 'spirit of the law' always seem to outshine the letter of the law, no?

● The wide open spaces and beautiful eco-protected environment of Australia is very well known. Being one of the largest countries in the world with one of the smallest population per kilometre ratios, Australia can enjoy larger houses and land than most people in the developed world. It is this fact which allows it to have statist policies and still be a worthwhile place to live, even for those with an anti-statist mentality. It may be statist in economic terms, but big brother isn't watching our personal activities like he is in the United States.

THE USE OF IMMIGRATION LAWYERS

Australia enjoys a very high standard of life and part of the way in which this is ensured is by the Department of Immigration keeping strict limits on the number and type of migrants who came to Australia to share in the benefits to Australians. The function of the Department of Immigration is probably more to keep migrants out than it is to allow them in. Given that Australia could not enjoy the high quality of lifestyle it does and still allow in every suitable migrant into the country, some good and talented people are quite probably refused. Those whose application is insufficient, unclear, or poorly presented are inadvertently taking the steps to ensure that they or their family are possibly going to be the ones refused. If you want into Australia and you don't go the extra nine yards to present the right appearance, or if you believe that you don't know how to present the right appearance, then contacting an independent migration service or an attorney specializing in such matters may be crucial.

Australian Immigration Law is fairly complex and the procedures implemented are exacting enough that the applicant who is close to the line in terms of qualifications may find in of value to use an immigration lawyer. The use of an Immigration Lawyer may significantly increase the chances of success of an application. We have heard it implied that in the vast majority of cases, the use of an Immigration Lawyer could make the difference between gaining a visa and being refused. In 1992, the Federal government of Australia introduced the Migration Agent Registration Scheme in response to the concern of the Department of Immigration and community ethnic groups that many of those practicing in the complex field of immigration assistance were below an acceptable level of competence or reliability. The Migration Agents scheme has been introduced to ensure that all those people giving migration advice had to prove their worthiness in terms of accountability, knowledge and reliability.

We understand that he scheme is tightly supervised to ensure the quality of experience and knowledge of those who give advice to potential migrants. For example, the vast majority of practicing Australian lawyers are unable by law to give advice on visa applications because this right is available only to those lawyers registered by the Federal government under this scheme. Anyone else seeking registration must pass a system of examination into the facets of the migration law. As in the United States,

288

the complexity of the law is such that the average citizen hasn't much of a clue as to what the hell is what. The Migration Act 1958 has, at the date of writing, 506 sections comprised of 1320 sub-sections.

Even a complete familiarity with the Migration Act will not give a workable familiarity with the possible visas available as these are contained in the delegated legislation of the Migration Regulations. The Migration Regulations are a vast body of law regulating the operation of the migration system as well as specifying the criteria that a potential applicant must meet to enter Australia. The Migration Regulations contain 184 regulations, hundreds of sub-regulations, 10 long schedules of further binding conditions and criteria and 107 visas. A single visa, for example a senior executive visa, can have 28 primary criteria as well as a points test involving many factors. On top of this, the spouse and each child must prove they satisfy 15 distinct criteria, as well. Almost all criteria are mandatory. This means that an applicant who manages to show that they satisfy 29 of the criteria cannot migrate to Australia. Another who satisfies all 30 criteria could be refused on the basis of failure to demonstrate that they satisfy a necessary aspect of one of the sub-regulations or subsections.

US STATE DEPARTMENT CONSULAR INFORMATION SHEET

COUNTRY DESCRIPTION: Australia is a highly developed stable democracy with a federal-state system. Tourist facilities are widely available.

ENTRY REQUIREMENTS: Information about entry requirements may be sought from the Embassy of Australia at 1601 Massachusetts Avenue N.W., Washington, D.C. 20036, telephone (202) 797-3000 or from one of the Australian Consulates General in Los Angeles, San Francisco, Honolulu, New York, Atlanta or Houston.

MEDICAL FACILITIES: Good medical care is widely available. Doctors and hospitals may expect immediate cash payment for health services. U.S. medical insurance is not always valid outside the United States. The Medicare/Medicaid program does not provide payment of medical services outside the United States. Supplemental medical insurance with specific overseas coverage including provision for medical evacuation may be useful. Information on health matters may also be obtained from the Centers for Disease Control and Prevention through its international travelers hotline at tel. (404) 332-4559. Internet: http://www.cdc.gov/.

INFORMATION ON CRIME: Australia's crime rate is low. However, foreign visitors from the U.S. or elsewhere are targets for pick-pockets, purse snatchers and petty thieves. Automobile burglaries and theft of personal belongings also occur. The loss or theft abroad of a U.S. passport should be reported immediately to the local police, and the nearest U.S. embassy or consulate. Useful information on guarding valuables and protecting personal security while traveling abroad is provided in the Department of State pamphlet "A Safe Trip Abroad." It is available from the Superintendent of Documents, U.S. Government Printing Office, Washington D.C. 20402.

CRIMINAL PENALTIES: While in a foreign country, a U.S. citizen is subject to that country's laws and regulations, which sometimes differ significantly from those in the United States and may not afford the protections available to the individual under U.S. law. Penalties for breaking the law can be more severe than in the United States for similar offenses. Persons violating the law, even unknowingly, may be expelled, arrested or imprisoned. Criminal penalties for possession, use, or trafficking of illegal drugs are strict, and convicted offenders can expect severe jail sentences and fines.

ROAD SAFETY: Visitors are reminded that all traffic operates on the left side of the road, and that all vehicles use right-hand drive. Visitors should use caution when driving and when crossing streets.

AVIATION OVERSIGHT: As a result of an assessment conducted by the U.S. Federal Aviation Administration (FAA) in November 1995, the FAA has found the Government of Australia's Civil Aviation Authority to be in compliance with international aviation safety standards for oversight of Australia's air carrier operations. For further information, travelers may contact the Department of Transportation at 1 -800-3227873.

REGISTRATION/U.S. EMBASSY 8. CONSULATE LOCATIONS: U.S. citizens are encouraged to register at the U.S. Embassy or a consulate. They may also obtain updated information on travel and security within the country at the U.S. Embassy or a consulate.
The U.S. Embassy in Canberra is located at Moonah Place, Canberra, A.C.T. 2600; the telephone number is (61) (6) 270-5000. The fax number is (61) (6) 273-3191.

The U.S. Consulate General in Sydney is located on level 59, MLC Centre, 19-29 Martin Place, Sydney NSW 2000; the telephone number is (61) (2) 373-9200. The fax number is (61) (2) 373-9184.

The U.S. Consulate General in Melbourne is located at 553 St. Kilda Road, P.O. Box 6722, Melbourne, VIC 3004; the telephone number is (61) (3) 9526-5900. The fax number is (61) (3) 9510-4646.

The U.S. Consulate General in Perth is located on the 13th floor, 16 St. Georges Terrace, Perth, WA
6000, telephone: (61) (9) 231-9400. The fax number is (61) (9) 231-9444.

The U.S. Consulate in Brisbane closed in March 1996. The consular function has been transferred to the U.S. Consulate General in Sydney.

AN INTERESTING & LOVELY LAND

A vast island continent, Australia is situated south of Indonesia and Papua New Guinea between the Pacific and the Indian oceans. It is the world's sixth largest country. Australia measures some 2500 miles east to west and 2000 miles north to south. A good deal of the outback is flat, barren and sparsely populated. Most of the population lives on the narrow, fertile eastern coastal plain and on the south-eastern coast. The Great Dividing Range runs the entire continent from north to south down the eastern seaboard, separating the coastal plain from the dry interior. The Great Barrier Reef lies between 30 to 200 miles offshore and extends 1500 miles from the Torres Strait to Gladstone. The only other barrier reef to even come close in size to the Great Barrier is the barrier reef off the coast of Belize.

Australia has the most unusual mix of flora and fauna on the planet. It's distinctive plants include the gum tree or eucalypt, of which there are some 700 species. Other common plants are wattle, banksia, waratahs, bottlebrushes, paperbacks and tea trees. Native animals include the kangaroo, koala and emu, and the platypus, echidna, possum, wombat and dingo. There are also a large number of interesting birds, such as parrots, cockatoos and kookaburras. Fauna to be wary of include Australian spiders (especially the redback and funnel-web), snakes (notably the venomous brown, tiger, death adder, copperhead and red-bellied black varieties) and both salt and freshwater crocodiles. There are more than 500 national parks, incorporating rainforests, deserts, mountain ranges and coastal dunes.

Australian seasons are the opposite of those in North America: summer starts in December, autumn in March, winter in June and spring in September. Seasonal variations are seldom extreme. It's rare for temperatures to drop below zero on the mainland except in the high mountains. In the north, the seasonal variations become even less distinct. Darwin, in the far north, is in the monsoon belt, where there are just two seasons: hot and wet, and hot and dry.

The southern states are popular during the summer months, but the best time to visit is probably in the spring or autumn when the weather in the south is mild, Queensland is still warm, and yet the humidity in the north is not overbearing and there are less flies in the bush. Spring in the outback can be spectacular if there are any rains to encourage wildflowers.

We have never met anyone who didn't like Australia and the Australian people.

CHAPTER EIGHTEEN
PHILIPPINES

"Where faith does not slay."
--Jose Risal

It would probably sound like an exaggeration to say that a full description of the Philippine islands would take 7,107 seperate books, one for each island. But they are undeniably spectacular islands with white-sand beaches and they are undeniably diverse in that way that makes a place seem almost timeless. The Philippines has almost 90 local languages. Some islands and some languages exist in isolation; what is there really to exaggerate? If we live there we can wander through the world's biggest city and live on an isolated island with white sand beaches an hour away. Impossible? Others are doing it. A couple we know imported twenty mountain bikes from Hong Kong, set up a concession on a resort island frequented by Japanese tourists. That was several years back; now they have an inn with a restaurant, a glass-bottom boat service, as well as a mountain-bike, motorbike and water-sports equipment rental service. In the U.S. this couple couldn't get a job pouring rainwater out of a cowboy hat, in the Philippines they are making several thousand dollars a month while living on a tropical island an hour away from one the world's most dynamic cities. How this couple managed to engage in retail sales, we cannot say, as the Philippines has some restrictions against foreigners operating retail businesses. We'll say no more other than that we know it is happening. In searching for comparisons to the Philippine Islands, the only thing that comes to mind is the Caribbean; admittedly a farfetched comparison. If we were young and just getting started and we had to choose between the Caribbean or the Philippines, knowing what we know, we'd pick the Philippines in a heartbeat.

The Philippines has some of the most innovative and best equipped Manufacturing Site/ Free Trade Zone/Free Port facilities in the world. Some of them are so well equipped that it's amazing that anyone could have afforded to build them.

One has a harbor that can dock *and* dry-dock 650 deep-water ships simultaneously. The place has thousands of modern air-conditioned buildings waiting for us to use for anything we want to use them for, with every imaginable type of infrastructure already in place. There are also facilities for sports, so we won't be bored and there are medical facilities, plus, would you believe it, a large airport. There are almost two thousand houses waiting and proximity to an exotic natural wildlife reserve that could be developed into an eco-tourist attraction that includes numerous species of wildlife such as monkeys, wild boar, exotic birds and other tropical species.

It cost so many billions of dollars to build this facility, that no one could have afforded to build it but the Deep-pocketed American field mouse... and that's who footed the bill.

Let's go and get some use out of it.

LOCAL NAME: Filipnas

TIME ZONE: GMT+8

AREA: The Philippines 229 thousand square miles encompasses an area similar in size to that of the country area of Italy.

STATUS: Republic

DATE OF INDEPENDENCE: July 4, 1946

POPULATION: 73,265,584 (40% of the population is concentrated in urban centers, 50% of the population live on the island of Luzon, and just eleven of the Philippines several thousand islands contain almost 92% of the total population.)

CAPITAL: Manila. A city with over 250 square miles of area to its credit, Manila is probably the largest city in the world. Almost twelve million people live in Manila making it the 11th largest city in the world in terms of population size.

LANGUAGES: The Philippines has almost 90 local languages. Its regionalism, and regionalistic languages, result from the fact that the Philippines consists of 7,107 sperate islands held loosely together, if they are held together at all, by an incapable government. English is the official language and most schooling, until recently, was instructed in the English language. Tagalog, which is the Filipino language is enjoying a patriotic comeback. Spanish is still spoken, but not to any great extent. The large number of local dialects, the lack of a full-blown media infrastructure outside of the major metropolitan areas and the physical isolation of many of the islands has prevented the evolution of a fully common language. Whether television and increased mass communications will ultimately create a universal television dialect is a matter of conjecture.

RELIGIONS: Roman Catholic (83%), Protestant (9%), Muslim (5%), Buddhist (3%)

PHYSICAL FEATURES & THE ISLAND LIFE:

With over 7,000 islands to its credit, visiting the Philippines is like visiting numerous sperate countries wrapped up in one. Each country, if we continue our analogy, is unique and mysterious in its own right and in its own way. The similarities between these disparate parts has less commonality than we would naturally expect; yet for expediency they are viewed as a political whole. Politics, as always, has little to do with reality.

STUPID STORY TIME: The islands themselves remind us of Polynesia, which isn't too far off. We recall arriving in the Philippines aboard a ship. The air was sweltering and smelled of mangrove. It seemed incomprehensible that anything could move in such heat, we stood on the deck of the ship in the shade of the fo'c'sle and stared at the shore. Nothing we had seen before was anything like what we were seeing now. If paradise looked like a place, then this was one of its prototypes. Later that day we drank our first San Miguel beer at a small cafe. Between that first beer and the morning of the next day we spent the best eighteen hours of our life.

To say that they are open and warm hearted is putting it lightly. They love to celebrate and will go all night if there is dancing and music. They are also very brave and loyal. The Philippines has some of the most friendly and alert people in the world. How can we forget that after so much abuse they reacted so wonderfully when the end came for Marcos. They didn't strike back, they rolled with the punches and they showed the world what they were made of when the vote was given to a housewife. Its hard to love them enough. We can and do.

294

I also love the islands they live on. Mountainous, green, tropical, surrounded by sea.

What sea! Every year a dozen or more typhoons affect these waters and about a half dozen actually strike the islands. We had the great privilege of riding one out in the Philippine sea. Unforgettable.

And when the waters are calm we can see the depths. A boat sitting becalmed casts a shadow visible on the bottom. At least outside of Manila harbor.

The Philippines is an a rich abundant land 25% of which is arable, 10% of the land is in permanent crops. Forty percent of the land is still forest, and while there has been some deforestation the mountainous conditions of much of the forest area has saved much of the forest from the chopping block.

ECONOMY: We'll go out on a limb and make a prediction: We believe that the Philippines is going to constitute one of the best manufacturing sites in the opening years of the 21st century. If viewed only in terms of investment, it has further to climb than the rest of Asia thereby allowing the greatest upturn potential. If we are correct and if we get on for the ride at the beginning either as manufacturers or investors, we stand to do better than most even if we start with less. We have no doubt that the ride will be bumpy.

The Philippines is working very hard to create positive incentives for investment. **Earnings from investment can be freely converted to other currencies and repatriated.** There has been a tidal wave of privatizations and deregulations which is adding excitement and incentive to foreign investors and investment. Recent years have demonstrated that despite their volatility the Phillipine financial markets have been some of the most rewarding securities markets worldwide. Because of the Philippines historic relationship with the U.S. it is more *accessible* than other Asian countries. Strategically located at the crossroads of international shipping and air routes; the Philippines is perfectly positioned (both geographically and culturally,) to be an intermediary between Asia and the rest of the world. The Filipinos are skilled, educated, (90% literacy rate,) and highly trainable workers. As they get out from under the burden of 'cronyism,' we can expect to see them excel as well as, or perhaps better than other Asian countries. The country itself is agriculturally rich in addition to having a storehouse of mineral wealth.

GDP: $160.5 billion
GDP PER CAPITA: $2,300 (1994 est)
CURRENCY: 1.00 Phillipine Peso = 0.04 U.S. Dollar at time of publication.

FREEDOM HOUSE RATING: Political Rights: [2] **Civil Liberties:** [4] The Philippines has a long history of 'cronyism,' and the rule of law has always been weak, with political power disproportionately held by economic oligarchies, wealthy landowners and political elites. Official corruption has always been rampant. Things are now beginning to turn for the better. Perhaps more than in any other country in the world, for the islands of the Philippines, tomorrow is the question.

TELECOMMUNICATIONS & THE WWW: Sadly, the Philippines telecommunication system leaves much to be desired. The good news is that it is improving. The local monopoly was **Phillipine Long Distance Telephone Company**, which in 1992 had a backlog of applications for telephone service numbering 800,000 of which 500,000 were in the city of Manila and its metropolitan areas. The government deregulated the industry in that year and now more the fifty firms are now providing service in the Philippines. While the increase in service since that date has been geometric, the density overall when compared with other industrialized nations remains quite low. Most regions will ultimately be serviced by at least two carriers, which will push the quality of service and the timeliness of installation. Since the deregulation service installation time has generally dropped to one month in the metro Manila area.

We find three (3) Internet Service Providers to the Philippines when we access the list of service providers. This doesn't mean that there aren't more; things change so fast in this area of technology that two weeks can make a difference. However, our recommendations to potential expats heading to the Philippines who will require Internet access is that they check things out fully before they leap.* By the same token, those who believe they can provide internet access might be looking to the Philippines as a place to set up operations.

The **Manila Bulletin**, This Phillipine newspaper has an Internet edition accessible at URL: http://205.136.64.60:10081/ We also recommend that readers access the homepage of one of the Service Providers at URL: http://dv.weblinq.com/welcome.html We found a number of other hits on the Philippines, but not enough to get us excited. The Philippines currently lacks Internet connectivity... as did everyone else in the world just a few short years ago.

Before we go too far describing the positive aspects of the Philippines we have to inform the reader that the Philippines has two rules that adversely effect the amount of fun an expat can hope to have there. The first rule is the one regarding the foreign ownership of its real estate. Beyond the ownership of yuppie-style condominiums that no one in their right mind would want to own, the purchase of Phillipine real estate is more or less restricted in the Philippines to Filipinos. This is a tremendous negative as far as we are concerned. We are not saying that it is impossible to overcome the problem; but it does present a tremendous stumbling block to potential expats who want to own real estate. All expats should probably read: *Culture Shock: Philippines* by Alfredo and Grace Roces; Graphic Arts Center Publishing Company, Portland, Oregon. telephone: 503·226·2402 The Culture Shock series is a series of books that more or less describes what it is like to live in certain countries. The information stresses cultural problems faced by expats, but it also includes much practical information about day to day living. We mention this, because the edition

* There is a list of Internet Service Providers for the entire world. It is available by going to: http://www.iworld.com This is the Home Page for a number of useful services. To access the list of Service Providers, click on the hot gif: >THE LIST<, which will give you a list of the almost 4,000 Internet Service Providers. The list is hot gif also. The Home Page of any listed Provider will come up. Listed by country, country code, area code, state, province, etc.

on the Philippines deals with the issues of renting property in the Philippines. The information there presented may prove invaluable. Having mentioned the real estate issue we have to stress that the Philippines looks quite good to us as a place to live in and to invest in regardless of the real estate issue.

The second rule is a rule regarding the operating of any retail business, which again is strictly prohibited to anyone but a Filipino. We know that there are ways around this, because we have seen evidence of such, but we have no idea how the rule is circumnavigated, nor would we be willing to venture to the Philippines in the hopes of quickly solving the problem. The Philippines are suitable for manufacturing and other ventures and in terms of real estate the majority of expats who venture to the Philippines enter into long term leases in order to manufacture and export out of the Philippines. Apart from marrying a citizen we see no easy way around these restrictions.

In the 1960's the Philippines was regarded as the second wealthiest country in Asia, surpassed only by Japan. After two decades of Marcos and 'Crony Capitalism,' a system that greatly rewarded and enriched a small group of large landowning families friendly with the ruling elite, the Philippines had run up U.S.$25 billion in foreign debt and was suffering from massive unemployment with more than half of its population living below international poverty standards. It is wonderful what governments can do to their own people. Should we bother to mention what forces kept Marcos in power to the detriment of his own people, or is it fairly obvious?

Today, under the presidency of Fidel Ramos, the Philippines has **16 Free Trade Zones** operating under three sperate guidelines. Two of the trade zones are attempting to set up as **Freeports**; the **Subic Bay Metropolitan Authority** administers the **Subic Bay Freeport**, formerly the U.S. naval base at Subic; and Clark Field, the former U.S. airbase.

We'd like to discuss the **Subic Bay Freeport** for a moment. We've seen this site and it is massive: It has a mammoth harbor that can dock and dry-dock 650 deep-water ships, thousands of buildings with every type of infrastructure already in place, sports and medical facilities, a large airport, almost two thousand houses and proximity to a natural reserve that could be developed into a eco-tourist attraction that includes many species of wildlife such as monkeys, wild boar, exotic birds and other tropical species.

The advantages of doing business at the site are:
✓ Duty-free import and export of all goods and materials;
✓ Unrestricted foreign ownership of business;
✓ No foreign exchange controls;
✓ Free-markets in gold, futures, and securities;
✓ No limit on the sale of goods into the Phillipine domestic economy (although to qualify for tax incentives, registered firms must export at least 70 percent of production);
✓ No taxes except for a 5 percent tax on gross income (compared to a 35% corporate tax in the rest of the country)

297

✔ Permanent residence visa issued to investors of at least U.S.$250,000 valid for the duration of the investment, and:

✔ An efficient, motivated, trainable and relatively inexpensive labor force; some 20,000 skilled and semi-skilled Phillipine workers who had been employed by the U.S. Navy are available to readily transfer to those private sector firms who establish operations at Subic Bay. They speak fluid English and they are extremely capable and honest. What more could anyone ask for?

We are convinced that for anyone who wants to manufacture in Asia that this is the absolute best country to work from. For information, contact:

Subic Bay Metropolitan Authority (SBMA)
Building 229, Waterfront Avenue
Subic Bay Freeport Zone
2200 Olongapo City, Philippines
Telephone: [63] (47) 222·5454, 222·2731, 384·5849
Fax: [63] (47) 222·5278
Manila telephone number: [63] (2) 817·3994

The Philippines are easy to visit and easy to enjoy. As stated, the majority of the people in the Philippines speak English and for the most part they like Americans. What animosity that does exist, exists in pockets. There are areas of the island of **Mindanao** which are said to be dangerous for foreigners. From what we have been able to gather as a result of our talking to expats and in reading between the lines of the available information, we suspect that Mindanao is much more dangerous for members of the Phillipine government than it might be for stray gringos. The conflict between the communists and the government proper has been healed to a great extent. As the problems of the average Filipino are mediated, the problems of the Philippines are mediated. No people are going to sit back and endure what Marcos and his cronies made the people of the Philippines endure. Least of all a people with a legacy of courage such that for which the Filipinos are justifiably famous.

Recreation in Philippines This site is mostly on Diving but we thought we'd include it anyway. URL: http://www.infohub.com/TRAVEL/ADVENTURE/RECRE-ATION/ASIA/philippines.html

World Trade Center
5th Floor, Pacific Star Bldg Makati Avenue Makati Metro Manila
Tel: (63 2) 819-7297 or 819-7204 Fax: 819-7205
Contact: Lilia B. deLima CEO

U.S. Foreign Service
American Embassy
1201 Roxas Blvd., Ermita APO AP 96440 Manila 1000
Tel: (632) 521-7116 Fax: 522-4361
Contact: John D. Negroponte AMB
August Maffry Jr. COM
Telex: 22708 COSEC PH

Ulanic from the University of Texas have their usual good page up on the Philippines.

URL: http://link.lanic.utexas.edu/asnic/countries/philippines/

Multiple linked pages. Many aspects of life in the Philippines.

There is a newspaper called the **Phillipine Reporter**

It is available on line or in a print edition. The Philippine Reporter is published twice a month.

Mailed Subscription Rates

6 months, 12 issues Cdn $10.00

12 months, 23 issues Cdn $20.00

18 months, 35 issues Cdn $30.00

Send check or money order to:

The Philippine Reporter

807 Queen Street East, First Floor

Toronto, Ontario M4M 1H8 <u>Canada</u>

You may reach them:

By phone: (416) 461-8694

By Fax: (416) 461-7399

By E-mail: reporter@web.net

URL: http://www.mabuhay.com/phil_reporter/

There is a very good book called: *Philippines Business*

The book is published by World Trade Books

1505 Fifth Avenue

San Rafeal, California 94901

They call their book: "The portable encyclopedia for doing business in the Philippines." I would tend to agree with them.

PHILIPPINES - CONSULAR INFORMATION SHEET

COUNTRY DISCRIPTION: The Philippines is a developing democratic republic consisting of approximately 7,100 islands, of which only 880 are inhabited. The two major islands are Luzon to the north and Mindanao to the south. Tourist facilities are available within the population centers and main tourist sites.

ENTRY REQUIREMENTS: Current information concerning entry requirements may be obtained from the Embassy of the Philippines, 1600 Massachusetts Avenue, N.W., Washington, D.C. 20036, telephone: (202) 467-9300, or from the Philippine consulates general in Chicago, Honolulu, Los Angeles, New York, or San Francisco.

INFORMATION ON CRIME: Crime is of serious concern in the Philippines. Reports of homicides, kidnapping, other crimes of violence, confidence games, pickpocketing and credit card fraud are common in the local press and usually involve Filipino victims. However, foreign tourists are sometimes victims of petty crimes and in the fall of 1995 were also victims in several unexplained shooting incidents in the Ermita District of Manila. Travel by public conveyance as well as private vehicle may be risky as traffic laws are frequently disregarded and drivers tend to be undisciplined. Travel off the national highways and paved roads, especially at night, is particularly dangerous. Lost or stolen U.S. passports should be reported immediately to local police and to the U.S. Embassy in Manila or to the U.S. Consular Agency in Cebu. Useful information on safeguarding valuables and protecting personal security while traveling abroad is provided in the Department of State pamphlet, "A Safe Trip Abroad". It is available from the Superintendent of Documents, U.S. Government printing Office, Washington, D.C. 20402.

DRUG PENALTIES: Travelers are subject to the laws and legal practices of the country in which they travel. In the Philippines, penalties for possession, use, or trafficking in illegal drugs are strict, and convicted offenders can expect jail sentences and fines. Capital punishment can be applied in cases of heinous crimes.

CARRYING FIREARMS: The Philippine Government has very strict laws regarding the possession of firearms by foreigners. Several foreigners have been sentenced to life imprisonment for bringing firearms into the Philippines.

AVIATION CONCERNS: In July 1995, the U.S. Federal Aviation Administration announced that it had found areas in which the Government of the Philippines' civil aviation authority was not in compliance with international aviation safety standards for oversight of Philippine air carrier operations. The Government of the Philippines was given a conditional rating. While consultations to correct the deficiencies are ongoing, Philippine air carriers are permitted to conduct limited operations to the U.S. subject to heightened FAA surveillance. The FAA is not providing heightened surveillance for operations to destinations other than the U.S. Travelers may contact the U.S. Department of Transportation hotline at 1-800-322-7873 for a summary statement on the assessment.

SECURITY CONCERNS: The Government of the Philippines is engaged in nego-tiations with Communist and Muslim rebels, and the security situation has improved in most areas of the country in recent years. Nevertheless, rebel presence and/or activity in certain areas of the Philippines pose potential or real security concerns. Most likely to be at risk are U.S. Government employees, missionaries, military per-sonnel, and resident Americans associated with organizations identified with the United States.

Activity by Communist guerrillas and armed bandits may make travel in the follow-ing areas potentially dangerous: in Northern Luzon, the provinces of Abra, Aurora, Cagayan, Isabela, Kalinga-Apayao, and Mountain (including Sagada and Bontoc); in southern Luzon, some areas of Quezon province and the Bicol region; in the Visayas, interior areas of Panay, Negros, and Samar islands. In Mindanao, crime and insurgent activity may also make travel hazardous to and within the provinces of Sulu, Tawi-tawi, Maguindanao, Lanao del Sur, Basilan, Zamboanga Del Sur, and South Cotabato.

The threat of terrorist action by extremists, both domestic and foreign, does exist in the Philippines and could pose a danger to U.S. citizens. There are periodic reports of plans for possible kidnappings or terrorist acts aimed at U.S. Government installa-tions, public and private institutions and means of transportation. Travelers may wish to contact the Consular Section of the U.S. Embassy in Manila or the U.S. Consular Agency in Cebu for specific threat information.

VOLCANIC ERUPTIONS: The June 1991 eruption of Mt. Pinatubo deposited large amounts of volcanic ash in a wide area around the volcano (located sixty miles north-west of Manila). The principal danger now comes from "lahars", or mudflows, which inundate low-lying areas and wash away bridges, especially in Pampanga and Zambales Provinces. These conditions will persist for several years, especially dur-ing the rainy season (May to November).

MEDICAL FACILITIES: Adequate medical care is available in major cities, but is limited in rural and more remote areas. Doctors and hospitals often expect immedi-ate cash payment for health care services. U.S. medical insurance is not always valid outside the United States. The Medicare/Medicaid program does not provide pay-ment of medical services outside the United States. Supplemental overseas medical insurance, including coverage for medical evacuation, has proven useful in some instances. The international travelers hotline at the Centers for Disease Control and Prevention (tel. (404) 332-4559) has additional useful health information.

REGISTRATION/ EMBASSY LOCATION: U.S. citizens living in or visiting the Philippines can register with the U.S.Embassy in Manila and obtain updated infor-mation on travel and security in the Philippines. The U.S. Embassy in Manila is located at 1201 Roxas Boulevard, 1000 Manila - Telephone: (63-2) 521-7116, exten-sion 2246. A Consular Agency was established in Cebu in October 1995, and is located on the 3rd Floor, PCI Bank, Gorordo Avenue, Lahug, Cebu City - Telephone: (63-32) 231-1261

PART IV

EUROPE

"The Closerie des Lilas was the nearest good cafe when we lived over the sawmill at 113 rue Notre-Dames-des-Champs, and it was one of the best cafes in Paris. It was warm inside in winter and in the spring and fall it was very fine outside with the tables under the shade of the trees"

-Ernest Hemingway *A Moveable Feast*

Europe has always been the traditional expat destination for most Americans. It is common knowledge, that France, after the first World War, was the home to many American expatriates, a number of whom were well known artists and writers. Europe is still probably high on the list of expatriate destination for most Americans and going there and living there is, (or seems to be,) many times simpler then going to other places. It is also more expensive. Paris is far from the bargain that it was in Hemingways day and even Spain and Italy are now quite expensive. Portugal is said to be a bargain, but it is certainly not a bargain when it is compared to a place like Belize. On the other hand, Belize has none of the grand historic culture that is available in Portugal; nor can we hop on a shuttle in Belize City and find ourself in London or Rome in a matter of minutes as we can from **Lisbon** (pop: 2,062,000).

PORTUGAL

Portugal is also entering the global arena and is scheduled to hold the last global Expo of the century. Known as **Expo '98** the event has been estimated as being an attraction that will bring a potential eight million visitors to the nation. With a population of around 10 million inside an area of 36,390 square miles, Portugal is just currently entering the global market. In 1995 it had a production growth rate of 2.7%, slightly higher than the rest of Europes and it is now a member of the so called **European Union**. It has re-privatized most of its key industries including such sectors as: transportation, communications, media, banking, insurance, cement, chemicals and steel. As a new member of the European Union, Portugal is gradually adjusting to an open economy after years of protectionism. The prognosis for the new Portugal is said to be good, according to the opinion of foreign investors who have investigated the scene and of expatriates who are currently living there.

Note that the Portuguese island of **Madeira** is now a **Free Trade Zone**. Located about 600 miles off the Portuguese coast, Madeira is actually fairly autonomous and is also an offshore financial haven of some note. The addition of the new Free Trade Zone status makes Madeira fairly attractive as a tax haven. For more information see the section on tax-havens, and/or check our Fax-On-Demand system. Web access for information on Madeira is available at: http://www.portugal.org/f8.html

Embassy telephone in Washington D.C., for Portugal is: 202·234·3800. Portugal has a Web Page at: http://s700/di.uminho.pt/homepage-pt.html

ITALY

IT HAS A RECORD OF ENDURING

Finer things engender finer thoughts, lasting things: lasting thoughts.

Italy, Canada, and Mexico all have a large number of American expatriates. We are not sure who has the most, because the official figures are misleading and inaccurate. Our guess is that Italy leads Europe in having the largest number of American expatriates and we would be surprised if it was not in the top ten expat destinations in the world. Although that may be changing even as we write these words. Immigrant Italians traditionally viewed America as a place to come to and earn money, but when the money was made, the intention was always to return home. Italy was home. This return to home did not always work out as planned. We know from talking to immigrants from other nations, that the idea of returning home was and is a fairly common view of many immigrants. But things seldom work out exactly as we plan them. We may certainly view one nation as a place to make money and another nation as home, but there is no guarantee that our children will have the same narrow view. The movie *Gaijin,* which we mention in our Brazil section is a movie which addresses this precise subject. The Japanese, are though to be very xenophobic, (it is said that Japan refused outside help during their recent disastrous earthquake because to accept outside help would have been tantamount to admitting that somehow, someone existed outside Japan who knew something that the Japanese did not.) In any event, the film *Gaijin* portrays this issue and the issue of children not holding the same narrow perspective that is held by the parent immigrant. The film portrays this issue quite poignantly, from the view of a Brazilian woman whose Grandparents were from Japan. We definitely recommend this film, made by one of Brazils brilliant young film makers, Tizuka Yamasaki.

Many of the Italian immigrants who came to America after the turn of the century came with the intention of returning home; most of them never did, or if they did it was as a tourist to visit the 'old country,' as it came to be called. Things did not go precisely to plan in America. Few immigrants got rich overnight, even though the monetary rewards were better in early twentieth century America than they were in Italy at that time, there was no guarantee of imminent success, or even of success at all. The immigrants got bogged down, children were born, the children were no longer really Italian. Home became America. My paternal grandfather never became an American as such, but remained an Italian living in a foreign land called America. My maternal grandfather on the other hand became American in spirit. He was the first Italian-American to become a police officer in the city of Kenosha, Wisconsin. His subsequent murder, which occurred in the line of duty is the subject of the novel, *The Bronze Factory Murder*, written by Joseph Dominic Gallo. My other grandfather who never really left Italy in spirit, may have wanted to return to Italy, but he had children born in America and returning to Italy for him ultimately became a logistic impossibility.

Despite all this, a surprising number of early immigrants did return. We believe that there is a return ratio that is inverted proportionately to youth. The younger an immigrant, the less likely the immigrant is to return to a place called: home. Many early twentieth century Italian immigrants to America returned to Italy. In fact, so many returned, that for a long while Italy led the world in absolute numbers of re- turned emigrants. Additionally, Italy has long led the world in the number of foreign tourist visits to it's shores. Add to these factors, the fact that even though the rules regarding foreigners living in Italy is subject to certain regulation and restriction, much as it is in other countries; in Italy the rules have never been observed in mod- ern history. (We do make exception of the Mussolini years.) Italy has traditionally been seen as the center of the world, a place to which everyone who is alive must ultimately return, like salmon must return to their place of origins. So, in addition to the number of returned Italians of actual Italian ancestry, there has been a historic return to Italy of Italians who are Italian by proxy. Land and housing prices in Italy were for a very long time a bargain. When Douglas Casey wrote the **Expatriate Investor** which was published in 1978, he made the statement that a small but modern farmhouse in Northern Italy, convenient to the Autostrada and a medium sized city, and on eight acres could be had in 1977 for US$25,000. The price for a renovated farmhouse in a rural area of Italy now cost from $75,000 to $85,000; and a farmhouse in the fashionable areas of Tuscany could easily cost around $300,000. Today, in much of Italy, prices for land and houses is comparable to prices in the United States and in some cases, the prices in Italy are in excess of U.S. prices. Italy is after all not a boundless land, despite its boundless history. It has a total land area that is only slightly larger than the state of Arizona. When we consider the very finite availability of land in this context of comparison, and recognize that todays average professional Italian makes just slightly less income than todays average Ameri- can; then the escalating real estate prices become understandable. As is our usual policy, we have something to say about real estate prices. Italy is socio-geographi- cally fragmented and has been for centuries. It is one of the distinguishing charac- teristics of Italy and the Italian people. They are not derived of a single background. They have lived as different and differing people for many centuries in City-States, isolated one from the other. This fragmentation caused a regionalism that existed for all practical purposes up until the time that television and mass-media created a more homogenized Italy. One clear result of the centuries of fragmentation is re- gional differences in economic conditions. These facts are more or less common knowledge. Historians have long discussed and pondered this phenomena ad infini- tum. There has almost always been a great disparity inside of Italy between the eco- nomic conditions of one region and another, one city and another, and even one town and the next.

To some extent this geographical-economic disparity between areas still exist. What is important to us is that the phenomena still exists in a measurable enough degree to create real estate bargains. Areas that have been traditionally depressed economi- cally, still lag behind their more prosperous neighbors, and real estate prices in these areas reflect this disparity. Additionally, while most Americans tend to be looking for sumptuous villas and/or modern condominiums, Italy has many cities with older areas filled with older homes that are being ignored. In some cases, these homes date back a century or more and they have few if any modern conveniences. Buildings and homes such as these can be had for bargain prices, (we would estimate that a price of around $15,000 might be a good place to start the bidding, and note that Italians barter well.) These bargains exist because more and more of the younger Italians desire only what is modern and stylish. This tells us that these properties should remain available for the near term, or at least until the next generation of Italians start looking around for their 'roots' and decide they would prefer to live in a historic apartment or house with it's 'traditional Italian ambience' rather than a contemporary condo.

Turning a vintage building into a modern house or apartment can be fun, but it can also be costly. Note that unless we can do our own renovation, that the costs of hiring the work could be usurious for those who do not speak Italian, or who do not know the 'ropes.' (It is difficult to out-Italian an Italian.) We believe that anyone with the capacity to remodel these older buildings themselves or who has enough experience to function as a knowledgeable contractor, would be well-served to investigate the possibility. Some of the cities in which such bargains may exist are cities that are lagging behind economically. These cities may take years to catch up, if in fact they ever do. Investing in Italian real estate such as this is good for the long term and may require that we ignore short term profits. It could give us a wonderful house to pass on to our children in a country that will endure. Those in hurry for profit might be better off looking elsewhere. We know this: Italy has been around for awhile and will continue to be around for a while longer. It has a record of enduring.

As a modern expatriate destination Italy has much to offer. Surprisingly so. Its economy is booming, its culture evolving; (while in the very same instant it contin- ues to remain fully Italian and comically paradoxical.) It is historically rich, yet amidst the historic ramparts and ruins it is also quite contemporary, almost smugishly stylish, and more often then not highly dynamic. Admittedly prices are no longer a bargain, yet what we get for our dollar is quite different from what our dollar buys us in the United States. While a $100,000 house in the U.S. is quite often little more than a modest house of impoverished character, a $100,000 house in Italy might easily be two hundred years old, built of stone, and have enough character to change our outlook on life itself. Finer things engender finer thoughts, lasting things: last- ing thoughts.

Contemporary Italy has contemporary opportunities. Though much remains imbed- ded and bogged down in the incompetent bureaucracy, such detainments do not delay the Italian. Everything functions despite the fact that nothing appears capable of being functional. What does hold the Italian back, if anything does; is the Italian's worldview as seen from the perspective that Italy itself embellishes. Two Americans recently went to Italy and opened a chain of Pizza Parlors somewhat along the lines of the trendy California Pizza Kitchen concept. The chain is a tremendous success. We mention this, not because it is an anomaly for Americans to go to a foreign country and have enormous success with a contemporary product or style. We men- tion this, for the obvious reason that pizza is thought to be the quintessential Italian food. We believe that any number of similar successful and stylish ideas can be imported, incorporated and done in Italy. Or worldwide.

306

Italy is definitely Internet connected, with some interesting Web Sites and some technologically intelligent Service Providers. There would be little if any problem dealing internationally from Italy over the Internet. There are so many interesting books on Italy that it would be impossible to begin to describe them. As the reader knows, we have a consistent habit of telling the reader to go to a country and live there for awhile before making long term commitments. Additionally we always stress that the rules of the road should be followed when we purchase real estate or make business investments. Find out what other expats are doing, but don't follow unthinkingly in their footsteps. We recall vividly how when we once lived in Guantajauto, Mexico with a number of other American expats that it was customary and stylish to ignore the Visa requirement that limited stays up to six months. Some friends of ours lost a great deal of money by not having the proper paper documentation at the proper moment. Life is lived in moments.

Italy is one place where the exception to this rule may seem to apply. We won't recommend it however. It should be enough to note that the Italian government seems to have a Midas embrace and that everything the government touches becomes chaos right after the first hug. Multitudes of expats live in Italy without ever applying for residency. At the very mention of the word government everyone in Italy instantly shrugs. Many centuries ago the Italian people realized that life was impossible. Impossible to understand, impossible to live in an orderly way and impossible to comprehend. It is said that for every two Italians you have three opinions; but one thing that most Italians seem to agree upon is this: Few Italians still believe that any form of government provides anything. Even so, they seem totally incapable of giving their governments up; they have had more governments in the last fifty years than any six nations combined. They are an impossible people.

SPAIN

"There is no people like them when they are good..."

There are some real estate bargains in Spain. For some reason, there are vast areas of the **Andalucia** region of Spain has been totally ignored by expats. When we include European tourists into the statistics, Spain has more tourism than any other country in Europe including Italy. Southern Spain is the most southern point of Europe. It is further south than Sicily or Greece and actually more southerly than a good deal of North Africa. The climate is excellent and very comparable to that of southern California. Even the terrain is similar to California. However, despite the excellent climate and it's extraordinarily beautiful architecture, with the exception of the resort areas along the coast, much of Andalusia is underpopulated. There is a book on Andalucia published by Passport Books, Lincolnwood, Illinois; which shows its exceptional beauty. To view the book is to be convinced.

Rural inland cottages and houses in need of total restoration begin in the $15,000 to $20,000 range in Andalucia.

BALERIC ISLANDS

The Balearic Islands are expatriate havens of long standing. **Majorca, Minorca, Ibiza** and **Formentera** are artist colonies of some reknown and also tourist meccas for many northern Europeans. It was on the Island of Ibiza that the famous art forger, Elmyr de Hory lived. He was a close friend of the Clifford Irving's and the subject of Irving's book, *Fake*, which was instrumental in inspiring the Howard Hughes caper which landed Irving a jail sentence. Irvings wife, the Baroness Nina van Pallandt and Irving himself were expatriate celebrities whose risky adventures were international headlines in the early 1970's. The February 11, 1972 issue of **LIFE** magazine featured their expatriate lifestyle and their daring, almost inge-nious attempt to publish a forged Howard Hughes autobiography. We have to assume that the entire affair was done as much for the fun as for profit. They brought world attention to Ibiza, and to the international expatriate community of artists and writ-ers that lived there. The islands are worth a visit, but real estate prices there today are affordable to most of us.

No one bothers with **France** anymore. Apart from some decent, but highly over-priced wines, France has little to offer. As an expat destination it is declasse and only posers and the uninformed still go there.

Instead of Paris, the place where the informed expatriates are now going to is: Prague.

PRAGUE

The Paris of the 90's

Fortune and time have treated **Prague** in a most extraordinary way. Despite its location, Prague has neither been touched by the ravages of war nor violated by the brunt of Bachus. What remains is a living architectural wonder of the old world. Prague has become **the Paris of the 90's**, with many expatriates moving there to enjoy the cheap rents, cheap real estate prices, the historic cultural ambience, the Pilsner Urquell, the art, music and the wonderful openess of this great city at a time of tremendous transition. We have had the pleasure of talking to some of the expats who have recently lived in Prague and they make it sound like good fun. We are told that every Friday evening people fly into Prague from Paris, London, and Rome to enjoy a weekend of wine and Jazz. The rents are so cheap that some people keep a Prague apartment just to have for these weekend jams.

The **Charles University of Prague** is now giving many courses in English, includ-ing medicine. We spoke with representatives of Charles University regarding their medical school. The course leads to a degree with the unfortunate acronym of MUDr; which stands for **Medicinae Universae Doctor**, or Doctor of General Medicine. The course lasts six years. Although the courses are taught entirely in English, students are expected to learn enough Czech by the third year to communicate with patients and hospital staff. The price is approximately $10,000 per year, which along with Prague's cheap rents, means that the school is a bargain. How the course stacks up in comparison to American medical standards we cannot say with absolute precision, but our impression is that both education and degree would probably much more than suffice for practicing medicine in many, if not most countries of the world. Those intent on returning to the United States to practice should seek further information regarding **MCAT** and **USMLE** scores of prior graduates before making a commitment to Charles University. We asked specifically about the number of hospital beds and the number of books in the medical library; and were told that there are hundreds of beds at the University Hospital, meaning the school has a sufficient on-site hospital where the students receive their clinical training; (a section of training that is difficult to obtain in some so-called offshore medical schools.) In response to the question about the library, the staff admitted to me that there was a shortage of books in English. English, (and possibly Italian and French) are the language[s] of medicine, with English playing a very heavy leading role. However, with the use of the Internet some of the world's largest medical libraries can be accessed from anywhere in the world, (including Prague.) This makes the existence of a well stocked on-site medical library slightly less crucial. Not all books and catalogues are currently available, but this is rapidly changing as computers move towards playing a major role in medicine. Charles University offers numerous other courses in addition to medicine; it is the oldest established University in Central Europe, and was founded in 1348. It is massive with many divisions besides Medicine. In Prague, telephone: 011-422-67-102-206, for the director of foreigner studies: 011-422-67-102-410; fax: 011-422-745-248 or 011-422-67-311-812; 3rd Faculty of Medicine also has its own massive Web Page which tells the history of Charles University and the Charles University school of Medicine. Bring up the Home Page at: http://www.1f3.cuni.cz/engl/intro2.html Those wishing to use email might try: EvaSamcova@1f3.cuni.cz or: whois@cuni.cz which gives information on the Charles University Address Book. We contacted them by post, through: **International Education Centre**, 29 Arthur Road, Heldelberg, Ontario, <u>Canada</u> N0B 1Y0 The actual University address in Czech: Ruska 87/2411, 10000 Praha 10 <u>Czech Republic</u>.

Our impression from reading about Charles University is very favorable. It was Charles University from which much of the resistance to foreign occupation has been launched. It was at Charles that **Jan Palach**, a Czech hero, burned himself to death to protest against the Soviet occupation of the country by invaders and against demagoguery, violence, and oppression. It was Charles University students who stood against the Nazis. 1,200 Charles students were deported to concentration camps as a result of their heroic protests. The school is excellent, the faculty excellent, and the education we could attain there; all things considered, would be second to none.

Those we talked to about living in Prague, tell us that it is a very exciting scene reminiscent of what Paris must have been like in the 20's. We imagine that it would be fun to go to college there living amidst such grand ambience and cultural richness. Those who have gone to Prague and started businesses have managed to fare quite well. Americans have started everything from English language newspapers to Discos in Prague. There is still said to be a shortage of fine restaurants, a hangover from the days of Soviet domination. An acquaintance spoke of being able to purchase some of the very luxurious older apartment buildings at very reasonable prices. There is a caveat however. Some of the communist created rent control is still in exsistence and it's binding obligations travel with the title to the property. This means that if we purchase one of these apartment buildings or hotels, we might be stuck with a large percentage of tenants who have bonafide lease-rights for life at rates of $25 per month. These buildings are incomparable. Classical architecture of the highest order. Artistic interiors with sculpture, fountains, and glass-doored elevators. It is one of those moments in history when opportunity exists. It would of course be difficult to own such a building, with perhaps forty apartments, three stories high, and find ourselves grossing only $800 a month in income. How would we be able to provide maintenance? How would we be able to meet outgoing expenses at all? What does heating cost for instance? These buildings might require two or three thousand dollars a month in maintenance alone. Such is the problem and the reason for the bargain prices. There is no simple solution and we want to stress that any clever solutions would not work very well in a country like the Czech Republic with its strong moral philosophy. One possible course of action in our opinion is to view the purchase as downpayment and the fixed-expenses as mortgage payments or condo fees. We might find ourselves living in a luxurious penthouse for three thousand dollars a month. Not a bad deal for those who can afford it. However, there is the purchase price which could be a million dollars. Which actually is not a bad price for a five million dollar building. Of course, commercial real estate prices are usually based on income. A building bringing in $800 gross per month is worth about $100,000 to $200,000; not one million. Additionally, maintenance can get complicated on such a large structure. A new roof, or elevator can be astronomical in price. Still, these buildings are works of art and someday the rents will reach market value. When? How? We leave these questions and this fantasy for the reader to ponder.

CASTLES IN POLAND
& THE ROAD TO
CONSTANTINOPLE

We've heard of castles in **Poland** going for $10,000. Lot's of castles in Poland going for $10,000. Very run down, but castles nonetheless. Tourist attractions? Restaurants? Bread & Breakfasts? Country hideaway? Well, as things become more global the Polish countryside might become a viable place to live. Once satellite access to the Internet is in place it will make little difference for many of us where we live. Oh, it would still be nice to go a bookstore in the flesh, or go out on the town; a fine restaurant, theater, or some good jazz. But if we are living in Poland we're actually not too far from many of the world's great cities. Perhaps we can't visit them nightly, but twice monthly might be possible. In exchange for the inconvenience or living remote, we get to live in an ancient castle, with no running water, no heat, no electricity, no kitchen, no telephone, and no toilet. Surrounded all the while by Polish neighbors who are sure that we are insane for living in a ruin, where we are seen spending most of our time installing those things that are readily available in the cheapest condominium. The Poles will understand, we are after all Americans. We are clever people, and we do clever things with our time.

Jim Rogers speaks of the area known as **Turkistan**, which is to the east of Central Europe. We will more or less quote Jim word for word, because we don't have any personal knowledge about the area of Turkistan, but we do respect Jim Rogers opinion. What he has to say is interesting to such an extent that we believe it is worth passing along to the reader. Readers are advised to get Jim's book, ***Investment Biker***, which we have mentioned elsewhere as being highly recommended. In fact, anyone who is serious about becoming an expat should consider Jim Rogers book essential reading; and we are quite sincere when we say this. (Such sincerity increases the latitude to plagiarize.) As Rogers and his riding companion Tabitha crossed from **Turkey** into **Georgia** they noted that the land on the Turkey side of the border was selling at around $20 per acre. This border and the route from Turkey into Georgia is a historic centuries-old route that is once again beginning to become a [modern] route into and out of the most prosperous sections of the Soviet Union. Where does it lead? Going in, it leads to agricultural and oil rich nations that are now being liberated from the Soviet Union. Going out, it leads into Europe. Rogers assets that this is going to be one of the heaviest traveled routes in the world in a few years. If he is correct and he has been surprising correct about many things of this nature, then buying land on the Turkey side of the border at $20 per acre would be like buying land at $20 an acre alongside the road from San Diego to Los Angeles. (Well, perhaps that is an over-exaggeration, but we'll let it stand because it emphasizes the point.) Buying this land for any type of future business would probably be a good investment, either for the land itself, or for a potential business of our own.

We realize that when we mention such oddball business ventures, that they probably seem inconceivable, highly complex and risk-laden to the point of absurdity. Let's pause for a moment and consider the conceivability, risk, and absurdity of such a venture. The first point we need to make, is that someone *will* do it. It will happen. The next issue we'd like to address is the complexity. Lets make a formula for complexity: in this instance, we are talking about a business venture, so any discussion of complexity is going to have to be based on an analysis of relative costs. In order to determine the feasibility of this business venture, we are going to have to do two types of homework; an analysis of the area done by gathering available information, and an analysis of the situation by going and visiting the area in the flesh. The book-research is going to be difficult if we try to use traditional research methods, because much is changing in this region on a daily basis. As an experiment, we did a quick search on the Internet looking for information on the City of **Tbilisi**. We pulled up 60 hits on the first try. If you don't own a computer and you don't have access to the Internet, being a global expat is going to be difficult. Not impossible; just difficult; people got along without computers before they were invented just as people got along without cars before they were invented. Even today, if we want to live without a car we certainly can, many do and live excellent lives; the same goes with computers. In any event, we pulled up 60 hits on Tbilisi, the capital city of Georgia, an important city within the area of our research. One of the first pages we brought up was: http://www.ten.nl/bizdevne/tbilisi.htm which is the **Tbilisi Business Communication Centre Home Page** which was set up in 1994 to assist investors coming into the region and to provide information. The services they offer are extensive and the information includes: 1] information regarding Georgian business, statistics, legislation, customs, procedures, etc.. 2] Market research, arrangement of exhibitions, fairs, and presentations. 3] Representation of foreign organizations in Georgia. 4] Secretarial and lawyer's services, interpretations, translations, printing services, accommodations, transportation, and full telecommunications services support. Their telephone: 011-995-32-988371   their fax: 011-995-32-987601 and we can email them at: bcc@access.sanet.ge This tells us that we can gain information on the area, and that at least one city in the area is becoming global enough to have a Web Page on the Internet. What is interesting to us, is that this city suffered a repressive attack by Soviet tanks in 1989 for staging an alleged anti-Soviet demonstration. In 1994 they have a Web Page; they have gone from living under a whip in an isolated city to being in virtual contact and a part of the free world in just five years. The news couldn't, and didn't get out of Tbilisi about the Soviet massacre until several months after its occurrence. Today, with freedom from Soviet rule, we can get email from Tbilisi in a matter of seconds; the massacres are over, or more precisely, the unrecorded massacres are over. Any area of the world that has open Internet access is open to the world. This will not stop governments from massacring their people, but it will make it much more difficult to do it with impunity.

Anyway, we can now see clearly the opportunities freedom of information allows us, and there is any amount of information on the region that will help us make an business venture decision. What we would need to do, is to search the Internet until we were certain that we had pulled up everything we could on the entire area concerning the Georgians, Armenians, the Azerbaijanis, and the Turkistans. Then, we would need to ask every question we could to determine the potentiality of our venture and to prepare ourselves to make a visit to the area.

Part two is the visit. This is more costly than Surfing the Net, but it is required. An extended trip to the area would tell us what we needed to know if we asked the right questions and looked in the right places. It would also allow us to determine not merely the price of the land, but the look of the land and the receptivity of the locals. Now how complex has this been? In terms of cost we probably learned what we needed to learn for considerably less than $5,000 unless we felt obligated to travel top-cabin. Additionally, if the price of land is $20 per acre we can buy 10,000 acres for $200,000. In the United States $20 won't even buy us a dinner and a bottle of wine. In Turkey it buys us an acre of land. This said, it would seem that it is no more complex, expensive or absurd to invest in land in Turkey then it would be to buy a $200,000 house in Santa Barbara. (If there were any houses available for $200,000 in Santa Barbara.) The upwards potential on the Turkistan land would be many times greater then the one bedroom cottage in Santa Barbara. Besides, its dangerous in Santa Barbara; they're running out of water.

We have to repeat what we said earlier; someone is going to do this. Someone is going to be on the road into and out of one of the world's transitional regions. There are said to be three things that are required for a successful retail business; location, location, and location. Perhaps old Turkistan is the place to be. There is no question but that **Istanbul** is a very fascinating city and that the Mediterranean Coast of Turkey is an excellent spot and would make an perfect location for a summer beach cottage. One such spot to consider is **Bodrum**. Bodrum is a town that had only 2,000 people a few years back and was for years a place where Turkish writers and artists lived. It is situated where the Aegean and the Mediterranean meet. Still considered a secret, Bodrum now has over 13,000 residents; and jet-setters like Mick Jagger and crew have been seen frequenting the local haunts. A lovely town of white-washed houses strung with bougainvillea, Bodrum is indeed beautiful. The water around Bodrum is unbelievably clear and there is long palm lined waterfront with a marina. The town itself climbs from the waterfront uphill with tiny twisting streets that are quaint and quite picturesque. From what we have been told, Bodrum is not exactly tranquil any longer but has rock music and party life in full swing much of the time. Not to worry, Bodrum is in proximity to many of the tiny Turkish fishing villages of yesteryear where real estate prices are better and the evenings unblemished by the scourge of rock and roll. The entire coast area of Turkey is pretty great. We have two friends who traveled through Turkey on a motorcycle along the coast. They said the Turkish countryside was lovely and the crystal clear waters of the Aegean magnificent. However, the girl was from Amsterdam and like most Scandinavians she wanted to sunbathe nude. Public nudity is considered rebarbative in the Islamic world. To accommodate themselves without offending Islam, they climbed down a cliffside on ropes unto a secluded beach where they camped for a week in isolation. The girl did mentioned to me that in Turkey the fishermen fished their boats closer to shore than the Scandinavians, a fact which she found exceedingly odd because it seemed to her that some of the fishing boats in Turkey looked very much in danger of crashing into rocks along the shore. No doubt.

313

We have heard that there is now a nudist beach at **Antalya**; called Club Mediterranée Kemer, that is set up specifically for Westerners and tourists. The coast is the most visited area of Turkey, and the most populated. A large number of rural Turkish people have chosen to move to the coast because there is more work, better schools for their children and the weather is perfect. But we started out talking about the border with Georgia. From what we've seen from photographs much of Turkey is interesting to look at, but we have not seen too much in print about the border region and we have not been there ourselves. So, to end this and move along, we will simply state: It appears that there is going to be some good opportunity in what was once the crossroads of the world. Perhaps a modern rebirth of the ancient caravan route that created the Ottoman Empire. The empire that sat at the gateway between three worlds: the Arabic World, the World of the Central Asian Republics and the continent of the Western World; Europe itself. Precisely what the border area with Georgia is like, looks like, and what living and working there entails, we cannot say. Email us an let us know.

CHAPTER TWENTY

IRELAND

We have so much information on Ireland that we couldn't possibly get it in a section. Ireland is for expats. There is every reason to go there and few to deter us. What has deterred others? The weather for one. Another has been the almost monotonous gloomy dreariness of the place. Some of these detriments are difficult to deny. Consider the bright side, almost half of the days are free of overcast; which is to say, that our beer-mug is half full -- and there is nothing monotonous about a stone cottage with a flower garden a half hour commute from **Dublin** center. Paris it's not. But who the hell really wants to be snubbed and insulted in Paris these days? We have a feeling that if Hemingway could return to life he wouldn't return to today's Paris. But he'd probably more than enjoy a couple of glasses of Guiness and a summers month in Dublin. There is little question that he'd love the countryside; and with the prices of real estate, he could buy a farm in Ireland for a price he might have paid in France many years ago. Ireland is a bargain, and its a pretty damn swell place to be.

We can still buy a cottage in Ireland for US$10,000. The language is an approximation of what Americans speak. The place has a very low crime rate. It is possible to live in Ireland tax-free. Ireland is becoming Europes new offshore haven. Ireland has great opportunities for both the young expat and the retiree.

FACTS AT A GLANCE

TIME ZONE: GMT

AREA: 27,129 sq mi

Note: The Republic of Ireland is slightly larger than the state of West Virginia [pop: 1,800,000]

STATUS: Republic

POPULATION OF IRELAND: 3,550,448 (July 1995 est) population growth rate: 0.33%

CAPITAL: Dublin (over 40% of population resides within 60 miles of Dublin)

LANGUAGES: Irish Gaelic and English

ETHNIC GROUPS: Celtic (94%) small English minority.

RELIGIONS: Roman Catholic (95%)

PHYSICAL FEATURES: Temperate maritime; modified by North Atlantic Current; mild winters, cool summers; consistently humid; overcast half of the time. Mostly level to rolling interior plain surrounded by rugged hills and low mountains, sea cliffs on west coast. Has zinc, lead, natural gas, petroleum, barite, copper, gypsum, limestone, dolomite, peat, and silver. There is about 14% in arable land with 71% designated as meadows and pasture land. Forest and woodlands make up 5%. Ireland has forestry potential with a government scheme to encourage forestry investment. There is some water pollution of lakes due to agricultural runoff, but the damage is not pronounced and the issue is being addressed.

CURRENCY: Irish Pound (1.00 Irish Punt = 1.61 Dollar at time of publication)

ECONOMY: Ireland is yet another one of those countries that seems to be doing a great deal right. The economy has become quite buoyant and the rate of inflation quite low; especially when compared to most countries in the European Community. A series of innovative incentives and subsidies brought a stream of foreign manufacturing companies into Ireland in recent years. Ireland has become a competitive niche player in the area in such high-tech industries as computer software design, electronics, and pharmaceuticals. Ireland is striving to become a major financial services center. They have developed a new (1993) International Financial Services Center. The new center coupled with a maximum corporate tax rate of 10% for foreign companies along with the access to the EC markets has provided a major boost to Ireland's economy. Agriculture still remains an important sector, although industry now accounts for over 80% of exports and employs 28% of the labor force. Ireland has worked hard to reduce is external debt and is doing a great many things to make itself an attractive destination for foreign companies and for expats.

GDP: $49.8 billion (1994 est.)

GDP PER CAPITA: $14,060 (1994 est)

FREEDOM HOUSE RATING: Political Rights: 1 Civil Liberties: 1 Apart from the highly emotional issues of divorce and abortion, the Republic of Ireland, unlike its neighbor Northern Ireland, is pleasantly trouble free. In November of 1995 50.3% of the electorate voted in favor of legalizing divorce.

TELECOMMUNICATIONS & THE WWW:

There are at least seven Service Providers that we know of in the Irish Republic. Our search of the Internet pulled up some interesting hits including a Migrating to Ireland Web Site at: http://pwaldron.bess.tcd.ie/ireland/migrate.htm There is a Virtual Tourist Guide to Ireland at http://pwaldron.bess.tcd.ie/ireland.htm and a Home Page at that Site for most question regarding cultural Ireland. We've found a Web Site which lists a number of real estate agencies throughout Ireland which can be accessed through the above URL. The Site, called Irish National Property Network is an extensive list that is made up of four sections:

- AGENTS
- BUYING IN IRELAND (which is a guide to real estate in Ireland
- PROPERTIES (listed by category)
- ARTICLES (on Irish and regional property issues)

In addition, there is an accompanying map showing each region of Ireland with a live click-on to view agents and properties in each area. The service looks good, however we cannot state how complete it is; whether it just lists prosperous agents, or it lists all agents we cannot say. What we have found is that the Site is complete in many ways and does list affordable properties. For instance; in the category of properties, we pull up three sub-categories which are further divided into three sub-categories:

- RESIDENTIAL PROPERTIES
  - Cottages £40-80,000
  - Period Houses £80-120,000
  - Up to £40,000
- COMMERCIAL PROPERTIES
  - Pubs, Factories, Warehouses
  - Offices, Hotels, Guest Houses
  - Retail, Investment Properties
- LAND / SITES
  - Farms/Land
  - Residential
  - Development

We have to admit that this is our kind of Web Site; its nicely laid out and seem very complete. The following shows a fine example of what we pulled up on the Farms/Land category on the very first try: Ballyhurst, Taghmon, Co. Wexford Old-style farmhouse which has been renovated. Standing on c. 8 acres of land, the farmyard is surrounded by stone buildings and lawns. The land is registered with the Irish Organic Farmers and Growers Association. The accommodation includes 2 rec rooms, kitchen, 6 bedrooms, bathroom and w.c. 8 miles from Wexford. Price: £90,000 (as of this writing [late 1996] the Irish Punt = 1.61 US Dollar) The property described includes a photograph, and we will state that the property is very attractive by any standard. A property of this description and style for US$144,900 would be a bargain anywhere, but in a highly civilized country like the Irish Republic with its rich cultural heritage, it's a steal! We repeat, we did not search for this listing, it was the first one we brought up in a random search. We are impressed both with the Web Site and to see our opinion of Ireland so quickly confirmed.

Additionally, there is another Site available through the same URL for the Migrating to Ireland page; Real Estate Ireland offers a free listing to all agents who wish to submit up to 20 residential properties including details and photos. Couldn't be better for us.

For a country with only 3.5 million people, the Irish Republic has very good Internet Access and highly useful and clearly comprehensible WebSites. We are impressed.

Telephone installation in Ireland will cost us £135 ($217) and the monthly billing will be on the order of US$20.00 We would use Callback once we were established.

RESOURCES ON THE INTERNET

Dual Citizenship FAQ:
Dual Nationality and United States Law
This document attempts to describe the current situation in United States law regarding dual citizenship. While it is not written by an attorney it is a fairly complete and detailed document written by someone who has gone through the process.
URL: http://yank.kitchener.on.ca/~richw/dualcit.html

The Irish Times Internet Edition
URL: http://www.irish-times.com/irish-times/paper/1213/hom.htm
email: itwired@irish-times.com
For just $129.00 a year you can have a copy of The Irish Times posted in the US on the day of publication once a week, 52 weeks of the year. Call Toll Free (USA only) 1 800 969 1258

Irish Universities
Good & Plenty
URL: http://pwaldron.bess.tcd.ie/univ.htm

INFORMATION FOR VISITING USA AND CANADIAN STUDENTS
URL: http://www.ucc.ie/ucc/admin/iso/us9596.html
Address: **International Student Office,**West Wing, Main Quad, University College, Cork, Western Road, Cork, Ireland
Telephone: +353-21-902543(direct) or +353-21-276871, ext. 2543/2810/2780/2918/ 2022 Fax: +353-21-273072 Email: adre8003@iruccvax.ucc.ie
Opening Hours:
Monday - Friday 09.15 - 13.00, 14.10 - 17.00

AYE TO IRISH

I will arise and go now, and go to Innisfree,
And a small cabin build there, of clay and waddles made:
Nine bean-rows will I have there, a hive for the honey-bee,
And live alone in the bee-loud glade.
-W.B. Yeats

We have so much information on Ireland that we couldn't possibly get it in a section. Ireland is for expats. There is every reason to go there and few to deter us. What has deterred others? The weather for one. Another has been the almost monotonous gloomy dreariness of the place. Some of these detriments are difficult to deny. Consider the bright side, almost half of the days are free of overcast; which is to say, that our beer-mug is half full -- and there is nothing monotonous about a stone cottage with a flower garden a half hour commute from Dublin center. Paris it's not. But who the hell really wants to be snubbed and insulted in Paris these days? We have a feeling that if Hemingway could return to life he wouldn't return to today's Paris. But he'd probably more than enjoy a couple of glasses of Guiness and a summers month in Dublin. There is little question that he'd love the countryside; and with the prices of real estate, he could buy a farm in Ireland for a price he might have paid in France many years ago. Ireland is a bargain, and its a pretty damn swell place to be.

We can still buy a cottage in Ireland for US$10,000. The language is an approximation of what Americans speak. The place has a very low crime rate. It is possible to live in Ireland tax-free. Ireland is becoming Europes new offshore haven. Ireland has great opportunities for both the young expat and the retiree. We can spend just a few months each year in Ireland and get full resident status. (Stealth-Expats take note.) In Ireland we can conduct business offshore and pay no taxes. The schools are good, the colleges first rate. (**Dublin's Royal College of Surgeons** ranks along side Israel's **Sackler School of Medicine** as having standards so high that they are in a class by themselves.) The living is easy and calmly paced. The land investments are sensational. Ireland is one of the easiest countries in the world to gain a 'First World' passport. Gloomy weather be damned, let's go!

To gain a Second Passport in Ireland is a refreshingly civilized process. No outstretched hand asking for a payoff; just a solid civilized procedure that is definitive and comprehensible. (If someone has their hand stretched out in front of them in Ireland its for a handshake.) The best and simplest way to obtain a Irish Passport is to be able to claim one by Right of Decent. This requires that one of our grandparents or parents was born in either the Island of Ireland prior to 1922, or in the Republic of Ireland after 1922. We can also obtain an Irish Passport if we have been married to an Irish citizen for three years.

Gaining Irish citizenship is also a rather straightforward matter involving the usual requirements of good character, self-sufficiency, and a declaration of fidelity. We must have lived at least one year in Ireland prior to making application. We cannot think of too many reasons why anyone would want to gain Irish citizenship beyond the gaining of an Irish Passport or to milk the Irish welfare system. The Passport is of value, but we personally feel that any type of public assistance should be the right and privilege only of senior citizens or those who have earned the dole through military service.

319

ESCAPE FROM AMERICA

The major problem with Irish citizenship in our eyes, is that like the United States, Ireland is one of the very few nations that taxes it's citizens on any and all income gained worldwide. There are numerous ways to live in Ireland without Irish citizenship. If the Passport is the incentive, then we would make sure that we had a second Passport from another country whose tax jurisdictional umbrella could ward off the deluge of Irish taxes. Ireland allows dual citizenship.

There are easier ways. The great blessing of Ireland is: it's solid culture along with its wholesome simplicity. This culture, plus the obvious bargains in real estate, in a geographical location that allows such quick and easy access to Europes markets & playgrounds, makes of Ireland a natural expat destination par excellent. Why spoil everything by gaining the obligation of taxation?

If we live in Ireland less than six months a year we are not considered legal residents. If we are artists, writers, or involved in any type of creative artistic endeavor for our income, we can live in Ireland full time and pay no Irish taxes. And there are other ways. Residency in Ireland does not require the payment of income tax to Ireland unless our income is derived from Ireland. All offshore activities can be set up to be free of Irish income taxes. In fact, from our position in Ireland we can invest into European Community opportunities that other Americans can only dream about. If our corporation is set up offshore, none of the European countries can tax us either.

Those of us who want to work in Ireland, or open a business in Ireland will be subject to Irish Income taxes. It might be fun to own a pub or similar business in Ireland; we leave this to the readers imagination. There are numerous tax-free investment schemes available inside of Ireland, such as forestry, aquaculture and so forth. It is possible to pursue tax-free or low-tax Irish based income opportunities. The Irish government will give free land to anyone who wants to engage in aquaculture. The types of aquaculture being pursued are lobster, mussel, sea urchin, and oyster. Anyone wanting to try oyster farming is given free land to use. The property ownership remains with the Department of Marine. Oysters sell for an average £3.50 per dozen on the local market, and less for wholesale to exporters. Or, we might consider exporting them ourselves. Grants of 50% for oyster farming are available for up to £20,000 maximum. That would put us in a £40,000 ($64,400) oyster farm on free land for an investment of $32,000. Not a bad deal. Contact: Department of the Marine, Leeson Lane, Dublin 2; telephone 353·1·678·5444

In order to work in Ireland we need a work permit. Work permits are easily obtainable; contact: Department of Enterprise and Employment, Davitt House, 65A Adelaide Road, Dublin 2, Republic of Ireland; telephone 353·1·661·4444

REAL ESTATE

As we made fairly clear in the paragraphs above, Real Estate in Ireland is a very good bargain. There are other places in the world where the price is lower, but few places with all of the many positive attributes that make up the Republic of Ireland. For example, a place like Mozambique may have the best real estate prices in the world, but when we compare the infrastructure, schools, market access, safety, and other factors, we will discover that one way or the other we pay for what we get. This is not to say that there aren't many who might prefer the excitement of a place like Mozambique and be able to make good and profitable use of its bargain real estate prices. Risk is usually a function of price.

Both the aforementioned Real Estate Ireland and the Irish National Property Network are excellent places to start looking for Irish real estate. Unfortunately, the Irish National Property Network, being a Network service, is available only to those with Internet Access. Real Estate Ireland can be contacted at telephone 353·1·833·9472. Fax at 353·1·853·0631 Their email address is: property@ibi.ie Their street address is: Internet Business Ireland 21 Fairview, Dublin 3 Republic of Ireland. For listings of upcoming property auctions in Ireland, contact: Irish Auctioneers and Valuers Institute, 38 Merrion Square, Dublin 2, Republic of Ireland. Telephone 353·1·661·1794. For Pub sales, contact: Irish Pub Sales Head Office, Church Street, Athlone, Co. Westmeath, telephone 353·902·72776 Also for Pub sales, try: Gunnes Licensed Division, 176 Pembroke Road, Ballsbridge, Dublin 4; Republic of Ireland; telephone 353·1·668·2588. There is no restriction on foreign ownership of Irish pubs. There are approximately 11,000 pubs in Ireland. They range in price from £45,000 ro £1.7 million. Until recently it was a simple matter of determining the value of an Irish pub. The measure was 1½ times the annual revenue. This measurement still applies in rural areas, but in Dublin and other larger metropolitan areas, we can now expect to see a good deal of blue sky attached to a pubs price.

In summary, the Republic of Ireland as distinct from its neighbor Northern Ireland, is an excellent expat destination. Some of the great opportunities we can enjoy include: excellent bargains in real estate, generous tax breaks for foreign companies and individuals operating as foreign corporations, tax-free living for individuals who earn their money from cultural or artistic works, easily obtainable citizenship, a picturesque country with a very low crime rate and Guiness beer.

Ireland can be viewed as a retreat from high cost, stress and crime. An idyllic country with a rich history, simple yet beautiful architecture, and a pervasive and pronounced culture all its own. It is a land somehow off the beaten track, yet close enough to the cultural center of things to provide a clear and current view of the world from the sidelines. It is a going back in time to an age and place where much of what is, still remains agreeable.

CONTACTS IN THE IRISH GOVERNMENT

Aliens Office, Department of Justice, 72 St. Stephen's Green, Dublin 2, Ireland
Telephone: +353 1 678 9466 (Visa Enquiries only)

Passport Office, Department of Foreign Affairs, Setanta Centre, Molesworth Street, Dublin 2, Ireland
Telephone: +353 1 679 7600 (General Information Day and Night)
+353 1 671 1633 (Business Calls 9:30-17:15 Dublin time Monday-Friday)
AMERICAN EMBASSY DUBLIN has a Home Page at:
URL: http://www.indigo.ie/usembassy-usis/
42 ELGIN ROAD
BALLSBRIDGE, DUBLIN 4 IRELAND

The Interactive Travel Guide to the best of Ireland
URL: http://www.iol.ie/~discover/welcome3.htm
This page Links us to just about every piece of information worth knowing about Ireland. A very nice resource page. (We estimate that this page has at least one hundred Links to everything imaginable from business to sports.)

US STATE DEPARTMENT TRAVEL INFORMATION

COUNTRY DESCRIPTION: Ireland is a highly developed democracy with a modern economy.

ENTRY REQUIREMENTS: For information concerning entry requirements for Ireland, travelers can contact the Embassy of Ireland at 2234 Massachusetts Avenue N.W., Washington, D.C. 20008, tel (202) 462-3939, or the nearest Irish consulate in Boston, Chicago, New York or San Francisco.

MEDICAL FACILITIES: Medical facilities are available. U.S. medical insurance is not always valid outside the United States. Travelers have found that in some cases, supplemental medical insurance with specific overseas coverage, including provision for medical air evacuation, has proved to be useful. Further information on health matters can be obtained from the Centers for Disease Control and Prevention's international travelers hotline at (404) 332-4559.

CRIME INFORMATION: Ireland has a low rate of violent crime. There is a high incidence of petty crime, mostly theft, burglary, and purse-snatching. Rental cars and tourists, particularly in the vicinity of tourist attractions, are targeted by thieves.

The loss or theft abroad of a U.S. passport should be reported immediately to local police and the nearest U.S. embassy or consulate. U.S. citizens can refer to the Department of State's pamphlet "A Safe Trip Abroad" for ways to promote a trouble-free trip. The pamphlet is available from the Superintendent of Documents, U.S. Government Printing Office, Washington, D.C. 20402.

TERRORIST ACTIVITY: On February 9, 1996, the Provisional Irish Republican Army (PIRA) announced the end of a ceasefire. The threat of terrorist violence in Northern Ireland and danger of violence spilling over into Ireland remains. The presence of police on the border regions will likely fluctuate depending on the threat of violence.

DRUG PENALITIES: U.S. citizens are subject to the laws of the country in which they are traveling. Penalties for possession, use, or dealing in illegal drugs are strict, and convicted offenders can expect jail sentences and fines.

REGISTRATION/EMBASSY LOCATION: U.S. citizens who register with the Consular Section of the U.S. Embassy can obtain updated information on travel and security in Ireland. Travelers to Northern Ireland may consult the Consular Information Sheet for the United Kingdom. The U.S. Embassy in Dublin is located at 42 Elgin Road, Ballsbridge, telephone (353-1) 668-7122, fax (353-1) 668-9946. The Consular Section is located across the street from the U.S. Embassy in Hume House, 3rd Floor, Pembroke Road, Ballsbridge.

SOME ARTICLES OF MENTION

There are three very interesting articles that we can view on the internet. The first of these is: *The New Refugees: Americans who give up citizenship to save on taxes*. Written by Robert Lenzner and Philippe Mao and published in the November 1994 issue of **Forbes Magazine**. The authors make reference to the fact that some prominent and wealthy Americans are renouncing their citizenship and taking up Irish citizenship.

"Why Ireland?" the authors ask.

They give their own reply: "...An Irish passport lets its holder travel hassle-free in any member of the European Union. It also has more panache than a passport from Belize or St. Kitts, two small tropical outposts. And, Dublin is being developed as a global money center with tax advantages for individual and corporate investors."

What does getting an Irish passport require ask the writers?

"Certainly no hardship, given what a pleasant place Ireland is for those with money. They need only buy a home there and reside there at least part of the year."

This article can been be seen at:
http://www.triax.com/4expats/escapeartist/forbes1.html

There is a second article called: *Flight Capital: Avoiding U.S. taxes by renouncing citizenship*. Also a Forbes Magazine article, from their February 1994 edition. and written by Brigid McMenamin. Excerpts from that article can be seen at:
http://www.triax.com/4expats/escapeartist/forbes2.html

This article is pretty much what the title implies. Several nations are mentioned, but Ireland again is mentioned as a fairly strong preference (as well as the Caribbean) by many of the more prominent, wealthy expatriates. We are not in disagreement with these articles. Although we do question the number[s] of expatriates listed in the articles. The authors of these articles are concentrating on fairly wealthy and fairly well-known people who have followed the course of action of renouncing their citizenship. We are not sure why it is somehow more relevant when someone in the top income brackets renounces their citizenship. We see it the other way around. If Joe up the street who is worth twenty million dollars renounces his citizenship there is no mystery to it. But if you and I who may just be good solid American field mice leave America, or renounce our citizenship; that is pretty damn relevant. In the former case it represents *flight capital* in the precise meaning of the term, in the latter case it represents the fact that more and more field mice are recognizing that they have been betrayed by their own government.

Of course, there are other reasons to go abroad in addition to the negative situation in the United States. That is to say, there are just as many positive things pulling us, as there are negative things pushing us. These two articles concentrate on the negative
324

economic factors at work inside the United States. There is another article that discusses more of the positives. Believe it or not the name of the article is, *Escape From America.* No, we didn't write it, nor did we even know the article existed until we started work on this book. The article appeared in the July1994 issue of **Money Magazine**. Written by Gary Belsky, it is an excellent article. In fact, if we don't have internet access, we should probably go to the library and seek the back issue of Money Magazine that has the article. If we are connected, try:
http://www.triax.com/4expats/escapeartist/money..htm

In the article, Mr. Belsky writes, "To understand why so many Americans are fleeing the U.S. is, in part, to plug into a pervasive sense of disillusionment and pessimism in the country today. According to MONEY's recent poll, three out of five Americans say the quality of life in the U.S. is getting worse, and nearly as many (58%) express similar feelings about economic and job opportunities. Little wonder, then, that nearly one out of every five Americans say they have seriously considered leaving the country. Of course, the idea of pulling up roots for an international move is hardly as dramatic as it was even a generation ago. Travel is easier and cheaper than ever and, especially for the well educated and wealthy, finding acceptance and jobs in new lands is not the daunting task it once was. Says Arnold Dashefsky, co-author of *Americans Abroad: A Comparative Study of Emigrants From the United States* (Plenum, $27.50): "As unbelievable as it may be to late-20th-century citizens of the U.S., emigration may be a more common trend in the next century."

We agree.

WHERE WE'VE BEEN

We've covered a lot of ground. But we've certainly got a great deal more to tell you. We've made this book as inclusive as was possible. As we pointed out early on, it is impossible to get the world inside of a book. What I have learned along the way would fill another two books.

When we started this book we had a general idea of what we wanted to bring to the reader. While the spirit of what we want to bring to the reader has not diminished, the quantity of information has increased exponentially.

That is not an exaggeration.

The temptation to add another ten chapters is great. The people who help me with the publishing part of all this have advised against it.

We've a WebSite up and running. It will be geared to the issues in this book. Our intention is to build an index of resources that are relevant to the topics covered in this book. We've made some progress. I want the reader to know that when I started this book I didn't know too awfully much about computers. As the book progressed, I found the computer more and more pertinent as a research tool. Somewhere along the line I tried to get a WebSite built. It took some time to find someone who would build me a WebSite the way I wanted. He did a great job. His artistic talent and his grasp of what I wanted was matched by his technical ability. We learned a lot about Web Site Construction.

What did I want? First of all, I wanted a WebSite that didn't have a globe image of the planet earth on it.

Second, I wanted nothing that moved, spun, zipped, jumped, vibrated, or distracted from the content of the WebSite. My general idea was that Web Site construction and WebSites should consist not of what they could be, but of what they should be; something I learned from reading the book *Creating Killer Web Sites* by David Siegel. The electrical nonsense on many WebSites is rather childish for the most part. It will pass.

Also, I was forced to learn how to build my own web pages and get them unto the internet. It was one thing to have someone build me a ten page site, it was quite another to be constantly involved in constructing page after page of resource material for expats and liberty seekers. I had to learn how to do it myself.

The site, *Escape Artist . Com* is located at http://www.escapeartist.com
Which is for promotion of this book.
The resource site is at:
http://www.escapeartist.com/going/home.htm
What started out as a Web Site for this book is slowly turning into an index, and hopefully eventually a search engine of sorts. We hope it is of value to you.

RESOURCES FOR EXPATRIATES

"...that is the great fallacy; the wisdom of old men. They do not grow wise. They grow careful." **-Ernest Hemingway**

OPENING SECTIONS

Harry Browne's Complete Guide to Swiss Banks By Harry Browne
McGraw-Hill Book Company 1976
ISBN: 0070084831 Probably out of print and slightly dated, but if you can find a copy of this book, buy it!

The Economic Time Bomb By Harry Browne
St. Martins Press 1989 ISBN: 0312921330

Crisis Investing For The Rest Of The 90's By Douglas Casey Published by Citadel Press ISBN: 0806516127

The Expatriate Investor By Douglas Casey Everest House Publishers 1978 Long out of print. If you do find a copy of this book its probably really worth buying.

Americans Abroad A comparative study of emigrants from the United States. By Dashefsky, DeAmicis, Lazerwitz & Tabory Plenum Press 1992

International Investment Opportunities
How and where to invest overseas successfully. By Adrian Day
William Morrow and Company1983 This book is quite dated but interesting.

Keep What You Earn:
Practical Strategies to Protect Your Assets from Taxes, Lawsuits and Financial Predators
By Terry Coxon
Published by Random House Trade
ISBN: 0812928288
A very important book!

I've Had It By Robert Hopkins
Holt, Rinehart and Winston 1972
Like Casey's book on expatriates, this classic by Hopkins is long out of print.

Investment Biker - Around the World with Jim Rogers By Jim Rogers
Published by Bob Adams ISBN: 1558505296
Having quoted this book as often as we have it is obvious that we believe it to be a very worthwhile book for expatriates. It is.

Tax Havens By Anthony S. Ginsberg
Simon & Schuster 1991 ISBN: 013886649
Fairly technical, for the serious investor.

Mark Skousen's Complete Guide to Financial Privacy By Mark Skousen
Alexandria House Books 1980 Although extremely dated, this does have some very worthwhile information in it.

Using Offshore Havens for Privacy and Profits By Adam Starchild
Paladin Press 1994 ISBN: 087364767
Starchild has a number of very interesting easy to read books on going offshore.

Grundy's Tax Havens By Grundy, Milton
Sweet/Maxwell 1996 ISBN: 0-421-47510-2
Very expensive book.

The Craft Of Investing By John Train
Harpers Business 1994
ISBN: 0887306268
Train is easy to read. He makes complex issues comprehensible.

The New Money Masters
By John Train Harpers Business Books 1989
ISBN: 0060159669
Includes some important chapters on Jim Rogers & George Soros.

Doing Business In Latin America And The Caribbean By Lawrence W. Tuller
Amacom Books 1993 I very much like Tuller's work regarding Latin America. This book is recommended.

The World Market Desk Book
By Lawrence W. Tuller
McGraw Hill Books 1993 Not as extensive and detailed as his Latin American book, though still quite nice.

Pick's Currency Yearbook By Albert Pick
München: Krause 1994 ISBN: 0873410025
International currency analysis, Pick is considered *the* authority on currency.

The International Callback Book By Gene Retske Available from: International Insider 1861 South Patrick Drive #206 Melbourne, FL 32937 Voice:407 779 8999 Fax: 407 779-8339
Covers most aspects of International Callback including information on how to set up our own International Callback company.

The World's Top Retirement Havens
Agora Publishing 1991

This book was published by the folks who publish **International Living**, which is a decent newsletter. We are reluctant to encourage readers to subscribe to newsletters because most newsletters are untimely and irrelevant. Newsletters are published for the most part to earn money for the publisher. This in itself is not a sin. But we prefer that all publishers earn their keep by being relevant and timely. International Living falls outside of the investment letter category, so we don't feel reluctant to recommend it. However before we do let's discuss newsletters in toto so that our definitions and our positions are clarified.

Here is what we would look for in a newsletter. 1] A Fax-On-Demand system to keep readers current of changing markets. 2] A hotline telephone number to update subscribers of crucial events. 3] Internet access to the publisher. 4] Global relevance. It does no good to follow the advice of the myopic, or of someone who thinks what applied last year applies today. The tried and true may have been good enough for grandpa, but grandpa wouldn't have a chance in today's world. More has changed in the last twenty-four hours than changed in grandpa's entire lifetime. 5] A newsletter should be the product of continuous day-by-day research from a number of different perspectives. Assuredly one of those perspectives would have to be a recognition that the nation-state is dying. Writers and publishers who are just making the motions without even a glimmer of comprehension of the true significance of the world changes taking place are doing their readers a disservice. The fact is: the world that we used to know isn't the world we are now dealing with.

Additionally, a newsletter should never rely on opinion, unless that opinion is the product of a thoroughly researched understanding of all the current possibilities and the probabilities being discussed as opinion. Mere opinion isn't worth too awfully much. Investment wizards and prophets are a dime a dozen. Especially these days. Those who have read this book don't have to ask the reason why there is currently such a proliferation of Wall Street wizards. We have learned that very little if anything happening today has any historic reference point. Yet, the same old prophets are trying to use the same old traditional methods to try to comprehend facts that no longer fit their opinions. It may help them feel comfy, but it won't tell us anything we need to know.

With that said, we have to confess that we're not too crazy about any of the newsletters out there. That is not to say that there aren't individuals whom we respect who are writing newsletters. **Harry Browne** for whom we have the ultimate respect publishes a newsletter. And we know few for whom we have a greater degree of confidence than the confidence we hold for Harry Browne.

Harry Browne Special Reports, Inc.
PO Box 5586
Austin, Texas 78763
512.453.7313
800.531.5142
Harry publishes the least sloppy newsletter that we know of. He is cautious; (at times to the point of immobility.) i.e. He always attempts to error on the side of caution and that means he never recommends anything overly-exciting. If we have money Harry will keep us from losing it, if we don't have money, we aren't sure that Harry can be as much help as he once was. He has become the Count Greffi of the Investment world. But we know of no one who is better. He has always known how to keep his finger on the pulse of things. Some years back he made several investment predictions that were so startling and iconoclastic that he became a sort of pariah of the investment world. We recall people like William F. Buckley insultingly questioning Harry's reasoning. Those who accused him of extremism ate crow and those who followed his advice made millions. The wisdom is still there in abundance.

Harry Browne has written a recent book discussing his views on Libertarianism and his bid for the Presidency.**Why Government Doesn't Work** By Harry Browne
St. Martins Press 1995 [We'd like to see Harry as President of the United States]

A number of years ago, before he got religion Harry Browne wrote one of the most interesting books we've ever read. It is still important and it is still relevant. Buy it, read it, tell your friends about it, send a copy to Harry. **How I Found Freedom in an Unfree World** By Harry Browne Published by Macmillian

NEWSLETTERS & MAGAZINES

International Living Agora Publishing Inc. 105 Monument Street Baltimore, MD 21201 We've always had a lot of fun reading this publication. Over the years it has been a source of some interesting information. They also publish some stimulating reports and manuals.

Island Properties Report PO Box 1596 Bonita Springs, Florida 33959 phone 813.495.1604 A source of information on the Caribbean and on Central America.

AMERICAS PO Box 98079 Washington DC 20078 Phone 800.222.5405 We admit that this is one of our favorite magazines. It is written on all of the 'Americas.' Art, Music, Literature, Travel, Photography. Everything from all over the Americas. An excellent magazine!

RESEARCH BOOKS

Freedom In The World
The annual survey of political rights and civil liberties from which we draw information that helps in analysis of a nation. The 1995-1996 edition Published by Freedom House 120 Wall Street New York, NY 10005

The End Of The Nation State* By Jean-Marie Guehénno University of Minnesota Press 1993 ISBN: 081662660 Originally published in France as: *La Fin de la Démocratie.*

The End Of The Nation State* By Kenichi Ohmae Published by The Free Press Books 1995 ISBN: 0029233410 **URL**:http://www.catalog.com/cgibin/ htimage/calypso/

The CIA World Fact Book A book that actually lists every country in the world and gives current information on that country. This book proves that the CIA does other things besides skullduggery; they actually do gather intelligence. In doing research for our own book we used many different additional sources for the hard data of the type that the 'CIA World Fact Book' provides. But we certainly <u>did</u> use and rely on CIA source publications and research. On average, there were less discrepancies in their data than in most sources. The reader might find it interesting to refer to what we wrote about the **GDP Per Capital in Chile**, where we spoke of several different and differing source-figures and where we ended up by necessity having to give our own opinion on which figure we believed was closest to reality. ORDER FROM: Superintendent of Documents PO Box 371954 Pittsburgh, PA 15250 tel: 202.783.3238 **URL:** http://www.odci.gov/cia/index.html

TechnoTrends By Daniel Burrus with Roger Gittines Harper Business Books 1993 ISBN: 0-88730-627-6 How to use technology to our advantage.

*note: Even though both these books have the same title they are seperate books. Guehénno's book was not translated from the French edition into English until 1995. No plagiarism occurred.

RESOURCE RESOURCES

Telephone Directories for Foreign Countries
It's difficult to imagine how much fun they are. Perhaps it's just me, but I do admit that I get an enormous pleasure in looking through foreign telephone directories. Our own set of foreign telephone directories isn't as fun as being in a place, but it is a lot of fun to peer through a foreign directory and dream about a place. In some ways it's more informative than a travel guide. Nothing quite explains a people like their advertisements. [Just as half the fun of watching foreign television can be the foreign commercials.] Just about every country in the world prints telephone directories. If we want one for a particular city or country we can get them by calling U.S. West at: 800.422.8793 or 303.375.0707
800.522.8793 There is also a Directories of Directories available.

BUREAU OF CONSULAR AFFAIRS
They have a Fax-on-Demand system that supplies Information Sheets and Travel Warnings about most nations. From our fax machine we call: 202.647.3000 and listen to the voice prompts. For information call their voice line 202.512.1530 There is also a WebPage:
URL: http://travel.state.gov/travel_pubs.html

WORLD TRADE PRESS BOOKS
World Trade Press Reference Books are well designed to help us understand a country from a business perspective and more. They have a number of different books. Their **Country Business Guides** which are available for more than a dozen different countries, each separate guide give a comprehensive view of a country's business life. Each country guide covers 25 topics relevant to international business. Sample chapters include: Economy, Demographics, Marketing, Labor, Business Law, Current Issues, Business Culture & Etiquette, International Payments, Opportunities, Import Policy & Procedure, Export Policy & Procedure, Industry Reviews, Foreign Exchange, Business Entities & Formation, Trade Fairs, Financial Institutions, Corporate and Personal Taxation, Transportation & Communication, and Foreign Investment. Each book also includes a 450 word/phrase Business Dictionary in the local language, 600-1100 important addresses and a set of regional, country and city maps in full color.

Their **Importers Manual USA** is a comprehensive single-source reference for the business of importing into the U.S. It is said to be relied upon by importers both large and small, international bankers, attorneys, foreign exporters and trade missions around the world. The new 1995-96 Edition has been fully updated and revised. In particular, the Commodity Index has been restructured according to the Harmonized Tariff Schedule and has doubled in size.

Seven tab sections include: Commodity Index—Detailed import "how-to" for the 99 "chapters" of the Harmonized Tariff Schedule of the US. From art to apparel and baskets to bicycles, from textiles to toys and watches to wood products, it's all here. Also, first-rate sections on U.S. Customs entry, international banking/letters of credit, international law, packing, shipping, insurance and 64 InfoLists on importing.

A Basic Guide to Exporting This is the U.S. Department of Commerce's introduction to exporting. The book is composed of 16 chapters divided into three parts and five appendices: Part A. Before the Sale; Part B. Making the Sale; Part C. After the Sale; I. Export Glossary; II. Directory of Federal Export Assistance; III. State and Local Sources of Assistance; IV. U.S. & Overseas Contacts for Major Foreign Markets; and V. Bibliography.
Dictionary of International Trade Every business has its own language, lexicon and lingo, and international trade is no exception. Consider: Ad Valorem, GATT, Most Favored Nation, NAFTA, Antidumping, GSP, Countertrade, CIF, Letter of Credit, and Harmonized Tariff Schedule.
The World Trade Press Dictionary of International Trade contains over 4,071 entries and is the only book that combines detailed definitions of international trade, customs, banking, shipping, legal and economic terms in a single reference. It includes acronyms and abbreviations, Incoterms 1990 (ICC Paris), an international dialing guide, currencies of the world, weights and measures, 11 maps and a source guide for the top 125 books, directories, country guide books, and periodicals of international trade.
They also have some **CD-ROM Products**
WORLD TRADE PRESS 1505 Fifth Avenue San Rafael, CA 94901 Phone: 415.454.9934 or 800.833.8586 Fax: 415.453.7980

BOOKS ON LIBERTARIANISM ON LIBERTY AND ON AYN RAND

In these pages we have mentioned some of the ideas and several of the authors of books on Libertarianism, on Liberty itself with a capital "L" and on the works and ideas of Ayn Rand. This was not a coincidence. If we had to admit to being any species of political bird we suspect that we would be a Libertarian. We would like to give the reader sources for such books. But before we do so we would like to clarify our position on Libertarianism.

Libertarianism is a philosophy whose time may never come. If it does, it will probably evolve naturally from real men and real women struggling in remote areas of the world where there is a situation of anarchy that has become free of governmental controls but where order persists. It is quite doubtful that freedom will arrive through the mostly ineffectual efforts of todays libertarian movement. Those who speak out for liberty today are for the most part myopic in their imagination and intellectually constipated in their ideas. Which is a shame. We find it extremely ironic that Libertarians have come to resemble the burdensome intellectualism that categorized much of the communist movement of mid-century. Just like the communist intellectuals before them, one faction of the Libertarian movement will spend all their waking hours bickering with the ideas of another faction of the Libertarian movement. Additionally, while this is going on, the ideas and the very legacy of Ayn Rand, unquestionably one of the movements more imaginative thinkers, have been repressed and held captive by a band of mental-eunuchs who are hiding under her intellectual skirts and who are incapable of speaking about anything other than in the litany she taught them.

Rands philosophy, Objectivism was once the occasional source of some more than interesting and seminal ideas. Today, for the most part the old guard live in a void blinded by the light of the moment that they resisted and missed.

For the very best explanation of Ayn Rand we recommend the very excellent book by Barbara Branden. It is doubtful that anyone alive knew Ayn Rand better than did Barbara Branden. The additional advantages that Barbara Branden has are obvious, she is extremely brilliant and she is a woman. All the other explainers of Ayn Rand are men and their explanations imprecise. We believe that only immature men believe they can explain women.

The Passion of Ayn Rand by Barbara Branden Published by Bantam Doubleday Dell ISBN: 0385191715

Laissez Faire Books offers what is probably the world's biggest selection of books and tapes on Liberty, Randism and Libertarianism.* They carry numerous esoteric titles and they can and do ship all over the world. Additionally, they published a monthly bulletin which they've been mailing out for almost 25 years. Their bulletin has a readership in the tens of thousands. **Laissez Faire Books** sells and ships Libertarian books anywhere in the world. They probably have books in their stock by Barbara Branden, Harry Browne, Douglas Casey, Jim Rogers and others. Their selection covers the whole range of libertarian thought and interest, Ludwig von Mises, Milton Friedman, John Locke Lysander Spooner, Ayn Rand, Thomas Sowell, Thomas Szasz and so on.
URL: http://www.lfb.org/
Laissez Faire Books 938 Howard Street, Suite #202 San Francisco, CA 94103
800.326.0996 or 415.541.9780
Fax: 415.541.0597 **email:** custsvc@LFB.org

*The 'Ayn Rand faction' of the movement, (more 'correct' than their counterparts,) also have bookstores and bulletins, though they will not carry [or read] books about Libertarianism because it is not of the true faith. (Which may give us some example of the idiotic pettiness that the movement has descended into.) Their reason? Ayn Rand told them not to, Libertarianism was not an 'approved' offshoot of the ideology. Which gives us a pretty accurate description of the intellectual scope of today's Randite's.

And then there is: **Liberty Magazine**. Admittedly good. Admittedly unique in it's perspective. It is always worth the read, especially if we want to understand todays world without media-doublespeak.

Liberty Magazine Box 1181 Port Townsend, WA 98368 Phone 800.854.6991 Fax: 360.385.3704 **Please note** that while Liberty Magazine has never once in six years responded to one of my faxed inquiries they have always sent anything for which I have paid, such as books or videos.

LIBERTARIAN LINKS There is a very good Libertarian Homepage that links to a multitude of Liberty Sites at: **URL:** http://www.wp.com/JIM/lib.html

Insight Guides

Argentina ((**B-P**#25101) $21.95
Brazil ((**B-P**#25102) $21.95
Buenos Aires ((**B-P**#25103) $21.95
Chile ((**B-P**#25154) $22.95
Ecuador ((**B-P**#25153) $21.95
Rio de Janiero ((**B-P**#25105) $21.95
South America ((**B-P**#25136) $21.95
Venezuela ((**B-P**#25163) $21.95

Insight Guides are simply the best! They are unequaled for full-colored photos and interesting background reading on just about every major country and city in the world. (And the writing is good!) The two city guides, Rio and Buenos Aires are admittedly fine. There are seperate guides for several South America countries and a complete guide of South America as a whole. We have a large set of the guides and we wouldn't part with them. Order your own. Get the one on Rio de Janeiro, put on a Jobim CD while you're reading it and we guarantee you'll be packing up your traveling bags by sunrise.
note: that there are also **Insight Guides** for **Belize, Costa Rica, Mexico the Amazon Jungle and just about everywhere else on this planet.**

BOOK SELLERS

Note: If there is a book you want that has the code **B-P** then it can be ordered from *Book Passage* They have an extensive travel book section. (I've included their book order # number code)

Book Passage Book Service
URL: http://www.bookpassage.com/home.htm
email messages@bookpassage.
51 Tamal Vista Blvd, Corte Madera, Ca 94925
Phone: 800.999.7909 or 415.927.0960
Fax: 415.924.3838

or, order them from:

POWELL'S BOOKS
Note: The advantage of Powell's Books is that they stock used books side by side with new books. If they have a used book of the title you are looking for it is listed in their WebSite. The savings can be as much as 50%. The condition of their used books tends to be fairly good. Powells has a massive selection.
Powell's Books:
Phone 800.291.9676 Voice: 503.228.0540
Fax 503.228.1142
7 NW 9th Avenue, Portland, OR 97209,
URL:http://www.powells.com
email: help@powells.com
Powell's Travel Store Division
Phone 503.228.1108 800.546.5025
Fax: 503.228.7062
701 SW Sixth Avenue, Portland OR 97204

Another excellent source of books is:

The Globe Corner Bookstore - Books and Maps for the Traveller
URL: http://www.globecorner.com/
For orders and information:
Fax: (617) 227-2771 Toll free: 1-800-358-601
Phone: 617-723-1676 email: orders@gcb.com

Amazon.com Bookstore
Supposedly the biggest bookstore in the world is now: Amazon.com. They have a WebSite where Amazon.com Books offers over one million titles Phone: 800.201.7575 or 206.346.2992 Fax: 206.346.2950 Standard mail: Amazon.com P.O. Box 80387 Seattle, Washington 98108-0387
URL: http://www.amazon.com/

RESOURCE S

BRAZIL

Brazil a Cooks Tour
by Idone, Christopher
Published by Random House Trade
ISBN: 0517595559
An excellent introduction to Brazilian crusine.

Brasilia; Capital of Hope
by Shoumatoff, Alex
Published by Putnam Publishing Group
ISBN:069811048
Brasilia & it's people.

Rivers Amazon by Shoumatoff, Alex
Published by Random House Trade
ISBN:0871562103
A very good read.

The Brazil Traveler by Selden Rodman
Delvin-Adaor Publishers
ISBN: 0-8159-5113-2
Always one our favorite writers. Writes about travel, art, literature, poetry and music. Goes and knows.

Insight Guides and the other travel books are available on Brazil.

MEXICO

Heroic Mexico: The Narrative History of a 20th Century Revolution By William Weber Johnson Published by Doubleday ISBN: 0385015518 One of my personal hobbies in an interest in the history of the Mexican Revolution of 1910-1940. We know of no better book on the subject than Johnson's. While this is admittedly not a purely relevant resource book for expats, it does much to explain the heroic attitude of the Mexican mind for those intent on Mexico as an expatriate destination.

Choose Mexico by Howells, John
Published by Moon Publications Inc
ISBN: 0933469047 Yet another fun book by the eternally happy optimist, John Howells.

Business International's Guide To Doing Business in Mexico By Gary Newman & Anna Szterenfeld ISBN: 0070093393 McGraw Hill

LATIN AMERICA

Choose Latin America By John Howells Gateway Books Yes, another book by Howells. He is an intrepid traveler. We think he is the one to read if you want some genuine enthusiasm about living in a place.

Lonely Planet Guides
Argentina, Uruguay & Paraguay (B-P#25156) $19.95
Bolivia (B-P#25091) $16.95
Brazil (#25128) $17.95
Chile & Easter Island (B-P#25050) $15.95
Colombia (B-P#25092) $15.95
Ecuador/Galápagos Islands (B-P#25026) $16.95
Peru (B-P#25028) $14.95
South America (B-P#25003) $27.95
Trekking in the Patagonian Andes (B-P#25158) $13.95

Lonely Planet publishers have a wonderful website at: URL:http://www.lonelyplanet.com They provide extensive coverage of South America with nine sperate guidebooks, ranging from the encyclopedic South America guide to the more precisely targeted Trekking in the Patagonian Andes. **Lonely Planet** guides give extra attention to out-of-the way places, local cultures and budget traveling.

COSTA RICA

Choose Costa Rica By John Howells
Choose Costa Rica gives advice on living and retiring in Costa Rica. Buying a home, healthcare, food, climate, language and culture. (This book also includes a chapter on retiring in Guatemala.)Published by Publishers Group West Inc ISBN:0933469268

Golden Door to Retirement & Living in Costa Rica by Howard Christopher
Published by Independent Publishers Group ISBN:1881233316 Very detailed and complete.

BELIZE

Sastun: Apprenticeship With a Mayan Healer By Rosita Arvigo
Harper Books 1994

Inside Belize: The Essential Guide to it's Society, Economy, and Environment
By Tom Barry
Inter-Hemispheric Education Resource Center 1992 The facts. Not a travel guide. Essential reading for those intent on living in Belize. Albuquerque, New Mexico. First Edition, 1992, 193 pp. $15.00 (paperback) ISBN 0-911213-39-2

Coral Reefs: Peterson Field Guide
By Eugene H. Kaplan
Houghton Mifflin 1982

Jaguar By Alan Rabinowitz
Anchor Books 1986
The establishment of a Jaguar preserve in Belize by an zoologist working in the field.

Belize: A Profile of the New Nation
By William David Setzekorn
Ohio University Press 1975, 1981
History for those intent on Belize.

Adventure In Belize
By Robert P. L. Straughan
A. S. Barnes & Company 1975
A early book on Belize that's in my collection. To look at the photographs in this book is to realize how totally isolated Belize was just a few short years ago.

Time Among the Maya By Ronald Wright
Henry Holt and Company 1991 Good writing! Good read!

Insight Guide to Belize, APA Publications, 1995. ISBN 0-395-71053-7, 332 pp., distributed in US by Houghton Mifflin Co., 222 Berkeley St., Boston, Mass. 02116-3764. Always our favorite Guide Books.

Belize Retirement Guide, Bill and Claire Gray. ISBN 1-880862-46-8. 3rd ed. 1995. 139 pp, US$19.95. Aimed at would-be expats

BELIZE PERIODICALS

Belize First, Lan Sluder, Equator Travel Publications, 280 Beaverdam Road, Candler, North Carolina 28715. Published bi-monthly. Emphasizes information of interest to the visitor or potential expatriate, no commercial advertising. Subscription US $29 per year. Email: 74763.2254@compuserve.com or: LSluder374@aol.com

Belize Currents, Belize Currents, Ltd., Memphis, Tenn. Published bi-monthly. Travel, business, glossy photos, lots of advertising.

Note: Most of the books, magazines and newspapers listed for Belize can be obtained in gift shops and/or local bookstores in Belize, or at the Belize International Airport gift shop. You can also purchase most of the travel guides listed in Belize. Some Belizean magazines and newspapers can be obtained via subscription in the US, Canada, and elsewhere.

Emory King's 1994 Driver's Guide to Beautiful Belize, Emory King, Tropical Books. Published annually. Mile by mile road guide to all sections of Belize, with maps. US $7.50. If you saw the movie Mosquito Coast, that was Emory in the bar scene. Emory is a Cigar-Smoking Belizean Legend who many years ago shipwrecked off the coast of Belize swam ashore and never left the place.

Belize: A Guide to Business Investment and Retirement, by George Rea: investment and tax information, demographics. We are not sure how we go about getting this. Possibly contact **The San Pedro Sun** for details. P. O. Box 35, San Pedro Town, Ambergris Caye, Belize Central America. The **San Pedro Sun**, is a weekly Ambergris Caye newspaper. Foreign subscriptions available at $40 for 6 months.

Other Belize Newspapers
Amandala, independent weekly newspaper.
Belize Times, weekly PUP newspaper.
The People's Pulse & Beacon, weekly UDP newspaper.
The Reporter, independent weekly newspaper. Phone: 501.2.72503 fax: 501.2 78278. Six month subscriptions to The Reporter are $40 U.S. The Reporter, 147 Allenby & West Street, Belize city, Belize, Central America.

ADOBE CONSTRUCTION

There is a very good book on Adobe Construction that covers every aspect of Adobe from design to production. We recommend:
Adobe and Rammed Earth Buildings
By Paul Graham McHenry
University of Arizona Press 1984
ISBN: 0-8165-1124-1

Myrtle Stedman has a series of books on Adobe that were first published in 1936 by Mrytle and her late husband Wilfed. The lovely old drawings in these books is worth the price of admission. Try:
Sunstone Press in Santa Fe, New Mexico
P.O. Box 2321
Santa Fe, NM 87504

There is a journal on Adobe construction:
The Adobe Journal
phone: 505.243.7801
Albuquerque, New Mexico

The Straw Bale House
By Athena Swentzell Steen, Bill Steen, David Bainbridge with David Eisenberg.
Chelsea Green Publishing Company 1994
ISBN: 0-930031-71-7
Straw Bale construction is not Adobe, but it certainly is very interesting to say the least and something worth considering for anyone who escapes to a nation that doesn't have idiotic building codes.

Also of interest:
Earth Sheltered Housing Design
University of Minnesota underground space center project.
Van Nostrand Reinhold Company 1979
ISBN: 0-442-28821-2

Underground Homes
By Louis Wampler
Pelican Publishing 1980
ISBN: 0-88289-273-8

Note: Using the earth as a portion of ones house makes the most sense. If you live in the United States and you have to battle building codes, forget it; just build it wrong, shut-up, don't have any fun and pay your taxes.

EUROPE

Ireland: The Owners Manual International Living/ Agora Publishing Inc.105 Monument Street Baltimore, MD 21201 phone: 401.223.2611 Ireland, is a manual prepared by the staff of International Living for expatriates considering Ireland.

That Fine Italian Hand by Hofmann, Paul Published by Henry Holt & Company Inc ISBN:0805017291 An explanation of modern Italy.

There is a particularly nice travel guide to **Andalusia** from Crowood Travel Guides
ISBN: 1852234466

WEB SITES OF NOTE

Obviously we have had to be fairly selective with the Web Site URL's we've listed here. We simply can't list every Web Site that's worthwhile even if we wanted to. Some that we consider of crucial note are:

UT-LANIC: Joint Projects and Hosted Databases on Latin American and the Caribbean.
URL: http://lanic.utexas.edu/
A Site that is put together by the Institute of Latin American Studies University of Texas at Austin, UT-LANIC covers every conceivable topic imaginable about Latin America and the Caribbean.

Library of Congress
Country Studies/Area Handbook
Search across all countries or any combination of countries. Deals with a particular foreign country by describing and analyzing its political, economic, social, and national security systems and it's institutions and examines the interrelationships of those systems and the ways they are shaped by cultural factors. This site is soon going to have color photos, charts and graphs.
URL: http://lcweb2.loc.gov/frd/cs/cshome.html

Links to United States Embassies and Consulates Worldwide. Just what it sounds like.
URL: http://travel.state.gov/links.html

U.S. State Department Bureau of Consular Affairs Home Page provides links to the following and a good deal more: ✓ Travel Security Information provided by the Overseas Security Advisory Council ✓Travel Health Info from the Centers for Disease Control and Prevention ✓Overseas Schools ✓Passport Information ✓Overseas Commerce ✓International Legal Assistance✓Visa Information✓Consular Information Sheet Travel Warnings ✓Quick Security Guidelines for Americans Overseas ✓Extensive Library Data and so on.
URL: http://travel.state.gov/index.html

International Internet Service Providers
How to get on the internet in Botswana? Well this list shows us how. For a list of service providers from every country in the world refer to this list from iworld. The URL's of the service providers from each nation are provided so that we can go and look at their work. It gives us a pretty good idea of what's going on there. Includes tech-info regarding the service providers themselves. Plus addresses of each type & phone numbers.
URL: http://thelist.iworld.com/country/country.html

The **InterNIC Directory of Directories** is an index of entries that point to resources, products and services accessible through the Internet These pointers provide descriptions of resources available to the Internet community. The Directory of Directories is compiled by the InterNIC Directory and Database Services at AT&T from contributions by members of the Internet community.
URL: http://ds2.internic.net/ds/dsdirofdirs.html
and/or try:
URL: http://ds2.internic.net/ds/dspg01.html

Timezone Converter Specify the time zone, time and date to convert from and the time zone to convert to. Results will appear at the bottom of the page:
http://poisson.ecse.rpi.edu/cgi-bin/tzconvert

Currency Converter We can view an exchange rate for any day since 1 January 1990 through yesterday. The O&A currency converter is updated daily at06:00 MET (Middle European Time) with information from the previous day.
http://www.olsen.ch/cgi-bin/exmenu

AIRLINE TOLL-FREE NUMBERS AND WEBSITES
We aren't sure, but this site appears to have just about every major airline in the world.
http://www.princeton.edu/Main/air800.html

Index

343

INDEX

INDEX

INDEX

INDEX

INDEX

EMPLOYMENT ABROAD

Looking for work overseas? We've figured out how to find it, including jobs in third world countries paying first world wages.

Yes, there are jobs overseas.

We purposely directed this book towards those interested in investing in foreign countries and towards those who want to start businesses abroad. We feel that the reasons for this are obvious. Nonetheless, there are jobs overseas.

Those of us who lack either the finances or the education to move into a ready-made situation should not despair.

While writing this book we spent a good deal of time considering what would be the best way for Americans wanting a worthwhile wage to find employment overseas. We believe we have hit upon a way of finding jobs overseas which would work across the board. We would put such a service in place if the demand was there.

FOREIGN REAL ESTATE

We debated whether to include specific names and contact numbers of those who have real estate for sale. Unless we can go and personally verify a situation we are reluctant, (for reasons that should be obvious,) to recommend specific real estate. We have learned the hard way never to trust any details without actually 'kicking the tires' ourselves. Few individual readers could afford finders fees and I am no longer interested in working for companies who determine where I am going. I pretty much go where I want to go and I like it like that.

We will provide a list of those real estate opportunities we find on the following basis:

- The real estate must be an absolute steal.
- The country profile must pass our criteria.
- There must be clear title.
- The property is not something that was 'discovered' ten years ago by a bunch of half-wits from Beverly Hills who've multiplied the price.
  [there are sufficient folks providing data on such properties]
- I must be willing to buy the property myself.
  [the property and the country in which the property exists have to be a place I'd invest in myself or I won't even discuss it.]
- There is sufficient interest in such information.

I guess what I'm saying is what I've already said and that is that I'm only interested in doing what I already do.

We would like to hear from you. At this point in time we have set in place the beginnings of a system to interchange ideas, resources and innovations with expats, freedom seekers and global thinkers worldwide. If you have information or questions to send our way we will relay answers, clues and current updated information to you and to other freedom seekers and expats. We will also welcome information from businesses that have services that would be of value to freedom seeking expats.

Thus far what we have in place is a contact line which we will try to maintain as a permanent contact line. That contact number is: 503-460-9313 We have a WebSite at **URL:** http://www.escapeartist.com and http://www.escapeartist.com/going/home.htm It is our intention to maintain this WebSite permanently. Our book order line is the toll free number 888-314-1592 which can be used to contact my distributor for purchase orders. The access information number 503-460-9313 will provide information as to how to contact us or our fax-on-demand system. We are working on a system which will allow the reader to contact us for help or with information, no matter where we are in the world and no matter where they are calling from and regardless of their level of technological sophistication. If you don't have internet access, don't despair! We are working on a system which should allow current information in each and every case.

What are we going to make available? We would like to concentrate on the entire issue of thinking globally; regardless if the reader is seeking freedom, the opportunity to make money, or to establish themselves in a new nation. Viewing the world as a world without borders gives you and I a unique perspective of growing opportunities that most people don't consider or are unaware of. Some of the things we'd like to make available and which we will emphasize:

● Real Estate Opportunities in Foreign Countries Updated & Current.
● Unique Nations with evolving opportunities
● Providing a Service that Works as a Modern and efficient Communications Interchange and Address for Expats
● Provide an Ongoing Analysis of Free Trade Zone & Tax Haven opportunities.
● Provide an Ongoing Analysis of Technological Innovations that Increase Liberty.
● A Continuous Search for Nations that may Offer the Best of Everything.
● Jobs Offshore, Jobs WorldWide. We are developing a NetWork of Sources and Contacts that will provide Worthwhile Job Opportunities in just about every Nation the World.
● Investment Opportunities. This is something which the confines of this book did not allow us to expand upon as we would have liked. We have numerous ideas about numerous places for both simple and complex Global Investments as well as the Development of American Businesses in Foreign Lands. Ideas that would create opportunities like Bobs of Brazil, Bikes in Belize or Teresa's in Teguchigalpa. Timing for this type of pursuit is important, so that's what we will be looking for.
● Updated Information on sources for Passports.
● A List of Out-Of-the-Way places that we know about, such as Artist Colonies and Jet-Set Havens that for reasons of exclusively and privacy are kept secret. The opportunities in these places is profound.
● A Constant Update of Tips & Tricks for expatriate living.

To maximize our opportunities in the new century we will need to learn to see our world as a world without borders. As Douglas Casey and Robert Hopkins before me said it, we will need: "foresight, flexibility, intelligence and capital: The foresight to anticipate trends and get out of countries which are decaying, no matter how great our emotional attachment to them. The flexibility to take advantage of opportunities throughout the world. The intelligence to see most governments for the con games that they are and to avoid taxes and other debilitating restrictions upon our life. As well as the capital to provide an island or tranquillity for ourselves amidst the turmoil of the world."

There is certainly some advice we would like to add to that. Nothing really holds quite the importance as our 'sense of life,' nor is anything quite so illusive. For us, learning to adjust attitudinally to a place may be the biggest challenge we face. After all, we are not going to a place as emissaries of a way of life. We cannot teach an Italian or a Frenchmen how to relax and enjoy life. We cannot teach an Argentine how to listen to Opera or to watch a Tango, nor can we can teach a Brazilian how to dance the Samba. If we want to gain from a new place as much as we contribute to it, then part of our gain will consist of gaining a new more peripheral and richer sense of life. In order to accomplish such an illusive goal, we are going to have to realize that at many things Americans are spiritual pikers. While it is absolutely true that our lack of traditional richness has been in many ways a form of mental liberation, that liberation has had a terrible cost.

What we have gained from being unencumbered is clear. Being unencumbered by the confines of tradition has given us the capacity to create technology and innovations unthinkable to many cultures; yes, even innovations as absurd as the hulla-hoop.

What we have lost is as valuable as it is illusive. We have lost the capacity to sit down to a four hour dinner of conversation with our family and our friends or even to sit quietly at a sidewalk cafe or a piazza and enjoy the ambience. Like Data, the television android on Star Treck, many of us can only pretend to be human, because like innovative robots, we have lost the capacity to live, or perhaps we never learned it in the first place. We have no sense of life because we had no reference points from which to draw it. Perhaps we were moving too fast and learning too quickly, but I don't think that was the problem. America is a rough-hewn nation as culturally crude as two by four made with an ax. And, we are tough; everyone who took us on learned that the hard way and suffered the consequences. And we are magnanimous and forgiving and compassionate. We did what no one else could do and we did it better because we didn't know that we couldn't do it. But in the process of building a better technology we lost a simple ingredient. Now it's time to go and reclaim it.

As the new expats we have an second chance at being alive. If we are smart we may have the opportunity to learn how to live all over again. While sharing what we have that is of value with other cultures we can learn to enjoy their sense of life. We can reconnect with ourselves, with our families and with humanity in the most important ways. The pleasure of that give and take and the pleasure derived from being fully free and fully alive may entail the greatest expat global opportunity of all.

PHOTOCOPY THIS PAGE AND MAIL* IT TO US

Hello Roger,

Place me on your mailing list in the following categories:
[check as many as desired]

☐ Employment opportunities overseas

☐ Real Estate opportunities overseas

☐ Investment opportunities overseas

☐ Artist colonies & Jet-set havens

☐ We have a service of value to expatriates

Other:_____.

NAME:_____.

ADDRESS:_____.

CITY:_____STATE:_____ZIP:_____.

VOICE: [____]_____FAX: [____]_____.

EMAIL:_____.

* Please note: try our update line at [503] 460-9313 to determine if there is a fax line or other contact line in place.
URL: http://www.escapeartist.com
URL: http://www.escapeartist.com/going/home.htm

738 East Burnside   Portland, Oregon 97227

Declaration of Independence

Adopted in Congress 4 July 1776

When, in the course of human events, it becomes necessary for one people to dissolve the political bonds which have connected them with another, and to assume among the powers of the earth, the separate and equal station to which the laws of nature and of nature's God entitle them, a decent respect to the opinions of mankind requires that they should declare the causes which impel them to the separation.

We hold these truths to be self-evident, that all men are created equal, that they are endowed by their Creator with certain unalienable rights, that among these are life, liberty and the pursuit of happiness.